Confessions of a Hypnotist

Confessions of A Hypnotist

Everything you ever wanted to know about
Hypnosis but were Afraid to Ask

Jonathan Royle

U.S. Library of Congress Number: 2005970932

British Library Cataloguing In Publication Data

A Record of this Publication is available
from the British Library

ISBN 1846850525
978-1-84685-052-3

Published January 2006 by

Prospect House Publishing
In Association With
Exposure Publishing, an imprint of Diggory Press,
Three Rivers, Minions, Liskeard, Cornwall, PL14 5LE, UK
WWW.DIGGORYPRESS.COM

An Ebook Edition of this book is also available from all good ebook retailers including www.amazon.com

Contents

WHAT THE EXPERTS SAY ABOUT ROYLE TRAINING

"I just finished watching Royle's 10-DVD training on 'There's No Such Thing as Hypnosis' and found his presentation style to be captivating and exciting. Many clinical experts out there (particularly here in the US) are good at taking a topic and making it complex and dry, but to me the real brilliance is taking a complex subject, boiling it down to its essence and making it seem simple, which is exactly what Jonathan does in this series. There is a tremendous amount of very applicable, real world advice in this set, even for hypnotherapists like myself using it in the trenches with patients, and I highly recommend it!!"

Eric B. Robins, MD
Board Certified Urologist
Co-author, "Your Hands Can Heal You"
Contributing author, "The Heart of Healing"
Certified Clinical Hypnotherapist
Advisory Board Member, Emotional Freedom Technique
www.yourhandscanhealyou.com

"I have trained in NLP and Hypnosis with Paul McKenna, but found this course invaluable. It gives a great deal of information and is written in an open, honest and easy to read manner, Jonathan keeps nothing back. I highly recommend this to anyone interested in hypnotherapy or stage hypnotism, no matter whether you are a beginner or an expert"

MATT CAULFIELD
NLP Trainer, Hypnotherapist and founder of The Birmingham NLP Training Academy
www.personalchange.co.uk

"I can wholeheartedly recommend the courses. They are brilliantly researched, analysed and presented for both the beginner and established professional. They contain all the information that is required to become a master hypnotist and are presented in a simple, clear and easy to absorb format. Nothing is left out. They are a fountain of knowledge on the subject. If hypnotism is your chosen area of interest..look no further"

JAMES BRANDON – MASTER ILLUSIONIST

www.illusionist.uk.com

"The course was better than Brilliant! You can quote me on that, or if ever you would like me to speak to any potential clients I would always speak very highly of you and your training materials!"

ANTHONY SMITH –LONDON

www.anthony-smith.co.uk

"The courses and products were overall very informative, interesting and well worth the money. Jonathan is without doubt, an extremely effective tutor. I am sure that the organisation will grow and continue to grow for many years!"

JAMES SMART – SCOTLAND

www.hypnosong.com

"The Complete Mind Therapy Structure as explained on the Secrets of Professional Hypnotherapy video is indeed very unique, in that it incorporates the most effective elements of every part of the course."

JOHN KAY – NORTHUMBERLAND

www.hypnotherapy-northeast.co.uk

"I am a Professional Hypnotherapist & Stage Hypnotist of considerable success and was taught the secrets of my craft by Jonathan Royle. Need I say more?"

CHRIS LEE – HALIFAX

www.chrisleetrance.com

"Thanks for the training which was excellent value for money and has provided me with a career for life which I enjoy immensely!"

BILL GRAHAM – ESSEX

www.hypnosis4u.co.uk

"I did your course in September 1999 in my real name of Kevin Washbourne, I learnt a lot from it and am now a busy working Stage Hypnotist as a result."

KEVIN STARR – NEWCASTLE

www.kstarr59.fsnet.co.uk

"I have read your course and whilst I think the techniques you teach would be more suited to the European performer I would certainly advise other students of Hypnosis to check your courses out for sure!"

Dr. MIKE STOWYER – AMERICA

www.hypnosisworld.com

"Having purchased and read your hypnotic courses, I believe that the educational content was very good and that you have managed to simplify and easily explain all the basic truths regarding Hypnotism. I feel they were all well worth the money and time to study them!"

BRIAN FOLEY – ENGLAND

www.alternativehealth.co.uk/hypnosischap

"I thought that the Hypnotic course that you sent me was an excellent purchase and I would strongly recommend it to any new or established Hypnotists. I found it informal, easy to understand, enjoyable to study and above all highly informative."

GARY WILSON – ENGLAND

www.gary-wilson.co.uk

"The course was fun, highly informative and well worth the investment, my hypnotic induction skills are now super fast and my confidence has soared to new heights!"

STEVE MACDONALD – LONDON

www.simplyhypnotic.com

"The only regret I have about buying Jonathan Royle's Compilation CD-ROM for £177 UK Sterling, is that I did not do it sooner! If I had got this earlier in my career I would now be a far more powerful and richer Hypnotist! The price he charges (£177) for this Compilation CD-ROM is way too low, he should charge $800 or more, I would. Bottom line is his stuff is hot and very good, you will never regret buying any Jonathan Royle training products!"

THESSALONIA DE PRINCE – AMERICA

www.super-hypnotism.com

"In my opinion Royle offers quite simply the most educational, entertaining and highly informative Hypnotherapy & Stage Hypnotism training available anywhere in the world today – this is a must take course!"

GLENN PERKINS – KENT

www.activ8life.biz

"After receiving your complete Stage Hypnosis and Hypnotherapy training pack I must say I was amazed by how much material there was. I read and re-read your books and decided to try it out on some friends at a party and guess what? It worked.... All I can say is that this stuff is PURE GOLD! I am now in the process of getting my Stage act together and embarking on a career as a Stage Hypnotist & Hypnotherapist – many thanks."

DAVID DUROSE – ENGLAND

"To say I learnt a lot and received excellent value for money would be an understatement, the course was highly educational in both content and presentation. In my opinion anyone wishing to pursue a career in Hypnosis need look no further than the products and courses available from Jonathan Royle as they are second to none!"

MARK HOWE – LONDON

www.hypnodrome.co.uk

"Having studied the training materials which accompany your courses, it is now my great pleasure to make you an honouree member of The South African Association of Hypnotists and a life member of The South African Academy of Hypnosis! This is your just reward for all the work you have put into Hypnosis, you have been acknowledged, elevated and exalted! This is indeed a wonderful time for the art of Hypnosis!"

MR MAX KAAN – SOUTH AFRICA

www.hypnoman.co.za

"The methods that Jonathan explains are both practical and professional and indeed for the modern publicity and success seeking Psychic Entertainer they should prove invaluable! Royle made his name almost a household word in the UK and in his book he generously reveals his bizarre and unique methods, for the very first time! I feel that all Mentalists, Psychics and Hypnotists can learn much from his modern & pioneering approach!"

MR EDDIE BURKE – STOKE-ON-TRENT

www.mreenterprises.co.uk

"I just have to tell you this, big time congratulations! As an NLP Hypnotherapist Master Practitioner I can't help myself from telling you how much fun I have had reading & studying your courses and your congruence surprised me! I can perfectly tell you that I am very happy that you have delivered what you promised, very insightful and entertaining, the best money I ever spent on Hypnotic training products & courses!"

SAN PICCIARELLI –EUROPE

www.nlplly.esmartdesign.com

"Just a short note to say how much Andrew and myself enjoyed our training day with you! The day was great fun and very comprehensive, and having read through the course handouts and post course materials I have been amazed at the depth of coverage you have included. We both now feel more confident and more informed as a result of attending the course. We enjoyed your style of training, highly recommended – it was a truly great learning experience"

PAUL BIRD – CHESHIRE

www.paulbird.com

"I recently purchased your complete guide to Stage-Hypnosis and Hypnotherapy and whilst I have not yet read it all, I would certainly say that it is very well written and very easy to follow! In short I believe that it represents excellent value for money and would recommend your Hypnotic training products and courses to anyone!"

MR CLIVE DINSEY – AMERICA

"Royle's Hypnotic Training course CD-ROM is well worth every penny. Be it to become the next Paul McKenna or to set yourself up as a caring, effective Hypnotherapist – I'm sure you'll find something of use within this course!"

FINDLAY HOSIE – MENTALIST

Member Mentalists Asylum Yahoo Newsgroup

"Mr Royle's suggestions, advice and routines are solid, practical and seem to be grounded in experience! Someone who tried this approach would probably recoup their investment quite quickly!"

MICHAEL CLOSE – MARKETPLACE SECTION

MAGIC MAGAZINE – JUNE 2002

www.magicmagazine.com

""I can not thank you enough for the information that you have given to me on your compilation CD-ROM! Your style of writing is so easy for me to understand and absorb that you created more understanding for me of Hypnosis in several hours than all of the other courses and training's I've ever taken put together! It won't be too far into the future when I buy a ticket to the UK to shake your hand, your candid approach is both refreshing and respected, I think your brilliant and your training materials without equal!"

VICTOR H. McCORMICK – AUSTRALIA

"Many thanks for the Compilation CD-ROM, my wife and I are both professional Hypnotherapists and a few months ago were seriously thinking of shelling out the £5K to go on the Practice Builders course – You have saved us a ton of money! I've learnt so much more than I ever could have done from their course, I just can't believe the value for money that the Course offers!"

KEITH ALEXANDER
BRITISH ASSOCIATION OF THERAPEUTIC HYPNOSIS

"If you want to become a Professional Stage Hypnotist or indeed a Hypnotherapist then you will find that Royle's Hypnotic Training Materials are amongst the best available in the World today!"

BLAKE ANDREWS
www.sleepwithblake.com

"Royles CD-ROM Compilation of all his books is excellent, it's full of all sorts of insights and secrets from the world's of both Hypnotherapy & Stage-Hypnosis. Indeed these countless insights are such that only a professional of many years practical experience such as Jonathan Royle would be able to impart them to the reader so clearly as he does in his texts!"

DAVID LYNN – HYPNOTHERAPIST
www.davidlynn.co.uk

"To say this course was impressive would be an understatement! Not only was it thoroughly enjoyable but also Jonathan teaches in a way that you cannot fail to learn, I'm proud to say he was my instructor and would recommend these ten videos to anyone with a serious interest in Hypnosis!"

GLENN PERKINS
http://bgentertainments.users.btopenworld.com
(Association of Professional Stage Hypnotists

"I've studied Royles – There's No Such Thing As Hypnosis DVD set and also his Secrets of Hypnotic Success and learnt far more from these than I have ever done from any other rival course! Indeed I once paid several thousand pounds and trained with a company called Practice Builders and in short these DVD's blow their course and the other courses I have done out of the water! If you want to be a successful Hypnotherapist – then you need these DVDS!"

DAVID RAMSEY
www.stressclear.co.uk
(Association of Complete Mind Therapists)

"If you want to learn Hypnosis in the quickest and most effective way possible then there is only one man to teach you and that's Jonathan Royle!"

HEATHER GREENE
www.stressclear.co.uk
(Association of Complete Mind Therapists)

"If you are serious about learning Hypnosis then I would recommend Royle as one of your trainers!"

ALAN JONES

www.enigmatist.org.uk

(Professional Organisation of Stage Hypnotists)

"Royle's Hypnotic Training Materials are well worth studying!"

BOB SPOUR

www.mindworkstechnologies.com

(Licensed NLP Practitioner & Certified Hypnotherapist)

"For Hypnotherapists who want to learn real world, tried, tested and proven to work marketing, advertising and promotion techniques to maximise their business and profits, I would recommend Royles Secrets of Hypnotic Success Series!"

CHRIS RUSSELL

www.entrancer.co.uk

(National Council for Hypnotherapy)

"Having already been a Hypnotherapist for 25 years, I recently bought Royles – There's No Such Thing and also his Secrets of Hypnotic Success DVD courses and was very impressed! He has obviously done a lot of research and has a lot of experience in the real world, which he passes on to the viewer. You cannot fail to learn many new and extremely valuable techniques form these courses and I would unreservedly recommend them to you!"

JANE ZATMAN

"Having watched Royles There's No Such Thing as Hypnosis DVD Home Study Course we would say that his training skills and knowledge are second to none! He is down to earth, his demonstrations and teachings are excellent and full of tricks of the trade which you will not find elsewhere! If you desire to become a Hypnotherapist or Stage Hypnotist then you need these DVDS and even if that's your job already you'll learn lots of new techniques here!"

TOM BOLTON & BEVERLEY ANDERSON

www.freeway-cer.com

(World Federation of Healing – Association of Meridian Therapies and Joint Creators of Freeway – Cer)

"Having studied Royles DVD courses I would say that his knowledge is excellent and his training skills different, but highly effective! Be willing to open your mind and if not accept, at least be willing to recognise the validity of Royles

opinions and real world insider techniques which
will help you become head and shoulders above the rest!"

MICHAEL HARDMAN
www.michaelhardman.co.uk
(General Hypnotherapy Register – British Society of Clinical Hypnosis)

"I have purchased practically all of Royles DVD training courses and I can honestly say that I have never been disappointed in either quality of content or volume of information taught! Because of my background in formal education I was originally drawn to studying with a recognised training provider, members of the General Hypnotherapy Standards Council (GHSC). My training with them was excellent, however it was greatly enhanced by Jonathan Royles material and indeed Royles material was excellent and far superior to the recognised course. His therapy skills are equal if not greater than the majority of therapists I have met to date and he teaches everything he knows in an open and honest manner. We need people like Royle to raise the profile of Hypnosis and I would recommend his courses to anyone who wants to become a better Hypnotist!"

Dr. WILF ARCHER – Phd.
www.mindskills.co.uk
(NLP Master Practitioner & EFT Advanced Practitioner)

"The contents and presentation are excellent and in short these ten tapes are a worthwhile investment for anyone wanting to learn Hypnosis or even for any practising Hypnotherapist and/or Stage-Hypnotist"

RAY RONSON – *www.hypnotist.uk.com*
(Former Member of British Council of Professional Stage Hypnotists – Member of General Hypnotherapy Register and The Hypnotherapy Practitioners Association)

"This Course was truly different; Jonathan has a no-nonsense approach and teaches things in a truly different way. These tapes are extremely informative and Hypnotically entertaining!"

BARRIE ST. JOHN – *www.comedyhypnoshow.co.uk*
(Member of UK Guild of Hypnotist Examiners)

"Jonathan's approach I must say is different to say the least, however having been a Hypnotherapist for some years as well as a Stage Hypnotist, I found the seminar both interesting and highly educational. The confidence that I had for working on stage has now increased and with Hypnotherapy I feel that I am now even better than before!"

MIKE BUTLER – *www.oakfieldclinic.co.uk*
(British Council of Professional Stage Hypnotists – National Register of Advanced Hypnotherapists & The National Guild of Hypnotists)

"A few years ago I attended a training run by Paul McKenna, Michael Breen and Richard Bandler, it was good and I learned a lot but Jonathan Royle's training course make's them seem like old nannies! There is absolutely no time wasting or useless information and Royle's unique manner of teaching makes everything very easy to learn and remember. This course is without doubt money well spent!"

FRANK LEA – *www.hypnosisandmore.co.uk*
(Founder Member of The Hypnotherapy Practitioners Association and Licensed Practitioner of NLP)

"Thank you for a truly great training weekend, I really learnt a lot, you packed so much valuable information into the two days it was excellent value for money"

Dr. STEPHEN BYRD – *www.synergy-international.net*
(Licensed Practitioner in NLP & Certified Hypnotherapist)

"At first Jonathan's style of training blows your mind, loud, proud, profanity is everywhere! But watch these videos you must because you will learn a huge amount of stuff and by the end you'll love his style! I applaud his level of honesty as to the true secrets of how Hypnotist's work!"

STEPHEN BISHOP – *www.myhypnotherapycentre.co.uk*
(Licensed Practitioner in NLP)

"Honest, Informative, Fun & Controversial are all word's I'd use to describe Royle's seminar. He knows so much and teaches things in a way that makes it so easy to learn. You'll discover everything you'll need to get started and become a Hypnotic Success!"

DANNY SMALL – *www.dannysmall.co.uk*
(Reiki Master Practitioner & Clinical Hypnotherapist)

"The course contains much unique material, which as far as I know is not taught anywhere else and will certainly make you a better Hypnotist, especially when presenting any public demonstrations!"

DAVID BOTSFORD – *www.corporatemedservices.co.uk*
(Graduate of The Jerry Valley & Ormond McGill Masters Ultimate Stage Hypnosis Training Seminar)

"I have been a therapist since 1986 now and this Hypnosis training seminar of Mr Royle's has a no nonsense down to earth approach which will shock some people, but the quality and quantity of information enclosed in these videos goes beyond any one course I have ever taken! His sense of humour and marketing techniques are useful both for the Therapist and Stage Performer and his Complete Mind Therapy brings together an infusion of some of the most powerful techniques available today and I shall be using it in my own healing clinic. He tells it as it is with no bull, this is refreshing to see, his knowledge is multi-facetted and he shares his wealth of knowledge in these videos!"

MR DEZ SELLARS – *www.meridianhealing.co.uk*
(A.A.M.T. & E.F.T. Advanced Practitioner & Clinical Hypnotherapist)

"This seminar was well presented in Royle's usual bombastic – plain English – no bullshit manner! Open your mind – Open your wallet and let go of your pre-misconceptions – Welcome to the real world as this is the best and only honest course currently available and is certainly the only course in Hypnosis that you genuinely ever need to take!"

MR STEVE OAKLEY – NORWICH
http://hypnogothic.mysite.freeserve.com
http://maxxvoodoo.mysite.freeserve.com

I would recommend the "There's No Such Thing As Hypnosis" video training course to everybody as there is no comparison with any other Hypnotic course I have ever taken! The honesty in saying that there is no such thing as Hypnotherapy is amazing. I thought I was missing something and wasn't as good as others, now I know I'm Not – I'M BETTER! These tapes are also great fun to watch and learn from and are very entertaining!

MR COLIN MASTERSON – (ESSEX)
www.re-balance4u.co.uk

"Jonathan's Hypnosis training e-books are a must read collection of Hypnotic tools. I highly recommend Jonathan's books to anyone who is considering becoming a hypnotist and to the seasoned pro that wants to go up a few levels. This is not a jump start program. It is more like being shot out of a cannon! Buy it now, don't sleep on it. If you snooze, you lose. Please add my link to your website with the review"

www.hypnoed.com

"I've been reading the Stage Manual and it's fantastic, I can't wait to watch your Stage Videos! I've just recently finished my certification in Hypnotherapy & NLP. I went to Thailand last year and did a Stage Hypnosis Course with Marc Cunningham & Mike Doubet and since then I've been studying everything I can on the subject! So far just from reading your manual I can honestly say that you explain things far better than anyone I've learned from. Your teaching is better than them all including Don Mottin & Milton Erikson to name just a few! You're a gentlemen and a scholar!"

MIKE JOHLES (*MICHAEL VECELL*) – USA

Having trained with Geoffrey Ronning, Alexander Duvall and other Hypnotic Experts I can honestly say that Royle's "There's No Such Thing as Hypnosis" is in my opinion a great set of DVD's produced as a quality package. They tell the "whole" story. The "complete" deal and contain much information I've never found on any other course or in any books! I suspect that many hypnotists will not like what Royle has to say at first, however, If they can open their own minds to get past this hurdle they will learn a lot more than they bargained for. On the other hand maybe it is best they don't buy them, then those that do will stand out from the crowd.

MARTIN COLE

www.martincole.com

"I learned a tremendous amount about all sorts of ways of making money, how to get more clients and the right way to approach them! Royle is very honest, outspoken and controversial, he kept me entertained and interested for the full two days and had 100's of useful tips to impart. In short I would recommend the videos of Royles May 2004 Hypnotic Marketing Success Videos to everybody as they are much better value and contain more information than any other similar seminar or training I've' ever been on!"

Dr. COLIN BARRON–GLASGOW

www.colinbarron.co.uk

"Jonathan is a motivational and enthusiastic speaker and on these videos you will see what he was willing to share about how he goes about increasing his business! A week after the seminar my head is still buzzing, normally by now I've forgotten most of what I learnt, that's a tribute to Jonathan as this course was head and shoulders above any of the crap I have been on before. Please don't sell these videos Jonathan as I don't want others to know where I got my ideas from!"

MR IAN EVANS–*www.retracforchange.co.uk*

"Jonathan Royle's training materials, videos and books are of the highest calibre and must have items for all Hypnotic students!"

DEZ SELLARS

www.completemindtherapy.com

"Royle's Unique Marketing Techniques are worth the entire price of this video training seminar course alone! Add on the other techniques you will learn and these videos represent the bargain of a lifetime – you owe it to yourself to order these one of a kind information packed videos right now!"

TREVOR DUMBLETON – *www.nlpfix.com*

(Master Practitioner in NLP & Certified Clinical Hypnotherapist)

Thanks for the training courses. Your insights into NLP and Hypnosis - and more importantly marketing - are helping me to finally expand my business. Since my motivation was always to help people, I completely missed the point that I can't do that without getting a stream of revenue! I feel that it's all coming together now. I appreciate the standard of training you offer and it has certainly helped me develop my skills to the next level. I would recommend your training's to anyone who's not faint-hearted, but who wants to hear what it's all about. Thanks again.

RICHARD HAGGERTY

www.accelerated-excellence.com

"I have personally studied many of Royle's amazing books & courses on Stage Hypnotism, Hypnotherapy, Mind Control, Hypnotic Skills, Hypnosis techniques and related subjects and would say his works are of the highest order. I would recommend them to all that visit this site!

www.portrayer.co.uk

"Before taking the course in Complete Mind Therapy I had qualified as a NLP Master Practitioner with McKenna Breen Ltd, but I have never come across the facts so openly presented and so richly portrayed as in your course material! It is wonderfully refreshing to find a competent person like yourself, who is prepared to impart those important small, but major facts that are normally missing, or appear to be in other courses. Thank you for such a richly rewarding and most wonderful learning experience.

John Brown (South Devon)

"The course gives you the real secrets from page one, it consists of the most valuable information I have ever learned from any course and/or book. This course can and will change your life for ever!"

Derrick Turner (Grantham)

"The course in CMT is very good and very easy for anyone to understand and learn from!"
Kevin Walter (Aldershot)

"My feeling is that the course in CMT is perfect even for the novice. Jonathan Royle's course has the power to change lives for the better for ever and indeed my own life has now improved in many positive ways".
Michael P. Jeffery (East Sussex)

"Having studied and attended many courses on the subject of Hypnosis. I have found that most seminars tend to skirt round the subject. I personally have found the whole course to be exactly what I have been searching for. Last year I became a NLP practitioner and have found that with the skills I have taken on board from Jonathan's course, the Hypnosis part of my interest is complete And I can now say that the techniques I use have come from the top people in the industry. The course is the most comprehensive and compelling I have ever studied!"
Dave Cunningham (West Sussex)

"A great in depth insight for anyone wishing to learn more about the magic of Hypnosis".
John Barry (Barnsley)

"I have enjoyed the course very much. He obviously has a very thorough knowledge of his craft and it shows. He has gone the extra mile to give value for money and a genuine grassroots account of real nitty-gritty details. He has been very generous in supplying information and advice over and above what is required of him".
Dave Gannaway (Southampton)

"The course itself is Hypnotic. You will not be able to put it down. A true insight. I'm now reading the course for the fourth time. Very absorbing".
Joe Phillips (Northern Ireland)

"I thought the course was excellent and very comprehensive".
Noel Qualter (Surrey)

"The course overall was very informative, interesting and well worth the money".
James Smart (Scotland)

"The Complete Mind Therapy session structure is indeed very unique, in that it incorporates the most effective elements of every part of the course."
John Kay (Northumberland)

"The course is easy to understand and good value for money. Your skills as a Hypnotic teacher are excellent. If you have a problem, you only have to phone and help is at hand".
Denis Holloway (Essex)

"Seek a professional with honesty and integrity. Study his teachings. Learn, explore and expand. You'll need a true expert - Jonathan Royle. His teaching skills are engaging, professional, communicative and entertaining".
Scarlett Robinson (Hampshire)

"Informative, good quality, easy to understand, excellent value for money and friendly advice when dealt with on the phone".
John McClean (Peterborough)

"Jonathan Royle is a black belt in the art of his craft.
This course is the best by far".
John Lawrie (Glasgow)

"As a Hypnotic teacher, his skills speak for themselves. I would recommend the courses with great enthusiasm".
John Buckley (Leigh-On-Sea)

"These items can not be improved. The techniques you learn will change your way of life for the better".
Derrick Turner (Grantham)

"CMT is particularly good. The enthusiasm comes through well."
Colin Lyne (Bolton)

"Very informative. You've read the rest, now read the best."
David Campbell (Glasgow)

"I spent thousands on courses, books etc trying to find new techniques and ideas. Within the CMT course I have found ALL I needed to progress and develop my skills on Hypnosis".
Alexander Johnstone (Inverclyde)

"The communication is good and the subject material easy to read".
Dr J. R. C. Hunter (Helensburgh)

"The contents are newcomer friendly and thus can be understood quite easily. True value for money".
Z. A. Tinggal (Kent)

"I have been entertaining as a magician for a number of years and in all that time I have had an interest in the field of hypnotism after seeing a stage hypnotist perform. His act was funny, mysterious and powerful , utilizing members of the audience and the use of the right type of music to compliment his act. He wasn't top of the bill but everyone was talking about him long after he left the stage. Surely that is what an entertainer strives for isn't it? For years after, I wanted to learn the art, but how do I go about it? My first step was to buy books on the subject from specialist bookshops, but although well written I found them to be more inclined to teach hypnotherapy rather than the stage hypnosis side of the subject. Then along came the internet and I found some useful sites dealing with stage hypnosis, more books became available to me which I purchased, but once again although well written they relied on the use of stooges in the act, not quite what I was looking for.

In the meantime I met someone who had been a hypnotherapist for over 50 years, and he gave me tuition on inductions and deepeners and more hypnotherapy. I have since been successfully helping people with ridding fears, phobias and vices, but I still wanted to be a stage hypnotist, and it was while I was surfing the internet again I came across your company Hypnotictraining.com I gave it a try. After all that time it was exactly what I was looking for.

What I liked about the courses was the way in which it was written, in easy to understand English. Jonathan Royle the author has been in the business a long time and it shows in this work. The stage hypnosis course not only teaches the art of stage hypnosis, it shows you how to construct a show including the type of gags to use, the types of music to use, the type of person to use, and the type of routines to use in different situations. It even tells you how and where to get more work. Nothing is left out.

The hypnotherapy course is also explained in the same vein making it easy and a pleasure to study . It is also pleasing to note that upon completion of this course and the others available one can qualify for diplomas.
I wish I had found this earlier, more than anything else this course has given me confidence. I am now on my way to fulfilling a dream thanks to you. I thoroughly recommend your products to anyone else who wants the same without wasting time as I did before I found your company.
May you go from strength to strength".
Alan Day - Magician (Stanford le Hope)

I am a qualified hypnotherapist with two diplomas on the subject. I have learned a number of things from you that neither of my previous courses taught me. This course has been excellent value and very worthwhile.
STUART KNOX - GLASGOW
Stuart Knox Hypnotherapy and Stress Consultancy
www.hypnosis-4u.co.uk

SPECIAL THANKS TO:

DELAVAR

As Ex-President of The British Council of Professional Stage Hypnotists and tutor of some of the worlds leading stage performers and therapists including your course tutor Dr. JONATHAN ROYLE (FORMERLY ALEX LEROY), Delavars help, advice and instruction has been invaluable in ensuring this course is the most comprehensive training course of its kind available anywhere in the World today!

ALL CORRESPONDENCE TO:

PROSPECT HOUSE PUBLISHING
Prospect House
P.O. Box 12,
Huddersfield, England. HD8 9YP
Tel or Fax: +44 (0)1484-861522

www.hypnotherapycourse.net

www.hypnotictraining.com

www.hypnotorious.com

www.box12.net

IMPORTANT LEGAL NOTICE

This training course in Stage Hypnosis, Hypnotherapy & Complete Mind Therapy is sold on the agreement and understanding that the purchaser and/or reader is responsible for their own actions at all times. Neither the author or publisher can be held in anyway responsible for misuse of these techniques and it is advised that you obtain suitable insurance cover prior to Hypnotising your subjects.

"Knowledge is not measured by its weight, height or length, but rather by its depth!"

DEDICATION

THIS COURSE IN:

COMPLETE MIND THERPAY (CMT)

IS DEDICATED TO:

MY DAD WHO TAUGHT ME THE ROPES IN SHOWBIZ,

AND

MY MUM WHO WROTE THIS POEM AND I LOVE DEARLY

ENTITLED

A BIRTHDAY WISH TO MY SON

The 13th of August 1975
Was the happiest day that I've had
When you came screaming into the world
The pain suddenly seemed not so bad

The years flew by so quickly
And at four you started school
That first day I was so upset
But you stayed oh so cool

Until it came to lunchtime
And then the tears came fast
You wanted to stay for your dinner
Home for lunch that day was the last!

Remember the Christmas production?
You were one of the Billy goats gruff
And watching you up there I felt so proud
But for you it wasn't enough

You wanted to go on performing
And went with your dad as a clown
You stole the show from the T.V. chimps
When you appeared in Newbrighton Town

Then again to Gandeys Circus
With your dad you once more set off
But you played in a place where you shouldn't
And a puma pulled your ear off

But it didn't stop you performing
Off to hospital for treatment and pad
An injection and sweet, then a quick change
And back in the ring with your dad

We moved to a house in Ainsworth
You didn't like it much there
But at church you sang a solo
And at home showed your magical flair

Then we moved back to Heywood
At one time we'd nearly a zoo
With rabbits (and babies) and pigeons
And then there was Smokey too

No time and you were eleven
And off to Siddal Moor
I was at work so each morning
You saw me off at the door

Then bad news we lost Grandad Nation
I couldn't be here for you then
He left us so many good memories
Don't you wish we could live them again?

You carried on with your magic
Fire-eating and juggling too
Then came the tarot and hypnotism
Is there anything you can't do?

Well your childhood has gone so quickly
We've seen all the illnesses through
Measles and mumps, German measles
And a bad case of chicken pox too

Now today your 18 and an adult
You've the rest of your life ahead
But I'll always remember your years as a child
When I'd watch you asleep in bed

And so to the future you're looking
I wish you good luck and success
Good health, good friends and a long life
I hope filled with happiness

But I'll always be there if you need me
You'll always have somewhere to come
And there'll always be someone who loves you
While I'm on this earth.....YOUR MUM!

I also dedicate this course to:

Mr. Paul Brady

One of Britain's leading mind therapists, a close personal friend and the man who originally taught me how to improve peoples life's for the better using the wonderful therapeutic power of Hypnosis and related mind therapies.

Paul McKenna, Andrew Newton, Peter Powers and Ken Webster.

These four people along with myself Dr. Jonathan Royle (Formerly Alex-Leroy) undoubtedly make up the top five Stage Hypnotists in Britain list. They are also people I am proud to count as either close personal friends and/or colleagues whom I have had the pleasure of working closely with in the past.

And last but not least this course is dedicated to:

YOU, THE READER AND MY NEW STUDENT IN HYPNOSIS.

I wish you luck in your new venture and promise that at all times I will do all within my personal power and capabilities to ensure that your career in both Stage and Therapeutic Hypnosis & related mind therapies is a long and prosperous one.

I thank you for choosing The Mindcare Organisation U.K. as your trainers, and assure you of our personal attention at all times.

Remember: "A journey of a thousand miles, starts with but a single step"

THIS COURSE IS YOUR NEXT STEP TO HYPNOTIC SUCCESS

"A COURSE IN COMPLETE MIND THERAPY."

"When man invented the telescope he looked into space to discover the new worlds. I believe that the greatest discoveries in life are yet still to be made by looking within ourselves and the untapped powers of our minds!"

"The mind is not one solid object. It is made up of thousands of mini sub-minds, by putting just a few of these sub-minds to sleep, especially in the analytical area of the mind the effects of Hypnosis become possible and this course contains all the secrets you need in order to put those sub-minds to sleep!"

"The only limitations which we have during our time upon earth are those which we impose upon our own minds.....so become a no-limits person!"

"What the mind of man can perceive and believe it can then achieve"

INTRODUCTION

Welcome to the mysterious world of Stage Hypnosis, Hypnotherapy and Related Mind Therapies.

So why did I start this book with all those testimonials from some of my past happy students? To show off? To be big headed? Well in truth my real motive is far from either of these.

I have told you all this not to show off, but so that you KNOW as a reader of this course that the information contained within is first class and not only is it worth a fortune it can also earn you one.

Having been taught by some of the leading experts in the business and having had the luck to get my break so early into my Hypnotism career, I have amassed a wealth of hands on performing and therapeutic experience from tutors who, in some cases have taken over 60+ years to gather.

I would hope now that you have confidence in me as your head tutor, as to benefit fully from what you will learn. You need to have faith in the skills that you learn and you can only have complete faith in these skills by first having faith in your teacher.

Nothing will be held back. This course will contain everything which is of value to a potential Stage Hypnotist and/or Mind Therapist who wishes to enter a profession which has mystified people for decades.

There follows, hundreds of pages, which explain in clear step by step detail all of the secrets, ploys and techniques that are used to become a safe and competent Stage and Therapeutic Hypnotist.

These skills will enable you to enter this lucrative profession which can open new doors in your attitude and lifestyle that you never dreamed possible.

I will introduce you to the professional art of Stage Hypnosis and Hypnotherapy and by so doing, initiate you into a profession, which will fascinate and astound people including yourself.

Stage Hypnotists are among the highest paid entertainers in the field of showbusiness, now this knowledge and power can be yours.

To finish this introductory chapter, allow me to explain that this course has been purposely written in a simple to understand manner with plain language and complicated words and phrases removed. As closely to the way the majority of us speak.

This has been established as the best possible way to learn, absorb and understand information which may be new and alien to us.

Grammar and syntax will be thrown away in the interests of passing on the knowledge easily, quickly, enjoyably and effectively to you.

Hypnosis is a much deeper subject than most realise, the majority of the population are of the opinion that all you do is snap your fingers or swing a shiny watch in front of their eyes and then they will just instantly drop off to sleep.

Well I can tell you here and now it is a great deal more complicated than that, yet at the same time if you are prepared to believe what I teach you it is also far easier to learn than you might at first imagine.

Read, study and absorb the contents of this course, it will without doubt place you on the road to ultimate success in both Stage Hypnosis, Hypnotherapy and related Mind Therapies.

I look forward to receiving a letter from you detailing your success as a Complete Mind Therapist, or a video of your "new" Hypnotic show. As I'm sure over the years to come this course will be responsible for the training of more Stage Hypnotists and Therapists than any other ever published.

That's lesson one by the way, always have 100% confidence in your skills and talents. When you exude this confidence to your audience or client it will make your job of Hypnotising them that much easier.

This is because through your body language and other actions including tone of voice etc. you will be transmitting the faith you have in your skills to them and, as such, they will then have total faith and belief in your ability to Hypnotise them also.

And if they have faith in you then they will believe you are able to Hypnotise them and if they believe you are able to place them into a trance then you can!

Yes that's right. If they believe you have the power to Hypnotise them then you will in turn be able to do so with ease.

IT'S ALMOST AS SIMPLE AS THAT.

Remember confidence begets confidence! Also remember that positive thinking is a most positive force and I would regard myself as an example of this.

I wish you luck in your future career, although if you absorb the contents of this course which is filled with liquid gold knowledge then your success is almost guaranteed.

For this chapter I'll leave you with a piece of advice given to me in a letter from Mr. Hypnotism himself - Paul McKenna.

"GOOD LUCK AND KEEP IT CLEAN!"
Paul McKenna, March 1994.

PART ONE

"BACK TO FRONT"

"Scientists say that we only use 10% of our brain power, well in that case what do we do with the other 47%?"

Seriously though, the potential of the human mind is literally unlimited and far greater than the average person could ever imagine.

As you will discover in this chapter the key secret to hypnosis is the belief and expectancy within your subjects mind, may the general public remain ignorant to the way their minds work otherwise we hypnotists will be out of business!

A COURSE IN COMPLETE MIND THERAPY

"The Professional Art of Stage Hypnosis and Hypnotherapy"

IMPORTANT WARNING TO ALL WHO STUDY THIS COURSE.

In order to have purchased this course and enrol as our pupil you will have had to have sent the supplier who sold it to you a signed declaration to state that the information enclosed will only be used for legal purposes.

We would not wish this course to get into the wrong hands as Hypnosis really is a far more powerful force than you could possibly imagine, as such anyone studying this course and putting the enclosed contents to use do so at their own personal risk. The publishers of this course, the supplier who sold it to you and the author Dr. Jonathan Royle in no way accept any responsibility whatsoever for other peoples actions and/or uses of this courses contents.

In this part I will reveal all the key secrets of Hypnosis. In other words, within the next few pages you will find everything you require to become a professional Stage Hypnotists and/or Mind Therapist like myself or Paul McKenna.

However as you will have, I presume, no previous knowledge of the subjects in hand you may think that the next few pages over simplify the art. The idea of this however is to show you the key points and then to explain to you why these are the key points. As such when you have read the last part of this course you will then realise and more importantly understand just how easy and simple it really is to hypnotise someone.

So this is if you like what most people would have made the last chapter of this course, but for reasons you will understand later, it has been presented "Back to front!" The main advantage of doing it this way is that you will learn both the cause of what you are doing and also the effect it has upon people. This will mean that you will automatically know more than a great number of Stage Hypnotists who just know the outcome of what they do and not what has caused it to happen. So always remember ***EVERY CAUSE HAS AN EFFECT*** and ***EVERY EFFECT HAS A UNDERLYING CAUSE.***

STAGE HYPNOTISM

Boiled down to the basics Stage Hypnosis is IDENTICAL to all other forms of Hypnosis. The only difference being the way in which it is PRESENTED and the speed at which the volunteers are placed into a DEEP hypnotic trance state. There are seven key points to follow for Therapeutic Hypnosis and below I shall explain how these key points also apply to the use of Hypnotism on stage.

SEVEN STEPS TO THERAPUTIC HYPNOSIS

1) Introductory talk to the client in order to obtain "rapport."
2) Induction of the hypnotic trance state.
3) Deepening of the trance state.
4) Ego-strengthening Therapy.
5) Carry out the necessary Therapy on the client.
6) Implant the major post Hypnotic suggestion.
7) Awaken the client from the Hypnotic trance state.

SEVEN STEPS TO STAGE-HYPNOSIS

1) Obtain rapport (done through one liner jokes at start of act).
2) Induction of Hypnotic trance. (Any fast method after handclasp).
3) Deepening of trance (giving suggestion that each time they are told to return to sleep they will go deeper.)
4) Ego strengthening Therapy (butter them up/compliments etc).
5) Do the Therapy (in this case the comedy routines of your act).
6) Implant the major post Hypnotic suggestion. (N.B. This is done at stage two when they are told that when you tell them to return to sleep they will go deeper and is done so that all suggestions given to them are cancelled before they leave the stage).
7) Awaken them from trance (awaken them and ensure they feel ok).

So you see, the basic structure is the same. In fact to be honest the best piece of advice I could ever give you is to go and see a Stage Hypnotist performing when they are in your area. Study them and also consult a Hypnotherapist and then you will see with your own eyes just how similar the two forms of Hypnosis really are. This will also be a most valuable learning experience as you can learn an awful lot by emulating (not copying) the style and manner of established experienced Stage Hypnotists. Basically speaking if you did what they did word for word and with similar actions on someone whom had been made to believe in your abilities then they would go into a *trance state and react to your various suggestions.*

THE KEYS TO HYPNOTIC INDUCTIONS

When wishing to place someone into a Hypnotic trance there is also a set procedure to follow which is:

A) BELIEF and EXPECTANCY
B) DISORIENTATION and CONFUSION
C) SUGGESTION and REPETITION
D) RELAXATION and SLEEP

Step A means that if you instil into them a belief in your powers as a Hypnotist and as such they believe that you are able to place them under trance, and they also expect to go under if you were to try it upon them, then they are in the correct state of mind to be very successfully and rapidly placed into a Hypnotic trance state.

Step B means that once they are in the correct state of mind to be Hypnotised you then use methods of disorientation and confusion to convince them they are starting to go into trance, and that's why they are feeling these strange effects.

As such if they believe this to be the case then they will expect to go under deeper and as such they will, as in the end its all down to their personal state of mind.

Step C means that once these things are starting to convince them they are beginning to slip into trance then you use methods of suggestion and repetition to confuse and disorientate them even further and also to convince them that they are going under more. If they believe this is the case and expect what you are doing to have an effect upon them, then indeed, in turn it most certainly will.

Step D is the end result of carrying out steps A, B & C and should be that if they believe what you have done to be Hypnosis and expect it to work then this will have the result of relaxation and sleep. And as all Hypnosis really is, is deep relaxation they will then be in the Hypnotic trance state.

So you see the secret to all induction's of any kind whether Stage or Therapy and whether slow, rapid or instantaneous is that if the subject sincerely believes that what you are doing does work and they also sincerely believe and expect it to work on them, then the end result will always be that it works on them. Basically, the key secret to all induction's is to have instilled into the prospective subjects mind, the belief in your powers and the 100% expectancy that should you as the worlds greatest of great Stage and/or Therapeutic Hypnotists picks upon them to be Hypnotised then it will work and as such they will enter a trance.

BELIEF AND EXPECTANCY EQUALS HYPNOSIS.

THE SPEED PROBLEM

Generally speaking if you place a person into trance via a long induction then they will remain in trance longer and go into a deeper state of relaxation. By the same token if you place someone into trance via a rapid or instantaneous induction then they will slip out of the trance state very quickly.

The general rule of thumb in the Hypnotism industry seems to be that:

"QUICKLY IN EQUALS QUICKLY OUT"

AND

"SLOWLY IN EQUALS SLOWLY OUT"

However, from experience I have found a solution so that instant induction's can be used to place them into a trance with the end result of them going into a deep state of relaxation and not slipping out of Hypnosis as might occur otherwise when you don't want them to! The solution is simply:

1) Use your instant induction's and place everyone into the trance.
2) Then use the group deepening method as detailed later to deepen the trance to such a level whereby they will not slip out of it.

So remember that if left to their own devices and a group deepening method is not used, then the subjects of an instant induction would probably slip out of the hypnotic state in a very short space of time indeed.

THE SECRET OF SPEED

The secret of speed induction's is just to make sure that you follow the keys which I have mentioned already and also to have an enormous amount of confidence. This confidence must be in your abilities. You must also carry out the instantaneous induction's with no doubt in your mind that they WILL work! This is so that this personal belief is transmitted to the subjects and they are then in no doubt in their minds that it will work. You must do instant style induction's with conviction, also a very commanding tone of voice and attitude and you must transmit to the subject that you expect to be obeyed by them. An element of shock is also used with instant induction's in order to catch them off guard and as such "shock" them into deep hypnosis so to speak.

THE THREE STEPS TO HYPNOSIS

An even simpler way to explain how Hypnosis works to place someone into a trance state is like this:

A) They must know that you are a Professional Hypnotist and can therefore do as you claim.
B) Ask them to close their eyes and to breathe deeply and regularly.
C) Suggest ideas of heaviness, sleep, tiredness and relaxation to them for a few minutes and then THEY WILL BE IN A HYPNOTIC TRANCE.

Once again I'm sure you can see how it all relates back to those two key words/secrets which of course are belief and expectancy.

PEER GROUP PRESSURE

A small percentage of people will react to your suggestions due to peer group pressure and the fear that if they don't then they will be tormented and subjected to ridicule by their friends as they are unable to at that time be a good Hypnotic subject.

THE I.I.C. SYNDROME

A phrase which I always use in my opening patter is this: "If you've got good powers of intelligence, imagination and concentration then you will be a good Hypnotic subject!" The psychological effect of this is that if they come up to try and be Hypnotised and did not react, then they think it will make them look an even bigger fool by not reacting than by taking part and being a "good" subject in the show. As if they were to return to the audience their friends and family would ridicule them for not having good powers of intelligence, imagination and concentration to be a good Hypnotic subject. So again in a way, this relates back to peer group pressure.

THE KARAOKE SYNDROME

The life of an average person is the set 9 to 5 routine, they lack attention and appreciation in their lives and would love to have the chance to be the centre of attention and to be given some appreciation by lots of other people. In fact the secret dream of many people is to perform on stage even if they do make a fool of themselves. It's the Karaoke syndrome and is exactly the reason why Karaoke nights are so successful. Those people that get up know they are awful singers and are making a complete fool of themselves and yet to them, its an escape from everyday life, a step into the world of fantasy and the chance to be a star! The fact other people are also prepared to make fools of themselves brings the sheep effect into play, so it then doesn't bother them either to make a fool of themselves. In just the same way a high percentage of people who volunteer for your act will have the Karaoke syndrome at work on their mind and as such you have got several more good subjects to partake in your act.

THE SHEEP EFFECT

The sheep effect is such that if one person is prepared to do something or make a fool of themselves, then others will "follow the leader" and they become one of the sheep following the crowd and doing what all the others upon the stage or in life are doing. (Never allow yourself to become a sheep!)

THE EXHIBITIONIST

These come in two forms, the first is the positive one who likes to have a laugh, be the star of the show etc and as such although not actually under Hypnosis, plays along and hams it up so to speak. As entertainment is the key word on stage, if they look convincing you would of course allow them to remain on the stage. Then of course there is also the negative form which manifests itself as the person who has a need to show off to his friends/family just how great they are and what an idiot you are. These people of course should be dismissed from the stage at the earliest opportunity. It is a wise idea to have a friend stood in the wings (side area of the stage) who can keep an eye on the subjects whilst you are facing the audience and have your back turned to the on stage volunteers. This friend can then, if they spot anyone, give you a hand signal which you would of course have prearranged between you to indicate which person is and in which chair they are sitting. You then return them to the audience and by so doing, are now in almost the same position as having eyes in the back of your head. By the way if this observant friend is trained in Hypnosis also, they can then also give you hand signals to indicate which of the on stage volunteers will be good to place into trance, which ones not to bother with and those which are under deepest when Hypnotised.

PEOPLE HYPNOTISE THEMSELVES

The Hypnotist only tells them that they can do it! Until he told them, they never knew that they could do it. In effect we are "directors" of the film and the subjects become the "actors" doing as we say. We just guide them into what is really just a deep state of relaxation and should really be classed as "Self Hypnosis". So much for the 1952 Hypnotism act, 1989 guidelines and 1996 government review then! These are covered later.

THE PLACEBO EFFECT

Most all of the previously mentioned rules also apply to the use of Hypnosis in a therapeutic context, although in this case the persons motivations rather than stardom are those of changing their lives for the better. One important thing that applies only to Therapeutic work, is that of the placebo effect. By the time your client has read your newspaper advertisement and/or been given a personal recommendation about you by a previous client, belief and expectancy are already going to work on their minds. It then takes a lot of courage to phone you and book an appointment for Therapy as this is then a conscious decision within themselves that things must change and will change for the better. The prospect of attending at your house or office is one that will fill them with much apprehension and this is why in some cases, clients will not show up for their appointments as the thought of change becomes just too scary. However when a client does show up as happens in 99% of the cases they are almost cured of their problem the moment they step into your consulting room, as they have already made a conscious decision by booking the appointment and attending on time that things must change! The other piece in the jigsaw is when you get them to hand over the payment for the session before you even start the Therapy. Most people do not like parting with money, especially not large amounts of it, such as the fee of around £40 per hour, which you will be charging them for your time and as such paying this fee makes them believe in your abilities to help them even more. The final 25% of the Therapeutic process is the actual treatment which you give them, although even if this were to be fundamentally worthless (which it is not), if the client is made to believe it will be beneficial then indeed it will!

GOLDEN RULES TO FOLLOW

RULE ONE:	Have total confidence in yourself and your skilful abilities.
RULE TWO:	Exude that confidence so that others will then have total **confidence in you and your abilities.**
RULE THREE:	Monotony and repetition is the trade of the Hypnotist so repeat, repeat and then repeat it again.
RULE FOUR:	Learn to use your voice so that it can sound demanding and also commanding.
RULE FIVE:	Follow the steps and instructions detailed within this course to the letter and your success is guaranteed.

YOUR HYPNOTIC TOOLKIT

As a Hypnotist, the only tools of use to you are self-confidence, which you must have in abundance, suggestion, commanding and demanding tone of voice, rhythm of speech (cadence), monotony, repetition, professional appearance, knowledge and experience. These are the only tools available to you. However, if you learn to use them all effectively then it will become a most powerful tool kit and will make your job far easier. So learn to handle these tools with finesse for they are the start, middle and end of all that you must do and know.

SOME OTHER MOST IMPORTANT POINTS

1) Hypnotists are not Hypnotists, they are merely actors playing the part of the image of a Hypnotist which people expect to see and as such react to.
2) All Hypnosis whether Stage or Therapeutic is really just self hypnosis.
3) Hypnosis occurs due to co-operation and not confrontation or challenge.
4) As Hypnosis is just a state of mind and compliance based on the subjects levels of belief and expectancy, there is no such thing as a "Hypnotised" feeling and this is because each person experiences everything that happens during the course of their life differently.

5) Belief and expectancy are the most powerful keys of all to success.
6) Suggestion correctly expressed is Hypnosis.
7) The correct way to express suggestion is in a commanding and demanding voice, and to keep on repeating it to the subject.
8) One willing co-operative volunteer is worth more than a hundred pressed men.
9) To make life easy for you, use the suggestibility test of hands locking together to find those subjects who will be the easiest to Hypnotise and who are obviously in the correct co-operative state of mind.
10) A Hypnotist is perceived as being a person of authority and people in general expect to be ordered by and to obey as a person of authority says. Just remember your school days and you'll realise both what I mean and also the fact most all people are conditioned in this way.
11) For suggestions of sleep, slow deep tones of voice with words suggesting a downward motion are used.
12) For awakening suggestions, a faster, higher tone of voice with words suggesting an upward motion would be used.
13) The salesmen's techniques of mirroring and matching are used to put people to ease, make them relax and to establish rapport easily.
14) Hypnosis is a state of heightened awareness and as such subjects can taste, smell, see, feel and hear things better than they usually would be able and are more, rather than less aware of their surroundings.
) If the mind is focused on one thing, or at least one thing at a time and is not allowed to wander, then as the normal worries of the day are not considered your subject will automatically relax completely.
When people relax they tend to lose a lot of their inhibitions and this could also explain why they are then prepared to do daft things.
Confidence begets confidence and as a man thinketh so he becomes, which proves that positive thinking is a most positive force.
t has to be in the mind first before it becomes an action (in every day life) nd it has to be in the subconscious mind first to become an action during ypnosis.
hen the imagination (subconscious mind) and the will (conscious mind) in conflict, the imagination always wins. So if you can get a person to us their mind on something to the exclusion of everything else, you are able to bypass the critical area of their minds and firmly embed a estion into their imagination without any conscious conflict! Then vards even if the conscious mind were to try and oppose the suggestion ar stronger force of the imagination would always win and the tion would be acted upon.
sis merely shuts down the analytical (critical) area of the mind that is between the conscious and subconscious. It acts as a kind of "gate- and processes all incoming information from the conscious mind is allowed to enter the subconscious mind where it is permanently file.

21) As we've already stated if the suggestion can be given directly to the subconscious mind (the imagination) then it will be acted upon immediately and as I've stated already all Hypnosis does is shut down that analytical (critical) area of the mind which in turn makes this action possible.
22) Talk success, think success, act success and dream success and then successful things will occur.
23) Remember positive thoughts breed positive actions, they are contagious and positive actions breed positive results.
24) Relaxation is the key, which opens the door to the subconscious mind. In this state, get the subjects to visualise your suggestions with implicit faith that it is so and so and it will be.
25) Co-operations with a highly developed imagination are the best qualities your subject can have for successful acceptance of your Hypnoti suggestions.
26) You want your subjects to have confidence, belief and faith with expectat of success, but it is no use just telling them this. They must be "sold" Hypnosis and its effects to possess these real qualities.
27) Rapport, observation, recognition and leadership. These are the four of inducing a Hypnotic trance. All are lead by the subject and followed by the Hypnotist as will be explained later.
28) Rapport should establish three things, trust, comfort and of course
29) Hypnosis is merely a form of communication. Tone of voice is all communication and indeed in Hypnosis also. It is also pos "secret" messages within a spoken sentence by changing your so that they have an almost "subliminal" effect.
30) You must take the venue or consulting room over. Show t alone are in charge. Demand instant respect, dominate you the subjects and condition them to react to your sugges they are in a trance. Give them orders and expect them and act in an authoritative manner and look at ease w their mind off what's happening at all times and then way to Hypnotic success.
31) If they believe that you have special powers then expect to be Hypnotised by you then they will be!
32) They are in a strange situation and environmen therapy) whereas you feel at ease. You have the at home upon the stage or in the room and the make them feel important, needed and appre them so that they sincerely believe they are o co-operate with you.
33) You know what's going to happen and th of them. You act in a routine manner as then work.

34) Ordering them around at the start conditions them to obey you. You are the salesman selling the great idea of Hypnosis to them. The sheep effect then makes them follow the leader and try to be a "better" subject than the others upon the stage.
35) Music which suits each routine in the background sets the correct style of scene and has a psychological effect upon them, that of making it all seem more real and easier to imagine.
36) The subjects who are in a deep trance are kept and used for the, harder routines. You then direct all applause to them and this reward makes them feel good and also conditions them to react throughout.
37) On stage always paint a verbal picture, so that the subjects know what is expected of them. They must know what you are saying as they cannot read your mind. The suggestions you give must also have one meaning only so that they cannot be misinterpreted.
38) A Hypnotist to be successful must be a self-motivated, strong minded, egotistical individual, who is confident in their skills. You must be a good showman and an artist par excellence. A smooth talker, persuasionist, salesman. Actor and adaptable at a seconds notice. In other words you must be able to think on your feet, use your common sense and have the gift of the gab.
39) Hypnosis is co-operation and not confrontation and the nature of your game should be imagination not humiliation.
40) You cannot see Hypnosis, you can only see the effects of it. This is my reason for saying that the use of props and music helps to make the whole show more attractive and more believable for both the on stage subjects and also for the watching audience.
41) Lastly for this part, allow me to explain how Hypnosis works between the subject and the Hypnotist in much the same way as a Bio-feedback machine. Also let me explain briefly how the human mind works, we'll elaborate later on.

THE HUMAN MIND AS I SEE IT

As I see it the human mind is made up of three separate layers making the whole, these three layers are as follows:

1) The conscious mind and/or human will.
2) The analytical and/or critical area.
3) The subconscious and/or imagination

We use the conscious mind to speak etc, the subconscious deals with the automatic actions of our blood circulation and breathing as well as being our imagination area of the mind. And lastly the analytical area analyses all incoming information before being allowed entry and storage in the subconscious mind as truth/fact. I will now make the analogy of the mind being a computer. The conscious mind is if you like the keyboard, which inputs new information. The analytical area analyses it for any mistakes in much the same way as a spell checker, then the "corrected" data, if of an acceptable nature, is allowed to enter the subconscious mind where it is stored forever in much the same way as storing data onto a floppy disc. To briefly explain if you told a fully conscious person that when you snapped your fingers they are Elvis and then snapped same said fingers, they would not react! Why? Well simply because the analytical area processes it and then compares it with the memory bank record in the subjects subconscious mind of who they are before rejecting it as it realises the statement to be untrue. All this of course takes only a fraction of a second to occur.

Under Hypnosis the mind and body of the subject relax, and due to the disorientation, confusion and repetition of suggestion the analytical area shuts down or goes to sleep. As such when told that on a snap of the fingers they will be Elvis the mind is then unable to process the information and find out that it is untrue and consequently it is believed to be true. It goes directly into the subconscious as being true and so is acted upon as an automatic reflex action. If only in a very light state of trance the will of the person may still go into conflict with the imagination or subconscious, but as we stated earlier when the imagination and will are in conflict the imagination always wins. As such they will react and be Elvis or do whatever you have suggested without question. Just as with any computer, programs placed into the memory which in the long term could be dangerous or more harm than good MUST be cancelled out or erased so that things revert to normality. So it is also with your subjects mind, all suggestions must be completely cancelled out before they leave the venue after the Hypnotic show. Otherwise they will remain in the computers memory bank to be automatically acted upon long into the future! Imagine the scene as the subject is driving home and Elvis comes onto the radio. This triggers off the memory bank association that upon hearing Elvis they must start to dance. They then do so and Crash! This is obviously an extreme example but expressed to implant firmly into your mind the importance of removing all suggestions and commands from your subject's minds except those of a beneficial nature such as in Therapy before they leave the room. You should always aim to leave them feeling refreshed and as good if not better than when they entered the venue that night. If you do this and abide fully by the 1952 Hypnotism Act, the 1989 guidelines and the 1996 Government review and generally put the safety of your volunteers first then you should be a most successful performer. This part contains all the keys you require for Hypnotic success, but I'll end by explaining how the mind is like a Bio-feedback machine. Observe Figure A and you will see the Hypnotist facing the subject. The final key to a most successful induction is as follows. The Hypnotist suggests things to the subject w… reacts to these verbal suggestions. The Hypnotist then ob… those suggestions and feeds back his observations as new… subject. The subject accepts and reacts to these, the Hyp… effects and then feeds back the observations as new suggest… and so the Biofeedback computer effect continues until the s… state of trance. In other words the Hypnotist's suggestions are a… his observations.

FIGURE A

THE BIOFEEDBACK COMPUTER EFFECT

An example of this so that you fully understand how it works would be as follows. The Hypnotist suggests that the subject will start to breathe deeply and regularly, this is then accepted by the subject and acted upon by them. They then start to breathe more deeply and regularly and perhaps also start to close their eyes. The Hypnotist observes this and then feeds back the observation to the subject as new suggestions along the line of "That's great and as you continue to breathe deeply and regularly, notice how your eyelids are now so heavy and so tired, in fact it's so much easier, just to let them close!" The subject accepts and reacts, the Hypnotist observes and feeds back the observations as new suggestions and so the cycle continues. This now means that you really do know how to Hypnotise someone, as with this technique the wording of your induction must always be ad lib and worded so as to contain your observations and as such

n. You would of course at all times be following the basic tone and speed of suggestions etc. And remember the key by most people with Hypnosis and a trance state are: sleep, deeper, falling, resting, calm, heavy, tired and all other words ch mean similar things to these.

atulations you now know more about Stage Hypnosis, Hypnotherapy ed Mind Therapies than most if not all of the "cowboy" Hypnotists currently flooding the industry. Now that you have the keys to Hypnotic s, lets look at them all separately and in depth so that your understanding nowledge of the subject is total. You will have noticed by now I'm sure, throughout this course, I will repeat many key points several times, the ason for this is that the trade of any Hypnotist is repetition and you can only earn through repetition. As such, this course has been written, not only to be enjoyable to read, but rather in a way that you learn the maximum amount possible in the shortest space of time possible. The fields of Stage Hypnosis, Hypnotherapy and Related Mind Therapies have made numerous Hypnotic multi millionaires and many more of us very rich and financially independent indeed. I promise that after reading the last page of this course, listening to the instructional audio-tapes, viewing the videos and possibly attending your personal training day, you will be in a position to, if you so desire achieve this same level of financial freedom and success. And don't forget of course that should you ever require any additional help or advice I am only ever at the end of a telephone line and as my old grandmother used to say "Two heads are better than one, even if they are sheep's heads in a pan of barley!" For now I'll sign off and see you in the next chapter.

PART TWO

"BE PREPARED"

"You can't see electricity but you wouldn't push your finger into a plug socket because you know that it does exist. In much the same way you can't see hypnosis as its all in a persons state of mind, however if the subject believes that it exists, then and only then does it genuinely exist! As in reality, all hypnosis is just a state of mind and state of belief!"

"Your subjects are over 90% of the way to being hypnotised deeply when they step foot onto the stage and/or into your consulting room. This is due to your pre show or consultation preparation and that is what we shall discuss in this part. The preparation which needs to be done beforehand in order to guarantee its success!"

Welcome to part two, here we will discuss the elements which when all are combined go some way to placing your potential subjects into a state of mind where they are over 90% hypnotised before they even start! How? Well your reputation as a hypnotist has preceded you, the "induction" of the people starts to happen long before you meet the people. The advertising or recommendations instils the belief of your powers into the subject's minds in advance of the day in question. It also creates within them the expectancy that you, as the great hypnotist, will make them unable to resist and as such will go under instantly! So they are over 90% on their way to being in a deep state of hypnosis when you first meet them.

Let's imagine it's a month before one of my theatre shows, you look in your local newspaper and see an article about me, my show and what a marvellous hypnotist I am. Or you see or hear of someone who has been treated. You start have read and as such phone up the box office and order a ...e to make an appointment. You make a note in your diary of ..., or a few days later a letter arrives, you open it and YES the ...red have arrived and so you place them inside your wallet for safe ...n the ticket it says Alex Leroy, World's No.1 Hypnotist. This ...u even more of my skills in an almost subliminal way. Over the few ...follow you mention the forthcoming show or appointment to friends, seeing adverts for the show in the local paper, posters around town, on the TV & Radio and in general you keep getting reminders of the ...which you are soon to see. Needless to say that all these reminders go ...way further to convincing you that I am a master of my craft and must be ...best thing since sex was invented. Each time you remove or place things into ...ur wallet you see the tickets and the show returns to your mind yet again. The ...ight of the performance arrives, you've paid £10 to come and see me, so you expect that the show must be worth this amount which would mean that I can hypnotise people including yourself if I were to pick upon you. You take extra special care to get ready and look smart, just in case you are chosen to go on stage and be hypnotised, which means that you must by now believe you might end up doing this which means in turn it would be easy for me to achieve. You arrive at the venue, the show is a sell-out and people are being turned away. This creates a feeling of excitement and expectation within. That the show you are about to see will be the best ever! You enter the foyer and a front of house display board shows my recent national press cuttings and photos taken during other past shows. You take a closer look at this display and see that other normal people, like yourself have been controlled and hypnotised by me. So then you believe 100% fully that as you are just as intelligent as the next man, you to can and will be hypnotised if I should approach you. You enter the auditorium, the lighting is dim and the background music gentle, relaxing and mysterious such as the music produced by Enigma. You take your seat and stare towards the stage waiting for the hypnotist to start his show. Your expectations are now high and belief almost total. And as we've stated earlier if a subject believes in your powers and expects you to be able to hypnotise them then you will be able to. The music starts. It is loud and mysterious, such as Thus Spoke Zarathustra from the 2001 Space Odessy soundtrack and recorded within it is my voice over introduction. This introduction may be in two parts as mine is. My intro music is "Are you ready for this?" By Two Unlimited. The track is a disco style tune and I personally have smoke coming off stage whilst coloured disco lights revolve on both sides of the stage sending rays of light shooting around the room like laser beams. The mid section of the track sounds all weird but changes in tempo and recorded upon this section I have a strange horror movie Orson Wells style disembodied voice which say "Ladies and Gentlemen, welcome to the show! Ask yourself this… are you ready to witness the most exciting, unusual and amazing show in the world today? Are you ready to let imagination become reality? Are as follows. The Hypnotist suggests things to the subject who in turn accepts and reacts to these verbal suggestions. The Hypnotist then observes the effects of those suggestions and feeds back his observations as new suggestions to the subject. The subject accepts and reacts to these, the Hypnotist observes the effects and then feeds back the observations as new suggestions to the subjects and so the Biofeedback computer effect continues until the subject is in a deep state of trance. In other words the Hypnotist's suggestions are always made up of his observations.

FIGURE A

THE BIOFEEDBACK COMPUTER EFFECT

An example of this so that you fully understand how it works would be as follows. The Hypnotist suggests that the subject will start to breathe deeply and regularly, this is then accepted by the subject and acted upon by them. They then start to breathe more deeply and regularly and perhaps also start to close their eyes. The Hypnotist observes this and then feeds back the observation to the subject as new suggestions along the line of "That's great and as you continue to breathe deeply and regularly, notice how your eyelids are now so heavy and so tired, in fact it's so much easier, just to let them close!" The subject accepts and reacts, the Hypnotist observes and feeds back the observations as new suggestions and so the cycle continues. This now means that you really do know how to Hypnotise someone, as with this technique the wording of your induction must always be ad lib and worded so as to contain your observations and as such capitalise upon them. You would of course at all times be following the basic guidelines of voice tone and speed of suggestions etc. And remember the key words associated by most people with Hypnosis and a trance state are: sleep, relax, drifting, deeper, falling, resting, calm, heavy, tired and all other words associated which mean similar things to these.

Well congratulations you now know more about Stage Hypnosis, Hypnotherapy and Related Mind Therapies than most if not all of the "cowboy" Hypnotists who are currently flooding the industry. Now that you have the keys to Hypnotic success, lets look at them all separately and in depth so that your understanding and knowledge of the subject is total. You will have noticed by now I'm sure, that throughout this course, I will repeat many key points several times, the reason for this is that the trade of any Hypnotist is repetition and you can only learn through repetition. As such, this course has been written, not only to be enjoyable to read, but rather in a way that you learn the maximum amount possible in the shortest space of time possible. The fields of Stage Hypnosis, Hypnotherapy and Related Mind Therapies have made numerous Hypnotic multi millionaires and many more of us very rich and financially independent indeed. I promise that after reading the last page of this course, listening to the instructional audio-tapes, viewing the videos and possibly attending your personal training day, you will be in a position to, if you so desire achieve this same level of financial freedom and success. And don't forget of course that should you ever require any additional help or advice I am only ever at the end of a telephone line and as my old grandmother used to say "Two heads are better than one, even if they are sheep's heads in a pan of barley!" For now I'll sign off and see you in the next chapter.

PART TWO

"BE PREPARED"

"You can't see electricity but you wouldn't push your finger into a plug socket because you know that it does exist. In much the same way you can't see hypnosis as its all in a persons state of mind, however if the subject believes that it exists, then and only then does it genuinely exist! As in reality, all hypnosis is just a state of mind and state of belief!"

"Your subjects are over 90% of the way to being hypnotised deeply when they step foot onto the stage and/or into your consulting room. This is due to your pre show or consultation preparation and that is what we shall discuss in this part. The preparation which needs to be done beforehand in order to guarantee its success!"

Welcome to part two, here we will discuss the elements which when all are combined go some way to placing your potential subjects into a state of mind where they are over 90% hypnotised before they even start. How? Well your reputation as a hypnotist has preceded you, the "induction" of the people starts to happen long before you meet the people. The advertising or recommendations instils the belief of your powers into the subject's minds in advance of the day in question. It also creates within them the expectancy that you, as the great hypnotist, will make them unable to resist and as such will go under instantly! So they are over 90% on their way to being in a deep state of hypnosis when you first meet them.

Let's imagine it's a month before one of my theatre shows, you look in your local newspaper and see an article about me, my show and what a marvellous hypnotist I am. Or you see or hear of someone who has been treated. You start to believe what you have read and as such phone up the box office and order a ticket, or telephone to make an appointment. You make a note in your diary of the appointment, or a few days later a letter arrives, you open it and YES the tickets you ordered have arrived and so you place them inside your wallet for safe keeping. Upon the ticket it says Alex Leroy, World's No.1 Hypnotist. This convinces you even more of my skills in an almost subliminal way. Over the few weeks that follow you mention the forthcoming show or appointment to friends, you keep seeing adverts for the show in the local paper, posters around town, adverts on the TV & Radio and in general you keep getting reminders of the show which you are soon to see. Needless to say that all these reminders go some way further to convincing you that I am a master of my craft and must be the best thing since sex was invented. Each time you remove or place things into your wallet you see the tickets and the show returns to your mind yet again. The night of the performance arrives, you've paid £10 to come and see me, so you expect that the show must be worth this amount which would mean that I can hypnotise people including yourself if I were to pick upon you. You take extra special care to get ready and look smart, just in case you are chosen to go on stage and be hypnotised, which means that you must by now believe you might end up doing this which means in turn it would be easy for me to achieve. You arrive at the venue, the show is a sell-out and people are being turned away. This creates a feeling of excitement and expectation within. That the show you are about to see will be the best ever! You enter the foyer and a front of house display board shows my recent national press cuttings and photos taken during other past shows. You take a closer look at this display and see that other normal people, like yourself have been controlled and hypnotised by me. So then you believe 100% fully that as you are just as intelligent as the next man, you to can and will be hypnotised if I should approach you. You enter the auditorium, the lighting is dim and the background music gentle, relaxing and mysterious such as the music produced by Enigma. You take your seat and stare towards the stage waiting for the hypnotist to start his show. Your expectations are now high and belief almost total. And as we've stated earlier if a subject believes in your powers and expects you to be able to hypnotise them then you will be able to. The music starts. It is loud and mysterious, such as Thus Spoke Zarathustra from the 2001 Space Odessy soundtrack and recorded within it is my voice over introduction. This introduction may be in two parts as mine is. My intro music is "Are you ready for this?" By Two Unlimited. The track is a disco style tune and I personally have smoke coming off stage whilst coloured disco lights revolve on both sides of the stage sending rays of light shooting around the room like laser beams. The mid section of the track sounds all weird but changes in tempo and recorded upon this section I have a strange horror movie Orson Wells style disembodied voice which say "Ladies and Gentlemen, welcome to the show! Ask yourself this… are you ready to witness the most exciting, unusual and amazing show in the world today? Are you ready to let imagination become reality? Are you ready for this?" At this point the music goes back up tempo, but this has had the psychological effect of making them believe this is the best show and the best hypnotist they could ever see in their entire life. The music continues and just before it ends an American style voice says "Ladies and gentlemen, hold onto your seats and leave your misconceptions behind as you welcome live on stage Europe's fastest, funniest and most outrageous hypnotist, the one, the only, the amazing Alex Leroy!" You applaud as does everyone else, the atmosphere is electric and I walk out onto the stage to the background (play on) music of "Simply the best" by Tina Turner. My posture is good (dance training helps here). I am smartly dressed in designer clothing although you may feel more at ease wearing an evening suit or tuxedo. Not a hair on my head is out of place, my stage make up gives the impression I have a lovely suntan, I am wearing expensive jewellery and in fact in every way possible I look to be a most confident and successful stage performer. I command the audience's attention instantly by my self confidence and appearance. I act as though I own the place, this is going to be the best show of my life and I must not have a single thought of failure in my head (self-hypnosis is useful here).

From this moment forward I must take the place over and must at all times act as if I am in charge. I must demand instant respect from the audience and I must them dominate them so much that they are in awe of me and have no doubts in their minds that I do indeed know my craft 100% inside out. This is then the point where my opening comedy lines and introductory talk (patter) are made to the audience and details of this follows in the next part. I then go into the handclasp routine in order to get only the best most suggestive subjects upon the stage. The people who's hands remain together are told to come to the stage as are any other audience members who would like to volunteer and enter my hypnotic world where fantasy becomes reality and there really are NO LIMIT'S. The Two Unlimited song "No Limits" then plays as they come to the stage. Once upon the stage I immediately start to give them orders in a confident and authoritative voice in order that they feel they must obey me. At this point you may leave their hands locked together or indeed unlock them depending on your style. You move them about the stage, ask them their names, where they come from etc, you get them to change seats in fact it matters little what you get them to do just so long as right from the word go they obey you and know they must do exactly as you demand. Question? Is the soldier on parade hypnotised to obey every order? Well in a way he is and the same situation is starting to happen here with you and the people on stage. You are ordering people to do certain things and they are unquestionably obeying your every command, which conditions them to continue doing so at all times. You now explain before proceeding with the induction those people that cannot be hypnotised (see chapter on opening talk). You then also explain that hypnosis is very much a two way thing and that you require the attention and co-operation of the on stage subjects to ensure success. By doing this the ball is now in their court, as, if they don't go into trance and react to your suggestions, then in the eyes of the audience it's their fault and not yours! You explain that hypnosis is a very relaxing and enjoyable experience and that they will enjoy every second of it! By saying this it makes them want to experience the state and so the whole self hypnosis thing comes into play. Then you explain that you can only hypnotise people with the correct powers of intelligence, imagination and concentration to be a good hypnotic subject and possibly the star of tonight's show. Lastly you say the audience will be laughing with them and not at them and that the audience will applaud to show their appreciation as without the onstage volunteers help and co-operation, there really would be no show.

By saying all this, they feel that if they don't go under, then they are stupid and will look stupid in front of an audience. They also feel they have the chance to be the centre of attention, to be a star for the night and as such they will grab this chance as detailed earlier in this course. They know the audience will appreciate what they do and now any objections they may have had will have gone and your job is literally as easy as saying that when you touch them on the head and say sleep they will immediately close their eyes, relax every muscle in their bodies, fall backwards into your arms and go to sleep....because this is the fastest form of hypnosis known to mankind!

So, you've told them how you expect them to react and you have instilled the belief into them that it will work as you say. Combine all these points with the fact that they want an escape from life, the chance to be a star, plus the fact that you have now on stage only those people most likely to go under (due to handclasp) who have 98% induced themselves before they get upon the stage and I'm sure you'll realise just how easy stage hypnosis really can be. You must have 100% faith in your abilities though and must feel 100% confident they will sense you are a professional who knows his craft and knows it will work so that in turn they will relax, believe and go into trance. If they don't actually go into a trance they will just play along and try to be the star of the show anyway. So what have you got to lose? Let them do this, as after all the audience won't know and the entertainment value is the most important factor with a stage show. Some people have one stooge planted in the audience who comes onto the stage at the same time as the genuine volunteers and then they appear to place the stooge into a trance first. The genuine people see him go under and fall to the floor asleep and now their belief in you and your powers is 150% complete. Now the sheep effect comes into play and they follow the leader and do as the stooge did or else they become the odd one out. To create the funniest situations upon the stage you must always give an air of competition so that the subjects feel they are in competition with each other. They will then respond in better and funnier ways. The remainder of the subjects after the stooge, should you use one (although its not necessary), are then placed into trance using one of the instant induction's detailed later before the group of people as a whole is given the group deepening instructions to ensure they are all in a deep trance. At this point you give them all the post hypnotic suggestion of: "For the rest of this evening you will react only to the sound of my voice, unless I indicate otherwise I shall only be talking to you if I place my hand upon your shoulder. So in a few moments when I awake you, you'll instantly be wide awake and for the rest of this evening whilst in this building whenever I say sleep to you, you'll instantly renter this state and each and every time you do renter this state you'll go deeper and deeper to sleep. Should for any reason you have to leave this building before the show ends then everything I've said up until that point will be completely cancelled out and you'll be as you were when you arrived here tonight! However each time I awaken you you'll have an overwhelming desire to do whatever I have suggested as an automatic reflex action and finally, you will not go anywhere near the edge of the stage, you'll stay well back and this is because there is an invisible forcefield around the edge of the stage which stops you going close to it. (The first comedy routine suggestion is now given) OK now everyone 1,2, wide awake."

Once all the subjects are induced, deepened to the correct state and have been given the above post hypnotic suggestion, then your comedy routines can begin which of course are limited only by your own imagination and time constraints. At the end of the first half of the show (usually one-hour in theatres) you give the volunteers separate suggestions each of what they are to do in and around the audience in the bar etc during the interval. You then give them all the post hypnotic suggestion that when you say "come and join the party", when you say "come and join the party", they'll all rush up from their seats and return to the stage as quickly and as safely as possible.

The interval then takes place, with a show going on all the time with no actual effort from yourself. Approximately 20 minutes later the audience is returned to their seats and no later than 30 minutes after the interval started the show recommences. The music is again loud and mysterious and as before the smoke, lights and special effects all go a long way to making the show look good. The voice over on your second half intro music introduces you once again as follows "Ladies and Gentlemen, please welcome back live on stage a unique comedy entertainer world renowned hypnotist Alex Leroy." Then you walk out as before with a good posture but in a change of costume so it adds to the professionalism and showbusiness of the whole thing. You do your second half of the show opening patter and then say "Come and join the party" at which point the subjects race up from their seats and join you on the stage where you question them about what they've been doing in the interval, which gets many laughs. You then put them all back under just by saying the key word "sleep", and your second half is then performed as per your own personal running order of comedy routines.

At the end of the second half of the show, after the final routine, they are all put back under and as a group they are all brought out of trance with all commands given being completely cancelled out in every way. This ensures they leave as they arrived, with no debris in their minds. Everyone lines up, you give them all a free ticket to see your show the next time you're in town as a "thank you" for participating in the show. They are given these both because they didn't see the show and also because it guarantees that you have some good hypnotic subjects at your next show at that venue. The subjects are sent back to the audience and your pitch for audio hypnotherapy tapes is made before saying "if you've enjoyed the show my names Paul McKenna and if you haven't then my names Alex Leroy" Your "Play off" music of Simply The Best starts as you walk off stage to thunderous applause. The audience then all goes home and they say very good things about you, which ensures a full house at your next show. Always remember that the very best form of advertising is personal recommendation and/or word of mouth. It is for this reason that it is always good if you can announce on the night of your show the next time you will be appearing at the venue. By so doing the audience will spread the word to their friends and also they will if they have enjoyed the show, purchase a ticket for your next appearance before they leave the venue that night which both gets you the money in early and ensures good attendance.

THE AWAKENING METHOD

"OK everyone just relax and sleep, I'm going to, in a moment count from 1 to 10 and on the count of 10 you will all be completely wide awake. There will be no side effects whatsoever and in fact you will feel better than you did when you entered this theatre tonight. All the things I've suggested to you will be completely cancelled out and no longer have any effect. In other words, you'll walk out of this building tonight feeling just as good if not better than when you arrived. Most of all, you will be wide-awake, full of energy and 100% normal in every way. 1, 2, 3, lighter and brighter. 4,5,6, coming up out of it now and beginning to breathe more normally, 7, almost as though your eyes are being washed by pure spring water. 8, feeling full of energy and optimism now as everything I've suggested tonight is with immediate effect erased from your memory banks. 9, full alertness and consciousness now returning and on 10 your wide awake, wakey wakey rise and shine!"

Well that's how the preparation works, the layout of a standard hypnotic theatre show and all that occurs prior to them being hypnotised to get them into the correct state of mind. It is also how my two and a half hour theatre stage show is structured. As the old saying goes, "If you follow a way that's tried, tested and proven to work then it will save a lot of trial and error on your part". Once again I will repeat one of the best pieces of advice in this entire course. If you want to be a Hypnotherapist go and consult a therapist and observe how he handles the session. If you want to be a stage hypnotist then do the same thing by watching as many hypnotists at work as possible, see you in part three!

PART THREE

"KNOW YOUR LINES"

"The man who said flattery will get you nowhere obviously knew how powerful it was and wanted to keep it to himself! Flattery will get you everywhere in life, in therapy and on stage."

"In this business it really is a case of "its not what you know but who you know", so try and go where the right people are and "accidentally" bump into them."

"If you've got to stay in a town overnight, stay in the best Five Star hotel even if it costs more than you can really afford! It is in places such as this that you have a far better chance of meeting people who can be of help to your career. So although it's a big expense, in the long term it's a major investment and will pay you dividends."

Also remember these two showbusiness adages. "The show must go on!" and "Always leave the audience wanting more!" There is of course the very true saying also of "Its not what you do but the way that you do it that matters" and this is the thing which will make you stand out from other hypnotists both in the eyes of the audience and potential bookers!"

Welcome to part three. Here I will give you examples of the patter, which I originally used in my shows when I started out. It should be noted that most of this patter was directly copied **from ANDREW NEWTON – (THE MAN WHO TAUGHT PAUL McKENNA)** and at the time was done without his permission. This information is now included here with Andrew Newton's permission on condition that you are aware that anyone who copies this word for word will have legal action taken against them, something which Newton has done several times successfully in the past against others who have attempted to steal his act in order to get more work or a TV show! This information regarding patter in this chapter is 100% Originated by and Copyrighted to Andrew Newton and as such you do not have permission to use it other than as a perfect example of how to structure your own opening talk so that it includes all of the Psychological points you need for success. Speaking of Newton there is much you could learn from him also and as such you are advised to visit the site of ***www.newtonhypnotictraining.com.***

Also in this chapter I will include examples of comedy gags relating to hypnosis which you may wish to include in your own patter when writing the script for your own show. You do not have my permission to copy my show word for word as it is detailed within this course for example only. Although to the audience it's not obvious what you are saying has been learnt word perfect parrot fashion this is actually the case and for good reason too.

As a hypnotist, you must be confident, decisive, straight to the point and shouldn't make any mistakes. By scripting as much of your show as possible you are far less likely to have "gaps" appear in what you say and do. And you can then be sure you'll be saying all that you need to in the least number of words possible and as such will appear far more confident and decisive. The examples given in this chapter are all ones that I either use at the time of writing or ones that I've used earlier in my career as part of my stage shows. Rest assured they all have the psychological effect of getting your potential subjects into a state of mind where they will co-operate as easily as is humanly possible.

NEWTON'S OPENING PATTER FOR THEATRES & LARGE VENUES

"Thank you, thank you and thank you too. Thank you very much indeed ladies and gentlemen for that truly overwhelming reception and welcome to what's going to be for most of you I'm sure, a truly interesting, informative and entertaining hour or so. Now the reason that I say most of you is because obviously tonight many of you will be hypnotised and for those of you who are hypnotised it will be a very relaxing, enjoyable if somewhat slightly unusual experience.

Now although you'll hear me say the word sleep rather a lot tonight, none of you will actually ever be asleep or at least I hope you won't. If you're hypnotised you'll be fully aware of everything that's going on around you at all times, you'll just have this overwhelming desire to do almost everything that I say. Now the reason I say almost everything I say is because it is impossible, despite what you may have read in the media to make anyone say or do anything which would contradict their morals or their values. So what I'm ideally looking for tonight are about a dozen or so people with no morals and with no values and then I'm sure we can all have a great show! Seriously though, although I say I want a dozen or so people to fill these chairs ideally I want about 40 or 50 people to come up to the stage and then we can pick out those with the best imaginations.

Actually to be truthful in an ideal world I'd hypnotise you all go to the bar, get drunk and then come back in an hour, wake you all up and tell you you'd all enjoyed a really wonderful show! Now basically speaking, virtually everybody can be hypnotised which is actually very true indeed. Every single one of you here tonight can be hypnotised, but its not always possible for me to hypnotise everyone that comes on stage right at the start and that's mainly due to the short time of space available as I'm sure you'll appreciate! Having said that of course it is virtually impossible to hypnotise anyone who does not wish to be hypnotised, so when I ask for volunteers, you have to come up here on stage with the idea of letting yourself go, relaxing and giving it a try. If you come on stage with an open mind that's all that really matters, the other things of course is that you can't hypnotise anyone who is drunk and the reason for this is that drunk people already think they are hypnotised! But I'm sure we won't have any problems there. And finally I can't hypnotise anyone who's asthmatic, epileptic, clinically depressed, suffering from any heart condition or indeed any pregnant women, although if your not pregnant see me after the show and we can sort that one out. Also I can't hypnotise the insane because despite popular belief in order to be a good hypnotic subject you need good powers of intelligence, imagination and concentration. Now I am aware of the fact that there are some families in the audience here this evening with younger children. This is very much a family show and I only mention this because when I ask for volunteers I would prefer it if the really young ones didn't come up to be hypnotised. It's not that there's any rule or anything it's just purely and simply that I hate kids! So if the really young ones could stay in their seats that would be much better all round. Are there any in by the way? (Wave at them) Hello, that was just a little joke by the way I didn't mean anything by it OK? (Pause) Jolly good, Father Christmas is dead.

Now I think that we've all got the gist of the idea now and I also think that covers just about everything that I wanted to say to you, so what I'd like you all to do now is take part in a little experiment which involves you all, even the people sitting upstairs in the cheap seats! Incidentally are you all right in the balcony? Well you won't be for long, it's loose!

NEWTON'S LOCKED HANDS PATTER

"Now all that's going to happen here is that when I say one, you'll put your hands straight out in front of you like so. When I say two you'll join your hands together, fingers interlocked, palms pressed tightly together and then you'll squeeze your hands together just as tightly as you can. And when I say three you'll just close your eyes and concentrate upon your hands. Now all that will happen with this experiment is, that if you concentrate, which I'm sure you will, then you'll find that your hands keep getting tighter and tighter all the time. In fact many of you will find that your hands get so tight that they will begin to shake violently like this (shake own hands to and fro). If this does happen to you, don't worry its perfectly natural, it happens all the time, you won't go blind and it won't last for very long! Now you may laugh at that bit, but there's a guy there with the big glasses and he knows exactly what I'm talking about don't you? OK, now remember this is just a little experiment to find out which of you have got good enough powers of intelligence, imagination and concentration to be a good hypnotic subject and possibly the star of tonight's show. So now is the time to put down your handbags and your purses and if the women could do the same that would be a great start. So here we go now, on ONE, hands out in front of you. TWO, join your hands together, fingers interlocked, palms pressed tightly together, as tightly as you possibly can, so that the fingers of the left hand are pressed firmly against the back of the right hand and so that the fingers of the right hand are pressed firmly against the back of your left hand. And on THREE, just close your eyes and concentrate on your hands and the sound of my voice.

(At this point Jean Michelle Jarre's Oxygene music starts to play)

FOUR, you can feel them getting tighter now, really concentrate its almost as though your hands are stuck together with the worlds strongest superglue. FIVE, Your hands getting tighter and tighter with every breath you take, every noise that you hear and every word that I say, tighter and tighter. SIX, they are getting tighter and tighter, and the tighter they get the more they will shake and the more they shake the tighter they will get. Seven, Eight, Nine, they're getting extremely tight now, tighter and tighter. TEN as you listen only to my voice and the sound of the music your hands are getting one hundred times tighter all the time. 11,12,13, They're getting much tighter now. 14, 15, hands getting tighter and tighter all the time now as they shake more with each second that passes by. 16, 17, 18, now lift your hands up above your heads, in the air now getting tighter and tighter all the time. 19, getting much, much tighter now as each second passes by so quickly and on 20, good now wherever you are, open your eyes and concentrate on me and me alone for a few moments. Now even if your hands are only slightly tight at this moment it does not matter, what I would like you to do now though is this. With your hands above your head, stand up in front of the chair your sitting in so that we can all have a good look at each other. Come on up, up, up, good that's much better. OK now hands in the air getting tighter and tighter and tighter. Now wherever you are, move out into the nearest aisle to you and walk this way up to the stage and we'll see you all up here in about a minute's time.

(The Star Wars theme tune then plays them up to the stage)

Right, now here we have a fair selection of perfect strangers, well actually they're not perfect, but by the look of them they are strange. First of all if one or two of you are feeling a little apprehensive about what's going to happen tonight, I'd like to assure you that whatever else happens tonight, I won't be making anyone run around the stage like a chicken or getting anyone to take their clothes off or anything like that! (Here turn to the audience wink at them and smile as if lying) Seriously though, fundamentally speaking you won't be asked to do anything, which contradicts your morals or your values. So firstly if there's any Estate Agents in, I won't be asking you to tell the truth and secondly if there's any Sunday Sport readers in I'll explain what fundamentally means after the show. For the next few minutes though, just stare directly at your hands not at me or anywhere else. Each time I count to three your hands will continue to get tighter and tighter all the time. 1,2,3 (click fingers) look straight at your hands and every time I count 1,2,3, they will continue to get even tighter. So 1,2,3, tighter and tighter now, so tight they'll start to shake and the harder you try to stop them shaking the more they are going to shake and quiver violently! Getting tighter and tighter now 1,2,3 tighter all the time. Really concentrate and think of nothing but your hands 1,2,3 tighter and tighter. OK all stand where you are, feet together, 1,2,3 tighter and tighter 1,2,3. 1,2,3. 1,2,3 tighter and tighter."

SPECIAL NOTE At this point you question the participants, names, where they live, jobs, have they been hypnotised before etc. and at all opportunities use normal one liner jokes for comedy impact. This entertains the audience and also gives you time to work out which will be the best subjects by observing who's hands are shaking most and who seems to be concentrating on their hands and following your instructions most. Then its back into the patter as follows: "OK right, well we'll start with you then sir, (the best subject who's hands are shaking most) by the way you don't mind me calling you sir do you? After all it's only in fun!"

NEWTON'S FALLING BACKWARDS INDUCTION ON SUBJECT A

Feet together, hands against your chest, tilt your head well back and close your eyes. I'd like you to take a nice deep breath in, then out, nice deep breaths, gets fresh air and oxygen into the blood stream and helps you to relax. Now when I count backwards from 3 down to 1, this time your going to feel yourself falling gently backwards into my arms, but I won't let you fall and hurt yourself, you'll just go into a beautifully relaxed state when I count from 3 down to 1. 3,2,1, falling back, back and sleeep (draw out the word sleep).

ROYLE'S FALLING BACKWARDS ON SECOND SUBJECT

"OK, now you know what's going to happen and you know you'll be completely safe at all times. So feet together, hands against your chest (for subjects with hands not together say hands by your sides), tilt your head well back and close your eyes whilst breathing at all times deeply in through your nose and then out through your mouth. 3 relaxing every muscle in your body from the tips of your toes to the tips of your fingers. 2 the deeper you go the better you feel and the better you feel the deeper you go and on 1 falling back, falling back and sleeeeep!"

ROYLE'S FALLING BACKWARDS ON REST OF SUBJECTS

"OK, you've all got the idea now so you're next. Feet together, hands against your chest (or by your side) tilt your head well back, close your eyes and breathe in deeply and regularly. On 3 relaxing, 2 relaxing and on 1 falling back, back, back to sleeep!"

THE WAY TO CONTINUE

Then from the remaining subjects with hands locked together pick as many as you need to make up the numbers who you feel using the information which I will detail later will make good subjects and then place them into trance by this or any other suitable method. Now you need to get everyone's hands separate so you can do this and at the same time deepen the state of trance they are in a little. To do this say "I'm now speaking to everyone upon the stage, in a few moments I shall take hold of your hands and the moment I do, they will immediately separate. I will then let your arms fall down by your side and as I do you'll feel yourself sink down into a 100 times deeper and 100 times more relaxing state of relaxation!" You then follow this up by going round all the subjects, separating their hands and as you drop their arms down by their sides you say "Deeper and deeper to sleep!" Its now time for the group deepening of the induction so that everyone will then be in a deep enough state of trance for the show to continue successfully.

ROYLE'S GROUP INDUCTION DEEPENING

"OK, now everyone listen only to the sound of my voice, as I count backwards from 10 down to 1 you'll find that with each count down it's like a step further down on a staircase to deep satisfying relaxation. So on 10, the deeper you go the better you feel and the better you feel the deeper you will go. On 9, deeper and deeper now as each second passes by so quickly. 8, now every muscle in the whole of your body from the tips of your toes to the tips of your fingers becoming so limp, so loose and so relaxed as they now feel so heavy and tired. 7, deeper and deeper still. 6, 5, 4. From now on, no noises will distract you whatsoever in fact they will simply send you deeper and deeper to sleep, even the sound of my voice will send you deeper and deeper to sleep. 3, should you have to leave this building tonight unexpectedly for any reason then everything I've said will automatically be cancelled out and you will return to normal in every way. 2, Deeper and deeper to sleep. Throughout the show you'll avoid going anywhere near the edge of the stage for your own safety. In fact its as if there's an invisible force field stopping you from going near the edge of the stage as you relax more with every breath you take, every noise you hear and every word that I say. And on 1, from now on I'm only talking to you if I tap you on the shoulder or indicate otherwise. For the rest of this evenings show, whenever I say 1, 2, wide awake, you'll instantly be wide awake and have an overwhelming desire to do anything I say as an automatic reflex action and whenever I say sleep, as quickly as that, (snap fingers) a snap of my fingers, you'll instantly renter this state except each time you renter it, it will be 100 times more relaxing and enjoyable for you!"

SUGGESTIONS FOR THE FIRST ROUTINE

At this point everyone is under hypnosis and the state has been deepened to a level ideal for the show to continue. The routines can now begin as whenever you have given them a suggestion to carry out, you need only say 1,2, wide awake and they will then awaken and carry out your instructions. Then when you wish the routine to end just say "OK everyone look at me and.... Sleep!" they will then return to trance and be ready for the next suggestion of the show.

END OF THE SHOW'S FIRST HALF

The routines continue until its time for the interval (usually one hour from the show starting). You can then give everyone a separate suggestion to act upon during the interval so that the show effectively continues within the audience before saying "OK everyone when I awaken you in a few moments, you will return to the audience and carry out the suggestions given to you a few moments ago. However the very moment that you hear me say come and join the party! The moment you hear me say come and join the party you'll return to the stage area, will still be carrying out your suggestions until I say otherwise and will, the very moment I say sleep return to this beautifully relaxing state. OK now everyone 1,2, wide awake!" At this point the subjects are returned to the audience and the interval takes place.

NEWTON'S SECOND HALF OPENING PATTER

"Welcome back ladies and gentlemen, now as you've probably already guessed, with hypnosis almost anything could happen. All that happens when you are hypnotised is that the imagination is enhanced by 10 times, maybe as much as a hundred times so that what is one minute purely imaginary, the next minute seems very real indeed and I'm sure you'll see many more examples in this the second half of the show. So I'd just like to say.... Come and join the party! Come and join the party!" (At this point the people under hypnosis will return to the stage and after some comedy banter about what they have been doing during the interval you say Sleep, they return to trance and the comedy routines continue as normal until the end of the show).

AWAKENING THEM FROM THE TRANCE

At the start of the second half of the show you may wish to demonstrate the world record high speed hypnosis method as detailed later, in which case you'd do the guaranteed locked hands test, as explained later, before demonstrating the high speed induction, again as explained later. The only other thing you must remember is to awaken everyone fully from trance at the end of the show and indeed this was explained fully with word for word patter in the previous chapter.

SOME EXTRA NOTES AND ADVICE

Once everyone has been hypnotised and the trance deepened, everyone is awoken and then given a seat to sit in for the rest of the show. The moment they sit on the seat you snap your fingers and say sleep and return to trance they will. The comedy routine suggestions are given to them with their eyes closed and when you say 1,2, wide-awake they will then awaken and react to the suggestions as instructed. It is also possible to tell them to carry out the suggestions immediately with their eyes tightly closed at all times and then you are able to say "1,2, wide awake" to let them realise what a compromising position they are in. You can also whilst they are reacting to one suggestion and are "awake" get their attention, look directly at them and give them an immediate change of suggestion without first returning them to sleep. For example they see the audience as being nude and you look directly at them and say the moment I click my fingers they will now all look like elephants and indeed the moment you click your fingers they will react in this different way. A huge list of suitable family and adults only routines is given later in this course, it's just a matter of choosing those you feel are best for you. Don't forget also that suggestions can be given either to specific individuals by stating you are only talking to the person who you are touching on the shoulder or to everyone by saying I'm talking to everyone on the stage. You can of course also get either the men or women to react by saying I'm talking only to the men or whatever is relevant for what you wish to suggest. See a stage hypnotist at work and you'll see with your own eyes the numerous different ways and times in which the suggestions can be given to them to carry out.

END OF THE SHOW PATTER

Well unfortunately we've almost come to the end of the show, but before we do end, can I just thank you all for being such a wonderful audience and may I also ask you to tell your friends if you enjoyed tonight's show. Please do come again next time as every show is different, people react in different ways and of course we also include some new routines from time to time. Anyone interested in how to stop smoking, lose weight or gain confidence amongst other things should see our range of hypnotherapy tapes which will be on sale in the foyer after the show. But for now lets have one final routine (then go into the world's greatest strippers routine).

***NOTES*:** At the end of this final routine put them all back under and do the awakening method as detailed in the previous chapter and of course suggest also that the moment they wake up they will wonder what they are doing and will get dressed as quickly as possible! Then everyone is returned to the audience as you leave the stage by saying "If you've enjoyed the show tonight my names Alex Leroy and if you haven't then my names Paul McKenna, thank you and goodnight!" You then leave the stage as your "theme" music plays you off and the house lights go back to normal in the venue as they have been dimmed throughout.

A COMPLETE SCRIPT

What I have just detailed is the complete step by step script to get you on stage, explain everything, get them laughing and relaxed, lock their hands together, induce and deepen the trance state, implant the post hypnotic suggestions, how to give the comedy routine suggestions, awakening them from the trance along with patter for both halves of the show and for the end of the show.

Use it as a guideline to word your own personal script, which should of course suit your individual personality. Obviously you have to just ad-lib the patter with regards to each of the comedy routines although seeing a stage hypnotist in action will illustrate examples to you and teach you all that is needed to know on this subject. But basically, give them the suggestion of what to do, awaken them and they do it, so in fact there is very little else to say here. Listed below are some one liner jokes all on the subject of stage hypnotism and/or those that can be used within your chosen routines.

Although I give a word for word example of Andrew Newton's stage show patter, I do advise you to construct your own using the advice and guidance within the next few chapters. It is always better to be the first Dr. Jonathan Royle rather than the next copy of him! Although to start with it will without doubt aid your success to emulate me and other stage hypnotists, in the long term you are well advised to devise your own patter and as such not get labelled as a copy. Patter which you devise yourself will also suit your style, personality and manner much better as well.

HYPNOTIC GAGS & GAGS FOR ROUTINES

A lot of people think that hypnotism comes from the brain, well they're wrong it doesn't, it comes from the hip.

Is this safe? Is this safe? Is the pope Jewish?

Seriously though I'd like to assure you that the chances of this going wrong twice in one week are very small indeed.

Hypnosis is just a very relaxing experience, rather like having a joint of Moroccan Black!

I'm both a mind reader and a hypnotist, which means I read minds and put people to sleep, I don't like the way I said that.

Several people have asked me tonight if hypnosis can be used to improve your chances with the opposite sex. Well I was going to speak a little on the subject later but I've got a date with Cindy Crawford.

Unfortunately as we are on TV, we can't show the full hypnotic process, it's on a list of things that can't be shown that also includes Jeremy Paxman's humility and Noel Edmonds bank balance.

Well, there are several different states of hypnosis, she's in a light state, he's in a medium state and she's in one helluva state.

I once hypnotised Mike Morris of GMTV, I tell you what I'll have to go and wake him up sometime.

I always ask women if they want to go under because if they say yes I know I'll soon be on top.

I'm a Jewish hypnotist, so I'll put you into a trance and steal your cigars.

Now there is no need to worry about the on stage volunteers, they will no doubt enjoy the show more than you. They've certainly got the best seat in the house.

All these people behind me have great imaginations, in fact they'd probably put the headline writers of the Sunday Sport to shame.

Now if you want to come up here you can always slip into something more comfortable, an altered state of consciousness perhaps?

If you'd like to be hypnotised, mesmerised, pulverised, pasteurised, sterilised (pause) Circum.......stances being as they are the best thing you could do is come up to the stage.

OK. Just tickle horsy under the chin, did he like that? Well he should have done your sat on him the wrong way round.

When you wake up you will not hit the hypnotist, I repeat you will not hit the hypnotist.

I hate it when my shows are really successful, there is never anyone left awake to applaud my act.

If I were a mind reader, I'd be offering you a refund Sir!

I actually managed to do this last week, it's just a shame I wasn't watching what I was doing at the time.

Some of you will be getting the impression that I haven't done this before, well I have its just that I couldn't do it the last time either.

You might be laughing at the volunteers now, but in an hours time you might wish that you'd slept through the entire show.

People tend to do strange things when they are asleep, I always imagine I am a Red Indian. Perhaps its because I have to sleep with an old battle-axe?

I tried to hypnotise my wife last week, she's got a speech impediment she can't say no.

I played Glasgow last week, the audience was full of insomniacs, evidently tickets for my show were cheaper than Valium.

When you wake up, the show will be over, I bet your glad you paid for your ticket now.

Now if your hands are stuck together you would be well advised to come up to the stage as if you don't your hands will be like this for three weeks, then they will turn blue and drop off.

This is all a case of mind over matter, if you don't mind then I don't matter.

What's your name? Correct!

What's your name? I was called that when I was a girl!

(Heckler) Quite funny Sir, only quite funny that's why I'm stood up here and your stood down there.

Next time you go to the loo Sir, you will get stuck to the seat for an hour.

Was that a round of applause or has someone put the chips in?
A lot of people say to me Alex how did you become a hypnotist, but I'm sure the question you'll be asking after tonight is why?

I've always been weird since the day I was born when I came out of the woman in the bed next to my mum.

This act is very educational, you'll go home tonight and say well that taught me a lesson.

We've been saving this chair for you Sir, for Rigormortis to set in.

You don't mind if I call you Sir do you? After all it's only in fun!

(Bingo routine) 6 and 9, excellent position.

(Send subject back to crowd) OK just go and join the other rejects.

You will not be made to do anything you don't want to do, but you will find that you want to do everything.

You may as well laugh now it doesn't get much better.

(Martians sketch) Nanu, Nanu! OK just go and join the earthlings.

(In love with hypnotist) When she awakens the more I click my fingers the more she'll fall in love with me. In fact would you excuse me a moment whilst we go back stage and I click my fingers a lot?

(Nude glasses) When you look through the glasses you'll see all the men in the nude but the hypnotist is the only one with anything of decent size.

(Nude glasses) Marks out of ten for presentation?

(In love with hypnotist) These are the perks of the job, if you want to learn how to do this Sir, I'll teach you after but it will cost you £500.

I'm good at putting people to sleep but not as good as a politician's speech.

What do you do for a living? (Taxman) Well in that case your hands are getting a Million times tighter.

(They keep moving when returned to Sleep) Well that just goes to prove that Duracell out last any other brand of battery.

(Weird reactions) Don't worry he's just excited about being up here, that's the kind of guy he is, a prat.

Hypnosis is a state like we all drift into everyday, for example like when we're reading a book or drinking our tea and don't hear someone talking to us or indeed like watching Emmerdale Farm.

(Prior to Falling Back) He looks just like a thunderbird's puppet. (Then as he falls backwards you pretend to cut the invisible strings, and then as he's awoken and stand up the Thunderbirds theme music starts to play)

Behind me are our 12 victims, oh sorry, Volunteers.

(Punter with loud clothes) There must be a Ford Cortina outside with no seat covers.

A lot of people find that if they drink coffee they can't sleep, well I'm the opposite if I'm asleep I can't drink coffee.

(Say to a man) OK. Just stare into my eyes, my goodness your attractive do you find me beautiful?

One night I dreamed I was awake and then I woke up and found I was asleep.

One night I dreamed I was Julian Clary, it was my own fault I fell asleep on a camp bed.

Talk about hypnotised, did you hear about the Politician who dreamed he was doing a speech in The House of Lords, then he woke up and found he was.

Scientist's say we only use 10% of our brainpower, well if that's true what do we do with the other 56%?

(Woman stands up when men should) Don't worry she's got a slight identity crisis, she's the one who entertains the men!

You'll do anything that the stage crew tell you to do when you wake up, you'll bend over backwards to help them in fact you'll have to.

Fall back and I'll catch you (let them fall) Whoops I lied.

(Put subject under by him staring at the microphone and then wave it to the audience as you say) Your all nervous now aren't you?

(Man has just fallen back asleep, now say to person next to him) That scared the living daylights out of you didn't it?

(Cardboard Razor Blade) I want to show you something that's very close to my heart; it's my liver.

OK Sir just move up a seat, I might be able to get a lovely young lady to sit next to you. Although looking at you I think not!

(As they get up off stage after falling backwards) Don't worry we did get the drivers name and we got his number.

What are you doing down there? (Pause) Oh I see getting up!

(Make noise like bad back) Oh dear you'll have to see the doctor about that Sir.

(Hippie Guy) Wow mans my heads exploding! Peace, Love and Brown rice.

You can go and sit in that seat now so we can switch it on.

It's OK Sir, we did sweep the floor before we started.

SOME GENERAL NOTES ON COMEDY

Basically it's up to you and the style you adopt as a performer to whether you use lots of one liner jokes in your act. In general though it helps to enhance the show if you have a good repertoire of one liners and Heckler stoppers to suit every possible occasion. You can then make a joke here and there as you find out the subjects names, occupations, where they live etc. On a weekly basis you are advised to buy The Stage & TV newspaper which can be ordered each Thursday from W H Smith's. Under the classified adverts section you will find several comedy writers advertising their services. It's from these sources that you can obtain material of use in the aforementioned ways and they can even write you original gags on the subject of hypnotism. My personal advice to you would be have a good stock of one liners to cover up any mistakes etc. If you can be a great comedian, your job as a hypnotist will be that much easier. Always remember that people relax when they laugh and also remember that the likes of Bruce Forsyth and Michael Barrymore grab people from their audiences and get them to do the most outrageous things without ever using hypnosis. If you can learn to get an audience in the palm of your hand, to get them to relax and then to do anything that you say, then either you're a hypnotist or an experienced comedian. Always remember on stage that entertainment value comes first and the hypnosis element comes last, after all the audience has paid to be entertained. Lastly, remember that the best possible teacher in life is experience, but the next best teacher is observation, so go and see as many stage hypnotists at work live as possible then you'll see in action how the contents of this course do work and how they are put to use in a practical situation.

PART FOUR

RAPPORT, OBSERVATION, RECOGNITION AND LEADERSHIP!

You have been offered the knowledge and wisdom required to act upon the opportunity to profit from being both a stage hypnotist and mind therapist! But as Sir Winston Churchill so rightly said and I quote:

"Most people will at some time in their life stumble over opportunity. Unfortunately for them, most will just pick themselves up, dust themselves off and carry on as if nothing had ever happened."

Another very old and famous saying from the sales industry, which I'll quote, is:

"Nobody ever got seriously rich working for somebody else!"

And Lastly:

"I'd sooner have 1% of the profits of 100 men than 100% of the profits of just one man!"

John Paul Getty (Multi-Billionaire)

Hi, welcome back again! Well lets deal in this chapter with rapport, observation, recognition and leadership. These are the four stages of inducing a hypnotic trance state. All are lead by the subject and merely followed by you the hypnotist. I shall take each step one at a time and lead you through the techniques involved.

However never forget that there is no substitute for practice and practical application! And after this, there is no substitute for real live stage shows or consulting room experience and if possible a little of both. Whether you practice on friends, relatives or colleagues matters little but practice you must do!

RAPPORT

The Oxford English dictionary defines rapport as relationship or communication, especially when useful and harmonious! This itself is a perfect description of the first stage of induction. The concept of rapport is not unknown to you. You see it around you all the time, in fact you are already an expert at it, yes you are! Take a look at your friends and family, at people in the street, at parties or in the bars and you will see people in rapport and also people who are quite definitely not in rapport.

A young mother or father with child, lovers looking into each others eyes, old friends comfortable in each others company, two supporters of the same football team recalling the high points of the match, the three people in the corner discussing their mutual concern about political matters and the two drunks who are at each others throats, these are all examples of how you have spotted if people are in rapport (or not) in the past.

Now wait a minute, there is something missing here isn't there? I was talking about and you were thinking about something that we could not possibly have observed, namely thought processes. When we see people together we can't read their minds can we? We can only observe their bodies and actions and listen to their voices. We don't know if the young lovers are really in love or if they are both secretly having affairs. We couldn't possibly tell if the two old friends are secretly plotting to rob each other or if one of the political discussion group is actually bored to death. What we base our assumptions on are the obvious signs of rapport, the smiles, the laughter, the physical closeness, the relaxed stances, in short its down to body language and voice tone. Most all of our daily communication is non verbal or tonal. That is to say, the way we move our bodies, change our facial expressions and raise or lower our voices communicates more than the actual words themselves do. This is what we have been watching and/or observing all these years and from this we have all become experts at reading peoples minds. I said you are expert at rapport and indeed you are, so much so, you cannot only use your body to mean much more than you say but you can even lie with it.

Imagine this situation. I am willing to bet you have done something similar to this many hundreds of times in the past, perhaps without even noticing it yourself. There is someone you need to impress, a potential employer or the bank manager. Someone from whom you need, but do not like. It may be a situation or an act that you feel is beneath your dignity, asking for a raise or a loan, or maybe trying to convince a policeman that although you shot through a red light you really are a responsible person that can be trusted to never do it again. At times like this your body sings out like an orchestra, your intent and meaning can be read like a neon sign from a dozen yards away, if you watched yourself on a video you would be astonished at just how brilliant you are, and all the time you probably didn't even know you were doing it!

In the hypnotic sense, rapport is exactly the same. Just as unconscious, just as easy and just as natural. Let us examine the mechanics and the purpose of it. The first necessity of rapport is "sameness". I would like to take you back to the two old friends we met earlier. How did you tell they were old friends and not just passing acquaintances? It was their "sameness", they were at "one", they sat facing each other, they spoke in the same tone of voice. If one whispered the other followed suit, if one laughed the other laughed, if one sat with his arms on the table or slouched back and relaxed so would the other. Always they looked into each other's eyes and paid attention. This much you could see but if they were genuinely friendly there would be other things happening that you could not see. Their thought processes would be exactly the same. They would be thinking consciously of the subject under discussion but subconsciously they would be examining each other and every examination of "sameness" would reinforce the belief within their subconscious that they are liked and trusted. Their breathing would become synchronised and their heart beats the same. The tonal qualities of their voices would stay within the same range. They would look into each others eyes at the same time without any obvious signal being given, they are becoming psychologically one, at least as far as is possible.

Before you start to think that I am now going into the realms of hocus-pocus let me assure you that I am not! There was an experiment carried out many years ago, one which would quite rightly be illegal today. Two Oxen were tied together at birth, they were connected at the neck, legs and tail so that they stood, walked and slept for many years side to side and could not move except in unison. When the bonds were removed some years later they naturally enough felt very insecure about this new situation. The bond between them was so strong that they still walked, ate and moved as one for many years after the fastenings were removed. Stopping for food and water at the same time, walking, stopping and turning heads together all as if still tied together. Bonding is as normal and natural in humans as it is in all animals. The bond between families and friends is as strong as the tethers that those poor Oxen were subjected to, but I hear you cry how is this of use in the hypnotic induction process? "Sameness" is the key! Get onto the subject's own level, don't try and impress or bully. Talk to them in their own style of language, be intellectual with intellectuals and be plain and simple with others. Move as they do, breathe as they do. Observe their body language and respond accordingly. People naturally like and trust people who appear to be the same as them, those who look into their eyes and communicate! If hypnotism can be summed up in a single small phrase then it is: "The art of communication and the avoidance of conflict!" The greatest sales people in the world are those who have learnt or have naturally the gift of sameness. This is something that you can try for yourself today. Go out and be with someone else whilst being someone else. The signs now that I have alerted you to them are glaringly obvious. One thing to remember though and that is sameness is NOT mimicry. In fact nothing is more likely to get you a punch in the eye than mimicking exactly what a complete stranger does. Be subtle, listen carefully, and note what he or she does physically out of the corner of your eye and copy it a few seconds later. Only copy what is obviously unintentional body language and not their deliberate actions. If your subject is smiling, smile too, but if he is tapping nervously on the table or has a nervous twitch in his eye then leave well alone. Match movement with movement, voice tone with voice tone, language with language, attitude with attitude. But do not attempt to imitate them exactly. Do all of this in a laid back manner and be non-aggressive at all times. Be sympathetic, be caring but never be patronising or condescending. Listen to what they are saying and always remember you have two ears and only one mouth so use them in these proportions. Avoid confrontation and contradiction, agree with what they say or say nothing at all. Praise the praiseworthy thoughts and ideas he or she is imparting and let stupidity and inaccuracy pass over your head unnoticed.

Everyone's natural instinct is to join in conversations, have their voices heard and their opinions too. They also wish to contribute to, or control the situation. But just for once put these quite normal and natural desires to one side, just for the sake of a single experiment. Listen to the other person's view and let that person take the lead. I promise you a very eye opening experience, which is also extremely satisfying, so go on, go and try it! You'll be astounded. For some this technique takes no more than a couple of hours to hone and polish but for others it can take months to undo a lifetime of habit, but it does work for everyone given time and genuine application. Remember it is you that you are trying to change at this stage not others. If you gain nothing else from this course then you will have been given the gift of friendship and ease in the company of others.

By the way these are also good methods to use when picking up members of the opposite sex! In a hypnotic induction the first thing to do is establish rapport. A nice friendly relaxed atmosphere, "sameness" is apparent to you both and you are communicating and feeling on the same level as the client. The subject trusts you and is confident to be placed into your hands, if this trust is not established, continue to work on it until it is. When you first start out, no doubt you will try to induce friends and acquaintances. Well YES, it is easier to establish rapport with them but it is also harder to establish trust in your abilities as a hypnotist. After all they know you are new to the subject and that you only bought this course recently. They will say things like "go on then hypnotise me!" and then sit there waiting for you to cast a spell over them. Be prepared for this, be calm, maintain the sameness, explain that it takes some time to hypnotise people and that you are new to the subject (only say this to people who already know the truth) and that you wish to proceed slowly. Make it a bit of a joke, you should both be enjoying yourselves. A professional established stage and/or therapeutic hypnotist does not have these problems of confidence and nor will you when your credentials have been established. Experienced hypnotists obtain rapport instantly and then recognising that the time is right, simply instruct the subject to "go into a trance now!" for them and me its easy (sometimes). The subject knows that he is going to be hypnotised, has paid for a ticket to see the show or for the therapy session, there is no doubt in his mind that he will succumb, so they do, its all down to the power of the moment. Rapport should establish three things as follows: 1) Trust 2) Comfort and 3) Belief. You are then ready to progress to the next stage, which is:

OBSERVATION

By now you will have sharpened your eye as to the body movements of others. Probably for the first time in your life you will really be taking notice of those that talk to you and those you talk to. Observation is an acute version of this. You must be aware of every single movement because these are the tools you will use to induce the first stage of hypnosis. Having established rapport you must now connect even further with the mind of the subject. I mentioned earlier that each stage of the hypnotic induction process is lead by the subject, this is a case in point. You must show them that you are able to feel what they feel, that you are sharing the same experience with them. In a way this is just sameness but is at a much deeper level. But how can you do this considering you are not a mind reader? Well you don't have to be, you just have to be a body reader. The following is an example of the opening words of a verbal induction. See if you can spot how it's done. It shouldn't be hard for a keen observer like you. Remember these are not magic words that will work for all people in all circumstances but they are typical of a keen and observant hypnotist at work.

"Just sit down and relax, lie back if that's more comfortable. That's right, feel your body being comfortably supported by the couch and the weight of your head sinking down into the cushions. Let the stress in your arms and legs flow effortlessly out as you relax completely and become calm, serene and composed. Take your time there is no rush as you feel relaxation flooding your entire body." Some of the language used here might seem a little strange, the phrasing a little unusual even. But pay no attention to that at present, these are things which I will explain later. What I want you to consider now is the subject matter of what is said. At first it may seem that the subject is relaxation, but look again and bear in mind that we are looking at observation in this section. Go on, go back and read it again. Can you see all the observations? The subject looked uncomfortable sitting up, fell back with a sigh and exhaled deeply when her head touched the cushions, she looked a little hurried and anxious and so had to be reassured, her arms and legs looked stiff and straight with toes pointing straight up and fingers clenched, in short she did not look comfortable in this situation and needed reassurance. The hypnotist (that's you) having obtained rapport, now establishes that they are sharing the same experience! That he has an insight into the subject's mind, knows what she is feeling and is a part of it. If you now take the trouble to go back and read those words again you will see that it truly is the subject that is leading and not the hypnotist. By using observations which are feedback to the subject as suggestions, as well as rapport, you start to enter the subject's mind and are then able to control it.

RECOGNITION

The subject will slowly begin to recognise that you are capable of understanding her thoughts. Her arms and hands are stiff for example and you observe this without being told. To her the experience of tense fingers is only a thought, she does not know how obvious it is to the trained observer. She is well aware that you are not reading her mind, after all she is not stupid, but the level of contact between you both is becoming more mental and less verbal. As this link is strengthened you can suggest and control more easily.

LEADERSHIP

You will have noticed in the earlier extract that there are some strange links and connections where different sentences, that are not really inter-connected are joined together in a cumbersome way. "Let the stress in your arms and legs flow effortlessly out as you relax completely and become calm, serene and composed." You are aware that the hypnotist's words are only a response to his observations. He has seen a physical tension in the arms and legs and is trying to use it to enter the subject's mind. So why not just say "I can tell your legs are tense?" Would this not have the same effect? NO! For one thing it would be far too obvious. The subject's mind would be trying to figure out how you did know, and lets face it, it wouldn't be too hard for her to figure out would it? And secondly by giving her a puzzle to sort out you are asking her to think alone and not be guided by you. This "guidance" is "leadership" in the hypnotic sense. There are two things going on, firstly you are addressing the subject's mind and secondly you are leading her in the direction you want, which is relaxation! Relaxation is not necessary or even important in inducing hypnosis, but it is what the subject expects and this is helpful. It also relaxes the belief mechanism to obvious benefit. The way in which this works is a little complex and will take a page or two to explain, so please bear with me. You cannot become expert without understanding this method of induction as it is the most basic and commonly used. Stress is an ancient response, sometimes called the "Fight or Flight" response. When our ancestors were still living in caves there were essentially two types of people...the quick and the dead! When suddenly faced with danger, perhaps whilst partaking of some pleasant and relaxing pastime like sleeping or eating, there had to be an instant and profound reaction. If a wild animal or some member of another tribe attacked them without warning then the entire body would have to be put on a "war footing" those that responded well lived and those slow died! It is not surprising that this particular process of instant and permanent natural selection had a profound effect on the human race.

The mechanics of stress, or the fight or flight response, is to flood the body with adrenaline, increase blood pressure, make immediately available resources of energy, stop any unnecessary functions like digestion, the energy of which at that time can be put to better use elsewhere, fill the muscles with Oxygen and get ready to fight to the death or run like hell! But what has this got to do with you and me today? Well the mechanism still exists and would still work today if called upon to do so. If a mugger or a rapist suddenly confronted you, the threat would create the exact same physical reaction as just detailed. But just analyse that for a moment, as a mugger is a person who looks much like any other person. They have one head and two eyes, two ears etc. The sight of a person would not normally trigger such a profound effect. Even a shady, wild looking individual if he just passed by you in the street would not produce such a reaction, so what is the trigger? It is your conscious mind that sets things into motion. You see him and compare his actions against the files in your memory banks and he matches one marked "danger" and it is then that things start into motion. Once you see that it is not his actual moves or words that trigger stress but in fact your analysis of and reaction to them, it is far easier to see how more commonplace stress is and how it is triggered. Your mind will push the stress button every time that you are threatened, even if it is only financially, emotionally or in any other way.

The stress function cannot be switched off as easily as it is on. You are prepared to fight but normally do not. While it is true to say that it would ease your stress considerably if you could punch your boss in the eye every time he denied you promotion it is not recommended if you wish to keep your liberty. So the chemicals keep on bubbling around your system causing all kinds of problems, sometimes for day, weeks or months on end, with each stressful event compounding the effect upon your central nervous system. What has all this to do with hypnosis? During stress your conscious mind is racing, checking everything, analysing all things, checking memory files and sorting out all new information. The entire system is on full alert. If you remember the ancient origins of stress you can then understand why this is so. In a situation where you have to be killed or kill it is your subconscious mind that is checking for every possible opportunity to strike. Checking your opponents every move or action in order to prepare a defence, looking for chances to flee or find a weapon whilst all the time controlling and moving your body in response to this immediate and very real danger. Even under only slight stress it is firing on all cylinders at 110% efficiency. It is, don't forget, this part of the minds operation that you are trying to bypass in order to make direct contact with the subconscious.

In this modern world we are all stressed, to some greater or lesser extent, most of the time therefore you don't have a hope of bypassing the belief system at least that is while the defences are up and checking every detail. Just as the mind can control the stress reactions of the body, the body can influence the mind. Don't believe me? Let's try a little experiment. Without doing anything special or putting this course down or moving I want you to do one thing for me - SMILE! No don't grin that inane little smirk with no real feeling in it, smile with your whole face, a realistic smile as if you were posing for a photo to be sent to a loved one and keep smiling for a full ten seconds. 1,2,3,4,5,6,7,8,9,10, strange how your mood has lifted isn't it? While you are stressed your body is tense. It remains tense until it is exhausted (and have killed your enemy) the system works like this:

Body still stressed **EQUALS** enemy still attacking
Enemy still alive **EQUALS** need more stress
More stress **EQUALS** more bodily tension
Body still stressed **EQUALS** enemy still attacking etc!

These are not just ideas of mine, I am trying to explain to you in written terms, the chemical reaction which is going on in your body during stress. It is a cycle that feeds on itself and all the stressful stimuli. The cycle can be broken in your hypnotic subject and it has to be broken if you are to quieten his or her conscious mind and its belief system. Physical relaxation will do this. Look at how the above cycle changes now that I have inserted an element of physical relaxation.

Relaxation **EQUALS** less stress
Body not stressed **EQUALS** enemy gone or defeated
No enemy **EQUALS** no need for stress
Less stress **EQUALS** less bodily tension
Body relaxed **EQUALS** mind can now rest

Remember that these are not the subject's conscious thoughts but a written description of a mass inter linked chemical and nervous reaction in their body. Through physical relaxation comes mental relaxation, a lowering of the defences of the conscious mind (belief and filing system). A good way to imagine the conscious defences is to liken them to a guard. Yes that's right a soldier or security guard. Lull it into a false sense of security (relaxation) and then create a subtle diversion (suggestions) before you slip passed without even being noticed. It sounds like a tall order does it not, controlling a person's innermost defence? That is until you remember that we are all slipping in and out of trances all the time. In your life there must have been times when you couldn't sleep or a friend or loved one has come to you for advice on the same problem and what did you say? Count Sheep! There is hardly a person alive who has not tried this or advised others to do so. This is a bypassing of and a controlling of the conscious mind and a giving up to the subconscious. The image of a sheep is a soft image to most people, that is to say anyone who has not actually seen them up close. We think of them as soft, cuddly and totally unthreatening. They are also completely unexciting. Counting wolves or spiders simply would not do. The job of counting is boring and dull to the extreme. It's so dull it is actually a subconscious activity, you just bring up the file marked counting and the system is fully automatic. To prove automatic counting, remember that time when you were counting something and your attention was distracted or your mind wandered. You lost count didn't you? We have all had this experience, countless times, this is why we count something that we have to imagine such as sheep and not just numbers. The visualisation of the sheep leaping over a fence is just interesting enough to distract your thoughts away from the exam tomorrow or whatever it is that is keeping you awake. The act of counting has no natural end, like reciting a poem has and so your consciousness is then centred on a soft, pleasant, unthreatening image. The worry/stress is put to one side and you consequently fall asleep at long last. I can hear you all shouting but I've tried counting sheep and it didn't work. Well its true to say these techniques are not fool proof and although they work for everyone they do so at different times in their lives. Incidentally if you do have trouble sleeping, due to worries that are so strong that the image of the sheep is not distracting enough, then try counting backwards from 1000, if you get to 500 and are still not asleep then count from there backwards in threes or sevens. If that doesn't work then try subtracting six and three quarters each time. Sooner or later you will find something distracting enough to quieten the problem which is keeping you awake and as such will go to sleep. Bear this in mind and you'll always have a good nights sleep for the rest of your life.

The conscious mind can only think of one thing at a time, so make it something that does not trouble you!

Now back to the plot, as with the sheep, the distraction of a swinging watch, flashing light or moving microphone is used to concentrate the mind of the subject away from the defence and then the hypnotist's suggestions seep more easily into the subconscious. Tone of voice is also essential and you'll discover in the next chapter to say certain words with a slightly different tonal quality, more slowly or at a lower pitch so that a new message entirely comes across in an almost subliminal way. Yes its possible to hide "subliminal" messages within normal spoken sentences even during normal conversation and then the "subliminal" sections will be acted upon. So basically, leadership is the process of taking control of the situation and using what you observe to best advantage by including it within your verbal suggestions.

So you see, there are an awful lot of similarities between the process of rapport, observation, recognition and leadership to those of the biofeedback style process of induction as detailed in an earlier chapter. Before ending this chapter it would be worthwhile to point out that 90% of reported illnesses are psychosomatic (caused by the mind) and of the 10% of unreported illnesses almost all of them are psychosomatic. Stress is by far the largest cause of many illnesses both of a psychological and organic nature and to this end the release of stress can be the best cure of all. Reread this chapter several times and you will without doubt be able to help people with all manners of ills and as such be a most successful therapist as well as stage hypnotist. They say that even the common cold is a stress related illness as if you had not been stressed in the first place then your bodily immune system would have been working to full effect and the germs which caused the cold would not have affected you. Even with an organic disease such as Cancer or Aids, stress is by far the client's worst enemy. Stress lowers the immune systems effects and also brings about a negative attitude to the illness in hand. Remove that stress and give positive thinking suggestions to the client and amazing results often do occur beyond their wildest expectations. How many times do we hear of Cancer/Aids patients who have been given six months to live still being alive, living an OK lifestyle some years later? These documented cases are all proof that positive thinking is a most positive force and when combined with relaxation/stress release can bring about apparently miraculous results.

PART FIVE

PRINCIPLES OF VERBAL PSYCHOLOGY

Suggestions can be both of a positive and negative nature, always aim to make your suggestions positive.

To briefly illustrate how strong a negative suggestion can be, imagine this scenario. A young child climbs onto a wall whilst their mother talks to a friend. The young child starts to run along back and forwards on top of the wall. Suddenly the child's mother turns round and sees her son and shouts out "be careful or you will fall!" The child in turn falls off the wall and gets hurt.

You see in the above example, until told that he could fall, the child did not know it was possible. The mother said "Be careful or **YOU WILL FALL!**" and indeed the negative suggestion of you will fall was then acted upon.

Now this chapter may appear to be very haphazard and of little point. However the point I shall be making and be trying to implant into your mind through the writings of this chapter is that every single word that you say upon stage or in therapy in your role as a hypnotist is of utmost importance. Things, which may appear like casual statements, can and usually do have a strong psychological effect on your audience, potential subjects or already hypnotised volunteers. Not only do the words you say have great importance, but even more so the way in which you say them matters also. For example if you said "OK now just close your eyes then sleep and relax" to a subject in a raised tone of voice as if shouting, do you really think they would relax? Of course not, however if it was said slowly, in a low tone of voice with each of the words being drawn out then your chances of success would be somewhat better. As a general rule of thumb, sleep/relaxation style suggestions should be given in a slow, deep, monotonous tone of voice with words drawn out and suggesting a downwards (sleepy) motion. For awakening style suggestions a faster, higher tone of voice with inflection/tone changes would be used and words suggesting an upward (awakening) motion should be used at all times. Monotony and repetition is the trade of the hypnotist. Although, of the two, repetition is by far more important, as whether you sing it, shout it or even whisper it, if it is repeated enough then it will start to have an effect upon the person. So repeat, repeat and repeat some more!

Learn to use your voice, it is a most powerful tool both on stage, in the consulting room and in everyday life. Listen to people when they speak and you will notice a lot can be learned about their emotions just by the way they are speaking. Are they happy? Sad? Upset? Or domineering? Well observe, listen and learn, you will soon uncover the secrets that lie within each person's tone of voice. When proficient at this with the people that you know well, you'll be able to tell when they are lying or holding something back. In order to help you exercise your voice so that you can use it in a monotone or in a commanding way as you would when giving a subject commands, I have included two little exercises below which you must do daily on a regular basis until you become aware how you speak and how to use your voice more effectively.

Firstly here is a poem, which to start with I want you to say with emotion just as the poet would mean it to have been said. When proficient at that, learn to say it in a monotone and then add a commanding overlay to that monotone.

EXAMPLE

I wandered lonely as a cloud that floats on high or vale and hill. When all at once I saw a crowd, a host of golden Daffodil.

WORDSWORTH WROTE IT WITH FEELING

I wandered….lonely as a cloud….that….floats on high….or vale and hill….when all at once….I saw a crowd….a host of golden Daffodil!

PAUSE AT THE DOTTED SPACES TO ADD FEELING TO VOICE

The next exercise must be spoken in a monotonous yet commanding manner of speech:

You are tired….very tired….you want to go to sleep….you cannot keep awake…….you are so tired that you must sleep….your eyes are tired….you cannot keep them open….you are so tired and sleepy….tired and sleepy….tired and sleepy….all you want to do is sleep….sleep….deep….deep sleep!

NOTE:

Repeat that over and over again until you know it off by heart. Master the commanding and decisive tone of voice and you will then be on the way to success as a hypnotist. Remember the craft of any hypnotist on stage or in therapy is suggestion. Yes that's right, repeated suggestion followed by cadence! What's cadence? Simple answer, that old fashioned sleep suggestion is nothing but cadence. Cadence is rhythm and rhythm is powerful. Remember the story about soldiers marching, who break step to cross over a wooden bridge, so that the cadence of the march will not build up resonance in the structure and cause it to collapse. Just as I mentioned earlier you can tell a lot about a persons emotions and state of mind through their tone of voice. So in the same way the subjects upon the stage who you wish to hypnotise can also tell a lot about you by your tone of voice as well. By now I will have said numerous times that as a hypnotist you must have 100% confidence in yourself and your abilities. Indecision will show both in your body language and your tone of voice. As a hypnotist you must be decisive which means everything will be suggested and spoken in the least number of words possible. You must also appear commanding and confident that any suggestions you give will be enacted upon by the subjects. Remember your subjects are told what to do by suggestions being repeated and also remember:

SUGGESTION CORRECTLY EXPRESSED IS HYPNOSIS

On stage my definition of "correctly" expressed is that it must be spoken in a commanding tone of voice, whereas in therapy it must be commanding with an air of empathy. Remember, as a hypnotist you are not asking people to do things, you must ORDER them to do things. You must therefore speak clearly and simplistically as does the majority of the population so that there is no doubt in the subject's mind what it is you expect of them. Back to cadence again. Do you know how to chant like the mobs do at football matches? A good piece of poetry is nothing but cadence, cadence is a rhythmic beat… one, two, three, four, up two, three, four etc. Repeat this giving exactly the same intonation to each word and then you have mastered cadence.

Positive and negative suggestions are things which you already use in your everyday life without a second thought. Always be positive where possible in the future! A verbal statement of a negative nature can ruin live's, for example parents often turn their brilliant children into dunces by always telling them that they will never be successful because they are dim and should try harder. How much better it would have been to praise the child on all the good things that it did, the child would be happier, feel better about themselves and go on to achieve far more in life! I repeat, always be positive in all that you say and do.

The words most spoken by a hypnotist are: I, You, Sleep and Awake. "I" meaning I am dominant, "You" meaning the subject you are talking to or the hypnotised group as a whole, the other two words explain themselves. Soon you will speak this way too. You will no doubt have noticed that I have written this course in the style in which I speak, in a dominant manner, but simple like a child. Remember also and I've said this before but it is worth repeating again, your subjects must ALWAYS understand what you are saying, never talk down to them but do speak in a most simplistic manner. Your commands must always be clear and decisive, if they are not so, they could be interpreted in a way which could be detrimental to your subjects. For example "Would you like to sit in the chair?" This is in fact a question and not a command, what should really have been said is "Sit down in the chair that is directly behind you." This last example is a command and has only one possible interpretation. Make sure all your suggestions are commands with only one interpretation both on stage and in therapy, as you must always give one meaning only commands. Remember also to use the language that all can always understand. Always be extremely careful what you say when your subjects are in trance, a casual word said by you might be taken as a command by one or more of your subjects, which as a direct result, they may then act upon now or in the future. Your voice must at all times be decisive, NEVER ever sound unsure of yourself, never whinge, your voice is your personality on stage and in everyday life or therapy. I will also say again that to learn anything in life you must keep on repeating it until you get it 100% right. In much the same way you must keep on repeating those sleep suggestions until the subject goes into a trance.

On stage, words are your paintbrush, even more so when giving the subject suggestions, so see what happens when you use bold precise strokes. By this I mean always paint a verbal picture with your words when giving commands so that the subjects know exactly what is expected of them. They must always know what you mean, as they are not psychic. For example I might say the following: "In a few moments when I awaken you it will be 4pm in the afternoon, you'll be sat in your deck chairs on a sunny Spanish beach and its lovely and warm. In front of you is a calm blue sea and you can hear the birds as they fly overhead, your feet are firmly on the sand and when you awaken it will be getting hotter and hotter all the time so you'll have to rub that suntan lotion in as quickly as you can because the quicker you rub it in the cooler you will become!"

With this example I have painted a picture with my words which in turn will paint a picture in their imagination. As we said earlier, when the imagination and the will are in conflict the imagination will always win. So here too they will really believe the scenarios presented to them and act upon it to the full. Now imagine if I'd just said "When I awaken you, you're on a beach and its hot." They could have been on wet mud, pebbles, in fact anything that their imaginations dreamed up as being reality to them at that time. So remember you must ALWAYS paint a picture with our words and set the scene of the play which our subjects are to act out clearly in their mind before we awaken them to perform their tasks. To briefly define hypnotism it is "The art of communication and the avoidance of conflict!" Now I hope you understand just how important your voice really is, as all hypnosis is just a form of effective communication. Tone of voice is essential in all communication. It is possible through the way you speak to hide secret (subliminal) messages in a spoken sentence just by changing the tone of your voice. Although this may sound a bit like science fiction allow me to demonstrate. You might say to a subject in hypnosis "As you lie there comfortably feeling the weight of your body being supported by the couch you are wondering how it is possible that you will go into a trance." Now obviously this is said in a monotone, you will also be at the same time establishing rapport, observation, recognition and leadership as detailed in the previous chapter. Now if you were to say certain words with a slightly different tonal quality, more slowly or at a lower/higher pitch then another message entirely comes across to the subjects subconscious mind and as such is accepted and acted upon without their conscious mind even realising what has happened. Incidentally this works during normal everyday conversation also, its just a case of making what you actually want the person to do seem like part of an innocent sentence so that when the subliminal voice change technique is used the event occurs and they think its their own idea!

In the following example I have underlined the words which are spoken in a different more commanding pitch/tone of voice. "As you lie there comfortably feeling the weight of your body being supported by the couch you are wondering how it is possible that you will go into a trance." The subconscious accepts "You will go into a trance" as a direct command but the subject does not realise this as they just assume it to be a casual part of the sentence. What is happening here is that the reality mechanisms are being bypassed and the subconscious mind is taking in the information unaided. It isn't as discerning as the conscious and it wasn't designed to be, so the ideas not only go directly in without being checked but are also acted upon without question. If a slightly different tone of voice is used, this is recognised by the subconscious and two separate messages are accepted where normally there would be just one. Below, to illustrate this "subliminal" technique further, I shall detail the working of a long therapeutic style induction. I have underlined the subliminal (hidden) messages, which are spoken in a slightly different tone of voice so that they are accepted as such. "As you lie there comfortably feeling the weight of your body being supported by the couch you are wondering how it is possible that you will go into a trance now. You don't know if you will go into a trance quickly or if it will take some time. (This includes rapport, observation, recognition and leadership) To really enjoy all these pleasant changes that are occurring in your consciousness. (This is recognition, but done in advance of the subjects actually feeling differently which you know they will because they are relaxing) "NOW take a deep breath and hold it, hold it, hold it, hold it, breathe out now and as you do all the tensions in your body will be exhaled along with your hot breath. (Of course their breath is hot, the subject has been holding it in their lungs which are warm for longer than usual! Recognition of this type is very powerful, they will feel the heat and they will relax because of the change in breathing rhythm. They also feel sure you have done this via your hypnotic powers and this reassures them that they WILL succumb to your suggestions.) You are lying here on the couch with your head resting against the soft leather. (The words "lying here" are reassuring. They mean togetherness, you are both experiencing this together, "lying there" means you are apart and is negative) As you close your eyes your heavy eyelids are shutting out the distractions of the world. You are listening only to my voice and are going deeper and deeper within yourself finding that pleasant comfortable place where you can relax totally. Now start slowly counting backwards in your mind from two hundred, 199, 198, 197, 196, 195, 194 and so on. (Here you have offered a gentle distraction for the conscious mind and you have started the counting verbally to reinforce that they must continue counting whilst you deliver suggestions directly to their subconscious mind. Herein lies another important rule of hypnotism, when the conscious mind is distracted and considering something else, any suggestions given to that person will then go directly into the subconscious mind and as such have a deeply profound effect. Whether you use techniques of disorientation and confusion as will be described in a later chapter or something for the subject to think of consciously as is the case here, it matters little. Just so long as you keep the conscious mind occupied on something else whilst suggestions of sleep and relaxation are allowed to go directly into the subconscious. As all hypnotic induction's are presentation to make the process look impressive, the only true value they really have is to distract the persons conscious mind whilst suggestions are given directly to their subconscious. For example a person is told feet together, hands by your sides, eyes closed, tilt your head well back and concentrate on your deep rhythmic breathing. This is all "dressing", however by concentrating on their breathing they are then distracting the conscious and all suggestions get to the subconscious with ease. This is also why people can be hypnotised so quickly and why to be a good hypnotic subject they must be able to concentrate. If they cannot concentrate you will not be able to distract the conscious mind and will find the induction much harder.)

"Keep counting back and back as you feel those muscles around your eyes relax and those beautiful feelings of relaxation and peace spread to your forehead and scalp and to the muscles of your jaw." (You are now in direct touch with their subconscious. The conscious is busy counting, you are not however fully in control yet and the trance state is still very delicate. Any noise or distraction could break the mood. As a person relaxes and stress is removed, certain bodily functions, such as digestion which were running slowly before may start to function again. Tummies rumbling cause the breakdown of trance more than anything else, but if this happens you can handle it like this. "Nothing can disturb us now. There are no secrets between us, no embarrassment or shame, and as you become aware of those comfortable, peaceful feelings of stillness and contentment sinking further down your body, your face relaxes, your expression is now one of serenity, down, down, further down. These (not those) wonderful feelings spread through your neck, shoulders, chest and stomach, right through your arms to your fingertips and through your legs to the ends of your toes." (Check for evidence here that your subject is still counting, lips slightly moving? Rhythmic head or eye movements? (Under the eyelids known as R.E.M's) does he or she seem to be paying more attention to you? Straining to hear your words or to internalise thoughts? If in doubt start the next passage with) "As you continue to count further down I wonder if you have noticed yet that your body is sinking down deeper into the couch. Becoming heavier as it is fully supported in total comfort. Noting the comfort spreading throughout your body as you go deeper your mind is becoming free, free to roam where it will in total comfort and safety. Free of cares or worries, your new awareness is a beautiful place and it is just within your reach. Between you and where you want to be is a tunnel, a tunnel of beautiful lights, a Kaleidoscope of warm sensual colour that you can move through with great ease. Your destination is now only a few paces away, and now you have arrived as you go deeper and deeper to sleep. (Your subject will now be in trance and is now where he or she always intended to go, roaming around the subconscious, but you must now act as a guide otherwise the trip will be wasted. It is at this point you would deepen the trance as detailed earlier and then proceed with your therapy or comedy routines).

Although this style of induction is a little longer than the others detailed elsewhere it is ideal for therapy and is also great for placing a group of say 12 to 20 people or more into a trance at the same time. In this way the time difference becomes minimal and as I said earlier, quick into trance means quickly out and so slowly in equals slowly out.

This style of induction is also ideal for psycho-analysis and past life regression, you just need to suggest that the special place they travel to, through the tunnel of lights will be their previous lifetime should they have one and in analysis you suggest that at the end of the tunnel they will have returned to their childhood ages 1 to 7 (the formative years). The subject can then be moved back in time through ages and lifetimes by each time suggesting a journey back through time by way of a tunnel of lights as is done above.

IT IS FRIGHTENING JUST HOW EASY IT IS TO HYPNOTISE PEOPLE WHO VOLUNTEER AND WANT IT TO HAPPEN!

To conclude this chapter on verbal psychology I shall give examples of "phrases" I have at one time or another used in my patter during shows when I was at the start of my career and was forced to work pubs and clubs. These venues are much harder to work than theatres and it's also much harder to hypnotise people in these venues as when all is said and done they are there to drink beer and you come second. Whereas in a theatre you come first and the beer is only available in the interval. So here are some example phrases and also the psychological reason why each statement is said in this way.

"You came here tonight of your own free will and you remain at your own risk" (This covers you if anyone is daft enough to try and sue you.)

"I am here tonight to hypnotise you, yes you! You are the stars of the show not me, I'm just here to see that you entertain your friends." (This flatters them because they think they are to be the stars and it motivates them to co-operate.)

"Everyone can be hypnotised given enough time, however, tonight my time is limited and I shall concentrate on those who are willing to be hypnotised and can both concentrate and co-operate!" (This makes a logical excuse for not hypnotising everyone, so therefore you will not be questioned when returning unsuitable volunteers to the audience.)

"Allow me to point out that no harm will come to anyone on stage, in actual fact they will all enjoy themselves, in fact many times I find that those that did not volunteer wish they had by the end of the show." (This reassures them that they will come to no harm. I also add that I never embarrass anyone, as I want them to come back again! Some hypnotists think that to embarrass people is funny, well it is not! Especially when it is in front of friends and in an area where they live and work. Yes it is easy to shock and embarrass but it is not funny!)

"A lot of you sitting down there saying that you will not come up had better watch out, now you have heard my voice many of you could find yourselves waking up on stage anyway so don't bother hanging back when I ask for volunteers!" (This can and usually does have the effect of getting you more volunteers to take part and as I've found, can also be so strong that some people fall "asleep" where they are sitting in the audience whilst the show is occurring as they really believe what you have just said! If this happens for you then just wake them up, get them to the stage and use them in the show.)

"You must be intelligent, strong minded and willing or you cannot be hypnotised. Some of the people we cannot hypnotise are very young children, mental defectives or alcoholics, and by the look of these tables I'd say there is a lot of the last group in tonight!" (When you tell them they must be intelligent this both gets a laugh and also brings the I.I.C. syndrome into effect. Also note that as this phrase is said as I walk around the concert room sending the fear of God up everyone making the belief syndrome even greater, it also gives you a chance to see the audience close up. Eye contact and a smile can reassure those that look over nervous. From a comedy angle, if a youngish female is around I will pat her on the head as I say very young children. For mental defectives, I pat someone on the head who is very well dressed or the person who is in charge. And after saying alcoholics I look at the tables and say it whilst looking at someone (not too big) with a load of beer glasses in front of them! On occasion you can add even more comedy to this situation by saying, "start the car" or "can I go and get my fee now then go home?")

"Some of those who did not come up will wish they had, your friends will be talking to you for the next year and if you are wise you will get them to buy the drinks before you say anything!" (This gives them an incentive to take part in the show namely FREE drinks)

"You might just find yourself upon the stage without knowing it, so I'd advise you when I do ask for volunteers to come up of your own accord at least that way you'll know why your up here!" (This takes the belief and expectancy thing another stage further, which leads to self-hypnosis within their minds)

"Do not at any time interfere with my subjects, they are not to be held responsible for their actions but you are for yours!" (This has warned the audience in a nice way not to try and mess up the show or else.)

"I now require some volunteers, so to start with I'd like 5 or 6 gorgeous girls to come up on stage, now the reason I ask for the girls first is that from experience I've found them more daring than the men!" (This both helps get more volunteers and sets off a competition between the males and females to be the best subjects, which of course leads to a funnier show)

SOME FINAL ADVICE

The last example given helps to get you volunteers easily. The women get up willingly to display that they do have more courage than the men and then obviously the men retaliate and want to participate in order that they look better than the women. So here, with a casual statement, you have brought the "battle of the sexes" into play and there will be an air of competition between the onstage volunteers, which helps ensure your shows success. A little note on the side is this.

Try to seat them so that any close friends, lovers or family members are NOT next to each other and as such cannot distract each other in any manner. As a general rule of thumb in a family show seat them boy, girl, boy, girl. This psychologically reminds them how they used to be seated at school and in turn this reminds them that just as they had to obey their teacher, so they have to obey you to. As a hypnotist you must learn most of what you will say in the show word-perfect parrot fashion. Although obviously it must not sound like you've done this to the listening audience, to them it's new! In ordinary everyday conversation, one may be forgiven for forgetting the proper words to use, but there is absolutely no excuse for a hypnotist. You are meant to be an expert who knows his/her subject inside out, as such you cannot when giving suggestions with a stammer, stutter or a search around in your mind for the correct words to use. All you say must be precise, it must fully and completely express the suggestion it intends to convey. It must also be constantly recurring so that the expression of it becomes monotonous, for monotony is, as you know by now the great allay of suggestion. Well that almost concludes this chapter on "verbal psychology" hopefully by now you will have realised that when used correctly your voice is a most powerful tool, which can have a most powerful effect upon people. My final example of how powerful the voice can be is to point out that the style of voice used by a Sergeant Major gets people to obey his every order whereas a doctors tone of voice reassures you that everything will be OK! So I'll end this chapter by reminding you of one most important thing:

Every effect has a cause and every cause has an effect, see you in the next chapter!

PART SIX

PRINCIPLES OF PHYSICAL PSYCHOLOGY

What we say verbally is only a minute percentage of what we are always communicating to others. It behoves us as hypnotists to have an understanding of non-verbal communication and body language. So for this chapter I intend to explain the basic points of this subject to you. After reading it, you would be well advised to train yourself to be aware of all your body movements in order to ensure that your non-verbal style of communication matches the message of what you are saying verbally.

Upon the stage you must always appear a most confident and dominant performer in your role as stage hypnotist. This means that both your verbal and non-verbal language must transmit the same message to the audience and that message must be the one that I've just outlined above. How many times for example have you heard someone say yes when asked a question and yet they are shaking their head negatively in contradiction to what they have said? Well in this example the true message was NO, and they were obviously lying, otherwise their body language would have coincided with their verbal speech and not contradict it. Have you ever met someone, taken one look and then decided you want to hit that person? I bet unbeknown to them they were transmitting very negative attitudes through their body language. Remember your physical behaviour is made up from your motives, thoughts, attitudes and feelings of an emotional nature and it is this behaviour that people see. Your behaviour and your appearance combined are the only bits of you that other people can see. It is therefore logical that other people's impressions of you will be based on the behaviour they see, as they have nothing else to analyse you on except this behaviour and your personal appearance. Your behaviour is like a transmitter, sending out signals to the people who you are dealing with, the signals you send through your body-language are vital because they influence the reactions of the other person and the faith they have in you and your abilities. Remember that behaviour breeds behaviour, also remember that at least 70% of communication is non-verbal and falls within the realms of body language. So it would behove us to at least have a basic understanding of the subject for use on stage, in therapy, or even in our everyday lives. Examples of ways in which non-verbal messages are communicated are as follows:

Vocal pitch and emphasis, speed of speech, breathing, posture, stance, facial expressions, eye contact, eye movements, pupil size, distances and territories, gestures, movements, clothing, dress, status symbols, choice of words and jargon amongst many others.

The most significant features of non-verbal communication are:

Body-language (which is seen/observed)
Voice (Which is heard/listened to)

The body language aspect includes movements, posture, sitting position, use of the arms. Facial expressions, eye-movements, handshake, way of walking, distance from others, style of dress etc.

So remember your success or failure depends on the mastery of body language and the degree to which your words and body language convey the same message that you are trying to transmit. At any given moment your brain can assume an attitude and communicate this to various parts of your body thus promptly responding with specific actions and expressions (body language). The unseen attitude will then have been conveyed to your potential subject without you even speaking and if this is of a negative nature, then you may find that they lose faith in your powers! A dancer is trained to, at all times, know exactly what their body is doing physically and as a hypnotist, you must train your body in the same way. If you didn't and were for example slouching around the stage looking depressed, do you really think the show that night would go well for you? So as a general rule of thumb your verbal and visual behaviours must compliment each other 100%. Now for some examples of conscious body language signals to set your mind thinking on others:

1) A raised, clenched fist = A threat.
2) A raised hand or finger = A request to speak.
3) A finger to the mouth = Be quiet.
4) Pointing to the clock = Time to stop.
5) Cupping the hand behind the ear = Speak up please.

Now follow a few examples of unconscious body language signals to set you're mind thinking on the many others which there are:

1) Dilation of the eyes = Interest aroused.
2) Raised shoulders = Tense.
3) Touching the nose = Uncertain.
4) Tilting the head to one side = Interested.
5) Arms and legs crossed = Defensive.
6) Touching of watchstrap = Impatient.
7) Hands behind the head = Feels confident/superior.

By the way, it is the unconscious body language signals which are the most interesting and significant when interpreting other peoples moods, attitudes and intentions as often they will say one thing verbally whilst they actually mean another which is shown through their body language. These body signals will always transmit to you the true picture of what they mean. However, do remember when reading body language that you cannot just look at one detail and draw a conclusion from it. In order to get a reasonably good picture of another persons thoughts and feelings from their body language, you should try to assess the body signals as a whole and see them within the context of the present situation as it arises.

Generally speaking, in order to be accurate, at least three signals should be pointing in the same direction. In short, if you observe people a bit and use your common sense it will become quite easy in a short space of time to become a master of body language reading. There are of course many books on this subject which you could buy or better still borrow for free from your local library which will tell you far more than I am able to tell you here. Confident people such as you must appear such at all times, consequently, you should always look people directly in the eyes and never break eye contact with them. Don't blink your eyes and thrust your chin forward. You should keep your hands and arms away from your face and if standing, should have them down by your sides or together behind you. If standing up, be bold and upright with your back totally straight at all times and if seated, lean back with legs out in front of you. When standing in one place, don't fidget and then you will appear a most confident and relaxed person, in control of both their mind and their body. Now in order that you know the signs to look for, which indicate a friendly and co-operative subject with whom you should achieve great success, I will detail some of the most important signs to look for.

FACE AND HEAD

Looks at the other persons face, smiles a lot, nods head as other person is talking to them, looks both interested and directly at you whilst talking.

HANDS AND ARMS

Have open hands, hand goes up to face occasionally, uncrossed arms when sitting down.

BODY

Uncrossed legs when sitting down, leans slightly forward, moves closer to other person who is talking.

REACTIONS

Will immediately do as you ask without question, will appear happy to help you, seems to be concentrating hard on all the suggestions you give and carries out any other instructions without objection or delay.

The reason I have given only brief examples is that by far the best way to learn anything is through practical experience, therefore spend some time in cafes, pubs and other public environments observing peoples body language as they react in different ways and say different things. Very rapidly you will become a master of body language interpretation. Obviously, experience of life and on stage or in therapy will tend to give you a "sixth" sense almost, as it becomes automatic to pick out the subjects whose body language indicates that they should react well to your suggestions. Also another very important point is that a persons name is to them the sweetest and most important word in the entire English language. It is also easier to get people to do things if you call them by name. Many excellent books are available on memory systems and as such you have no excuse for forgetting the names of your on stage subjects! You could however make life easier and have an assistant who writes all the volunteers first names onto white self adhesive labels which can then be stuck to the subjects upper clothing as a constant visual reminder of their names throughout the show.

Although you can hold your radio microphone close to the subjects when they are speaking during a comedy routine so that they can be heard clearly by the audience, it is much better to have the stage miked up with mikes in the fly's (above the stage). Also have mikes at the footlights (front of stage), between them, these microphones will pick up all the speech of the on stage subjects and as a result, the audience will be able to hear the at all times unless they are whispering of course! Another alternative is to kit them out at the start of the show with their own clip on tie clip radio microphone which at least one well known stage hypnotist always does.

Anyway back to the plot and the secret of how to never break eye contact. To do this you simply look them not in the eye, but instead stare at the bridge of their nose. To the subject it appears that you are staring them directly in the eye and as they will always have to break eye contact first this will make them feel very uncomfortable (inferior) and as such confirm that you are the person in authority who must be obeyed. When a subject is talking to you always look directly at their lips and this way they can never catch your gaze unless you allow them to. Once again, you are in the dominant position at all times. Another way, although longer and harder to achieve, which can be used to stop you ever having to break eye contact and also to stop your eyelids fluttering too much in a nervous manner is to practise staring at a point on the wall in your living room. Now practise this until you are able to gaze at one spot without your eyes watering or tending to close. It could take a long time, but once you have mastered this you will never again have to break eye contact and doing it this way you will genuinely be staring them directly in the eyes! This ability to fix a gaze on anyone or anything for long periods of time without your eyelids fluttering excessively is a most mysterious and unnerving ability to have. Also look in the mirror and practise so that you can adopt a penetrating gaze of a stare with both your eyes and facial expression whenever you so wish. Of course, it is this stare which you would use to help induce the subjects into a trance.

I'll move next onto the subject of image, that is how your physical body looks and the state of health you are in. Now you may be thinking what has this got to do with being a hypnotist? In fact it is very relevant indeed, as for example would you visit a smoker to stop smoking? Would you visit a fat person to lose weight? Of course you wouldn't and in just the same way, as a hypnotist, it does little for your credibility to be a smoker, to be overweight or to be dressed in cheap clothing. So stop smoking if you do it, lose some weight if you're a little on the large size and buy the best outfit that money can possibly buy so that you look like a million dollars. If you can't afford a real Rolex then a fake one, which looks convincing will do. The psychology behind this from an subject's point of view is that if you are dressed in expensive gear then you must have loads of money and to have lots of money you must be good at your job and so you must be a good hypnotist. And as I've said numerous times now, if they believe in you and your powers then your job will be easy due to belief and expectancy! A little note on the side, if you're a non-smoking person of an average weight don't be surprised if you sell far more of your hypnotherapy tapes after the show. Believe me this in itself can be very profitable with over £9-00 per tape (when sold at £10) profit you only need to sell to a small proportion of the audience and you can enhance your appearance fee in this way. Your face and skin are also part of your physical appearance so make sure you treat them well.

To sum up in a few words, make sure that from tip to toe, teeth to fingernails and all in between, that all aspects of your physical appearance are clean, smart and tidy and project that successful image which you require. As this chapter is called physical psychology I will now reveal a secret which many hypnotists use but have for a long while kept secret. They place their hands gently on the subject's shoulders and say sleep? Or do they? Well my experience has shown me (I'll explain how I discovered this in a moment) that although the hand appears to be gently resting on the subjects shoulder, in actual fact the fingers are pressing firmly into the small gap under the bone at the front of the shoulder (you will find it with a little practise). When a little pressure is applied here it can be quite painful, however if you then tilt your head forward onto your chest, as you would if entering trance on stage then the pain suddenly disappears due to the position which your body is now in!

This can very quickly become a conditioned response rather like Pavlov's dogs, and as such each time you just apply a little pressure at this point as you command sleep, the person by then having been conditioned to realise what will happen concludes that in order to feel no pain they should immediately close their eyes and let their heads flop down onto their chests!

How did I discover this? Well, prior to becoming a hypnotist, I did a lot of research and some of this took the form of going to hypnotism shows, volunteering and then playing along as if hypnotised so that I could then get an idea of what went on from the stage situation point of view. Were stage whispers (talking off mike) used? Were other forms of trickery used? Well the answer to both these questions is - yes they were used, in abundance alongside the principles of genuine stage hypnotism. This is something that you can do, but please don't make life difficult for the hypnotist, do exactly as they say and in return you will be rewarded by learning a great deal. I had this conditioned pain response ploy used upon me by a quite well known Blackpool hypnotist and I noticed that he was only using it on the subjects who he could tell were not genuinely under hypnosis. As a kind of non-verbal warning to play along as they were doing. Not to be awkward, or else they would pay for it! Believe me, it worked very well for him indeed and since then has worked well for me also. Now to dispel a long time misconception, as lots of people believe that if you swing a watch in front of their eyes and say sleep then they will go into trance. Well indeed, if they believe and expect this to happen, then it would become 100% total reality and would be the quickest induction you could use on such a person with a belief system like this! However all that the action of staring at the swinging watch does or the point on the wall or the bright spotlight is to strain the small muscles at the corners of their eyes and also to blur their vision out of focus. These are natural physical effects, which are ordinarily caused by staring at one fixed point for a long time. However the hypnotist capitalises upon this by suggesting that the eyes will get strained, vision will blur and so on. So when these natural effects occur to them, the subjects believe them to be due to your suggestions and allow themselves to slip into trance more readily. Although this has been quite a short chapter you will find through experience that it has been a most important one too!

PART SEVEN

WHAT IS HYPNOSIS?

My pre-chapter piece of advice this time is to recommend to you four videos that you should purchase and watch as soon as possible as you will learn an awful lot by watching them and these videos are:

1) **"Leap of Faith" starring Steve Martin.** This tape will really open your eyes and illustrate the point I've been making throughout this course, namely if they believe you can do it then you can!

2) **"The Hypnotic World of Paul McKenna".** This tape shows you the top TV hypnotist at work and contains numerous ideas, which you could adapt as routines for your own show.

3) **"Ken Webster Live in Blackpool!".** This tape is a two hour video of Ken's live show in Blackpool and upon it you'll see him using the hands locking together test and various induction methods as well as presenting a show which is unique, hilarious and well worth seeing.

4) **"Harry the Horny Hypnotist."** This tape features a stage hypnotist doing an adults only show and to be honest is best viewed as an example of how NOT TO do a hypnotism show!

Tapes one, two and four can be ordered from any good video supply shop both to rent and/or buy. Tape three must be purchased by either going to see Ken Webster perform in Blackpool on the Pleasure Beach or by entering his name into the "Internet", visiting his world wide web site and ordering it by credit card for the price of £14-95. Watching all four of these videos after having read this entire course will prove to be a most valuable learning experience. Having read this course you will have the pieces of the jigsaw for hypnotic success and then by watching these videos the pieces will all fall into place and your understanding of the subject will be complete. Numerous Royle Live Show videos can be also be got via the author.

Derived from the Greek word "Hypnos" meaning sleep, Hypnosis is seen as being a power when in fact it is, as the Oxford English Dictionary says. "A form of communication where suggestions can be given most effectively by one person to then be carried out be the receiver of those suggestions."

The answer I give when asked this question of what is hypnosis? Is the one which I learnt from Delavar's excellent training manual "The Hypnotists Bible" and it goes like this:

Hypnosis is that small moment in time when the Ego gives way to the I.D. and vice versa. With hypnosis, we can extend that fraction of a nano second into a period of time as long as we like. We are then at this time in communication with both the Ego and the Id. We have the Ego, that is you (when awake) and the I.D. (you when asleep). To clarify further, the I.D. controls your body all the time but has no control over the Ego, whereas the Ego has no real control over the body, only the emotions are affected by it. You breathe, think, taste, smell, feel pain, keep your heart beating and so on only because the I.D. is there to see to it! The Ego is the part, which makes you walk down the street with a swagger because you feel you are the best thing since sex was invented. It is also your Ego that allows you to go on stage as the world's No.1 hypnotist or invite clients into your consulting room. We need both the Ego and the I.D. However they cannot both be in charge at the same time, so we say the Ego when awake and the I.D. when asleep. OK so this is true but what is hypnosis? Well the I.D. can always overrule the Ego, Ego awake and I.D. when asleep. So this then really is an explanation of what hypnosis is or what happens when it occurs.

Now there comes a time twice a day (normally) when the Ego and the I.D. need to communicate with each other, can you remember going to sleep? Can you remember waking up? (Nobody can!) Before you go to sleep or awaken there is a transitional period of a few seconds. That period is the time when the Ego and the I.D. give instructions to each other, the only time when they can if you like come together. To get to this period, we always dream, we drift off to sleep and awaken with a dream also (It acts as a distraction for the mind as in the hypnotic induction process). It is this transitional period when the Ego and the I.D. are exchanging dominant positions and it momentarily confuses the brain function. This is what the hypnotist uses and his induction methods if you like, merely extending this transitional period from a few seconds into very long periods of time and it is this we now call the hypnotic state. A few extra points on the side, under hypnosis (deep relaxation) the I.D. can take full control of all the bodily functions, but the Ego is still in a watchful state as it never likes to give up full control. During sleep of a normal kind, the I.D. has a free hand to repair some of the damage caused by the uncaring Ego. In a hypnotic trance we do not cut off the supply of Oxygen to the brain as happens in normal sleep, we do in fact go straight to the dividing line between the Ego and the I.D. so that the subject is neither awake nor asleep. They are in that mid point between the two points/states. It's this midpoint which is hypnosis. In layman's terms I will now explain how this state (in trance) feels and also what its like/what it is.

WHAT IS A TRANCE STATE?

Nobody really knows, there are many theories, however in scientific terms a trance is measurable by changes in brain activity and behaviour. Auto-suggestion, Yoga, meditation and self-hypnosis all induce a trance state. The reason why the trance state is so hard to understand is because they are so commonplace that it is hard to tell when you are in one or not. The closest I can come to an explanation of a trance state is the state in which the mind selects what it is consciously going to pay attention to. For example when you are watching a Western on TV, you are not sitting in your living room observing an electronic device, you have suspended disbelief and if it is a good film for long periods of time you will feel that you are actually in Dodge City observing those gunslingers in action! You are ignoring the sound of the traffic outside your window because it is not part of the story, you are unaware that you leg has gone to sleep or that the dog has just chewed its way through the newspaper, this then is a trance state.

A Boxer is hit many times during a bout but only the really hard blows hurt. All the little jabs and ineffective punches that would under normal conditions hurt the Boxer as much as you and I, go by unnoticed. The Boxer is concentrating on his opponent's moves and actions to the exclusion of all else, even pain! This too is a trance state.

Another example is a good driver, one who does not consciously think about the physical act of driving, changing gear, moving pedals and so on, but instead concentrates on the road ahead and the other drivers around them. He/She has turned the driving over to the subconscious and this too is a trance state.

When so engrossed in a book that you don't even hear a persons offer of a drink, this too is yet another example of a trance state. All of these examples are trance states and all of them are normal and safe. If the adverts come on whilst watching TV, the bell goes off during the boxing match, or the car engine makes a funny noise whilst driving, you simply change your focus of attention from the trance state to the new scenario. You are in fact fully aware and awake at all times, just as the hypnotic subjects on stage and/or in therapy are. You are under nobodies "control" but your own, you have not become deaf or had any of your senses dulled and above all the transition is so quick that it goes by unnoticed. I'm sure you will have experienced many such examples in your life in the past and so you see you already know from personal experience what a trance state is and what it feels like to be in one.

In the hypnotic trance state you can still be fully aware of your surroundings and situation, the only real difference is that you are no longer in control of the switch which operates the normal automatic control systems. You have willingly and happily given this power to another. Many people who have been hypnotised, especially those who have only been under a low key influence, for example like when being told to stop smoking, will feel that they have been tricked because they have not yet lost full consciousness.

If only they knew that hypnosis is a state of heightened awareness.

This feeling of having been tricked is due to their own misconceptions and preconceived ideas of what hypnosis is all about. They often complain to their friends "What a rip off the whole thing was" yet they never again touch another cigarette.

One way to imagine how the mind works is to imagine it as an art gallery full of beautiful pictures. A person is walking through it, the gallery is the subconscious mind and the person the conscious. As the person looks upon a picture, he is all absorbed by its beauty and form, but all the other pictures are still there. They are just not being paid attention to at this time. If you think of the conscious mind as the real you (your personality), the part of your mind that thinks in language, then you are misleading yourself. You are in fact far more complex that that! Let us imagine what you are doing right now whilst reading this course. First your eyes are scanning the page and the meaning of the words are coming into your brain. You are not consciously thinking A is for apple, N is for nightie, D is for daisy and so on, instead you just read the word AND. These other things were committed to your subconscious mind and became conditioned into you so that they now work as an automatic reflex action and all this was learnt as a child. What happened is your conscious mind decided to sit and read the course and to open a channel to your subconscious mind, to the bit in the "computer file" marked "reading and how to do it". This in itself is a trance state (a distraction of the conscious mind) which your conscious mind was in until I alerted you to the situation. Also until I alerted you to the situation, your conscious mind was lost amongst all these new ideas that I am sharing with you. Therefore you are not thinking about the Gas Bill or next Sundays weather, you have not either considered your surroundings at all or the fact that you may be standing or sitting. It could in fact be argued in a very real sense, that I have hypnotised you or induced a trance state into you without us even meeting in person, for what has just been described is the essence of the hypnotic induction process.

One person's control of another's conscious mind by keeping it occupied with but one thought. That is what hypnosis is, not all that frightening now is it?

During hypnosis, it is the belief system and processes which must be overruled and controlled. Now the only way one person can control another persons belief mechanism is to bypass it completely and that is what hypnosis enables us to achieve. This is what allows us to convince subjects they are Elvis or Madonna. Because the belief system is not being consulted, it does not realise the discrepancy with fact and as such is not objecting to the command, as would usually be the case. If the belief mechanism were to check with the subconscious, it would find that it has been temporarily reprogrammed. The hypnotist bypasses the belief and understanding systems (reality safeguards) in the mind of another and influences the subconscious mind directly. This is hypnosis at its simplest form. Just as when counting sheep in your mind at night to promote sleep, the distraction of the swinging watch, flashing light or moving hand is used to concentrate the mind of the subject away from defence so that they relax. Once they have relaxed, the hypnotist's words will seep more easily into the subconscious where they will then be enacted. Basically speaking, hypnosis is easy to achieve through fixation of attention and distraction of the subject's mind away from what they are doing. It is the thinking behind the words you say and the flexibility and ingenuity you have as a hypnotist that matters. You may have seen a trance induced or been hypnotised yourself and been amazed at just how simple it really is. It may have followed the almost comical form of "go to sleep, you are in my power!" etc. But the true power of the hypnotist lies within the mind of the subject and the words and/or actions used are not dictated in advance but are lead by the actions and reactions of the subject. It is this understanding that makes a major difference to the success you will achieve.

In the mind of the subject, it is the "Belief and Expectancy" which matters most. Now it shouldn't take too much common sense, after all I've told you, to see that what I've said is all actually 100% true. Now, if the words were all important and you could induce a trance simply by uttering them, then the entire audience would fall under the spell and act in the same way at the same time at each and every show you did which of course is not the case in reality.

In reality, hypnosis occurs due to a persons belief and expectancy and as we mentioned earlier the best kept secret of all is that all hypnosis is really just self-hypnosis, with us just acting as directors of the trance state. Now its time for a very brief history lesson:

Hypnosis is a condition in which willpower and a person's consciousness is suspended but other functions remain unimpaired. The subject of hypnosis is then exceptionally suggestible to suggestion, may be made insensible to pain and will carry out instructions (post hypnotic suggestions) at once or long after being awakened from the trance. Discovered by Anton Fredrich Mesmer (1733-1815), an Austrian physician who claimed he could reduce people to a trance like state by applying a technique he called Animal Magnetism. The subject's willpower being entirely subordinated by his own.

The police expelled him from Vienna and he created a sensation with stage and public demonstrations when he moved to Paris in 1778. But again in 1785 he was denounced as a charlatan despite his obvious powers. He was really just an early experimenter in what we now call hypnotism or hypnosis. It was however at the time called Mesmerism and was called this for many years afterwards also. A surgeon by the name of James Esdaile Braid then, many years on, studied Mesmer's work and coined the name hypnosis from the Greek word Hypnos meaning sleep and so a whole new life was given to the suggestion technique. James E. Braid performed operations with only hypnosis as the anaesthetic and brought it as a science almost to the attention of the medical profession.

Another key peg in the development of hypnosis and its use in medicine and psychotherapy was Milton Erikson who's great books are available on general sale and publications authored by, or co-authored by this man are unreservedly recommended to all students of this course. From a stage performance point of view it was Peter Casson who made stage hypnosis so popular back in the 50's although obviously many Music Hall performers had been doing it for many years prior to this. It was due to Mr. Casson that the 1952 Hypnotism act was implemented, otherwise stage hypnotism shows may have been banned completely in England in 1952 no thanks to the actions of an American hypnotist called Ralph Slater who brought the industry into disrepute and for this we have a lot to thank Peter Casson for.

In more recent years there have been people such as Paul McKenna, Andrew Newton, Ken Webster, Peter Powers and myself presenting hypnosis on TV to millions of people at one time, bringing it to a much wider audience and so making stage hypnotism shows more popular than they have ever been.

So all in all, its roots are set many years ago and its an art that is tried, tested and proven to work. Well let me rephrase that. Hypnosis is a skill anyone can learn, but the practice of it is an art which can only be learnt through practical experience. Just as anyone can play a piano this does not automatically make the a great concert pianist and in the same way it follows that each and every hypnotist will have a different level of skill and only those with the highest skill levels could be classed as the concert pianists of stage hypnotism.

In 1952, the hypnotism act was introduced (amended 1972) to protect the citizens of the UK from the humiliating, dangerous and pornographic stage hypnotists who gave the subject a bad name for many years. Other similar laws were passed in countless other countries at about the same time. Now licenses must be sought for any public show and strict controls and regular inspections are now normal procedure. Stage hypnotism is now a safe and highly recommended form of family entertainment, performed by the skilled without trickery and watched by the enthralled without embarrassment. Hypnotism is a form of power over people, and any power when misused can be dangerous. This knowledge, like any other knowledge is given in trust to you, to be looked after, used for the good of all and shared with other like-minded people. Most importantly let me state that nobody has ever come to any harm under hypnosis or as a direct/indirect result of it despite what may have been said in the media (during 1993/1994) about the tragic death of one Sharon Tabarn, the daughter of Margaret Harper some five hours after a stage hypnotism show conducted by Andrew Vincent at the Roebuck Public house in Leyland (Preston) Lancs. Despite the fact that several people including her family and so called experts who should have known better, including top Hypnotherapist Derek Crussal, backed up Mrs. Harpers allegations of death by hypnosis and formed (C.A.S.H) The Campaign Against Stage Hypnotists she did in fact die due to natural causes.

Well the real truth as I understand it and it has been related to me is as follows. The coroners report, the pathologists report and all other expert reports concluded that her death was due to natural causes and has no connection whatsoever to the hypnotism show or the hypnotic trance state. In fact I am led to believe by what I have recently heard that excessive traces of alcohol and chemicals (not just prolactin) were found in her bloodstream and it is now generally believed within the industry that this is why she died tragically in her sleep by choking on her own vomit. So despite the false impression given by the mass media there was no connection whatsoever between hypnosis and the death of Sharon Tabarn and in fact there is no recorded case in history backed up with proper facts and evidence of anyone ever dying due to hypnosis.

Always remember that hypnosis is a totally harmless state, which is why as detailed earlier, it is a natural part of our everyday lives. At this point it would be interesting to note that in 1989 the government attached model conditions to the granting of licences for hypnotism shows, then in 1995 the government appointed an expert committee to investigate if stage hypnotism posed a threat to the public and as such should it be banned? Then as a result of the 1995 investigation declaring that stage hypnotism posed no serious risk to the public, the 1996 Government review on stage hypnosis came into force along with a revised set of model conditions to be attached to the issuing of licences. A full copy of the 1952 act, the 1989 Guidelines, the 1995 safety report and the 1996 Government review and revised conditions are included along with a letter from the Home Office in a separate chapter within this training course and you are advised to become fully conversant with the contents of all these documents in order that your shows and practices are 100% legal at all times. A little note on the side here is that upon completing this course you will be granted upon successful application membership of (P.O.S.H) and (R.I.H.P.) which are The Professional Organisation of Stage Hypnotists and The Royle Institute of Hypnotherapy and Psychotherapy.

Following the laws by the letter and providing proof of public liability insurance, details of your past three successful shows and a copy of your membership certificate should almost certainly always result in you being granted licences with ease. If however you do encounter problems do not hesitate to contact us and we will be pleased to assist.

So to return to the subject in hand, hypnotism is the effect of the thoughts, feelings, imagination and will of each particular subject. When the subject's mind is in agreement with the mind of the hypnotist, according to a given suggestion, then this is hypnosis. Take a look in your dictionary and the definition of hypnosis will no doubt mention sleep, it is a sleep like state, a trance if you like, in which the condition of the subject becomes passive and the subconscious mind accepts the hypnotists suggestions, providing of course that these fall within their moral code. Very briefly put, hypnotism is a psychological method of selling an idea by an operator (the hypnotist) to a subject under certain conditions. These conditions can be divided under two headings:

1) Conditions applying to the operator (hypnotist).
2) Conditions applying to the subject

It is also interesting to note that it is now an accepted fact that a subject under the influence of hypnotism will only carry out the hypnotist's requests when they are not against their morals or internal beliefs. This is not, to be honest, strictly true as in fact once a person has given their consent to be hypnotised and is under hypnosis they can be made to do anything you wish just so long as the suggestion is phrased correctly. By correctly, I mean worded so that to the subject it appears that they will be carrying out a perfectly pleasant act which ties in with their morals, but which has the end result of them doing as you wish.

An example is. The person would not pick up a loaded gun and shoot someone at your command under normal conditions. But if you convinced them they are four years old, playing cowboys and indians and that it's a cap gun which they will use to shoot the big bad chief indian, then they would carry out what seemed to them something normal, but which would actually result in them committing murder. For this reason, you should ALWAYS think very carefully before giving suggestions.

You should by now, realise that when a subject enters hypnosis, although they may themselves not believe this to be the case, (remember belief and expectancy) they are in fact going under by means of their own free will. They co-operate with you the hypnotist, to bring about this state of mind which is actually self-hypnosis.

POSITIVE THINKING IS A MOST POSITIVE FORCE

AND

CONFIDENCE BEGETS CONFIDENCE

From your point of view, the key secret of hypnosis is the faith in your abilities is the means and confidence is the weapon of execution.

IT HAS GOT TO BE IN THE MIND FIRST BEFORE IT CAN BECOME AN ACTION LATER

So quite simply, make sure all the suggestions you give are clear so that they do go into the mind first and then become actions late. Another important point is to always be enthusiastic in whatever you are doing then you will automatically become more successful as a result.

ENTHUSIASM IS ESSENTIAL - A NEVER TIRING ENTHUSIASM

Now, so that any fear of failure you may still have can be forgotten, allow me to state what is a very true fact indeed and that is:

Anyone can, if they so desire, become a competent professional stage hypnotist and mind therapist. The only qualities which are 100% necessary are an outgoing personality and the ability to force ones own personality onto others as described in these training course manuals which you now hold in your hands. The only difference between you and the majority of people on planet earth is that you have, I assume a desire to practise the art of stage hypnotism and mind therapy and also an inner belief that you can do it! You should by now have the self confidence that by the end of this course you will be able to, without doubt present your own stage hypnotism shows and/or treat people with mind therapy. Basically speaking all hypnotic induction's and trance deepening's have the following characteristics:

A) The subject's attention and concentration is focused upon one stimulus or a range of limited stimuli. You can ask the subject to gaze at a bright light or at a spot on the wall or ceiling, at the tip of your finger or indeed at their clasped hands. The subject could even be just concentrating on the sound of the hypnotist's voice or the regular beat of a metronome. The subject can focus upon feelings in their body or the ebb and flow of their own breath to mention just a few possible examples. The key secret here is to have the subject focused and concentrated upon one thing and make it seem important at all times.

B) The hypnotist repeats continuously, suggestions of relaxation, letting go, sleep, heaviness, calmness, going down deeper and deeper etc.

C) The coupling of A & B combined, e.g. focusing their attention by a suggestion. For example, with each breath you take you are letting go more and more, as your eyes are getting heavier and heavier you find yourself drifting down deeper and deeper, or, each time your hands shake more rapidly, so in turn you drift deeper and deeper to sleep. These are all good examples of how to do this.

These three key points are present in one form or another in all the induction and deepening methods that you will ever encounter or indeed will ever use. Remember that the power of hypnosis does not lie within the hypnotist, but rather the real power is within the minds of the subjects. The hypnotist just utilises the simple techniques within this course to unlock that power, and here I refer once more to the principle of belief and expectancy within the subject's mind. Another important rule to remember so that you realise that hypnosis really is as easy as I've made it appear is that when an idea takes root in the subconscious mind, then it must show up later in the motor (psychical) actions of that person. This brings me back to the rule that when the imagination and the will are in conflict the imagination (subconscious) will always win.

BE SIMPLE POSITIVE AND DIRECT IN ALL THAT YOU DO

AND

WHAT THE MIND PERCEIVES THE BODY ACHIEVES

To explain, let me put it this way. Once a person under hypnosis perceives that what a hypnotist suggests will take place, (Coue's law of reversed effort) then whatever else is suggested will have a stronger influence upon that person with even greater ease than the previous suggestion. The suggestion that everything will be cancelled out of their minds at the end of the show and that they will be just as they were when they entered the building is given, as you will recall at the very end of the show, a show in which volunteers have responded in a way that you wanted them to many times and so you need have no worries that they will also respond to your suggestions to awaken them and to cancel out previous suggestions before they leave the venue. This itself is a logical illustration of the rule I have just mentioned above. Another clever ploy is after giving a subject a suggestion to act upon, before "awakening" them to act upon it you say to them **"Now just nod your head if you understand."** As long as they nod their head you need have no worries, as you can then be certain they have both heard and accepted what you have just suggested and as a result it will be acted upon as 100% total reality.

This works also in therapy, as when they nod to confirm that they understand, it is both a conscious and subconscious affirmation by themselves and to themselves that indeed they have understood your suggestions. They will therefore act upon them in the correct manner, it, if you like, cements the suggestions into their subconscious mind in a manner that guarantees success.

COUE'S LAW OF REVERSED EFFORT

The French physician Emile Coue (d.1926) who was most famous for the short positive thinking statement of "Every day in every way I am getting better and better" was well aware that the subconscious mind was directly responsible for the imaginative processes of each and every one of us. If you imagine that you are going to feel uncomfortable and ill at ease when you have that meeting with the boss later, then a suggestion/idea will take root in your subconscious mind and therefore must show in your motor actions. Consequently when you arrive at the meeting the harder you try to relax, the more the idea will pop back into your head and will occur in reality and you will feel uncomfortable and ill at ease.

Emile Coue teaches that no matter how hard we try to consciously stop something from happening, whenever a persons imagination grasps hold of an idea, then the conscious will stands no chance whatsoever of exerting any control over the situation because as we know already "When the imagination and the will are in conflict the imagination will always win." So the law of reversed effort means that any conscious effort that is used is reversed into the exact opposite.

FEAR AN EVENT HAPPENING AND IT INEVITABLY WILL

So due to the law of reversed effort as detailed above, we are able to achieve any things in our role as a stage hypnotist and mind therapist. For example when doing the handclasp test to lock the subject's hands together we say after all the suggestions have been given:

"OK, now just TRY to separate your hands, but the harder you TRY the more they will stick together!"

Because the idea has taken root in the imagination that their hands will be locked together, the law of reversed effort comes into play here to ensure as reality that their hands do indeed stay locked together. The way the last statement of **TRY** to separate your hands is worded is also very clever and has an extremely strong psychological effect. The word **try** is in fact a very strong suggestion within a suggestion so to speak. It means that you believe their hands are now locked together and as such they cannot possibly separate them, but they can try anyway! In other words it implies in the one word **try,** that should they bother to try and separate their hands then they will be unable to do so. This technique of using the word **try** in this manner, along with the law of reversed effort can be used after many other suggestions, the wording of which you can devise yourself but remember to always paint a word picture of the end result you desire. So some other examples of how this ploy can be used are as follows:

A) OK, now just **TRY** to say your name, but the more you **TRY** the more you will be unable to remember it.
B) OK, now just **TRY** to open your eyes, but the more you **TRY** the more they will remain stuck together.
C) OK, now just **TRY** to lift up the chair, but the harder you **TRY** the more you will be unable to lift it.

The technique I have just detailed is more powerful than you could ever imagine. Using it, you can lock peoples hands together, make their arms or legs rigid, stick their eyes together and much more, all just by using the suggestions that these things will occur and then by using the word **try** and the law of reversed effort to ensure that they don't.

As all these things are done without actual so called hypnosis, the subject is fully awake and conscious at all times. Hence these things are often called suggestibility tests. This is known in the trade as conscious hypnosis or waking state hypnosis.

In general, those people who react readily to such suggestibility tests will make excellent hypnotic subjects and can be placed into trance with the greatest of ease. Experiment with this and you will see what I mean as you should never forget that practical experience is the best teacher in life. Always have 100% confidence in yourself and your skills because if you fear failure, remember the law of reversed effort which states that if you fear an event happening then inevitably it will. One last most important point for this chapter and that is to say that don't forget that doing one actual show or therapy session will teach you far more through practical experience than this or any other course ever could teach you. A close second to this is that participating in stage shows and therapy sessions will also teach you far more than just reading this course ever can, although now you will obviously be able to observe with far more expertise. Don't forget also that just like myself and every other person in this industry you can never, and will never know all that there is to know on this subject as new developments and discoveries are made daily. So you will never stop learning if you want to become a really expert professional hypnotist.

REVERSE PSYCHOLOGY

Reverse psychology works in much the same way as Coue's law of reversed effort and I will mention it only briefly herein. You can of course find detailed explanations of it in any practical psychology book available from your local library. My one main example of how it does work is this. When I was a boy and at school one day the hardest lad in the entire school started to pick on me and call me names etc. Believing in the law of reverse psychology I started to criticise him back (this in itself shocked him), then when he threatened to hit me if I didn't shut up, instead of shutting up I said "OK then just TRY and hit me!" He just stood there for a minute and did nothing, then he said "Be careful or I will hit you!" To which I replied "Why wait a minute try to hit me now if you can!" He then just looked bemused by my reaction and after calling me a complete Pratt walked off without so much as touching me. You see I'd said exactly the REVERSE of what he would have expected me to say in such a situation and this use of reverse psychology combined with the law of reversed effort helped me to avoid a good bashing that day. When you say something which is the exact reverse of what people would expect you to say in a given situation it stuns them and this shock makes them unable to think clearly or indeed be able to carry out the original actions they had planned as in this example.

For now I'll see you in the next chapter when we discuss suggestibility tests!

PART EIGHT

SUGGESTIBILITY TESTS

"I want you to imagine in your minds eye that I've just cut a lemon into two halves. I have then picked up one half of this bitter, sour, horrible, juicy lemon and placed it into my mouth at which time I've sucked all the bitter, sour juice from inside it and now all that bitter, sour, citric lemon juice is now running down my throat!"

"OK now, TRY to whistle! I bet you can't, in fact I bet your mouth is now awash with saliva making the action of whistling impossible. In fact if you truly imagined what I suggested for you, this will indeed have occurred in reality and by the way this is an example of a most simple suggestibility test!"

THIS IS AN EXAMPLE OF THE POWER OF SUGGESTION

In this short chapter we will deal with the subject of Suggestibility tests. All of these work due to the word **TRY** as detailed in the previous chapter and indeed also due to the law of reversed effort, an element of pure suggestion and the persons ability to be suggestible to this comes into play also. These suggestibility tests are used whilst the subject is fully conscious at the start of your act or therapy session if desired in order that you can easily and quickly decide which of the people will make the best hypnotic subjects. Some hypnotists perform these tests upon the entire audience at once and then ask those it works on to come forward to the stage and these people are then narrowed down to the best subjects who are then used in the show. Others who are more confident of their skills ask for volunteers to come up to the stage and then they do the tests only on those onstage volunteers, the logic behind this being that one sincere volunteer is worth one hundred pressed men. So either way should be most successful for you if presented correctly, confidently and believably.

I would however in your early days advise you to do these tests upon the entire audience, as then the law of averages will be in your favour. Don't forget, the more people there are in your audience by far the more chance you have of getting more people under hypnosis. It really is all just a numbers game at the end of the day. Incidentally, as in your early days you will be working in pubs and clubs to audiences of about 80 to 150 people you will not have the advantage of 2000 people in a theatre to choose your subjects from and so in these situations the suggestibility tests are an essential part of your show and should be done on the entire audience. When your career develops and you move onto larger capacity venues, you will then be able to safely and confidently ask for volunteers who wish to be hypnotised to come forward to the stage before you have even done any suggestibility tests. Once upon the stage these volunteers are subjected to the tests and the best reacting subjects are singled out to be hypnotised. Remember that in a theatre which seats 1000 to 2000 people when you ask for volunteers at the start you will get around 80 to 100 people coming up to the stage. Not only does this look dramatic and impressive to the rest of the audience, but also effectively it means your volunteers each of who is worth a hundred pressed men wants to be hypnotised. In a theatre situation, you will have almost as many volunteers on stage as would be in the entire audience during the early days of your career in pubs and small clubs! So you see, it really is all down to the law of averages and the numbers game. In general your shows will always be more successful in large capacity venues such as night-clubs and theatres than those held in pubs and social clubs. Don't let this deter you though, as upon having read this course you **WILL** be able to do an excellent show in pubs and clubs until you progress to the larger venues. The only problem, or should I say difference there is really between working in a pub and a theatre, is that in a theatre they have paid to come and see you and so you are the main thing of importance and alcohol comes second and will only be available in the interval anyway!

WHEREAS IN A PUBLIC HOUSE

They have come to have a few pints and you the poor entertainer have got to work really hard to keep their attention. Also in pubs it is not wise to let your show start too late as, due to the drinking and the fact people who are drunk cannot be hypnotised, it is wise your show starts before they have all had one to many to drink. Some of the components that make up these suggestibility tests or the induction's which follow later are of a physiological and/or physical nature. In other words, in many of the cases if you got them to do as I describe then it would be physically impossible to separate their hands or open their eyes even without the verbal suggestion element coming into play! However as these tests are all presented in a manner which makes the subject believe that whatever occurs is due to our suggestions, when these things do occur for whatever reason whether physical, physiological or suggestion, the subject comes to believe that it was all due to your suggestions and so will more readily accept and react to any future "genuine" suggestions that we may give them.

In other cases such as in the induction's detailed later, due to natural physiological causes, they may be made to feel dizzy or disorientated and because we know this always happens and is a natural feeling we can suggest that it will happen before it actually does happen of its own accord. Then when it does occur, as indeed it will, the subject always believes our verbal suggestions to have been the cause of what they now are feeling and/or experiencing and so in turn this compounds their belief in our powers even more and from that moment any "genuine" suggestions will always get a successful response as the subject is now conditioned to belief they will and expect they will work and so in turn they will.

So hopefully, you now see that little known naturally occurring phenomenon are used by the hypnotist to make the subject experience strange sensations which the subject then connects to your suggestions and as a direct result, increases their belief in your powers and takes them further down into the trance state.

Examine closely all the suggestibility tests and induction's which I teach you and you will, without fail, see that each one has an element of it either being guaranteed to happen or of some part, feeling or sensation being guaranteed to occur which the subject then comes to believe are due to your verbal suggestions and in turn cements into their mind the belief and expectancy that all future suggestions will indeed be 100% effective also.

These suggestibility tests also get the subjects to focus their attention and concentration onto one thing which of course you will also command them to do later when inducing the trance state. This conditions them to react in a certain way when asked certain things and makes your overall job easier. So I suppose we should really call these suggestibility tests pre-induction's or light induction's as when anyone is focusing or concentrating on one thing they are in effect in a very light hypnotic state. This is because the key element of trance is fixation of attention and concentration on one point of focus. It almost goes without saying that the people whose hands lock together are better subjects than those whose don't! So what? Well in a pub or club situation you will probably have only about 8 or 10 people come up with their hands locked together and so it would be wise here to hypnotise as many of these as possible before asking for other volunteers if needed. On theatre shows however you will have loads of people with their hands locked together so how do you choose which will be the best subjects to use? Well very obviously those people whose hands are shaking violently as opposed to just locked together are by far the most suggestible subjects, as indeed they have so far reacted better to your suggestions than anyone else. To narrow down the numbers even more remember always that one volunteer is worth a hundred pressed men so first of all return anyone to the audience who does not wish to remain there.

Next you would of course eliminate people who seem drunk or high on drugs, people who appear under the age of 18, anyone who looks petrified being on stage and lastly if there are enough people on stage with their hands locked together those people who just volunteered without their hands being locked together. However, where numbers are smaller than usual, the volunteers without hands locked together are used as potential hypnotic subjects also.

From the remainder, the "handshakers" are excellent subjects. Next, those people who have been hypnotised before on stage or by a therapist are easy to place into trance also and then it's a matter of observation. Although experience of performing will give you an almost sixth sense of who to pick here follow some important signs to look for which are indicative of a potentially good subject. Those that take what you say seriously and appear to concentrate on things when you tell them to, appear to do as you say when you tell them to and generally seem sincere in their efforts will also make excellent subjects. The reason for this being that hypnosis is co-operation and not confrontation. Also during your initial banter/patter with the on stage volunteers, the answers they give to your questions will on many occasions give you an indication of who will make a good subject and who won't! For example those who have been hypnotised before in the past can usually be made to enter trance just by commanding them to close their eyes and Sleep!

If the people have been hypnotised successfully before, even if it was not by you, then as they have entered the state of trance before, know how it feels and know what to expect and how to react they will make the most excellent of subjects and can be placed instantly back into trance as their belief and expectancy in the powers of hypnosis is 100% complete and based on prior practical experience of being hypnotised. They have experienced the state of hypnosis before so they know it exists and now they just need a catalyst if you like, to renter the state and you serve this purpose for them. With these kind of people it is often as easy as snapping your fingers in front of their face and saying sleep to make them enter trance with ease. So what actual visual clues are there that people are indeed doing as you suggest and taking it all seriously? Well basically, it's a case of using your common sense here. If they do as you say the moment that you suggest it, then obviously they are taking it seriously and are concentrating on your instructions and so in turn are a potentially very good subject. For example, if you suggest that their hands are getting tighter and tighter together all the time and you can visually see that their hands are turning red with the pressure they are using to squeeze their hands together then obviously they are reacting well to your suggestions.

Having given you all this guidance, it is however true to say that the selection of who to use is something that each person must master for themselves through practical experience. Body language plays a part, those that will be good subjects will usually have similar patterns of body language which of course you will learn through hands on practical experience. Basically however, having used the correct patter to open the show and due to all the other psychological elements in our favour as discussed earlier, if you are adaptable and suit your induction to the personality of your subject then you can hypnotise given enough time **EVERY PERSON** that steps onto your stage.

Anyway, enough about what the suggestibility test is used for or how to spot potentially good subjects, lets now explain a few actual suggestibility tests, which can be used to narrow down the selection process. This is all "Waking State" hypnosis if you like and does demonstrate to the watching and participating audience that all suggestion correctly expressed does have a most powerful effect.

THE ARM DROP TEST

This test, if used at all, is used right at the start to find which people in the audience are already in a nicely relaxed state and as such would make potentially good subjects for use upon the stage, it also shows you which members of the audience are able to relax when they want to, as once again these type of people make excellent subjects. You get everyone to close their left hand into a fist and then to extend their left forefinger so that it points up in the air. They are then told to place the lower part of their right arm (near the wrist) resting upon the top of their extended left forefinger. They are told to allow the full weight of their right arm to be supported by the forefinger of their left hand. Next they are told to relax every muscle in their bodies and especially in their right arm so that all the weight of the right arm rests upon the left forefinger. You explain that you will now count to three and that on the count of three they are to pull their left forefinger away from under their right arm rapidly. You count 1,2,3, and on the count of three they take their fingers away. The people who are able to relax best and have followed your instructions to the letter will find that having allowed the weight of their right arm to rest fully upon the left fingertip, that upon removal of the left hand's finger, their right arm will immediately fall into their laps like a sack of potatoes.

Their arm will have fallen, as it will be limp, loose, relaxed and heavy and that's what you are looking for, the people who have relaxed easily in this manner. Those who did not react due to not relaxing enough will probably have remained with their right arm still suspended in the air upon removal of the finger or at least it would have fallen far more slowly into their laps than the really suggestible people. So in this test the idea is just to see who can relax quickly when asked to and indeed those people whose hands fell into their laps rapidly have passed this test with flying colours! This one is not a suggestibility test as such it's more a way to see who follows your instructions to the letter and who can relax easily. I would therefore use at least one actual suggestibility test such as the handclasp after this experiment prior to inducing the Trance State in order to ensure success.

FINGERS CLOSING TEST

This is a suggestibility text of a natural type. By "Natural Type" I mean that what occurs would do anyway for most people automatically without any suggestions, so it's a physical trick, if you like, but this instils more belief into them prior to the handclasp test. You ask them to interlock their fingers so that the fingers of the left hand are against the back of the right hand, and the fingers of the left hand are against the back of the left hand. Palms pressed tightly together and thumbs resting on top of their interlocked fingers just as in the handclasp text, which is fully detailed with complete explanation and patter in the "Know your lines" chapter of this course.

You then ask them to extend their two forefingers, so that the tips of each outstretched finger are touching. They are then told to separate the tips of the fingers by about an inch and a half, and lastly they are told to stare directly at you and not at their hands. You yourself have got your hands in the same position as their hands, as you suggest that by the count of 3 their fingers will be touching just as they were beforehand, that should the try to keep them apart then the fingers will just draw nearer and nearer together. You then count as follows:-

1 It's almost as though there are strong magnets on the tips of your fingers, drawing them together, more and more, bringing them nearer together.

2 They are getting so close now, that they are almost touching as those magnets become so powerful and pull your fingertips together. And on,

3 The magnets are so powerful that your fingertips are now touching.

N.B.

As you do this, you close your own two fingers together slowly, so that by the time you say the number three, your own fingertips are touching. Many will take this as a non-verbal suggestion that their own fingers are getting closer together.

You then get the people who's fingertips were touching by the count of three to place a hand up, this makes it easier for you to gauge the response level which with this test is usually extremely high. At the end of the fingers closing test, you can then go into:

THE HANDCLASP TEST

The way to do this is fully detailed in the "Know your Lines" part, so it is not necessary to repeat it all.

I will however, mention how it can be used differently when working in smaller venues where there is not enough room to have lots of people coming to join you on the performance area.

In these cases, you would carry out the test as described in the earlier chapter until you have counted up to 20 and given all the suggestions. At this point, you would say, "OK now, everyone, still believing in the worlds strongest superglue which sticks your hands tightly together, I'd like you to try and separate your hands (law of reversed effort takes effect here), but you'll find the harder you try to separate them the more they will stick together tightly. OK, now, **try.** (give them a few seconds then say) Right, that's enough, just relax your hands now and stop trying." Those people who's hands are now still stuck together I'd like you to stand up, because if you don't, your hands will be like this for three weeks, when they'll turn blue and drop off. Also anyone else who just found their hands difficult to separate who wishes to experience the state of hypnosis, please come this way towards me.

N.B.

In this way of using the text, obviously fewer people will end up with hands locked together. However, it solves the limited space problem. Those who's hands are shaking are usually the best subjects, those with hands just locked together, next best and those whose hands separate, but it was harder to do than usual come next in order of preference and lastly, those people who just volunteered to take part anyway. Remember though, as with anything in life, there will always be exceptions to the rules and as such, you must always use your common sense and learn to think on your feet.

In all methods of using the test, here is how to separate their hands for them. You simply suggest that the moment you tap them on the back of the hands their hands will spring apart, as if two magnets were repelling each other. You then go round to each person whose hands you wish to separate and touch them on the back of the hands, whilst at the same time, saying to each of them, "It's O.K. now you can separate your hands, you CAN separate your hands."

Just as imagination allowed them to stick together due to suggestion, so it will also allow them to part due to suggestion. Usually most people would separate all the subject's hands and then do the induction's on them. As you will have noticed in the "Know you Lines" chapter, on large theatre shows only, I separate their hands straight away, if I wish to return them to the audience, or, if I wish to use one of the induction's from the next chapter which requires them to have their hands separate at the time. Otherwise, I would place them into trance via the falling backwards induction, using the patter as detailed in "Know your Lines". Their hands would still be locked together and they would be held against their chest area. This being to case, the top half of their body would now be much heavier than the rest of their body, and, as such, they are now going to find it much harder to stop themselves falling backwards into your arms, when you start the induction of falling backwards. Once on the floor with their eyes closed, I would suggest to them, that their eyes **will** remain tightly closed at all times until I say otherwise and then, that when I take hold of their arms, their hands will immediately separate. The moment you have said this you take hold of their arms, one in each hand and say, "OK just separate your hands now." The moment they separate their hands, you use this as an opportunity to deepen the light trance they are in by saying, "The moment I drop your arms to the floor, it will not disturb you, in fact, it will serve to send you deeper to sleep, 10 times deeper to sleep" (then drop their arms to floor as you say) "Sleep and Relax".

LIGHT AND HEAVY HANDS TEST

With this test, the audience is told to close their eyes and extend their two arms out straight in front of themselves at the same level. Their Right palm to be face down towards the floor and their left palm to be faced upwards towards the ceiling. You now tell them to close their eyes and suggest to them that their left hand has got a pile of very heavy leather bound library books upon it, which are so heavy, that their hand is being pushed downwards lower and lower with every breath they take.

You then suggest that tied to the middle finger of their right hand is a large helium filled balloon which is pulling their right hand high up into the air, as it floats ever upwards, rising higher and higher with each breath they take.

You keep suggesting things along these lines, that the left hand holds the heavy books and right hand is being pulled up into the air by the helium balloon.

You will find that the people who really are open to suggestion, will allow their arms to react accordingly. As such, their left hand will move downwards, as if a heavy pile of books is upon it, and their right hand will move upwards, as if tied to a helium filled balloon. You then tell everyone to open their eyes, and many will be amazed to find that their arms are now in very different positions with a huge gap between them both.

THE PERFUME BOTTLE TEST

You remove a fancy cut glass bottle from your pocket and explain that it contains the most powerfully scented perfume in the world. You state that, in a few moments, you will remove the lid of the bottle and allow the scent to travel around the room for everyone to smell, as it really is that strong. You tell everyone to raise their hand into the air the second they smell the scent come their way, which, as it's so potent, will take only a few seconds. The bottle's lid is then removed and the people start to raise their hands, once several hands are in the air you explain that the power of suggestion has worked upon them, and in fact the bottle contains nothing more than water, with a little added food colouring. You then drink the contents to prove your point and people will be amazed as they will swear they smelt the scent travel around the room, trust me, this does, if presented convincingly, work.

WARM FINGERS TEST

This is sometimes used prior to the handclasp test. You have them place their arms outstretched in front of them, and get them to place their hands flat against each other, you then command them to start rubbing their hands backwards and forwards against each other, as quickly as they can. You say you'll count from 3 to 1. All the time they are to keep rubbing their hands together and, if they concentrate, then by the count of 1 their hands will be getting hot and sticky, as if coated with superglue. You then say 3, getting hotter and hotter, 2, the hotter they get, the more sticky they become, and the more sticky they become, the hotter they will get, and on 1, just interlock your fingers like this (you then demonstrate how they should put their hands for the handclasp test, which you immediately go into). OK everyone, as you hold your hands interlocked, the warmth and stickiness you felt, is already locking them tightly together (you then go into normal patter for handclasp).

Now just to explain briefly, the idea of his test is that if you rub your hands back and forth against each other rapidly, they do indeed become hot and sticky. But, as this is so obvious, people don't realise this to be the case and attribute it to your suggestions, which not only gives them a greater belief in your powers, but as they feel their hands are hot and sticky, do not be surprised if it becomes easier for them to believe that there is super glue on their hands, sticking them together tightly.

THE ORDER OF TESTS TO BE DONE

So, in your very early days when you lack confidence in yourself, you may wish to use all the tests, if you do however, please ensure you do them rapidly, as you're meant to be a dynamic showman and not a boring lecturer. So the order of tests would go:

1. Arm drop text
2. Finger closing test
3. Warm fingers test
4. Handclasp test
5. Actual induction of Hypnotic Trance

The psychology behind them being placed in this order being that:

1. ARMDROP TEST

This shows you which can relax easily and quickly, and which do exactly as you tell them to, it's just a relaxation exercise, however it gets them used to doing as you say.

2. THE FINGERS CLOSING TEST

It is natural for the fingers to close together anyway and, you will have a high success rate with this, the success of it then increasing their belief in your powers.

3. WARM FINGERS TEST

This takes but a matter of seconds to do prior to the handclasp and should, as just described, take the belief in your powers, another step further.

4. THE HANDCLASP TEST

By now they BELIEVE in you, and EXPECT it to work, so you should have a high success rate here.

5. THE ACTUAL INDUCTION

As the people you are using, have probably reacted successfully to tests 1, 2, 3 and 4, you can be sure as they are now conditioned to do as you say, they will enter the Hypnotic Trance.

GAIN PRACTICAL EXPERIENCE A.S.A.P

Do as many shows as possible, as soon as possible and once you've gained confidence in your skills, you will then be able to speed up the whole process. By then, just coming onto the stage, doing your opening talk and then going straight into the handclasp test from which you induce the Hypnotic Trance state in your volunteers.

The only thing which you may not quite have now, which will enable you to do this, is 100% faith in yourself and your new skill. But, if you have already got this faith, then start out like a master and just proceed as if you're a very experienced hypnotist (after all the audience doesn't know). I will end this chapter by telling you of a "Handclasp" style test in which it is, if they do as you say, physically impossible for 99% of people to separate their hands. This art which is unknown to the general public means:

A You are guaranteed a high percentage of people who can't separate their hands when asked to try, and

B It ensures that their belief in your powers is then greatened, so that it becomes extremely easy to place them into the trance state.

I personally use this method of "Handclasp" at the start of the second half of my theatre show, in order to get some new people upon the stage, whom I can then use to demonstrate how I am able to place between 12 and 40 people or more into trance in less than sixty seconds. Have fun using it, it's also a great way to quickly establish your credentials and a volunteers belief in you when at a party etc. before placing them into trance to demonstrate your art.

THE GUARANTEED HANDCLASP TEST

With this you stretch your arms out with palms facing yourself. Fingers wide open and thumbs up in the air. Bend wrist, so that although arms are out stretched, palms are facing your body. Interlock your fingers and push in together as closely as you can. Turn thumbs towards you, until back of your hands are facing you. Now push arms out hard, until elbows crack, and push your palms away from you as much as you can. Now I will count to three, and on the count of three, your hands will be stuck fast together, and in fact, the harder you try to pull them apart, the more they will stick together tight so on 1, staring directly at the backs of your hands as they stick together, tighter and tighter. 2, just lift your hands up above your head now and push your palms up towards the clouds, as high up into the sky as you possibly can and on 3, keep pushing your hands up high into the sky, and now just try to separate your hands, the harder you try, they stick tighter together.

(GIVE THEM A FEW SECONDS THEN SAY)

OK, just relax and keep your hands together as they are until I say otherwise. OK, everyone, firstly I'd like you all to stand up where you are so that we can all have a good look at each other, now walk this way, towards the stage, and I promise you, I will not keep you up here if you don't want to take part.

N.B.

At this point, loads of people will come towards the stage and as they do so you say:

"OK everyone, the moment I touch your hands, they will immediately spring apart and it will feel as though you've received a slight harmless electric shock in your arms."

You then quickly, go to each person and knock the underside of their arms firmly and sharply, so that their hands do indeed spring apart. For anyone who still keeps their hands together, just get them to reverse the procedure which got their hands into this position in the first place. From those who do come up to have their hands separated, you ask for volunteers to take part in a quick 3 minute test after which they may return to the audience. You get between 12 to 24 people to come up, dependant on the stage size etc. and the rest of the people are now returned to the audience to a round of applause.

It is at this point, that the 12 to 24 people are lined up in a straight line, when you can follow the details in the next chapter, in order to be able to place all of them into a trance in less than sixty seconds. That's about 2 to 3 seconds per person only to get them into an instant deep hypnotic trance. And that's where this chapter ends. In the next chapter, I will reveal what you have all been waiting for, and that's the secrets of the actual induction methods used to place people into trance. So hold onto your seats and leave your misconceptions behind, as we enter the hypnotic world, where there really are NO LIMITS.

For now, good luck practising the art of suggestions and the tests, as outlined in this chapter.

PART NINE

INDUCTION METHODS

"The simplest things are usually the most effective in life and hypnosis is no exception"

"The process of hypnosis is so easy to carry out, that, for most, it's hard to believe it works and yet, that's exactly the reason why it's so effective as people believe you must be doing something complicated to place them into trance."

"But you should have learnt the true secret off by heart now and that's the fact it's all down to belief and expectancy and following the simple steps, which I am explaining to you in this course, then success will be yours."

Well welcome to the chapter which you've been waiting for, how to place people into the Hypnotic Trance. By now, you will have hopefully assimilated all the other knowledge which I have revealed to you, if not, then please go back to page one, read through it all again and digest until you do understand what I've said. As you must understand what I've said in order to understand how these hypnotic induction's actually do work.

Basically speaking, the success of the hypnotic induction relies on the belief and expectancy within the mind of your potential hypnotic subject. All the other elements of the suggestibility test, your opening patter and the fact that people are already 90% on the way to already being hypnotised before they step onto the stage, due to your advertising etc. also help in a huge way.

If you have followed all these points and the subjects on stage or in your consulting room believe you are a professional hypnotist, with the skill to place them into trance and they also expect whatever you do to work, then as hard as it is to believe at this moment in time, it will work.

So step A is the belief and expectancy within the volunteer's mind. Step B, of disorientation and confusion is catered for in the way which these hypnotic inductions have been designed. They themselves, if carried out as instructed, will either confuse them, disorientate them, or in some way do both. When this element is combined with step C of suggestion and repetition, you will almost always get the end result of relaxation and sleep, which of course is step D.

So follow the guidelines and you'll have great success with your hypnotic induction's. There are two general rules of thumb I should mention at this point, and these are also applicable to every hypnotist on earth.

1 The more confident you are in your own skills and talents, the more successful you will be as a result in all that you do. As it says in the bible "As a man thinketh so he becomes"

2 The more experience you get of actually hypnotising people, the faster and more effective your induction methods will become and the greater a percentage of people upon the stage or in the consulting room you will be able to get into a trance easily and effectively.

So practise, practise and practise some more. Remember this though, don't try it out on family and friends and expect a huge success, as they knew you when you weren't a hypnotist, so that most vital element of belief and expectancy will not be there.

Instead practise on new faces in bars etc. in conversation say what you do, and present them with one of your business cards to establish belief and expectancy and ask if the group wants a free demonstration, then go ahead and practise your skills. But remember this, you are the only one that will know this is the first time you've ever done this, as far as they are concerned, you've been doing it for years and are a true master of your craft. So once again belief and expectancy come into play here.

Anyway, I've tried to dispel any doubts which you may still have and hopefully I've done that, if not, you'll have to pluck up the courage to try it all out and then hindsight will tell you that what I'm teaching you is 100% true in every way.

As a hypnotist, the most important thing you could possibly need is supreme self-confidence, so here goes with an induction method which can be used very successfully on stage and in some cases even in the consulting room situation.

FALLING BACKWARD INDUCTION

You get the subject to stand with both feet together on the floor, hands down by their sides unless this is being done after the locked hands in which case they are told to place their hands closely against their chest. This means there is then more weight at the upper area of their body and they are even more likely to fall back than usual. You stand to the left of them and place your right foot flat against the back of their heels so it can act as a pivot if required. Your right hand middle finger pushes onto their forehead, as you say, "and tilt your head well back as you close your eyes." You have now still got your right middle finger on the centre of their forehead, just above the bridge of their nose, as you count from three to one and give the suggestions of relaxing and falling back, as I will describe in a moment, you draw your middle finger lightly across the centre of the subjects forehead, so that by the count of 1 it is almost ready to slide towards the top of their head. This acts as a non-verbal suggestion to fall backwards, and believe me, even without the verbal suggestions, it usually has the effect of the person falling backwards. When you have given your suggestions and the person starts to fall back, all you need do is lower your right arm from their head, down to their upper back area and just cushion their fall back so they don't hurt themselves. In actual fact, you are just lowering them down onto the floor at which point they will be in the hypnotic trance.

On some occasions, if I feel it is a difficult subject, I will prior to getting them to tilt their head back and close their eyes, get them to take some really deep breaths in, hold them a few seconds and then out. This has the effect of slightly "hyper-ventilating" them. This means that when you tilt their head back and tell them to close their eyes, they will then feel a little dizzy already and this brings the self-hypnosis angle into play again. This will occur even more strongly if you, as they breathe deeply, knock them with your right hand on their back at the place where their lungs are. This has the extra effect of knocking them off balance and disorientating them even more. Remember, that you must read these instructions several times and get it clear in your own mind the whole process of physical actions and verbal suggestions, as they should take just a few seconds from starting point to the point at which they are lying upon the floor in trance. From a verbal point of view, the whole lot would go as follows:

"OK sir (or madam). Just stand there, feet together, hands down by your side (or hands against your chest). Tilt your head well back and close your eyes. I'd like you to take nice deep regular breaths in, hold them a few seconds and then breathe out as this will help you to relax more quickly.

In a few moments, I'm going to count from 3 to 1 and on the count of 1, when I say sleep, you will feel yourself falling back, but I won't let you fall and hurt yourself, instead you'll just fall into a beautifully relaxed state.

1. The deeper you go the better you will feel and the better you feel the deeper you will go.
2. You can feel yourself falling backwards now into a beautifully relaxed sleeplike state.
3. SLEEP (They fall) falling back, back, back and sleep and relax."

THEY WILL NOW BE IN THE HYPNOTIC TRANCE

N.B.

If the subject does not start to fall of their own accord, you can always use the fact that your feet against the back of their heels acts as a pivot to tip them back gently, so that to the audience it appears as if they have just fallen back into your arms. Another point worth mentioning is that on the count of one, you immediately remove your hand from their head and tap them firmly on the back as you say SLEEP. This has the effect of knocking them even more off balance and as a result they then fall backwards into your arms. So your next step is to get your wife or husband and use them to practise the actions on, until you can do them without hesitation, then you will have one of the quickest and most effective inductions that there is available to you.

The great thing with this induction on a theatre stage is that all the volunteers can be lined up in a straight row and one by one, after each other, they can be placed into trance using this method. Once all of them are upon the floor under your spell so to speak, you then proceed by deepening the level of trance for the whole group at once, which makes it slicker and quicker. In this case, the volunteers would be face on to the audience and they fall backwards away from the audience. As with all the induction methods, which I will explain to you in this chapter, I will tell you the basics, and your own common sense would tell you the rest. For example, in a funny shaped venue, you might have to have the subjects standing sideways onto the audience before making them fall backwards. This is really an excellent induction to use. It's quick, safe and works well, I wish you much luck with it.

FALLING FORWARDS INDUCTION

This is, in essence, almost identical to the falling backward induction, except that they fall forwards. The reason it works is the same, and even without belief and expectancy being considered, if this is done correctly, then people will feel themselves falling forwards into your arms.

You stand facing the subject, they have their hands down by their sides, stand up straight rigid, feet together and stare directly into your eyes. They are told to keep staring directly into your eyes at all times and then you proceed as follows:

Verbally you say something such as, "I'm going to count backwards from 3 to 1 and on each descending number you'll feel yourself falling forwards, but I won't let you fall and hurt yourself, instead you'll just fall into a beautifully relaxed, dreamy, sleeplike state. So,

3, the deeper you go the better you will feel and the better you feel, the deeper you will go.

2, You can feel yourself falling forwards, more with every breath you take, ever noise you hear and every word that I say.

And on 1, you can feel yourself falling forwards, falling forwards, forwards and to sleep."

As you say this or similar, the physical element is as follows:

From the moment you start talking, your fingers of each hand are placed firmly, flatly and gently on the sides of their head in line with their forehead. As you talk you are gently pulling your fingers forwards in a smooth motion towards yourself and this has the effect of both distracting them and also disorientating them a little. But, perhaps more importantly, as your fingers are firmly against their head, it has the effect of gently pulling their head forwards towards you, and also acts as a non verbal suggestion to do the same. This as a result will mean their body will follow suit and they will start to move forwards. At the same time to promote this further, you take one small step backwards, as you count each number and as they are to stare into your eyes at all times, it will have the effect of their eyes following yours, and as such their body will move forwards more. Also bend your legs slightly as you get nearer to the count of one, so that your eye level becomes lower. This means that to keep their eyes in line with yours, they have to lean over slightly and when they do, they will reach that point of no return, and will suddenly be falling forwards into your arms. You must catch them and then very gently lay them upon the floor, so that their head is to one side. Combine all this with belief and expectancy and the shock element of you commanding SLEEP, just as they reach that point of no return and now I'm sure you'll be able to understand why this induction works so well.

THE FLOATING ARM INDUCTION

For this induction, have the subject sitting in a chair, feet together and hands resting upon their lap, with eyes tightly closed. You then proceed as I will detail in a second, although you'll have to adapt things for each person. The method of this induction is to first get them to lift up their middle finger of the right hand, due to suggestion, then to allow their hand to lift up, followed by their arm. The moment their arm has floated up to their face and touches their nose, it will instantly fall back into their lap and they drift into an instant deep relaxing sleep.

This is really all down to suggestion, and is a 100% genuine induction. The standard phrases, which are used by all hypnotists and which are detailed at the end of this chapter, are inserted at appropriate points, to relax them even more. This will give you a brief idea of what to say, but this is really a case of what suits your personality, you now know it's all down to suggestion and what you want to achieve, so now here's an idea of what to say.

"As you breathe deeply and relax more with every breath you take, every noise you hear and with every word I say, you'll notice that the deeper you go over the next few minutes, the better you will feel and the better you feel, the deeper you will go. I'd like you to concentrate on your right hand middle finger, and as you do, just notice how it almost feels like a helium balloon is tied onto it making it so light, so light, that it no longer wishes to remain resting upon your lap. And just notice that with each breath you take and ever noise you hear, your finger now becomes so light with that helium balloon attached, that it is lifting up off your lap and up into the air. Now just imagine that helium filled balloon, floating up higher and higher into the air, and as it does your hand is starting to rise up, up off you lap and into the air, as it's now so light, as light as air, in fact, so light it floats up higher into the air. (Proceed in this fashion until their hand is up off their lap, and starts moving upwards) You now notice that as your hand floats up higher, being pulled up higher into the air all the time by the helium filled balloon, that your arm is now so light and follows suit. (Continue in the same vein, until their finger, hand and arm are up in the air). Now just notice that your hand is floating towards your face, nearer and nearer to your nose, all the time (Continue in this vein etc.) And realise now, that the moment your finger touches your nose, your hand will suddenly become as heavy as lead, will fall instantly down back into your lap, and you'll sink instantly into a state of relaxation 100 times deeper and 100 times more enjoyable than that which you are already in. (Continue in this vein etc).

N.B.

If you follow this basic outline, they will do as you intend and the moment their arm falls back onto their lap, you will also have a visual indication that they have now entered trance. Remember, paint a picture with your words, leave no doubt in their minds what you wish to occur and as such belief, expectancy and the power of suggestion will do the rest.

EYES GLUED TOGETHER INDUCTION

This can be done with the subject standing up straight, hands down by their side and eyes closed, or whilst they are sitting down, feet together with hands on their lap and eyes closed.

You place your right hand middle finger, firmly onto the central area of the head, just above the top of their forehead. You explain that they must imagine, that there is a hole in their head at the point where they can feel your fingertip and as such, they are to stare through the hole in their head and up at your fingertip. To do this they will have to push their eyeballs upwards underneath their eyelids.

Once in this position, you then suggest that by the count of one their eyes will be stuck together and the harder they try to separate them, the more they will stick. As long as you make it clear that even when you ask them to try and open their eyes that they must in actual fact keep staring upwards with their eyes as if staring through the hole in their head, then this will work. The reason for this, being that when your eyeballs are in this position it becomes physically impossible to open your eyes anyway.

The subject will believe his failure in opening his eyes is due to your suggestions, and then so that it comes very unexpectedly, you suddenly tilt the subjects head forward onto their chest as you say, "Eyes tightly closed at all times and just sleep". They will remain like this now until you command to them otherwise, obviously the trance will be deepened along with everyone else a little later on into the act.

INSTANT INDUCTION

Here follows the wording of a very effective and quick, induction method. Having finally got you subjects lined up on the stage, you begin in a very strong and commanding voice, "Close your eyes, begin to breathe deeply and regularly, you will find that your eyes will begin to stick together. They will become tightly stuck, in fact, you cannot open your eyes. Then walk up and down the line speaking to each person in turn. Try if you want to, but you cannot open yours eyes." (Each of them tries and can't, they believe they are now under hypnosis and shock themselves into a deep trance).

Then continue up the line saying "And neither can you, or you, or you, etc. In fact the harder you try the more they stick together and the more you enter trance. OK, now everyone, eyes stuck together, but your feet are now stuck to the floor, yes your feet are stuck, rigid to the floor, you cannot move from where you are standing, however hard you try. OK just try and move from where you are standing, but the harder you try the more your feet are stuck solidly to the floor, (continue for a few seconds, then say). Relax, relax, stop trying and relax as you go down completely into trance. In fact, from this moment forward, you will listen to and respond only to my voice. Whenever I say, 1, 2, wide-awake you will instantly be wide-awake, and do whatever I have told you to do. In fact, you'll carry out everything I say as an automatic reflex action. And whenever I say SLEEP, as quickly as this, (snap fingers) a snap of the fingers, you will instantly return into a deep sleep, but each time you re-enter it, for you it will be 100 times deeper and 100 times more enjoyable."

N.B.

Now whenever you say sleep, they will re-enter the trance state, but each time go deeper and deeper into trance. It is for this reason, that the harder to do routines are left until near the end of the act, as by then everyone will have gone in and out of trance several times and now will be so deep that almost anything is possible. A last word here, and that's the simple fact that as a hypnotist who wishes to master rapid and instantaneous inductions, you must have 100% faith and confidence in yourself to be a success. I will also take this opportunity to give you the address of a company, who can supply you with numerous books on Stage Hypnosis.

If you wish to get more books on the subject contact: - Magic Books By Post, 29 Hill Avenue, Bedminster, Bristol, England BS3 4SN. Send them an S.A.E and you'll get a catalogue by return of post.

HYPNOTIZING HECKLERS (CEREBRAL ANOXIA)

Allow me to point out here and now, that this method is included for information purposes only, I would never, ever dream of using it myself and anyone who does try it, does so at their own risk. **THIS CAN KILL PEOPLE. BE WARNED.** Do you know what Cerabral Anoxia is? Well it usually means a dead person, dead from a lack of oxygen to the brain. You may be asking what has that got to do with you? Well, it is very easy to render someone unconscious by pressure on the Carotoid Arteries, leading to the brain. Even until a few years ago some stupid idiots would pass this off as a quick way to hypnotise people, or a way to hypnotise hecklers, even today, the odd person uses it, but if I were you, I would not even contemplate its use. Under many byelaws, laws of a country etc. its use is now forbidden. In fact, part of a permission to perform in the UK will read that only psychological methods may be used to induce hypnosis. Well, cerebral anoxia, is what they are referring to here. It is absolutely forbidden, for any member of P.O.S.H. or A.P.S.H to use it in any circumstances, any reputable person would never dream of using it on someone.

However, should you ever come across a "new method" from someone which resembles this, you will be aware of it's existence and avoid it at all costs. Here's how it is done for information purposes only.

Stand in front of your subject, then place the fingers of each hand at the side of their neck, just below the ears and slightly towards their throat. Do this with their head tilted way, way back. Whilst in this position your fingers should now be directly over the large veins in the neck. There is one on each side of their neck, you can often see them, and if not, you can feel them very easily as they pulsate and throb beneath your fingers. Press gently on those veins, but also firmly at the same time. Now ask the person to breath deeply, keep the pressure on until the person goes limp, if the word sleep is shouted at this time, as far as the crowd watching will be concerned you have just placed that person under hypnosis. The moment they start to go limp remove all pressure and allow them to fall to the floor or back into their chair, like a sack of potatoes. However, should you accidentally keep the pressure on a few seconds later, the person may end up dead or a cabbage for life, with permanent brain damage. You could be arrested for murder, at the least manslaughter. If you did not kill them you can be convicted of attempted murder or assault, with intention to endanger life, or grievous bodily harm. So the golden rule here is ***never, never, ever attempt this technique on anyone at anytime***. Should you ever see someone use this method then please report them to the Mindcare Organisation and we will investigate, as anyone using this method is not fit to call themselves a hypnotist.

This by the way is what is known in the trade as the "Carotid Artery Induction" and yet as I'm sure you've realised, it has nothing to do with hypnosis and, as such, should not be used.

THE CRAIG WILLIAMS MICROPHONE INDUCTION

This is an induction method, which is excellent and a very good up and coming hypnotist, by the name of Craig Williams, has made it a masterpiece in his hands. Anyway, here goes with the technical inside information on how it's done.

This induction is very quick and looks amazing to the audience, it is usually done whilst the subjects hands are still locked together. You get the subject to stand so that you're both facing each other, and yet, at the same time are both sideways on to the audience so that they get a good view. You tell the subject to stretch out their arms, straight out in front of themselves, this means that the distance between you must be such that it gives them room to do this. You take hold of their right arm with your left hand and make sure that you have a firm grip upon it. In your own right hand, you have got hold of the microphone. You explain that they should stare at the top of the microphone at all times and for no reason whatsoever should they remove their eyes from it. You also instil into them the belief and expectancy that the moment the microphone taps them on the head they will instantly relax every muscle in their body from the tips of their toes to the tips of their fingers and that their eyes will immediately shut and remain closed until you say otherwise. You then hold the microphone, which is in your right hand up in the air as high as you can comfortably hold it. It is held at a slanted angle, pointing towards the subject's forehead. They have been told to stare at the top of the mike at all times and in order to do this, as the microphone is above their eyeline they will have to strain their eyes in order to do this and here, once again, the belief factor will be taken a step further by the strange sensation which the will feel in their eyes. You then count backwards from three to one and use the standard phrases as you would in the falling backwards induction etc. With of course the addition that the moment the microphone touches their head, they'll fall back into a relaxed dreamy sleeplike state, as you won't let them fall and hurt themselves, and of course their eyes will instantly shut and remain closed until you say otherwise. Then on each descending number you bring the mike closer towards their eyes, so that by the count of one, and the word sleep, the microphone will tap them upon the head and act as the trigger to enter hypnosis. Also to keep their eyes upon the top of the mike as it gets closer to their head, they will have to tilt their head backwards a little. As they do so, if you take a small step towards them, then they will start to fall backwards anyway, but as you have a firm grip of their arm you don't let them fall, instead you just allow them to lower to the ground in a smooth, steady motion. With the combination of belief, expectancy, suggestion, eye strain and visual disorientation, plus the added element that they will, if you do this correctly, start to fall backwards anyway, means that you now have in your armoury of techniques, a most powerful and quick induction, which should only take about 30 seconds from start to finish.

Once again, as with all things detailed in this course, experience will teach you more in one show, than any book, video or audiotape ever could. A last point here is, that should you wish to place a person under hypnosis with this method whose hands are not locked together then for the sake of the induction just have them clasp their hands in to the correct position, then, in both cases, the moment they are in trance and lying upon the floor, you can separate their hands for them and so suggest that as you drop their arms down by their sides, they will sink 100 times deeper in trance, so it even has a built in trance deepening method.

THE BODY FLOP INDUCTION

For this dramatic looking induction, your subject is sitting in a chair with a low back, this is so that you will be able to push the upper area of their body forwards by leaning against their back area, so obviously if the chair back was too high then this would not be possible.

They are sitting in the chair, upright with feet and legs together, so that feet the are flat upon the floor, and their arms and hands are rested upon their lap, with palms facing upwards. You then get them to close their eyes and at this point you must be standing directly behind them and the chair in which they are sitting. You place a hand upon each of their shoulders in a relaxed fashion and then say something along these lines.

"OK, (subjects name here) just relax. I'd like you to take nice deep, regular breaths so you can relax a little quicker and I'll keep my hands upon your shoulders so that we can get our rhythm of breathing into alignment. (Here pacing, leading and rapport come into play strongly).

I'm going to count backwards from 3 to 1 and on each descending number, you will find that the deeper you go, the better you will feel, and the better you feel, the deeper you will go. The moment that I say sleep, you will instantly drift into a deeply relaxed sleeplike state. OK (their name) here goes.

Three : With every breath you take, every noise that you hear and every word that I say, you are relaxing more and more as you concentrate only on your thythm of breathing which is now so deep and regular.

Two : Every muscle in your body becoming so heavy and so tired, each muscle now so limp, so loose and so relaxed, as you go deeper and deeper. And on……

One: Sleep, deeper, deeper and deeper to sleep."

Whilst this is being said you are massaging their shoulders which is a great stress reliever and will help them to relax very quickly, it also acts as a distraction for their mind. As you are coming to the words "And on one", prior to saying the trigger word sleep (drawn out), this is the point of importance. At this moment in time you must rest your chest area against their back lightly, as you lean over them from behind, very smoothly, but very quickly, your hands now move off the subjects shoulders and down to their lap ready for the sudden physical element which shocks them into hypnosis. As you say the word sleep (which is drawn out), your hands lift their arms up off their lap and sweep them off, so that they quickly fall off and down besides them hanging in mid air, at exactly the same time you lean forward so that your chest area pushes the upper area of their body over and their head flops down almost into their own lap.

This, by the way, must be practised so that you can carry out both actions simultaneously. This is a disorientation method par excellence, as one minute they are being massaged on the shoulders and the next second they are simultaneously flopping forwards with their head falling towards their own lap and their arms have fallen off their lap at exactly the same time. This strange combination of distractions for the mind acts as the trigger and into hypnosis they do go rapidly. To the audience it looks so impressive, as the subject suddenly seems to flop forward in their chair like a rag doll as you command sleep.

THE LOCKED HANDS INDUCTION

This is an instantaneous induction method which one of my hypnotic tutors Mr Peter J Fox has a great success with and which I have seen him use many times. This is 100% reliant on belief, expectancy and your supreme self-confidence as are all instantaneous induction techniques, which you will ever use.

In practise you get a subject, lock their hands together and just a few seconds later after you've said, "OK, just try and separate your hands, but the harder you try the more they will stick." You suddenly, whilst facing the subject, place your right arm on the back of their neck and pull them gently towards you, with the end result of their head being rested upon your shoulder. This is done at exactly the same moment as you unexpectedly say in a loud and commanding voice, "just sleep and relax, going deeper and deeper to sleep". As their mind is already on something else, it's already distracted (see keys to hypnosis) and with the shock element of suddenly moving towards you and commanded to sleep and very quickly followed up with commands to go deeper etc., it also acts as a disorientation and confusion method. The moment they do have their head against your shoulder, you must follow up immediately with a quick trance deepening method, as explained elsewhere. Then you awaken them, get them to sit down and the moment their bum touches the seat you click your fingers in front of their eyes and say sleep, and back under they will go. This induction works because of the shock element being so unexpected at the time it occurs and as they have been trying to separate their hands with no success they have no reason to disbelieve any further commands as such they will be acted upon instantly.

THE HANDWAVE INSTANT INDUCTION

This is the method which I have both used myself and have also seen Paul McKenna use with great success. You ask your on stage subjects, if any of them have been hypnotised before. Those who answer yes are asked when and by whom, you remember this information and then place 2 or 3 people into a trance with inductions such as falling backwards etc. During this, the people who have been hypnotised before are watching and this takes the belief and expectancy concept one step further. As, don't forget, it's easier to hypnotise someone rapidly when they've just seen you place other people into trance, and as such know that you can do the same to them. You then return to the subjects who have been placed under hypnosis before and ask three quick questions.

1. Do you wish to enter this lovely dreamy state of hypnosis tonight? (YES)
2. Can you remember that the moment you enter hypnosis, your eyes close, your heavy head falls forward onto your chest and you breathe deeply and listen only to the sound of my voice? (YES)
3. Well (their name) in that case, may I have your permission to use the fastest form of hypnosis known to man, to make you instantly re-enter this lovely dreamy sleep like state? (YES)

N.B.

The moment he/she has said yes to answer all three questions, you immediately, without any time delay at all, so that it comes as a complete shock, just do as follows:

"Well in that case (their name) just sleep and relax."

As you say this, your right hand is lifted up in front of their face and as you command sleep, in a raised tone of voice, your right hand moves in a downwards motion in front of their face, so that the fingers are outstretched and move down from above head, past their eyes and downwards, which in itself, is a powerful non verbal suggestion of sleep. It also gives them something to psychologically connect entering the trance state to and something for them to believe in. Remember, that as they've been under hypnosis before, they know exactly how to react and your three questions prior to the instant induction have done two things.

A It has psychologically conditioned them to enter the trance state immediately that you say the word sleep.

B It has acted as a brief reminder to them of how to act in trance. If they have been under before and have answered yes honestly to the three questions that you ask, then you can be sure that they will instantly enter trance.

Someone who has been hypnotised before is, by far the best type of person on whom to do instantaneous inductions, as they know how to act in trance and their belief is 100% complete, as they have experienced it first hand. Also, as a general rule of thumb, the more recently they have been hypnotised, the more easily that they can be made re-enter trance. I'm sure you can now see why you need to have enormous confidence in your abilities in order to make instant inductions work.

HANDSHAKE INSTANT INDUCTION

Before I describe how this induction is presented, allow me to make this point. As long as the subjects' belief and expectancy in your powers is totally 100% complete and as long as you truly have tremendous confidence in your skills, and this is transmitted to the subjects through your actions etc., they will then both expect what you do to work and also know that you expect it to work. As such the Handwave and Handshake instant inductions can be done without asking any questions. In fact, the moment a subject said that they had been under before, then you could just say:

"Well in that case, (their name) Just sleep and relax"

The hand movement, handshake or whatever was being used as the trigger would be just the same and of course, your voice must sound commanding and demanding. However, the point which I am trying to make here is, done with belief, they will instantly re-enter trance without any additional psychological conditioning. This even applies to "Hypnotic Virgins" who have never, ever entered trance before, as long as their belief is total, then when you command them to sleep, they would do so however the induction had been presented as it's just the trigger word, sleep, which they expect to hear to make them enter the state and, if this is what they believe, then for them, it's very true indeed. You of course would only use instant inductions on the most susceptible subjects (see elsewhere) this means the odds are then even greater in your favour of it working.

Anyway, to the handshake induction. This really is as simple as it sounds, you approach a subject, who you have observed will be very susceptible after having unlocked their shaking hands etc. You ask their name, and upon their reply you extend your right hand as though ready to shake hands as you say:

"Nice to meet you (their name)"
Still holding their hand as though ready to shake hands you quickly say
"Have you ever been hypnotised before (their name)?"
Then, whatever answer he/she gives you, immediately follow up by saying
"Is it OK with you (their name) if I hypnotise you right now, instantly?"
If they answer yes, it's an easy subject and all you need do is just say
"In that case (their name), just sleep."

As you say the word sleep, you lift their arm into the air slightly, and then move it down rapidly towards their lap, as you command in a loud voice, "sleep." This hand (downwards) movement acts as a non verbal suggestion of sleep and that's why this is called the handshake induction, as the audience just see you go up to a subject, shake that persons hand and say "sleep" and at that moment the person has gone under your spell. Incidentally, I have found from experience, that the downwards motion of the handshake is more effective when made on an outbreath of the subject (as they breathe out), all suggestions of relaxation and sleep are more effective also when made as the subject breathes out, as this psychologically implies letting go etc. This induction, can of course, with confidence and experience, be done in the way which is used by experienced hypnotists. In our version, we simply go up to a subject, ask their name, the moment they reply, we extend our hand and clasp theirs and then do the handshake motion, as we say "Ok (their name), just sleep and relax." This is all so sudden for the subject, that it shocks them into trance and they connect entry of trance to the handshake. Lastly, if the person says no when you ask if they will allow you to hypnotise them quickly, you simply reply by saying "Well in that case (their name), I can't be bothered wasting my time on you. Sleep". Because he feels he has one up on you by saying no, he suddenly feels small when you say you can't be bothered wasting your time with him and here, the shock/surprise factor comes in, as you shake his hand and in a raised voice command him to sleep. As with all instant inductions, they do work, but only if you have enough confidence.

CAN'T BE BOTHERED WITH YOU INDUCTION

This induction only works, because what you do comes as a real shock to the subject and because you do it with such faith, confidence and conviction, that they will instantly enter the trance. They sense your confidence and as such, belief and expectancy again comes into play. They would of course have just seen you place other people into trance and will be waiting, anticipating, almost rearing, when you'll come and do the same thing to them.

Proceed like this. You do an induction such as the falling backwards technique and prior to this you've had several susceptible subjects stand directly in front of their chairs, which you've said they will sit in. They are standing right next to the chair, so that when made to fall back they will fall into the chair, and not fall and hurt themselves. You have just placed someone into trance, and now walk along the line as if deciding whom to pick to hypnotise next. As you do this you must stare directly into each person's eyes and send the fear of God into them. You walk along the line and when you reach the subject whom you are going to use this induction upon, you stop for a moment which you did not do with the others, you say nothing and just stare at him for a couple of seconds, this will scare him to death, he will be so relieved 2 seconds later when you continue along the line, that he will relax more, and let his defences down. You then come back along the line, and the moment you reach him, your right palm is pushed against his forehead, and he falls back into his chair as you simultaneously say in a loud and commanding voice. "Oh, I can't be bothered with you, Sleep." This will come as such a shock, especially when he thought he had escaped. It works due to shock, belief and expectancy, in short, it's the power of the moment and the power of the unexpected which will make him close his eyes as he's seen the others do (he's been conditioned), and he then enters trance. Although I shall give you several more presentation examples for inductions, the bottom line is, that if belief and expectancy are 100% total, then any trigger can be used to make them enter the trance instantly. Remember this and you can always adapt to suit any venue, audience or show situation.

AEROPLANE INDUCTION

The moment you have just placed someone into trance, you turn to the person sitting next to him or her and say, "you wouldn't do anything daft like that, would you?" They, of course say no. You then tell them to watch the microphone as the moment is taps them upon the head, their heavy eyes will shut tightly, their head will fall forwards onto their chest and they'll breathe deeply as they go to sleep. You then hold the mike in front of their face as if it is about to tap their head, then suddenly, for a few seconds prior to unexpected tapping them upon the head with the mike and commanding sleep, you move the mike up, down, sideways etc. and make funny noises as if the mike is an aeroplane. This will cause the audience to laugh and the person upon the stage to think you're crazy, but as the beliefs already there and he expects to go under when the mike hits his head, guess what? As such he will go under. This "aeroplane" gag, can also be used when the person has already been placed under hypnosis and you just want to add a little variation, so, instead of using the trigger word sleep for them to re enter trance, you use the aeroplane induction which takes only a few seconds and helps add an extra little comedy elements to the proceedings.

Another comical way to make two people re enter trance, is to apparently knock their two heads together and then they go back to sleep. Of course, the real reason they've gone back under is because you've used a stage whisper to put them back under by quickly and audibly to them (but not through the mike) saying sleep. To the audience however it looks hilarious, as you appear to knock two people's heads together and they then re enter trance instantly.

Yet another comical way you make them re enter trance is to say to them

"You wouldn't go to sleep if you slapped yourself across the face would you?"

(They say no) "Of course you wouldn't. I'll tell you what though, give it a try." He then slaps himself across the face and as he does, so instantly re enters trance, he would do anyway, but if in doubt, use a stage whisper to say sleep to ensure that he goes under as he slaps his own face. These few ideas are all very simple to put into use and all looks hilarious to the audience and as entertainment is the key thing on stage you are onto a winner here

THE FINGER STARE INDUCTION

This is also a very quick induction and should take no more than 40 to 50 seconds to have the person enter a deep trance state.

They should be sitting on a chair, feet together firmly flat on the floor, upright and looking directly at you, the hypnotist. Their arms and hands being rested upon their lap with palms upwards, you then proceed as follows. You extend your own right arm and then extend your own right hand index finger, whilst the rest of the hand remains like a clenched fist. This extended finger is then held slightly above the level of the subjects eyes and a few inches away from them so that they must strain their eyes to look upwards at your fingertip.

You explain that you want them to stare at all times at your fingertip, they must not move their head, only their eyes in order to follow the route which your fingertip will take. When you are sure that they have understood this full you say something such as;

"In a few moments, I shall count from 3 to 1, and by the count of one you'll notice your eyelids will be so heavy and tired, in fact the harder you try to keep them open the more they will want to remain shut. The moment that I say sleep, and tap you upon the head, you'll instantly drift into a deep, relaxing, dreamlike state. So on 3, the deeper you go, the better you will feel, and the better you feel, the deeper you will go. On 2, you can feel your eyes starting to strain as they get so heavy and so tired, it's so much easier to just relax and let go. And on 1, eyes closing tightly now, as with every breath you take, every noise you hear and every word I say, you go deeper and deeper to sleep. Now that you're asleep, in a few moments I am going to tap you on the head. The moment I do, you'll sink instantly 100 times deeper into trance, so just sleep (here head is tapped) and go deeper."

N.B.

As they start off staring at your fingertip, which is above their eye line, the key here is to strain their eyes as much as possible, as quickly as possible. To do this in a steady motion, during the count from 3 down to 1, you move your fingers both nearer to them (they go cross eyed etc) and at the same time in a downwards motion. So on 3 it starts above their eyeline, on 2 in line with their nose and 1 in line with their chin, which means by this time, as they will still be trying to keep their eyes on your finger, their eye lids will have shut naturally anyway, and because their eyes have been very strained, it's so much easier to leave them shut as you say sleep. Without pausing you follow this up immediately, with the quick trance deepening method, of telling them that the moment you tap their head they will go 100 times deeper into trance, you then tap their head and remove your finger quickly, as you say sleep and go deeper. This usually has the effect of pushing their head back a bit, they resist and as such push forward onto your fingertip with their forehead and then you suddenly remove your finger as you say sleep and go deeper, which means that their head then falls down onto their chest. If this does not occur, you can literally just place your hand upon their shoulder, as you say, "and your head is now so heavy, it falls down onto your chest." Whilst saying this, you simply use your fingers as a lever against the front and back or their neck to make them move their head down against their chest. In practise, the whole induction takes between 40 to 60 seconds maximum.

THE SWAYING HANDCLAP INDUCTION

For this induction you have the subject standing just in front of their chair. Their legs and feet are together, hands down by their sides, eyes shut and they must breathe deeply in through their nose and out through their mouth. You then say something such as:

"As you stand here, with your eyes closed, you notice that with each and every breath that you take your body is relaxing more each second that passes by. I'd like you to relax completely, so I'm going to gently sway you backwards and forwards in rhythm with your rate of breathing." (This you then actually do) "So breathe in and out, in and out." (They are swayed back and forward in time with their breathing) "Don't forget that the moment I tell you to, your whole body will relax, your eyes will remain tightly closed and you'll enter a sleep like state."

N.B.

Throughout all this talking, you've been progressively swaying them further backwards and forwards, so much so, that if you were to set them off swaying backwards again and did not stop them falling with your hand, then they would indeed, fall backwards into their chair, or at least it would be very difficult to stop themselves. You capitalise upon this fact, and the moment you've said, "and you'll enter a sleep like state," you have timed this as you will be ready to set them back on their swaying backwards direction movement. The moment they are moving backwards, you clap your hands by the person's ear, as you simultaneously and very loudly command sleep. This is immediately followed in a quieter tone of voice by, "and going deeper, and deeper to sleep." As you clap in the direction they are going anyway, the sheer shock of the noise knocks them off balance and they'll fall all the way back into their chair, it also quite literally shocks them into hypnosis.

THE PROGRESSIVE RELAXATION INDUCTION

This induction, as the title suggests, is a slower, more progressive style. It is the type of induction which can be suitably used in the therapists consulting rooms, as well as upon the performance stage. In a stage situation, it is usually used to hypnotise a group of several people simultaneously so although it takes longer, you are actually placing several people into trance at once, therefore overall, there isn't too much difference timewise. For these styles of inductions the subjects must be sitting on their chairs, feet together and flat on the floor, with hands and arms resting upon their laps, with palms facing upwards and they should be sitting up straight, as comfortably as is possible. You will find that the wording for such an induction (with added subliminal effects) is in the verbal psychology chapter of this book, and basically, it just relies upon the principles of rapport, observation, recognition and leadership, which are also described in full elsewhere.

What you say to the subject/s will be different each time and dictated by the way in which the subject/s react to you suggestions. (Always use what the majority do as your guide.) Of course the standard phrases, which all hypnotists use at some time, and are included at the end of this chapter, will come in extremely useful during a progressive relaxation induction. Follow all that you've been taught, and the example induction as given in the earlier chapter and you will be able to carry out a progressive relaxation induction, both in the therapy room and upon the stage. As you will by now know, the basic techniques of what makes an induction work and of how rapport, observation, recognition and leadership dictate what you say to the subjects in a progressive relaxation induction, I will now give a few examples of additional distractions which can be offered to the subjects mind to promote the onset of trance more rapidly.

THE SIDNEY FLOWERS BLINK METHOD OF P.R.I.

This is in essence a progressive relaxation induction (P.R.I), which is also combined with a method to strain the subject's eyes. The subjects are seated as for other P.R.I.'s and are told to focus upon a spotlight, or a point on the ceiling, which they are not to take their eyes off (this also helps strain the eyes). You then explain that you will be counting, and on each number everyone will get more and more relaxed, and within a few short moments, everyone will find it so much easier to let their eyelids, which will become so heavy and tired, to shut, rather than trying to keep them open. You also explain that on each odd number as you count, they should close their eyes and on each even number, they should re open their eyes. For example:

On 1…. eyes shut
On 2…. eyes open
On 3…. eyes shut
On 4…. eyes open
On 5…. eyes shut
On 6…. eyes open
On 7…. eyes shut (etc)

So that on each alternate number, from one they have to shut their eyes and then re-open them on the next even number count. Combine this with the fact they are staring at one point all the time and I'm sure, you can understand why their eyes become strained so quickly. And as the littler muscles in the corner of the eyes do become tired, they will find it much easier to allow their eyes to remain shut. You use your normal patter, which is formulated at the time through a combination of the standard phrases and the things that come to mind, due to rapport, observation, recognition and leadership. Obviously you will also keep suggesting that their eyes are becoming so tired and that their eyelids are becoming so heavy, so tired, so limp, loose and relaxed, as each second passes by. By the count of thirty, most, if not all people, will have had their eyes closed for a while already, however, if their should still be the odd one or two with eyes open, this is now the time to command everyone to close their eyes, and you then proceed directly into your trance deepening patter, to take them all to a deeper level of trance, in a very short space of time.

SPOTLIGHT EYESTRAIN P.R.I.

To cut a long story short, the principles used are identical to any other P.R.I., except, that here, it is very bright spotlights that strain their eyes and disorientate them, as you deliver your suggestions of relaxation as usual. The lights should be in the fly's (the area above your head at front of stage) or front of house. For the consulting room, it can simply be a spotlight mounted on a wall. In either case, the lights should be above the subjects normal eye levels, so that they must strain their eyes in the first place in order to see the light. Add to this the intensity of the bright white spotlight itself and maybe now you can see why they become lethargic, their eyes glaze and then close and they do exactly as you say.

MUSCULAR RELAXATION P.R.I.

Very briefly, the principles are the same except here, they start with their eyes closed and you suggest that, as you mention different areas of their body, they are to imagine the muscles in that area of their body as ropes tied together in knots, and as they mentally undo the knots in their mind so that they become separate lengths of rope, so, in reality, all the muscles in that bodily area, will become so limp, so loose and so relaxed, as they also become so heavy and so tired. You start with their feet, and move around their body, getting them to imagine the same thing happening for their ankles, lower leg area, knees, upper leg area, hips and thighs, groin area, stomach, chest, back, spine, shoulders, shoulder blades, the whole arm area, wrist, hands, fingertips, neck, jaw, cheeks, brow muscles etc.

Each time getting them to visualise the relaxation and each time telling them that as the knots untie and the ropes become separate, so in reality all the muscles in that area, will instantly become so limp, so loose, so relaxed, so heavy and so tired, with each and every breath that they take. You also, at various intervals along the way, insert some of the standard phrases, such as "The deeper you go, the better you feel and the better you feel, the deeper you will go." By the time you've gone round their entire body in this vein and have reached their heads, you will find that they are in a deep trance, and at this point, you would immediately deepen the trance further in the standard way. At the end, you would then say "Sleep" firmly and implant your post-hypnotic suggestions. This induction when done nice and slowly, which is why it's called a P.R.I., should take between six to ten minutes, dependent upon your speed of delivery. Remember that the techniques, which you have been taught in this course in other chapters, can also be combined into any basic induction outline, which I may give now or later.

THE COUNTING BACKWARDS INDUCTION

To do this induction upon the stage to best effect, you should have your voice recorded onto the background music, which you would use for any normal style of induction. Upon this voice on music tape, you must say something such as that in the example induction given in the verbal psychology chapter. For example:

"As you stand up straight upon the stage, or sit comfortably in your chair, you will retain perfect balance at all times. From this moment forward I'd like you to listen only to the sound of my voice, and you'll find that with every breath that you take, every noise you hear and every word I say, that you will go deeper and deeper to sleep.

Now, you don't know if you will go into a trance quickly, or if it will take some time.

To really enjoy all those pleasant changes that are occurring in your consciousness."

YOU THEN CONTINUE, AS PER EXAMPLE IN VERBAL PSYCHOLOGY CHAPTER.

The whole induction, which should be changed by making the example of how to count backwards in their mind longer, so that you keep setting the pace of counting in their mind until you've gone back to 180 and then it's left to them to continue doing so in their minds, which distracts their conscious mind, so that all suggestions given go directly into the subconscious mind. Your pace of wording should be such that it suggests relaxation and then you end the induction as per the example in verbal psychology chapter. These are all dubbed over the induction music and reverbs is added to the voice, with an occasional "sleep" or "relax" added between each count backwards, to add an element of confusion too. This whole induction should last no more than five minutes in total, from start to finish and is "overdubbed" onto the induction music such as Jean Michelle Jarres "OXYGENE" or TRANQUILITY, which is a tape available from new age supply centres. This tape is set ready in the player and the moment the lights dim, as will be explained in a moment, is the exact moment when the tape is started.

Now imagine this, you have completed a few quick inductions and placed a couple of people into trance, but still have about 60 or more people upon the theatre stage, who have come up to have their hands separated. So why not try to hypnotise them all at once and then base your selection of the 12 best subjects, upon the 33 observable signs of trance and a few quick text routines?

To do this, you proceed as follows:

You ask everyone who is sitting down and not already in trance, to sit up straight in their chairs, feet together and flat upon the floor, with hands and arms rested upon their laps with palms facing upwards. Anyone who is standing up and not already in trance is told to stand with feet slightly apart, so that they stand firm and steady, hands down by their sides (unless still locked together) and then everyone in the audience is told to remain silent for the next few minutes whilst people enter the trance state or hypnosis, and then the fun will begin.

Everyone upon the stage is then told to close his or her eyes and listen to everything that you say and then imagine it as 100% total reality. You also say that should you touch them upon the shoulder at anytime they will pay special attention to what you say and ignore what you tell everyone else, whilst still counting backwards in their minds. At this moment, the stage lighting grows dim, so that the figures of people in chairs, or standing up can be seen, but only just, everything appears as a silhouette. This dim atmosphere in itself helps to promote the onset of trance. It also means, that for the next five minutes, whilst the recorded induction plays, you can go around the stage (with your radio mike switched off) pretending to talk into the microphone. The audience will assume what they hear coming out of the speakers at the time is what you are saying live, there and then. In actual fact, you are either just miming and know that the studio recorded induction sounds better than you could ever do it live, or you are saying other things to separate subjects whose shoulder you have got your hand upon. I will leave you to work some of this out for yourself, but they've already been told, if you look back through what I've said at the start, that should I touch them upon the shoulder they will ignore what you say to everyone else and will know you are speaking to them and them only. As such, they will then take special notice of all you say. This means that you can touch people on the shoulder, talk to them and as the radio mike is switched off, the audience will be unable to hear you and will assume that what you are saying, is what they hear coming through the speakers. This means, everyone is being hypnotised, to a certain degree, just by the voice upon the tape and for dramatic effect, you can go up to those you feel are very susceptible, place your hand upon their shoulder and speak audibly into their ear to do a falling backwards induction on those standing up, or a body flop induction upon those who are sitting down.

As the audience will only be able to see an outline of each person, it will look most impressive to them as they listen to the induction, which they assume is you speaking live, to also see people falling backwards onto the stage or flopping forwards in their chairs like rag dolls, it will look most impressive indeed. And the moment the "subliminal" style induction recorded on the audio tape reaches the point where the lights on the stage go brighter, the tape will now be playing just relaxation music, the audience will be amazed to see people scattered all over the stage, and you now go into your group deepening immediately, this being done for real through the radio mike, which by this time will have been switched back on.

The post hypnotic suggestions are then given to everyone and lastly, in order to narrow down the onstage 60 people to the best 12 subjects, you go through a quick process of mind imagination screening, which is also quite entertaining to the audience, as well as serving it's required purpose. Those people who are obviously not in trance are dismissed immediately, and then simple suggestions are given, such as, it's a cold day, a hot day, you're milking a cow, you're a washing machine etc. You will be able to tell visually, by the subjects reactions to these simple, yet fairly amusing tests, who will make the best subjects, and of course these are the people who are kept on stage, the rest being slowly dismissed, once fully out of trance. So, in other words, the show begins and continues, whilst the selection of good subjects and return of not so good subjects is still being made. This means that the fun, entertaining routines start a lot quicker and from the point of view of the audience, the show is much slicker and quicker than many I could mention.

If you ever get the chance to see Paul McKenna work live, in a large capacity venue, then you'll know exactly what I mean. You, at the end of all this will already have extracted many laughs from the audience, who will be thoroughly enjoying themselves and also will have selected your best subjects for use throughout the remainder of the evening.

So, here for your reference purposes, is the running order of events, which would make up a very professional and entertaining hypnotic stage show.

1. Intro music with voice over introduction recorded upon it.
2. Play on "Theme Music" as you walk upon the stage and take a bow.
3. Your opening comedy lines and talk about hypnosis.
4. The locked hands test, with suitable background music.
5. People have got to the stage area, whilst loud and exciting music plays.
6. Get to know the people etc. and establish rapport.
7. Do a quick induction, or two, such as falling back etc. to get about five people into trance very quickly and to establish total belief and expectancy.
8. Then go into the "subliminal" induction on tape procedure as detailed above, whilst you also do several more instant inductions on suitable subjects, whilst the tape with your voice upon it plays.
9. Group deepening of induction is done in normal way.
10. The major post hypnotic suggestions are implanted into everyone's mind.
11. Everyone is awoken and obviously unresponsive subjects returned to seats.
12. Everyone left is then put under again, at same time, by just saying sleep, and using the handsweep techniques below.
13. The mind/imagination screening begins and good subjects selected.

THE HANDSWEEP TECHNIQUE

This is a quick way to return everyone to the eyes closed hypnotic state once the major post hypnotic suggestion has been implanted in the subjects minds. It saves the time needed to go to each person in turn and snap you fingers prior to saying sleep, it also looks a little more dramatic than just facing everyone and saying "OK everyone, I'm talking to you all now, so just Sleep" (This is said as you snap your fingers in a downwards movement, facing the whole group, they then all go back under at the same time).

To do this, stand facing the audience and suddenly, you do a 360 degree turn on the spot, rather like a dancer would do and as you turn your hand is open, fingers outstretched and you say sleep (drawn out), so, that as you turn, each and very subject sees your outstretched palm pass by their point of vision as they hear command sleep and they all return to the eyes closed hypnotic state immediately. It's quick and very impressive.

Of course, anyone who does not react immediately is told to sleep and if they don't react this time they are, of course, dismissed as an unsuitable subject. This should not worry you however, as by this stage of the show, all the onstage subjects should be real diamonds and worth their weight in gold many times over. From a time length point of view the running order I've just mentioned would be as follows:

1 Intro music and voice over introduction to show **(3 mins)**
2 Play on music, enter stage and take a bow etc **(3 mins)**
3 Opening comedy lines and talk on Hypnosis **(5 mins)**
4 Locked hands test **(4 mins)**
5 Getting people on stage as music plays **(3 mins)**
6 Getting to know them/rapport/one liners **(3 mins)**
7 About 6 instant inductions, with more one liners **(5 mins)**
8 Group subliminal induction of everyone at once **(5 mins)**
9 Group deepening of trance **(1.5mins)**
10 Group major post hypnotic suggestions **(1.5mins)**
11 Return those not under to audience **(1 min)**
12 Put all group under with handsweep and oneliners **(1 min)**
13 Start the first sketch/imaginations screening **(30 secs)**

So, from the point when first piece of music begins for the start of show, up until the point where everyone is under and the first comedy routine begins takes:

A TOTAL TIME LENGTH ON THEATRE SHOWS OF THIRTY SIX MINUTES

Which, done in first half of the show, leaves about twenty four minutes for comedy routines, so that the interval comes one hour into the evenings' events. The interval in a theatre show realistically ends up being 20 to 30 minutes and then the second half of the show is done, which also keeps to the one hour each way format, this makes the complete theatre show, including intervals, two and a half hours inclusive, which for a stage hypnotism show is standard practise these days.

In the second half of the show you have, of course, only to come back on stage to do a few one liners (say 4 minutes) then you say "come and join the party" at which point all the subjects race back to the stage (2 minutes), you return them all to sleep after questioning them about the comedy routines they are still doing, which they did during the interval in and around the audience (4 minutes). This means 10 minutes into the second half, the show starts again properly, leaving 50 minutes in which to do comedy sketches. Or course, if you do the guaranteed handclasp text and the world record induction of over 12 people in 60 seconds, then this will take up about another eight minutes of the show. The end result being, however, that you have more volunteers to use if you wish, it kills time and there would then only be 32 minutes to fill up with comedy sketch routines. Obviously, the show would end by all suggestions being removed from the subject's minds and then them being awoken properly.

Please note, this is just an example running order, you are free to devise your own and indeed, I would advise you to do so. The point I am trying to make is this though. The hypnotic induction can be made as much a part of the show as the comedy routines you get the subjects to do. In fact, the general public are truly amazed watching people being placed under hypnosis rapidly, it does not bore them, so have no worries there. In a club or pub show you would have a smaller audience and you'd have less people to deal with, as result the whole procedure being much quicker. Ideally, in pubs and clubs, you want everyone under hypnosis with 20 minutes of your act starting, so that there is 40 minutes left for the actual comedy sketch routine section of your one hour spot, which incidentally seems to be the standard time required in pubs and clubs these days.

I hope this has not only given you an excellent idea for use of the verbal psychology induction, but also, I hope it has given you a better understanding in the way a hypnotic show is engineered and routined to make a "whole" that is both fascinating and entertaining whilst looking slick and professional.

THE LITTLE BOY INDUCTION

Yes, yet another different method of induction. However, I hope you have noticed that with all of the methods I've detailed, belief and expectancy in the subjects mind is the biggest factor which works in our favour.

This is a method which I would only use upon a very small in height subject, so that I could make a logical reason for what follows by delivering a few one liners aimed at how small the person is, and how they remind me of a little boy.

I would stand upon a chair, with the subject on the left hand side of me, with their right arm stretched up into the air, as high as they can get it. I would then take hold of their upstretched arm with both of my hands and tell them to stare forwards, preferably at a bright white spotlight, otherwise at a small point high up on the wall facing them. They are to stare at this point at all times, you are now ready for the induction. You explain that you will count backwards from 3 to 1, and that, by the count of 1, when you say sleep, they will find it so much easier to just relax every muscle in their entire body, let their heavy eyelids shut and continue to breathe deeply and regularly.

"So on 3, as you stare intently at the bright white light, your eyes begin to strain and you just want to fall into a beautifully relaxed state. On 2, you can almost feel your legs becoming so weak beneath you, that you feel as though you will fall to the floor in a heap. But I won't let you fall and hurt yourself, instead I'll just let you fall into a beautifully relaxed state. And on 1, you can feel yourself falling to the floor, your legs are like jelly and cannot hold your weight as you sleep. (the word sleep is drawn out.)

N.B. As this is said, all the way through, in time with their breathing, you pull their arm upwards as much as you can on their in breath and then let it go slack again on their outbreath. This does two things, it acts as a disorientation method and a distraction for their conscious mind and also, for some strange reason, it blurs your vision. There is a pressure point in the armpit, which if hit hard, can make you pass out or vomit. Well, obviously, we are using nowhere near that kind of pressure and the pressure which we are using is indirect, as opposed to being directly on the pressure point. I believe it is possible however, that this indirect pressure to the point in question is responsible for the blurring of vision, combine this with the straining of the eyes caused by the bright white spot light and the power of suggestion and that's where the disorientation element comes in, it's also the reason why they end up collapsing in a heap to the floor when you command sleep, which, as you imagine, looks highly impressive to the audience.

What I have said may seem hard to believe, in this case I leave it to your experience to give you a true picture. But, I do know personally from use of this method that, if done correctly, it most definitely does work. This method although effective, is really just included for completeness, although I'm sure at some point in the future a performer will make a masterpiece of it.

100% CONFUSION INDUCTION

We have already established earlier in this course, that confusion and disorientation, play a large part in the success of all hypnotic inductions. Well, now to an induction which relies totally on confusion and disorientation, I will only explain how to do this induction briefly, because if you've already really studied the rest of this course, then you will be more than capable of working the rest out for yourself. Basically, you would proceed with saying things such as:

"Just notice how your left hand is hot and your right hand cold, whilst you left leg is light and your right leg heavy.

Now experience the sensation of your hot, right hand becoming cold and your cold, left hand becoming hot, as your heavy, left leg becomes lighter and your light, right leg is becoming heavier all the time."

You would continue in this vein for a while and then suddenly inject your suggestions of relaxation and sleep amongst the illogical confusing statements, which confuse their conscious mind, as one moment a hand is meant to be hot then it's cold etc., all this becomes too much and within a short time the conscious mind shuts down and doesn't even bother to analyse the rubbish which you are presenting to it. It all goes directly into the subconscious mind of the subject and disguised suggestions of relaxation and sleep are then enacted upon. The rest, as I am sure, you can work out for yourself, to finish however, here's an example of how to start adding sleep/relaxation suggestions to the confusion script.

"And notice now, how as your hot right arm tingles and your cold left leg feels heavy, that you relax more and more and your heavy eyelids start to shut."

SHOCK HYPNOSIS

This is just literally finding a most susceptible subject, whose hands have locked together well, observing their body language to check that they feel uneasy upon the stage, and then suddenly and most unexpectedly going up to them and both loudly and firmly, shouting sleep into their ear as your right arm pulls them back from a standing position to the floor, which disorientates them. Or you can literally just throw them back into a chair, as you make the command sleep, the end result will be the same.

I have seen a very well known adult stage hypnotist do this very successfully, on a regular basis, but believe me, it takes enormous confidence and works because you shock the person into hypnosis, you literally scare the person so much by your sudden actions, that they do everything you say and are in fact then scared to do otherwise.

I'll end this explanation of "shock hypnosis" by telling you how one well known stage hypnotist uses this method. To the audience it looks as though Mr? just walks up to the subject, who is staring at their shaking locked hands and knocks them on the back of the neck with the flat part of his right palm, as he commands in a loud authoritative voice "sleep." The subjects legs then fly up into the air and they literally fall in a backwards motion to the floor. Yes, your absolutely right, it looks very impressive, one moment they are standing up, the word sleep is said, and suddenly their legs fly up into the air and they fall down to the floor like a sack of potatoes, asleep.

Well, how? Firstly, let me say, that this is not a method which I condone or recommend any one to use, as it's very easy for someone to get hurt doing this. However, for information purposes only, here's what you do.

Your subject would be standing on the right hand side of you, staring at their hands, which are shaking (sign of good subject), you then simultaneously bring your right hand up, flat against the back of their neck and your right foot literally just knocks the back of their ankles very firmly, causing their legs to fly up into the air and, as such, they'd normally fall straight to the floor with a thud and hurt themselves. You however, have got your right hand on the back of their neck and can "cushion" their fall to the floor. To the audience however, all they will ever remember seeing is a person standing upright one moment, who, the next minute, goes flying in the air as you tap their neck and command them to go to sleep. It should go without saying that this is a very dangerous stunt to use and my advice would be not to use it, anyone doing so, does so at their own risk.

Obviously, as you knock their legs from beneath them is the moment when you shout sleep, which acts as a misdirection so that people do not realise what you've done. As I am sure you can imagine the shock of hearing the word sleep shouted into your ear is very extreme to say the least, let alone the shock of flying up into the air and then down to the floor. This is a very extreme form of disorientation and the rest, once again, is down to belief and expectancy. Impressive as this looks, and despite the fact I have, in the early days of my career, used this technique, **USE AT YOUR OWN RISK**.

THE RUBBER LEGS INDUCTION

To the audience, this induction appears as follow:

The audience see 12 or more people standing on various parts of the stage and all are staring at their hands, which are locked together and shaking violently. As you verbally suggest that the people are relaxing etc., people start to fall to the floor "asleep" all over the stage, almost as if their legs had turned to rubber beneath them. Yes, just imagine that, you are standing nowhere near them at the time, but they all start to collapse to the floor "asleep" as if their legs have turned to jelly or rubber. As I'm sure you can imagine this looks a real showstopper and absolutely unbelievable from the audiences' point of view. So how is this miraculous induction done, I can hear you say? Well, you would proceed as follows:

You choose the 12 most susceptible subjects from those whose hands locked together and they are spread out around the stage, so that there is room surrounding each of them when they fall to the floor "asleep". They are all told to stand so that their right foot is on the left hand side of their left foot and both feet are flat on the floor. By that, I mean their feet are crossed over and are placed next to each other in this position, whilst flat upon the floor. They then have to stare directly at their locked hands, which by now are shaking violently. Once all of the people are in this position, you explain that this is one of the fastest and most powerful forms of Hypnosis known to mankind. Very loud and exciting music, such as the Bladerunner Theme, or music from the Witches of Eastwick, begins to play at this point. As this music is loud and exciting and as we know excitement breeds excitement, the onstage volunteers will be getting more apprehensive all the time about what is to occur (belief/expectancy). As you will have, if you're sensible, already placed a couple of people under hypnosis with quick inductions, their belief and expectancy levels will be high and working in your favour. The lighting should also change to suggest that something dramatic is about to occur. Verbally, you now suggest to all the subjects who are standing in this strange position, something along the following lines:

"I'm going to count backwards from 3 to 1, and as I do, many of you will find that as you stare directly at your hands, which will continue to shake more violently, the harder you try to stop them, the more they will shake. In fact, the more they shake, the more you will be going deeper to sleep with every breath you take, every noise you hear and with every word I say. Many of you will find your legs will turn to jelly and give way beneath you, when this happens you will not fall and hurt yourself, you'll just fall into a beautifully relaxed, deep, dreamy, sleep like state. You'll enjoy every minute of it, as the deeper you go, the better you will feel and the better you feel, the deeper you will go to sleep."

N.B. At this point you then turn to the audience and say. "Well, ladies and gentlemen, be prepared to be amazed, as this one of the most powerful and dramatic forms of Hypnosis know to mankind. Your attention please."

(Turn back to the subjects and say) " OK, now everyone, so on 3, already many of you will be experiencing that rather strange sensation as your whole body becomes so relaxed and as you stare intently at your hands, your legs are becoming like rubber, so weak they cannot hold your body up any longer and you just want to go to sleep. And on, 2, as you hands shake so violently now, you notice also that your whole body begins to sway. You cannot keep your balance, you can feel yourself falling, as your legs become more weak and rubbery with every breath you take, every noise you hear and every word that I say, so it is so much easier to relax and sleep. And on 1, your whole body so relaxed now, it's hard to keep your balance, now all you want to do is relax and enjoy that feeling of serenity as your legs turn to jelly, as your whole body begins to sway, as you feel yourself falling and you all go to sleep (say sleep in drawn out fashion).

N.B. At this point, anyone who may be standing up is approached from the rear, so that they don't see you coming and you hit the upper side area of their right leg sharply with the side of your hand, as if doing a karate chop. This is enough to knock them totally off balance, so that they do fall to the floor as you once again shout sleep and shock them into hypnosis. Most people will have gone under and fallen to the floor by then however and of course, this additional "push" can be given to those that you feel may be resisting a little, as you actually deliver the count back with patter from 3 to 1. If you are unsure that anyone would fall to the floor, then stand as I've detailed, place your hands as if locked together, and shake them around violently whilst staring at them as the onstage subjects will be doing, I'm sure you'll see that in less than a minute you will fall over too. Then see what happens when someone knocks you on the side of the leg as detailed, whilst they also shout, sleep, firmly into your ear, this time I'm 100% certain you'll end up on the floor. Now do you believe me?

WHY WON'T THEY BE HURT?

Well, the reason is simple, any intelligent person will, as they start to fall to the floor, feel this is occurring and probably try to stop themselves. As they move towards the floor, their legs will naturally bend at the knee, which brings them nearer to the floor, before they "fall" properly, which means they will not freefall as far. When you combine this with the fact that they will probably fall sideways down onto their knees, and then sideways to the floor, this means that their journey to the floor will be far more gradual than it actually appears to the audience. Try it yourself, and you'll see what I mean, it's almost an automatic thing to "fall" to the floor in this way, which is very similar to a sideways fall which some stuntmen use, so that they do not get hurt. Obviously, there is still a small element of danger and this can also be eliminated by softening the surface which they are to land upon. To do this many hypnotists who work theatres regularly, have a nice soft carpet (size of an average stage) which they fix to the floor with gaffer tape, along all four edges, so that no one can trip up accidentally. This, then cushions that small final fall to the floor and the incident of people hurting themselves is practically non existent. However, as with all I describe in this course, proceed at your own risk.

THE ARM SPIN INDUCTION

For this one, the subject sits in a chair, feet together, whilst flat upon the floor, they interlock their fingers, as with the handclasp text, but leave them held loosely, so that when you wish to, you can immediately pull their hands apart and they will separate instantly.

They are then told to close their eyes and relax their arms, so that you are then holding the full weight of their arms and if you were to let go of them, they would fall down into their lap. Indeed you can do this suddenly to check that they have complied with your commands if you so wish.

All this should take but a few seconds to sort out and then you physically proceed by rotating their hands around in a circular motion, which in turn will move their arms in the same way also. This must be done in a steady circular motion, as you deliver your verbal suggestions of relaxation and sleep. The rotation must be done "rhythmically" and at the same speed throughout, so that it both distracts them consciously and also acts as a very low level disorientation method, whilst having a calming "rock a bye baby" affect. You then deliver your usual kind of verbal suggestions having already "conditioned" them to believe that the moment you say sleep their eyes will remain closed at all times until you say otherwise and that they will enter trance at the moment in time. The moment you command sleep, you simultaneously pull the subjects hands apart and, as you will be holding each of their wrists in a separate hand, you not only pull their hands apart, but also in a smooth motion you pull their arms slightly towards yourself and downwards at the same time. The effect you want to achieve is to have them move forward in their chair, with their head moving down towards their lap, as in the body flop induction, except here we achieve it by jerking their body forward by use of their arms (again it disorientates).

The moment you have done this, you allow their arms to drop down by their sides so that they feel lots of physical movements of their body which act as non verbal suggestions of sleep, as they are downwards movements.

All this should be practised upon a willing friend, so that at any performance, you are able to carry it all out so it just takes a matter of 2 or 3 seconds for all the end actions to be done with the result of them being flopped forward in their chair. In other words, you must be able to do it without any hesitation.

When done correctly the subject will start sitting up straight in their chair and the moment that you've said sleep and carried out the physical movements, their hands will be down by their sides and their head down in their lap with the upper area of their body slumped forwards, which, of course, looks most impressive to the audience. Verbally, you would do the normal thing of, "I'll count from 3 to 1 and on 1, when I say sleep you'll instantly enter a beautifully relaxed state and your eyes will remain closed at all times, until I say otherwise." Then you'd count from 3 to 1, usually using the standard kind of phrases along the way and on 1 when you say sleep, all the actions are carried out quickly. I hope you have noticed, that besides belief and expectancy, another reason why this and most inductions work is because of the ritualistic actions you carry out and the importance which you attach to them, which in itself also heightens their belief and expectancy. Also your verbal suggestions begin by explaining in a disguised form what you expect to happen to them when you say sleep, they then know how to react and belief will do the rest for you. As we said earlier, co-operation is a key word in hypnosis.

WORLD RECORD HIGH SPEED HYPNOSIS TECHNIQUE

What I am about to explain to you, is presented to any audience as the fastest and most powerful form of hypnosis know to mankind. And, indeed, to them, that is exactly what it will appear to be. You, as a knowledgeable hypnotist, will know that there is a lot of "psychological" conditioning done in your lead up to demonstrating this method of hypnosis, which is usually done at the start of the second half of the show, by which time everyone has seen you place people into trance rapidly and, as such, their belief and expectancy is complete. You do the "guaranteed hand clasp test" prior to getting people up to be instantly entranced for your world record attempt. The way you present this as a world record attempt, not only enables you to get free, large scale publicity at every large show you do, but also it makes everyone anxious to see you succeed and, as such, it puts them in the perfect frame of mind in which to do instant inductions upon them. The people whose hands are locked together, via the guaranteed hand clasp, are brought up to the stage and their hands are then separated, as detailed in the last chapter. You will no doubt, have many people who were upon the stage at the start of the show and wanted to be hypnotised but, as you sent them back, they missed their chance, or so they thought. So, when you ask for between 12 to 20 volunteers to remain on the stage and take part in the world record high speed hypnosis attempt, you will have many takers, as they will want to grab this second chance to be a star in any way that they possibly can.

The rest of the people are returned to the audience to a round of applause. The people are standing with a slight gap between each of them, in a straight row across the stage. They are standing so they are facing the audience and in a

position ready for the falling backwards induction. You then use the I.I.C. principle to condition them that they might be an idiot if they don't enter the hypnotic state especially as this is the fastest and most powerful form of hypnosis known. You then make sure they are standing feet together and hands down by their side, as in the falling backwards test. Next, you get each and every person to stare at the bright white floodlight which should be high up front of house and facing the stage. All front of house lights are switched off and the stage lighting is also made quite dim, so that the light which they are staring at intently literally "blinds" them and blurs their vision. (So don't look at it yourself!). In fact, if you have a modern image, a pair of dark sunglasses would not go amiss during this routine, so you can continue with no risk to your own vision. Next everyone is told to stare directly at the bright white light at all times, and now the Bladerunner theme begins, which is a very loud and exciting tune, which will put a sense of fear into them. You then do your psychological conditioning of what will occur by saying something such as:
"Ladies and Gentlemen, in 1993, a famous television hypnotist, by the name of Alex LeRoy set a world record for high speed hypnosis. He placed over 12 people into a hypnotic trance in less than 60 seconds. Well, tonight, ladies and gentlemen, I don't intend to break that record, oh no, I intend to smash it.

In a few moments you will witness the fastest form of Hypnosis known. It is also the most powerful method of hypnosis. To this day, nobody has been able to resist it's most powerful effects." (Now turn to your subjects).

"OK, now I'm talking to everyone, as you stare directly at the bright white spotlight, listen only to the sound of my voice. In a few moments I shall touch each of you upon the forehead, and the moment that I do, you'll instantly fall back into my arms and enter a deep, deep hypnotic state, as this is the fastest form of hypnosis known.

Now, I won't let you fall and hurt yourselves though, you'll just fall back into a beautifully relaxed state."

(Turn to audience). "OK, ladies and gentlemen, prepare to be amazed."

At this point the induction starts and everyone is placed under hypnosis as I will detail in a moment.

(Once all under say) "Ladies and gentlemen, the fastest form of hypnosis know." (Here take a bow at your applause). At this point, you either awaken people and return them to the audience, or implant the major post hypnotic suggestion in their minds and use them in the second half of the show. Or, implant the post hypnotic suggestion that, when you say goodnight at the end of the show, they will all jump up out of their chairs and shout out loudly,

"WE LOVE THE WORLDS GREATEST HYPNOTIST JONATHAN ROYLE, OH YES WE DO!"

The moment they have done this and leave the building, all suggestions will, of course, then be completely cancelled out. Just imagine it, you say goodnight to end your show, and as you leave the stage 20 or more people jump up and shout out, "We love the worlds greatest hypnotist, Alex LeRoy, oh yes we do!" This is the kind of ending to a hypnotic show that guarantees a standing ovation.

OK, so what do you do physically? Well, quite simply, if the people saw you coming to touch their foreheads, then they would anticipate it occurring and could try to resist. That is exactly why we don't do that. Instead, we start at the left hand side of the stage, working along the row rapidly until we reach the right hand side. Always, when doing what follows, you must be standing on the right hand side of the subject as you stand behind them. Your right hand is then lifted up behind the subject's back and above their head. You then, suddenly, bring your hand down flat over their eyes, which they won't expect, and at exactly the same moment in time your left hand presses flat against the lower back area of your subjects. So as your right hand pushes your subject's head backwards, your left hand pushes their stomach area forwards, they then very quickly reach that point of no return and fall back to the floor, with you cushioning their fall slightly.

To cushion their fall, you lift your left hand up at the last moment to their upper back area and lower them slightly to lessen the impact. All this, in practise, should take one to two seconds to carry out, as detailed. One moment the subject is standing up, staring at a bright white light and the next moment, everything goes dark as your hand unexpectedly goes over their eyes and they fall back to the floor as you shout "sleep" firmly into their ear, if that's not enough to shock anyone into hypnosis, then I don't know what is. Add to all this, belief, expectancy and suggestions and you really do have a most powerful technique to add to your repertoire.

As the timing of the induction, from a world record point of view, only starts when you touch the first subject by placing your hand over their eyes, it is easily possible to place 40 or more people into trance in less than sixty seconds. This is a very impressive demonstration of hypnosis, which can also get you much free, large scale publicity to promote your theatre show in each town you go to. It really is the fastest form of hypnosis known and will make you a lightening speed hypnotist, use it and be careful.

HYPNOTISING THE AUDIENCE

The induction used for this would be a progressive relaxation induction of an eye straining nature. The techniques of rapport, observation, recognition and leadership would be used with the majority being catered for, so that the end result of many people going into trance whilst still sitting in their seats within the audience is achieved. The standard kind of phrases are used as suggestions along with the classic suggestions of "Your eyelids are so heavy and so tired, that they want to close, in fact the harder you try to keep them open the quicker they will close."

The focus point for the entire audience is a large Hypno-Disc, which is a large black and white spiral effect disc with a motor rotating at a steady speed and giving a blackhole effect as if being "drawn" into the disc. The whole audience is told to stare directly at the spinning disc as your suggestions of relaxation are given in the usual way. The end result will be that as the disc both has the effect of straining your eyes and disorientating you, most of the people who do stare at it will fall to "sleep" in their seat and you will have to go out into the audience to awaken them and bring the subjects you want to use up onto the stage to take part.

I saw a hypnotist called Mark Maverick, use this method most successfully in early 1994 at The Garrick Playhouse in Altringham, and it was most successful for him, with a large majority of the audience going to "sleep" in their seat. These Hypno-Discs are available in a small size for the therapists office from Mr Kevin Gray, I am sure he would, however be able to make a large stage size motor operated Hypno-Disc for you to order, he can be contacted at:

Mr Kevin Gray (I.A.H)
2 Old Row
Burton on Stather
Scunthorpe
South Humberside
England
DN15 9DN

Tel: + 44 (0) 1724 720706
Tel: +44 (0) 1724 720909
Fax: +44 (0) 1724 720877

When you contact Kevin, also ask for full details of all his other "Hypnoquip" products, which will be very useful indeed for your hypnotherapy consulting room.

THE EYE TO EYE FASCINATION INDUCTION

Watch the Jungle Book film and witness the snake staring at the young boy, as he says "look into my eyes", and you'll have an idea of how this eye to eye fascination induction works. I usually take hold of the persons left hand in my right, and this establishes an instant rapport and instant bond between you both. Then using the method explained earlier in the course, make them think that I am staring directly into their eyes and at no point do I blink or lose eye contact, this has a strong psychological effect upon them and, not only makes them feel slightly uncomfortable, but also makes their eyes become heavy and tired, via the eyestrain technique, already explained. I then start talking in a low tone of voice, at a steady monotonous speed, suggesting that they can feel themselves sinking into the chair, their eyes becoming heavy and they want to close them, as they feel warm, tingling sensations in various areas of their body, as they wish to go to sleep, etc.

Continue along these lines, only stopping for a second to take breath. The key with this induction being to keep their eyes fixed upon your gaze and bombard them with suggestion, after suggestion until their eyes close and they go under. At which point, you quickly deepen the trance, as usual, and they will then be your suggestible subject. The belief factor also comes in here very strongly, as people believe all you have to do is stare into their eyes, tell them to go to sleep and they will, well in this case, great, let them carry on believing, as it makes our job easier. The suggestion of sinking and a sensation of falling down a black hole creates powerful pictures in the imagination and, as we know, when the imagination and the will are in conflict, the imagination will always win. This method can have a person in trance in less than 60 seconds, and is ideal for use in a social party situation. It's funny, but I've noticed that lots of women want to be around you when they find out you are a professional hypnotist. Oh well, I suppose there must be some perks to the job after all.

INDIRECT INDUCTION METHOD

Another powerful technique, which I have found always seems to work, is to say the following sentence at the start of your show.

"If you do not volunteer, it does not matter, you have already heard the sound of my voice and many of you will find that you go to sleep by yourselves whilst sitting in the audience, but don't worry I will wake you up, as the deeper you go, the better you will feel and the better you feel, the deeper you will go."

By implanting this suggestion into the whole audience's mind, it will go into some peoples subconscious and in a short time have the effect of making them react to the sleep suggestions you are giving to the onstage subjects. On more occasions than I care to remember, I have had people enter trance whilst sitting in the audience and I've had to go out amongst them to wake up the ones who have gone under. This, too, is the reason why the full hypnotic induction cannot be shown on TV or broadcast over the radio, as people would most certainly enter trance around the country. Now you should be starting to realise just how powerful suggestion really is.

Incidentally, Mr Peter Casson, The Chairman of the Federation of Ethical Stage Hypnotists, was on BBC 1 many years ago, with the end result of cameramen and the production crew entering the hypnotic trance during the live broadcast, yes, it looked amazing and caused a sensation, but, it also lead to a ruling that the full hypnotic induction could not be broadcast on TV or radio.

VARIATIONS ON INDUCTION

The point that I wish to make here, is that, as long as you follow all the guidelines, which I set out in the first part of this course, then your induction's will still work, however you should decide to alter them to suit your own style. This in itself is a most important point, you must be relaxed in all that you do, then you will appear more confident and professional and so ultimately, you will have more success. An example of a slight variation or an induction is as follows:

You tell the subject, that you'll count from 3 to 1 and say sleep etc. Instead, you suddenly just say one and sleep, and they will, if a good, responsive subject, still fall back into your arms and enter trance. I suppose the shock element also comes into play here.

Another example, is they stand as with the falling backwards induction, but with eyes open, you tell them to follow the microphone with their eyes and the moment you command sleep to close their eyes, enter trance and fall back into your arms. You then move the mike towards their head at an angle, then continue past their head, so that in order to follow the mike's path of travel, they must tilt their head back more and so on, until they reach that point of no return and start to fall back into your arms, which is of course the moment when you command them to sleep.

CREATING YOUR OWN INDUCTIONS

By using the tried, tested and proven to work principles which have detailed in this course and the example inductions which are in this chapter, you should be more than capable of creating your own new unique to induction. Perhaps you yourself will write a book detailing your creations in years yet to come. A good source of material is any literature/books/tapes etc. which you can get by a gentleman from the U.S.A., called Mr Gil Boyne. Mr Boyne, is an American therapist, who specialises in instantaneous inductions. He has literally hundreds of quickie inductions and any literature which you can obtain detailing his methods would be of immense use to you. Another book, which I recommend, is one that was recommended to P.O.S.H. and after reading it, I too, wholeheartedly recommend it, entitled Trance-Formations, the book is by Richard Bandler and is very interesting reading on Hypnosis.

Another subject, which I would recommend you to learn, in order to become an expert at rapid induction, is anything on the subject of Neuro Linguistic Programming (N.L.P.) which is an extremely quick way to change perceptions of the mind and the way in which people think. It is also a very useful subject to have knowledge of for use in the hypnotherapist's consulting room, should you wish to pursue that avenue of financial gain. Remember, that old saying "Knowledge is Power", well, that is very true.

You may also wish to consider adding subliminal messages within the sounds of your induction music that you use to place them into trance. These verbal commands are not consciously audible to people listening to the music, but they are very quickly acted upon by their subconscious mind. How useful it would be to have suggestions of relaxation and sleep subliminally recorded within your induction music. A full kit, containing subliminal overmasks, sound effects, instructions and a full training manual are available to teach you how to make your own subliminal recordings. These can be used both as just mentioned, and also, to make therapy tapes, which can be sold separayely.

Details of the full kit are available for a S.A.E. from:
Mr Martin Windebank
6 Gwynne Close
Windsor
Berkshire
England
SL4 5PY

Another supplier of very unusual Hypnosis related items, which may be of use is:
Lifetools
Freepost KS1852
Poynton
Stockport
Cheshire
England
SK12 1FZ.
Tel: +44 (0) 1625 85885 or
Fax: +44 (0) 1625 850551
And ask for a free catalogue.

They supply relaxation music suitable for induction, subliminal tapes, books and training materials on hypnotherapy and mind control techniques. And devices, such as the lucid dream machine, which makes you have "virtual reality" dreams, their catalogue is well worth getting.

The very best audio tapes I have come across to date, which include countless different subjects for therapy including cancer treatment, childbirth, infertility, exams, esteem, alcohol abuse and much more are available (free catalogue on request) from:

PILGRIM TAPES PTY
P.O. Box 107
SHREWSBURY
England
SY1 1ZZ

I would also advise you to obtain, either from a book shop or your library, about 2 or 3 books by the following people:

Sigmund Freud, Carl Jung, Milton Erikson and anything, also by prolific psychology writers on the subject of personality types and the human mind. This will all be "heavy" reading, but will gain for you two things which are.

A You will have a thorough understanding of how the human mind works and how the damage caused by everyday stresses can be repaired in the consulting room and

B You will also have learned how to spot different kinds of people, how to get them to do different things etc., and this is the kind of information you need as a hypnotist.

So if anyone falsely accuses you of having no knowledge of hypnosis and psychotherapy, then having studied this course and acting upon my advice, will be a qualified Hypnotherapist, with a sound knowledge of psychology and the human mind. This will set you far above most of the stage hypnotists who are currently at work, they, having been plumbers one minute and after reading just one book by Paul McKenna, they are stage hypnotist the next. You are advised by me to study several other peoples viewpoints on hypnosis and to then make your own decisions, then, and only then, will you be happy and confident in all that you do. The hypnotism industry is one of the most cut-throat and competitive area of showbusiness, then it's also one of the most lucrative. Should you join a stage hypnotism society, whether it is P.O.S.H., or some other, never be influenced by what other members say, they are no better than you, although they may think they are God.

Integrity is a key word in this business, which, unfortunately, many hypnotist don't seem to have. You must never talk about people behind their backs, you must never spread nasty rumours and certainly you should never try to stop a fellow hypnotist from getting work.

TECHNIQUES OF BRAINWASHING

Deprive a person of all sense of touch, light, sound and taste and they will very quickly become disorientated. Soldiers and police do it, when they make people stand with their hands flat on the wall and feet wide apart It is not just a safety measure, it is also a hypnotic technique and that technique is disorientation. Another technique is to place subjects into a tank with warm water as the only support, deprive them of all external stimuli, they cannot see, hear or feel anything, and after short time, they will be at your mercy. Once in this disorientated state, you can then alter their personality, believes, in fact, anything that you could wish to change.

Place a microphone at the top of the tank, so that it is unidirectional in effect, now, giving any commands that you wish to have carried out, repeatedly, giving them in a slow, quiet, monotonous, firm tone of voice. After six or seven hours, you will have changed the victims' whole personality and can let them out of the water tank. Remove their blindfold and let them out of the dark warehouse. Male to Female. Nice to Evil. Or vice versa, with brain washing, anything is possible and you can get anyone to do anything.

Anything is possible with brain washing and that's why these details are included, for information purposes only, and have been kept deliberately vague, so that you will not be tempted to use them.

Relaxation aids are on sale now, from Lifetools in Cheshire (address elsewhere), for example, goggles that keep on flashing a red light in the wearers eyes at pulse rate, this will both make them enter trance and also start to brainwash them. If they were to then hear music, which contained subliminal commands within this, then the hidden commands would most certainly be enacted on.

PRESSURE POINT INDUCTION

These really have nothing to do with hypnosis, and if anything, are what has given hypnosis a bad name over the years. I detailed Carotid Artery induction earlier in the course and also the Little Boy induction, both of which rely on pressure, either directly or indirectly upon pressure points, which are all capable of knocking you unconscious. Unfortunately, if too much pressure is applied, or pressure applied for too long, then it can kill the person. So I wouldn't use these techniques. However, a book called "The Black Art of Death" gives full details of these kind of techniques and it's available by contacting the following company:

Coach Harness Books
C/O Haughley
Stowmarket (SFK)
England
1P14 3NS
Tel: 01449 673258

It would also be worth searching the Internet for an American Publishing Company called Loompanics Unlimited as they sell many bizarre books containing information of use to the Hypnotist which are unavailable from any other source.

SELF HYPNOSIS BRIEFLY EXPLAINED

Self hypnosis is remarkably simple and the results can be absolutely astounding.

To hypnotise yourself, the easiest way is to make up your own treatment cassette on which you record the hypnotic induction, (P.R.I.) deepening and suggestion therapy, which of course, should be aimed to programme your mind that you have got 100% self confidence, then, at the end goes the awakening method.

Full details of all the components that make up the finished whole are contained within this course.

The tape would then be played to yourself whilst lying down on your bed, in a dimly lit sitting room/bedroom and will have basically the same effect upon your mind, as would be obtained, if someone else suggested the positive changes to you.

Just like medicine, although not dangerous in anyway, the tapes should only be used by the person it is intended for and as a hypnotic induction process is used upon these tapes, they should never be listened to in the car whilst driving or when operating machinery. Incidentally, these home hypnotherapy tapes are also ideal and in fact, I would say essential items, for a trainee hypnotist. Listening to them, you can learn first hand, how the hypnotic induction is correctly delivered verbally and how different suggestions have different effects. Also, perhaps most importantly, they enable you to experience the hypnotic state for yourself.

These tapes can be sold individually, or given to clients attending for therapy to help reinforce the treatment they receive.

The other method of self hypnosis, is to literally, mentally think the wordings of the whole therapy session through in your minds eye.

To induce self hypnosis, the procedure is similar to a guided induction and is as follows:

Make yourself comfortable somewhere warm where you will not be disturbed. Release all tight clothing and remove your shoes. Make sure your feet are not touching each other and your hands are resting slightly away from your body. Close your eyes, take a deep breath in and hold it for 5 seconds. Then release it slowly, all the way out, as far as you can, all the way to the bottom of your stomach. Repeat this a further 3 times. Each time you exhale, allow yourself to relax and just "let go". Let your body start to feel limp and heavy and let all the tensions flow away.

It is very important not to try too hard, as the secret is to allow things to happen naturally, with no effort at all.

Then start to count backwards, in your mind, from 10 to 1 and with each number you count, allow your mind and body to relax even more. Let your mind just drift away to anywhere you like and your body to become heavier and more relaxed with every number. Repeat this as many times as you like until you know you are physically and mentally more relaxed than when you started.

Next you need to bring in the visualisation technique. Imagine, in your "minds eye" the muscles in your feet and around your toes and FEEL them relaxing. Let them go limp and heavy. Let all the tensions fade away. Then move up slowly through your calves, the tops of your legs, your buttocks, your stomach, your chest, your shoulders and neck, down your arms and into your fingers and thumbs, up the back of your head, over the top and down your forehead. When you reach your face, pay special attention to allowing all the little muscles round your eyes, your eyelids, your cheeks, all round your mouth, your jaw and even your tongue. You may find, at this point that your jaw sags open slightly with the pleasant feelings of total relaxation.

Do not be afraid, as you will not loose control or become "fixed", but you may find that with the first few attempts you drift into a light sleep! Part of the knack is to stay more or less awake while being totally relaxed in order to give yourself positive suggestions. The idea is to program your mind to slip into relaxation to the trigger of backwards counting and physical relaxation.

The process can take a little time in the early stages – maybe 15 to 20 minutes – and sometimes needs quite a bit of practice to perfect. But when you have mastered the technique, the state can be entered very quickly indeed, in a matter of seconds with some people.

When you have entered self hypnosis, you can make any suggestions you wish to yourself eg.

I am gaining in confidence.

I feel relaxed and happy at all times.

Every day in every way I am getting better and better.

I will approach people and situations in a more positive manner.

I will be appreciative and receptive to people.
Should you have an event in the future to confront, an excellent way to approach it is by visualisation during self hypnosis, eg.

Suppose you have an important meeting or a public speech to make. You would induce self hypnosis and then go through the whole event from before the start to the finish in your mind BUT with the situation in a controlled and relaxed manner. Go through, in your mind, all the things you will do on that particular day, right from getting up in the morning, but this time you are calm, relaxed, in control and not at all agitated (almost a new you). Continue through the whole day, making special emphasis on the event, while remaining in this controlled state.

This is an accepted form of therapy and is equally effective when used with self hypnosis.

When you have completed your session, simply say to yourself that you will wake yourself up by counting from 1 to 5 and when you wake up you will remember all the suggestions and (importantly) you will feel refreshed, relaxed, revitalised, confident and full of energy (repeat these thoughts). Then simply say to yourself 1, feeling relaxed. 2, I am feeling refreshed. 3, feeling revitalised and starting to wake up. 4, I am full of confidence and waking up more with my eyes starting to open. 5, feeling full of energy, eyes open wide awake feeling on top of the world.

Practice this technique to perfection and you will be astounded at the results. It's almost like a wonder drug which will not go in a bottle but with no side effects!

STANDARD PHRASES WHICH HYPNOTISTS USE

To end this chapter on induction methods, I will give you some examples on the kind of "Standard Phrases" which would be used by a hypnotist during the induction process. The rules I explained in the verbal psychology chapter, would of course be followed when giving these suggestions to the on stage subjects, or the client within the therapy room. Firstly though, allow me to recap a little. Hypnotism becomes possible through five essentials:

1. The fixation of the gaze of the hypnotist.
2. The execution of certain passes that the hypnotist must know.
3. The delivery of commands of suggestions must be in a voice filled with conviction.
4. The ability of the hypnotist to concentrate on the suggestion which he wishes to impart.
5. The ability of the subject to assume a passive state, to concentrate on the suggestions given and their willingness to accept same.

Another piece of advice is this, your nose will tell you an awful lot about a person, very often, what they eat on a regular basis, do they smoke? Their place of work (eg. Mechanics smell of oil, nurses smell of ether etc.) Now go out and do the same, you will, with a little practice be able to smell the odour of fear, when someone is terrified upon coming to the stage, or coming to visit you in your consulting room. When you get close to a subject, it's all very well to be able to determine things about them, through the way that they smell, but always make certain that they cannot tell what you have eaten and always smell sweet. Bad body odour can, and will interfere with your image and you may not, at the time, realise why.

Let all your bodily senses work for you, not against you, train them all to perfection. You will then almost be psychic and will have mastered E.S.P. (Extra Sensory Perception} training your senses to work better than most people) and not addition sensory perception as most people believe. These sorts of powers are within reach of all of us.

Another example of how your sense of smell can be used is to determine when any woman is on heat, this may sound unbelievable, but yes, it truly can be done, as they give out Pheromones, which I have mentioned elsewhere, so do men when they are feeling randy. Why do you think a dog smells the genitals? It tells him just how powerful you are, your position in the family group. So observe life and then learn from your eye opening observations. Atmosphere is another component, a successful hypnotist must use to best effect. The atmosphere must, as I explained earlier, always be such, that entering the hypnotic state seems obvious and easy to the subject. Let me present you with an example of how atmosphere works, then you will not be able to tell me that you cannot sense atmospheres, as you in fact do this every single day of you life. Have you never walked into a room where a terrific personal argument was going on, just before you entered? You knew nothing about the argument, in fact, you didn't even know that the couple could fall out. However, you could cut that atmosphere with a knife, couldn't you?

So ensure that the subjects are always seated comfortably, no tight items around the throat. You will have already informed them of what you intend doing, you state you will not give them any commands that are harmful, in fact, any commands that you give them will be only beneficial to their life.

The last subject I feel that must recap in, is something, which even some very experienced hypnotists seem to forget, and that is to cancel out all the commands which you have given to the subjects after they have been carried out. In other words, all commands must be cancelled out completely before a person leaves the building unless they are beneficial. This is a most important point and one which you forget at your own risk. In fact, I usually mention it in my opening patter and awakening speech in a similar way as follows:

"Whenever you leave this room/building/theatre/area etc., all my commands will be completely cancelled out."

Or

"When I awake you in a few moments, you will feel on top of the world, full of energy and optimism and in fact, you will feel better than you have ever felt in your entire life. You will not have any headaches or side effects of any kind. You will, in fact, feel really great. When you leave here tonight, all my commands and suggestions to you will be completely cancelled out, in other words, you will be as you were when you first came in here tonight."

Obviously, this only applies when on stage. During therapy sessions you should reinforce all suggestions as much as possible and encourage your client to REMEMBER the messages for the rest of their life.

Notice, the strong emphasis on "You", this tells the subject, that you are speaking to them and them alone. This kind of emphasis must continue all the way through, it is you, the hypnotist, that they must relate to all the time. If they start to notice what the audience is doing you will have lost them, unless it was you who brought the audience to their attention. Anyway, back to the original subject in hand, that of standard phrases which you can use during your hypnotic induction.

STANDARD PHRASES FOR HYPNOTIC INDUCTIONS

"The deeper you go the better you will feel, and the better you feel, the deeper you will go to sleep."

"With every breath you take, every noise you hear, every word I say and every thought that you think, you'll go deeper and deeper to sleep."

"Every muscle in your body from the tips of your toes to the tips of your fingers, now becoming so limp, so loose and so relaxed."

"Each and every muscle in your body, now becoming so heavy and so tired."

"Your eyelids are feeling so heavy and so tired, in fact, the harder you try to keep them open, the more they want to close tightly, as you relax completely."

As you sit (or lie) there in the comfortable chair, it almost feels as though every movement would be a great effort, as though you are sinking down deeply into the chair and into calm, satisfying, relaxation."

"This feeling of warmth and relaxation, is now travelling around your entire body and as you continue to breathe deeply and regularly, you are drifting deeper and deeper to sleep."

All the worries, stresses and tensions of days gone by, are leaving your mind and leaving your body now, allowing you to relax completely."

"In a few moments, when I awake you, you'll have an overwhelming desire to do almost everything I say, you'll find that you'll enjoy living your part in tonight's show to the full, and will carry out all that I suggest, as an automatic reflex action."

"Just as your subconscious makes you breathe at night, or circulates the blood around your body, in just the same way you can faithfully rely upon your subconscious mind to help you eliminate this problem from your every day life."

"It becomes habit in your subconscious mind to smoke (or whatever) and now your subconscious mind will make it habit not to smoke (or whatever)"

"Something that you thought would be difficult to achieve, will turn out to be ridiculously easy to do."

"Each morning when you awake, from this moment forward, you will awaken with an inner warm glow of confidence, a renewed optimism to life and a more positive attitude to get things done."

"Every day, in every way, things will be getting better and so much easier to cope with."

"You have made a promise to yourself to (whatever) and whilst it may be alright, on occasion, to break a promise to a friend, your subconscious mind will not allow you to break a promise to yourself and, as such, success is guaranteed."

NOTE: I hope these above examples will give you a much better idea of how on stage or therapy room suggestions, should be worded for maximum, positive effect.

Common sense and a little thought is all you require to word your own suggestions to give your own on stage subjects, just remember the golden rule, that there must never be any doubt in their mind of what you want them to do. Good luck with your induction's and enjoy "entrancing" people, but don't let the feeling of great power go to your head or else you'll end up like far too many other hypnotists in the profession, who have a Messiah complex and treat others like dirt, as they believe they truly are the best thing since sex was invented. This is OK on stage, but if it is carried over into your personal life, then you'll end up with no friends and your family will turn against you. To end this chapter, below are two little techniques, which can make life easy for you.

HANDSHAKE TECHNIQUE

This is basically just a way to tell, in the time it takes to shake a subject's hand, whether or not they will make a good subject. When you shake their hand press your fingers against the palm of their hand and feel how much moisture is there. The drier their hand is, the more relaxed the person is already and, as such, the easier it will usually be to hypnotise them. On the other hand, the more the subjects hand is perspiring, the more nervous they are and the harder it will be to get the subject relaxed for a normal style induction. These people, with waterlogged palms, are either not used to, or are shocked into hypnosis, as they are already too tense for the slow P.R.I.

TWO ARE BAD SUBJECTS PLOY

This is just a psychological ploy, which can be used to increase the chances of people wanting to be hypnotised and also the number of people who end up under hypnosis. At the start of your act, once the subjects are on stage ready to be hypnotised, you say.

"Well, I must say ladies and gentlemen, that there are two people on this stage who cannot be hypnotised, or at least I think they can't. The reason being, they don't have the correct powers of I.I.C. and we will not be able to use them. I won't point them out however, as they might surprise us and start concentrating a bit more." This, which you have just said to the audience, is pure waffle, however, as each person on the stage starts worrying if it's them, they'll all put 100% effort in to being hypnotised. Now your chances of success are considerably increased. Just imagine how daft people will feel, returning to the audience, having not gone under, when you have said something like that. My experience shows me they are more likely to remain on stage and act hypnotised and take part in the show before looking a complete fool and returning to audience.

See you in the next chapter.

PART TEN

"BITZ 'N' BOBS"

A CHAPTER OF GENERALLY VERY USEFUL KNOWLEDGE

"Each man and woman will, in their lifetime stumble over opportunity. Unfortunately, most will simply pick themselves up and go through life as if nothing ever happened."

"You have, with this course, been offered a complete business plan, on how to earn big money from the hypnotism industry. I hope you have the vision to see the bright future, which can now be yours, if you so desire."

This chapter has no particular format at all, that's the way I intended it to be. By having no format, you will have to put your own mind to work more to see the truth of what I'm saying and teaching to you, so here goes.

Always remember, that positive thoughts breed positive actions, as they are contagious, and positive actions bring positive success. To be a successful hypnotist, you must have a "magnetic" or attractive personality. This personality is a sum total of your health, appearance, habits and attitude. This type of personality is a plus personality, and a plus means that something is added. Negative, is an away sign and you cannot possess negative qualities and be successful. Therefore, any negative qualities you possess must be removed. Keep healthy, reasonable hours, good wholesome food, keep clear of colds, no over indulgence and treat others as you would sincerely expect to be treated yourself. Then you will develop for yourself a magnetic personality. Also remember, that it is vital to master self control. As you will never successfully control others if you cannot control yourself. This point is often overlooked, except by the successful few. Strive always to be healthy in mind, body and soul. You may have some negative attitudes or nervous habits, which must be eliminated, if so strive to get rid of them rapidly. Cut pride and any desire to be important, this is not easy when you know that you have the secret for success, which by the end of this course you will have. Keep this secret to yourself, but ensure that you carry out the formula. You must master your negative desires, before you can possibly hope to master others. Listen with respect, to the views of others, and always find the good in what is expressed. Do not try to show that you know more about the subject, even if this is the case. People who do this have very poor self control. Never interrupt with objections, better that you spend time saying what is good about the discussion. You will always gain more influence over others by giving credit for what is good and very intelligent. Agreement, more often expressed makes and keeps friends, you just forget the rest, it is better to do so than disagreeing, the latter is negative and to you a loss. So in future, observe the things that you do wrong. Unconsciously these are bad habits, done with little or no conscious thought, they are your disabilities now and they have to be corrected.

Nervous activity is the responsible source for most bad habits. This activity is power, so it is much better to put it to a positive use, learn to control all of your bodily actions and mental actions.

The most important qualities, which a good subject should possess are confidence, belief and faith, with expectation in the power of hypnotism. The qualities just mentioned alone, will lead the subject to co-operate with you, as a result they will be very susceptible to your suggestions. Make certain that your publicity ensures a good attendance on every appearance. A good audience is what makes a successful hypnotist, a good write up in the local paper is a must. If you can manage it, get a good publicity man at the very start, it will cost a lot, but will enable you to get free, large scale national publicity right from day one. Remember, the bigger the audience, the better chance you have to get some good subjects, who will go under quickly, you will, in fact, have the law of averages on your side. Always live by this saying and think positively. "Best, better, best, may I never rest, until my best is better than my betters best." Another very important phrase to believe in and live by is "Every day, in every way, I am getting better and better."

You may not know, but it is not legal to show the full Hypnotic induction process on TV. The reason for this being, that, in 1946, a hypnotist called Mr Peter Casson, inadvertently hypnotised the engineers on the control panel whilst doing a broadcast for the BBC. This alone should prove that hypnosis is a genuine phenomenon. But still, many so called learned men, argue about its reality. In fact, a man, by the name of Theodore Barber, believed that you could get the same effects without going through the hypnotic induction process. Well, if that were true, I'd like to see him go up to someone and get them to imagine that they are a washing machine. The way that your personality comes across on stage or in the consulting room is a most important part or heart of any hypnotist. Confidence, directness, assertiveness, being totally positive in everything that you do, are all very vital qualities that you need to develop for your career to be a success. You must be able to confidently force your personality, in a non aggressive way, onto the volunteers or your clients, as this is an important part of the induction process. Observe Paul Daniels, Bruce Forsyth and Michael Barrymore in action, they are all masters of forcing their personality upon the audience, each of them is able to get people to do the most ridiculous things, and yet they use no hypnotism at all. So, if you can come across to an audience as they do, then it goes without saying, when you add the power of hypnotism, then you have a very strong hand of cards to play with.

Now, also believe this. Everyone on stage at the start of your show, will be hypnotised, they may not know it and albeit it will be in varying degrees, but everyone will be hypnotised to some extent. This is the point where I will now mention the subject of stooges. Some hypnotists, including myself, on occasions of importance, do have a friend or two, who they enjoy working with. Now, by occasions of importance, I mean when members of the media are to be present and the success of your show is vital for your future publicity. In these cases it may be as well to employ the services of someone you know who is guaranteed to co-operate and react in the manner you wish. Also remember, that one stooge is useful to bring the "sheep" effect into play, as once the subjects have seen one person go under quickly, then they will follow the leader so to speak, and follow suit themselves. Stooges come in two forms

A Those people who are good actors and you pay to play along to your stage suggestions.

B Those people who really have been hypnotised by you before, and allow you to place them under hypnosis again prior to the show to implant a post hypnotic suggestion that, when they come up onto the stage that night they will go back into trance instantly. This kind of stooge is genuinely under hypnosis, but you have paid them to be there, as you know they will react well to your suggestions.

It should go without saying, that in either case, should you ever actually use stooges, the audience must never know, in fact, the only people who should ever know are you and the stooge, don't ever tell your agent/manager, as it could ruin your reputation. I will end the subject of stooges by saying, they are not required if you do as outlined in this course, then you will have a most successful and

100% genuine show. However, it is worth bearing in mind stooges should you ever have to do a TV show performance, or you know that the media in general will be present at one of your shows.

During the early days of your career, it is advisable to proceed with a fairly standardised induction, such as the falling backwards or P.R.I. Then, when you have a few hundred or so inductions under your belt, you can become more daring and start to use instant inductions, as by then, you will have the enormous self confidence levels required to make instantaneous inductions work for you. When talking to the onstage subjects, you must have a forceful tone in your voice, yet, at the same time talk in an assertive manner. By forceful tone, I mean a tone of voice that suggests that you mean business. Remember your aim is to hypnotise them not scare them to death. Should you touch the subjects when you say the word relax in your induction, and later when you say sleep, then always touch them in the same place for whatever you are suggesting to them. Never confuse them by altering things.

When you command sleep or relax, if you should move your arm, always ensure that it is a downwards movement. Then later when you say wide awake, let them observe an upwards arm movement, this conditions them psychologically to react in a certain way to each type of arm movement, even if you later were not to speak to them.

When counting for relaxation or sleep, count downwards, ie. 5,4,3,2,1, and when terminating the state count upwards, 1,2,3,4,5, etc., so that you are doing the opposite thing, it has the opposite result. Whenever you should click your fingers, make sure that it is the same number of clicks for whatever suggestion you are giving. By that I mean, use the same suggestion for the same number of finger clicks, so that once again it becomes a conditioned reflex.

When you've got the subjects upon the stage and are suggesting their hands are getting tighter and tighter, walk amongst them and suggest that the more they stare at their hands the more relaxed they will become. You then get hold of the subjects to be tested by holding their arms, which you then push in towards their own chest, at the same time you push their head down towards their clenched hands. You do not require much physical force when doing this, but your voice must sound direct and positive, as you suggest hands getting tighter and tighter. You then let go of the subject's head and arms, as a general rule of thumb, if they spring back into their original positions, then you can safely say, that there will be more responsive subjects. However, if they stay exactly where you positioned them, then you know they have obeyed your non verbal command, and as such are good people to place into the hypnotic trance.

Another clever technique to use within your act, when performing the induction process, is this, you say to subject, "OK, just take a nice deep breath in (the word in being drawn out), hold it and then out (the word out being drawn out)." The words, in and out, are drawn out to coincide with the subject's inwards and outwards breathing rhythm and has the effect of verbally "mirroring" their breathing rhythm and helps to establish a stronger rapport. This then allows the subject to relax more and as such the trance state sets in.

Another general rule of thumb, I have found, is this, when the subject breathes out, in other words, on the outbreath, is the best time to suggest things such as, sleep, deeper, relax etc. Psychologically, subjects associate breathing outwards with letting go and relaxation, and this is the best time to suggest such things

There are several different states of hypnosis which it is possible for everyone to enter. However, when a volunteer is in trance, the depth will fluctuate, just so long as they don't drift into the somnambulistic state, then you will be OK. If they do, then awaken them, stand them at the side of the stage and a few minutes later, when you are sure they are fully alert, return them to the audience. If in this somnambulistic state, they will be so deeply relaxed, that they will not react to your commands and will not be of use to you and your show. There are five states of hypnosis, and these are:

1 THE WAKING STATE (HYPNODIAL STATE)

This is the initial stage of hypnosis that begins the moment you ask them to clasp their hands together. It is a lovely lazy state that we all drift into prior to sleep or, although fully conscious, just before we wake up. Many volunteers in your show will be in the hypnodial state, but that's OK, as they will be relaxed enough to react to your suggestions, to let the ego be subdued and to throw themselves into the routines you suggest.

2 THE LIGHT TRANCE (LETHARGIC)

This is the next level of hypnosis, and in this light trance, as the title suggests, the subjects feel quite lethargic. A flickering of the eyelids is often noticed or a movement of the eyeballs under the lids (known as R.E.M.'s , Rapid Eye Movements). This merely shows that the subject is entering a deeper level of trance. When the subject is in a light trance, it is easy to work with them for the same reasons as when they are in the waking state.

3 THE MEDIUM STATE (CATALEPTIC TRANCE)

In this state, the person feels detached from their surroundings and very often has a hazy recollection of events when the hypnotic state is ended. This state will cause you no problems, as the subject will still respond to your suggestions. In fact, for information purposes, this is the state of trance you'd want a subject in to make their body rigid and support them like a plank of wood across the back of two chairs. Or to move a blow torch across their arm with no pain as will soon be described.

4 THE DEEP STATE (SOMNAMBULSTIC)

This state is an absolute nightmare for you in your role as a hypnotist. The reason for this being, in this state, they will be enjoying hypnosis so much, that they will want to be left alone and will not want to participate. If any subject should enter this state, then awaken them, stand them at the side of the stage for a few minutes and then return them to the audience, when you are sure they are fully conscious.

THE POST HYPNOTIC STATE

This is the state they are in when you say, wide awake, they are apparently removed from trance and then react to your suggestions. I prefer to call this, an eyes open trance state, as even with their eyes open, in this state you can suggest more things to them and they will immediately react. You can also tell them that when you snap you fingers in front of their face they will realise what they are doing and be really surprised.

SPECIAL NOTE

The only other state after somnambulism is the COMOTOSE state, which as the name suggests resembles the state of coma. To get someone into this state takes a lot of trance deepening and will not even bother you upon the stage. However, as in this state the body mechanisms are slowed down, it is the state of trance that would be required for such a genuine stunt, as the sleep for a week in a shop window, which Peter Powers did in 1993, upon a man in Liverpool. A much greater understanding of the body, the mind and hypnosis should be gained before ever even contemplating to place someone into this state. In the meantime, you can always engineer a fake version of the stunt if wished.

IDENTIFYING THE TRANCE SUBJECTS ARE IN

The oldest known, and most mentioned scale of hypnotic susceptibility, or scale for measuring the trance state depth, is the Davis/Hubard scale of hypnotic susceptibility. Another scale, is that of Leoron/Bordeaux, and both of these can be obtained from any good book store, contained within the pages of various hypnotherapy literature. I will not mention them here, as to be honest, 95% of the population are most likely to go into a light (lethargic) trance, which is ideal for us. Of the population as a whole, only 55% are likely to enter the medium trance, which again will still be of use to us. As for the somnambulistic trance, which will cause us problems, only about 20% of the population can enter it, and on stage this is highly unlikely, as it would usually occur in the consulting room. Should this occur during your therapy session, you will be able to verbally guide your client back into the state required. As a general rule of thumb, the better they react, the deeper in trance they are, with the exception of somnambulists, when the opposite applies.

HYPNOTISABILITY OF THE ENTIRE POPULATION

5% Unable to be hypnotised
95% Light trance, so the majority of people can participate in your show or be suitable for therapy.
55% Medium trance…….. Cataleptic.
20% Deep trance…….. Somnambulistic

A few indications that a person is in hypnosis I will briefly mention. A full list however has been given in the previous chapter, these listed here are the ones I most commonly find however. Once you've done a few shows or therapy sessions it will become second nature almost to spot these things which indicate the hypnotic state. For now, here are the main ones to spot.

THE FACIAL FLUSH

The skin tone colour changes as the hypnotic relaxation sets in.

EYELIDS FLICKERING

Eyelid flickering indicates the onset of trance, or a deeper level of trance.

WHITES OF THE EYES

You will notice with some subjects, that their eyes have floated upwards behind their lids. There is no cause for concern, if you observe the whites of their eyes through their slightly parted lids, in fact, it just means they are certainly in a trance.

EYES REMAIN OPEN

If this occurs, but the person is actually in trance, then there will be a kind of glazed look upon them. In this case just close their eyelids gently with your fingertips.

THE SCRATCH

Some subjects may begin repeatedly scratching themselves on various parts of their anatomy. Don't worry, carry on, they do not consciously realise they are doing it.

QUASIMODO RESPONSE

Some subjects, as they relax, will distort their features into the most laughable of unpleasant shapes. This is an involuntary action and they are unaware of it occurring.

OBVIOUS RELAXATION

If their heads fall forwards, or to one side, their jaws sag open, facial and bodily features relax etc., then the suggestions of relaxation, which you have been giving, are influencing the motor actions of their body.

CATATONIC STATE

Sometimes this occurs without suggestion. Some or all of the subjects' muscles become rigid or stiff. If this occurs of it's own accord, try to reverse it with suggestions of muscular relaxation.

SLEEEEEP

With somnambulists they demonstrate all the signs of actual, genuine sleep. However, they are just in a very deep trance. They will not react to you and their speech will be slurred and lazy. You must awaken these people, make sure they are full conscious and return them to the audience.

TIME DISTORTION

When a person is in hypnosis, time distortion is experienced to a factor of two to two and a half times. A two hour stage show will, to the subject, seem like about 20 to 30 minutes, and they will be sincerely amazed when they realise the truth. In a rare case or two, it can be the reverse and the odd subject thinks it was twice the length of the time it actually took.

ABREACTION'S

Abreaction's, as the name suggests, are abnormal reactions, which are sometimes experienced by a subject in trance and you should certainly be aware of this. You may never experience a person on stage have an abreaction, although if you enter the field of therapy, then they will become a regular occurrence to you. On stage abreaction's occur so rarely, that should it occur you will be knocked completely of guard and it will come as of much of a shock to you as to the audience.

When under hypnosis, a person relaxes the critical (analytical) area of the mind. The ego switches off, so this can enhance a subject's long term memory. If an abreaction did occur, it would just mean that the subject had drifted back through their thoughts. Back in time to an earlier period in their development. Back into their childhood, the subconscious mind retains within it's memory banks, past experiences of traumatic natures, as well as numerous other incidents/events which have long been forgotten. The reason these things are "blocked out" or "repressed", is because as a youngster, they were far too traumatic to deal with, but now, from an adult viewpoint, it would be easier to come to terms with them.

These repression's are often the cause of fears and phobias that the person has. (The phobias become an outward expression of an inward problem). The moment an abreaction occurs and the traumatic event (repression) is released, so the cause of the problem will be removed and as such all the symptoms will disappear. You see the mind is like an electric kettle, when the water becomes too hot and has boiled, the thermostat in the kettle causes it to switch off, so that it does not boil dry. So it is with the mind, that if a young mind experiences an event of a traumatic nature, then it may be too "hot" for that young mind to handle, so their emotions repress that memory and lock it into the subconscious mind. But the person believes they have forgotten it and even, in some cases believes the traumatic event never took place. In fact when they release the repression, people are usually unaware it was there, or that the repressed event ever took place. So, just as it takes emotion for the event to be repressed, it also takes a lot of emotion to release it and that's all an abreaction is, an emotional release of a repressed memory.

The fears or phobias which that person may have been experiencing then stop, as they were created by the hidden problem in order that the subject be consciously drawn to finally sort out those fears/phobias, which in turn also ensures that the repressed problem is eventually dealt with.

Although it's very dramatic to witness, the end result for the person it's happening to, is that their life will improve no end, and fears/phobias they once had will now no longer trouble them. So the result of an abreaction is strong, emotional and/or bodily reactions. Now as a therapist, we'd just let them continue experiencing the state, until they came out of trance naturally, as it would in a therapeutic sense, do them tremendous benefit. On stage, however, we are there to entertain, so stop this state of emotion spreading amongst the subjects (remember the sheep effect), if one person cries, another will. So if this occurs, we on stage must say to the group as a whole:

"I am talking now to everyone upon the stage, just relax, feel good, I am talking to everyone now. Just imagine that you have got that nice Sunday morning lazy feeling and you will carry on experiencing this until I touch you on the shoulder, until then, nothing can, or will disturb you."

Then release the abreacting subject from trance by saying:

"I want you to bring your feelings out now, up to this moment in time, forget about the past, feel relaxed, feel good, feel like you did before you came on the stage tonight." (this is said with hand on their shoulder). Continue in this manner until their feelings return to normal. If necessary, explain to the audience what has happened and that no harm can be caused with hypnosis, then return the abreacting subject back to the audience in a fully conscious state and continue with your show. The audience will respect you for putting your subject's feelings first. Now just go and tap the others upon the shoulder and they will once more start reacting to whatever you say.

HARD TO AWAKEN SUBJECTS.

If they don't awaken when you give them the commands, don't worry, they are probably just more relaxed than they've ever been. Blow in their ear, lift their arm, shake them. These may awaken them. If not, ask them why they will not wake up and rephrase their response back to them in order to awaken them. If unsuccessful with that, then suggest that when you count to 3, you'll prick their arm with a sharp pin and they will immediately be wide awake. Then count to three and just touch their arm with the tip of a pencil, they should believe it to be a pin and as such, will awaken. If not, don't worry, they'd just slip into a normal sleep state and awaken in an hour or two. However, on stage, you may not be able to wait that long, so, as a last resort only, lean over them, whisper the word DANGER in their ear and get out of the way quickly. When in hypnosis and you mention the word danger, they will react in a primitive fashion, but it will release them immediately from trance.

PACING AND LEADING

Pacing and leading, is where you match your speech rhythm to the volunteers rate of breathing. When you are in sync with their breathing, slow the pace and rhythm of your speech even more and the subjects breathing will deepen. Ask the volunteer to close his eyes and concentrate on the sound of your voice, then ask the subject to pay attention to his breathing. As the depth of breathing gets deeper, match your "relaxing," "letting goes" etc. with the ebb and flow of his breath. Then, when you are ready, lead the subject into trance by acting the way that you want them to and they will react in turn.

MY SECRET OF HYPNOSIS

When I go on stage, I think this phrase in my mind, and I follow it to the letter, knowing that if I follow it, then success is GUARANTEED.

"I want them to believe I can do it. They will then believe I can do it and as such, I am able to do it."

Once again we are back to belief and expectancy, which are the two main keys to anything connected with hypnosis.

You now have an extremely good knowledge of hypnosis. Hypnotherapy and Psychotherapy form an ideal partnership and combined with the stage can provide an excellent business. It will not only open up more earning potential for you, but will also set you a few steps above most hypnotists in the business who know very little about their job. So good luck, and happy studying.

PART ELEVEN

THE LAWS, REGULATIONS AND RED TAPE OF THE HYPNOTIC INDUSTRY.

This chapter deals with all the hassles you are likely to encounter in your quest to become a top professional hypnotist. It also gives you all the solutions, so you don't have to spend two years finding all this information. As such, this chapter is worth the price of the course alone, many times over.

I always say, that if something is man made, then it is there to be man broken, in much the same way, if you search long enough, there is a loophole which can be legally exploited in every law of the land. Some of these loopholes are detailed in this chapter.

BRITISH ACTORS EQUITY MEMBERSHIP

British Equity is open to all professional show business performers, be they circus or variety artistes, actors/actresses, stunt men or even one of us poor misunderstood comedy stage hypnotists. You, once you are a professional stage hypnotist, could join this independent trade union, if you so desire. (Personally, I would recommend it.) I, myself, am a member, but in the end, it's your choice to join or not. At the time of writing, to join equity, all applicants have to supply contractual evidence, detailing their professional engagements. The requirement is a minimum of eight one off contracts at professional fees, these are the ones which should be submitted when wishing to join. Of these, two should be for shows within the last month, two should be for forthcoming shows and the other four should be for shows that you have done within the last year. When you have got a few shows under your belt, and a few bookings in advance, I am confident that your membership will then be processed without any problems, I will, of course, as your tutor, sponsor you for membership. Equity are our representatives, so to speak, in important matters, and here I quote Eddie Saville, the Assistant Secretary of Variety for Equity, in a recent letter.

"Clearly, Equity monitor all aspects of the industry, and we are aware of the current publicity which stage hypnotism is getting. We will watch very carefully the developments in this area of our business, and will react accordingly to defend our members interests, should this be considered appropriate."

This statement is clearly an expression of the Trade Unions support for stage hypnotists, a much misunderstood area of the showbusiness industry. For more information on joining criteria etc., send a S.A.E. to:

Equity, Guild House, Upper Street, Martins Lane, London England, WC2H 9EG. Telephone: 0171 379 6000

Equity, 65 Bath Street, Glasgow, Scotland, G2 2BX. Telephone 0141 332 1669.

Equity, Conavon Court, 12 Blackfriars Street, Salford, Manchester, England, M3 5BQ. Telephone 0161 832 3183

Equity, Transport House, 1 Cathedral Street, Cardiff, Wales.
Telephone 01222 397971

As a note on the side, once you have got your equity card, if you get a photograph and CV done and sent off to several Theatrical Casting Agencies, (see Stage and TV Paper). Then you may be able to earn some extra money doing television and film extra work or small parts. Not to mention the possibilities of TV Commercials etc. When you are a member of Equity, they will gladly advise you on how to go about entering this field of work, also give you any advice on the show business industry in general, which you feel you may need to ask.

PUBLIC LIABILITY INSURANCE.

Hypnosis is, I've already state several times, a totally harmless state, however, because the effects of it are all in the mind it would be very hard to prove that the ex-subjects are not a result of our hypnosis. We know it's just not the case, they know it's not the case, but if someone did decide to sue you, in a way like this, for psychological damage or making them feel ill. It would then be your problem to defend yourself in court and prove that it was not hypnosis that did it. So unless you are very rich, an incident such as this example, which by the way, is highly unlikely to occur anyway, (but better safe that sorry), would make you bankrupt trying to defend yourself in court. Unless you had taken out suitable public liability insurance, which would then cover you for the costs of legal cases etc.

Another reason for getting public liability insurance, is that it also covers you if someone falls over your equipment, or your speaker drops onto their head. Once again, the compensation, or the legal costs, would be paid for you by the insurance company.

Lastly, and probably, most importantly, another reason you must have public liability insurance is to be able to get your licences for the shows you do granted in most UK towns. Although it's not part of the 1952 hypnotism act, most UK towns will now only give permission for a hypnotic show to take place if you have got one million pounds worth of public liability insurance cover. This cover must also cover members of the audience, who are actually going to be hypnotised. So all in all, as a working professional, it's a necessary expense, which of course is tax deductible.

If you intend to practise in therapy only, the insurance premiums are more easily obtainable and carry far less premiums – around £50 per annum- and an application form is supplied . You may be required to provide a copy of you're Qualification Diploma which can be obtained by visiting our site of **www.hypnotherapycourse.net**

A million pounds cover, which includes the people being hypnotised, can be obtained direct from Lloyds Insurance in London. As an individual going to them who's just started in the industry, you'll be quoted between £1000 to £2000 per year for insurance cover.

It is, non the less, possible to obtain one million pounds worth of insurance cover, which also includes the people being hypnotised, for just a few hundred pounds per year. You can get this by joining one of the professional bodies for the stage hypnotism industry and then applying for insurance cover through them.

As a member of a respected society the insurers, see you as a competent person who, in their eyes, is a lower risk and that's why lower premiums are available to members.

For more details please contact:

The Professional Organisation of Stage Hypnotists (P.O.S.H) Incorporating The Association of Professional Stage Hypnotists (APSH)

And for Therapists contact The Royle Institute of Hypnotherapy and Psychotherapy (RIHP) incorporating The Association of Complete Mind Therapists (ACMT)

BOTH MAY BE CONTACTED AT THIS ADDRESS

The President, Dr. Jonathan Royle – BSc (Hon)
C/O Prospect House Publishing
Prospect House, P.O. Box 12, Huddersfield, England, HD8 9YP
Tel: +44 (0) 1484 – 861522 or 07050-377579.
www.hypnotherapycourse.net– www.hypnotictraining.com

By joining one of the above societies, the insurance companies, know then for certain, that you have signed a legal document to agree that whilst a member of the society you will:

A Abide by the 1952 Hypnotism Act and Amendments of 1972.
B Abide by the 1989 Government guidelines for hypnotists.
C Will only work in a venue with permission by the council.
D Are a working professional Stage Hypnotist who knows their craft.
E Will, in general, do a clean, safe, ethical show, which cannot harm anyone.

In other words, they then know that you are an extremely low risk and as such, it's highly unlikely that they will ever have to pay out.

To join this society, I'd advise that you send them a S.A.E. for membership details. In general, however, you need to show several contracts from past and future shows, as with joining Equity. You usually have to already be an Equity member and you also send them a copy of your publicity materials and agree to abide by all the points that I've just mentioned. All such societies have a membership fee, some cost more than others, some give value for money and some don't. So it's it up to you which you join. Once a member, you can then approach the insurance companies and get your one million pounds cover for a modest fee. Most of the societies will send you details and application forms for the insurance upon you joining them, you then just pay your fee, and they do the rest for you on your behalf.

For interests sake though, here are the details of a UK Based Insurance company which offer Stage Hypnosis insurance cover for people located anywhere in the World.

StoneLynx Insurance Services
15a East Street, Okehampton,
Devon, England, EX20 1AS
Tel: +44 (0) 1837-659-359
www.stonelynk.com

At the time of this publication (2005) a colleague Jonathan Chase also claims to be offering members of his group Stage Hypnosis Insurance Cover for anywhere in the world and he can be contacted on:

The Academy of Hypnotic Arts
P.O. Box 186, Falmouth,
Cornwall, England, TR11 4WB
+44 (0) 870 – 777 – 8896
www.hypnoarts.com

And another English Hypnotic Source who claims on their site to be able to supply Stage Hypnosis Insurance is:

www.davidknight.net

And here are the contact details of a UK Based Insurance Company for Hypnotherapy Insurance.

SMG Professional Risks
31 Clarendon Road
Leeds, England, LS2 9PA
Tel: +44 (0) 113 – 294- 4000
www.smg-professional-risks.co.uk

For those in America and indeed anywhere else in the World I would recommend that you Join The National Guild of Hypnotists as they will help you source suitable insurance cover and their contact details are:

The National Guild of Hypnotists
P.O. Box 308, Merrimack,
NH 03054, USA
Tel: (603) – 429 – 9438
www.ngh.net

To become a full member of R.I.H.P. and/or P.O.S.H. the only requirement, after studying this course is to complete the final test paper which can be obtained from **www.hypnotherapycourse.net** The test is not difficult, provided that you have studied this course thoroughly, you will be asked questions on varied subjects. The aim of the exam is to confirm your knowledge of hypnosis, how it works, how to deal with various problems which may occur and to ensure that you have started to think like a professional, safe and ethical hypnotist.

You can, however, be confident that when you pass the test paper and be awarded your certificates, then you will be more than able to safely and competently conduct your own successful comedy stage hypnotism show, or practise as a competent theapist and be able to enter a most exciting, interesting and very lucrative industry.

INSURANCE, CATCH 22 SOLVED

To get insurance for stage work, you are placed into a catch 22 situation, as to join certain societies which can get you the insurance, you need several contracts from past shows to give them. And to do many shows these days you need the public liability insurance, which is where the catch 22 situation is created. The obvious way around this would be to make up some fake contact, which could then be used to gain membership to both Equity and your chosen hypnotic society. However, although you may get away with this, I don't recommend it, as it's fraud.

What I do recommend is this, contact SMG Professional Risks, the insurer in Leeds (address elsewhere) and ask them to send you the application form for one million pound cover for a hypnotherapist. When the form arrives, you fill it in and send it back along with a copy of your hypnotherapy diploma, This copy of diploma and the completed form are returned along with a cheque to the company. Then your cover note of insurance is sent back, and you are covered as a hypnotherapist for 12 months, for any claim up to one million pounds, this will include all people who you will hypnotise. This is worth every penny, as:

A. It means you can open up a therapy clinic and treat people with hypnotherapy for their emotional problems and:

B. You will also be able to get your licences for shows granted by the local councils, but how, I hear you cry.

Well, quite easy really, the proof of insurance certificate will say on it Hypnotherapist Public Liability cover, which includes hypnotised people and also have on it your name and contact details etc. You must send this along with your application for permission to be granted. On your covering letter, which should be sent typed upon your letterhead, it says you are a hypnotherapist, not a stage hypnotist and you want permission for a light hearted demonstration of how hypnosis can be used for entertainment and for therapy. As you will be agreeing to the 1952 hypnotism act, and as far as they are concerned you have your insurance cover, which says Hypnotherapist, and as it says the same on your letterhead, they have no reason at all not to grant you permission. Even from a legal point of view it's not fraud, as you will be a qualified hypnotherapist, that's why you got the insurance cover. And hypnotherapists sometimes do public demonstrations for research purposes, so if ever a claim was made against you to the insurers, you'd say the demonstration was for research purposes, which a hypnotherapist is entitled to do without even being granted permission from the local council. So, because of loopholes in the 1952 hypnotism act, technically speaking, if you say the show is for research purposes every step of the way, then you'll be covered by the insurance and not have to apply for permission to be granted by the councils before your shows go ahead.

If you do operate things in this way, then there is one more thing which I would do. That is to inform the audience right at the start of your act, that anyone who comes up onto the stage is volunteering to take part, and as such, takes full responsibility for their actions. Here, the line, "You came of your own free will, and remain at your own risk," comes in useful. Before you place the people who come onto the stage, under hypnosis, you ask them for their permission, now, if they agree and they were to hurt themselves or tried to sue you for side effects, then they would not have a leg to stand on. The reason for this being, English law states that if a person willingly place themselves in a position of possible danger, then they are the only ones who can be held responsible for any consequences as a direct result. So you always warn them, that, if the partake they have volunteered and also gain their permission to hypnotise them. Then as long as you don't break the 1952 hypnotism act, all the risk then becomes theirs, as they have willingly placed themselves into a potentially dangerous position of possible danger. We will now move on to the subject of how to get permission for your shows granted by the councils legitimately.

THE 1952 HYPNOTISM ACT

In order to perform as a stage hypnotist at public venues, by that, I mean pubs, theatres, civic halls etc., you need to apply by law for permission from the relevant local councils licensing department for your show to go ahead. Failure to do this can result in a fine for you, a fine for the venues licensee and the venue can lose its entertainment licence. As a professional and ethical stage hypnotist, who agrees to abide by the 1952 hypnotism act and 1989 government guidelines, being a hypnotist who's got public liability insurance and is a member of both a professional hypnotic society such as P.O.S.H.. and also in Equity, your permission will usually be granted without any problems whatsoever.

If, however, the permission is not granted, then you can make an appeal through the Magistrates Court. If this ever needs to be done, just phone up the clerk of the court and explain that you want to make an immediate appeal against the decision, he will advise you of how to go about it, as would your professional hypnotic society. This court appeal can also be used in towns who say they have "banned" hypnotists, and it is possible to have the "ban" lifted in court so that your performance can go ahead. So never think that anyone can stop you from performing. The only snag with this, is that the council themselves have seven days to appeal. So from the date of your appeal, until the date the permission is granted by the court will be about 10 days, so if your show fell within those 10 days it could not go ahead. If you give the council their 28 days to process your application and allow extra time for court appeals, then there should never be a problem and your shows should always go ahead as planned. It has to my knowledge, never happened yet, but if your appeal in court also proved to be unsuccessful, then you could always go ahead with the show anyway by doing it in the way that I will explain later and your show would still be operating 100% legally.

By the way, doing it this way, you would not be in a position where they could sue you. Now there are a few important points to remember, the first is that you are only responsible for getting the permission if you are promoting the show yourself, ie. when hiring a theatre etc. However, when you are booked to perform at a venue with your show, then it is the person who has booked you and given you the contract for the show who is responsible for seeking this permission from the council. If neither of these is the case then the venue itself is responsible for applying for the permission. For example, if booked for a pub, through an agent, it would be the pub licensees problem. You would be well advised, however, to inform all venues and booking agents, that they have to apply for permission from the local authority for your act to go ahead. Should you then be booked and no application has been made, as will usually be the case, then the show would go ahead with no problems. But if a police constable did enter the premises to check if permission had been granted then as you'd warned them, legally you would not be in the wrong, this could be stipulated in your show booking contract.

To apply for permission, when promoting your own shows, I would advise that you follow the following procedures:

1 If possible, go to the relevant councils licensing department (or phone) and obtain the appropriate application from them for permission for a hypnotic show to be granted.

2 When the form arrives, fill in all the details and send it back by registered mail, or recorded delivery, so you have proof of it's postage, along with the following items:

A Your Equity membership number

B Copy of your public liability insurance certificate

C Copy of your professional stage hypnotists society diploma

D A copy of your hypnotherapy diploma

E A copy of your first aid at work diploma if you have one

F A brief outline of the shows contents, so that they know it's not obscene

G A couple of complimentary tickets for the show, with the request that, if they are not satisfied with the enclosed, they are welcome to send anyone to attend the show to view it and check that it is as you've detailed to them.

H The names, addresses and contact details of six venues, at which you have performed within the past six months and who will, if the council ask for it, supply them with a reference that your show was conducted safely etc.

I Also, if you have one or two references from venues/agents etc., already, which state that they felt your show was conducted safely, ethically and also professionally, then send these as well.

This whole package should be sent at least 28 days prior to the performance date so that they can consider it. If you want to allow time for a possible court appeal, then the package should be sent at least 35 days prior to the show.

3 Call them the next day, after sending the package, to confirm that it has arrived and is in the hands of the correct people.
If you have heard nothing by the end of the second week, then call up again and pin them down to a definite time and date upon which the decision will be made. If need be you have also here another chance to send copies of everything to them if they have "misplaced" it.

4 You will, by the time of the show, either hear that permission has been granted, or not. If not, continue with the court appeal and I'm sure the show will go ahead. If you should hear nothing, which sometimes happens, then as you've made every possible effort to help the council come to a decision and can prove this, I would just go ahead with the show anyway. As if they did try taking you to court, they would be laughed at when you told the judge you had carried out the above mentioned procedures to the letter.

If you follow this procedure to the letter, then there is no reason at all why they can possible not grant you permission for your show.

Oh yes, and one last point, some councils charge a fee for processing the permission, in Trafford it's £16.50, and in Blackpool, I was quoted £110. But they are allowed to add any extra conditions they desire, unfortunately. Also some councils, such as Bury, Bolton and Preston, have a complete ban on hypnotists at public shows, however, this can usually be remedied in court. The councils which do impose a ban cannot, however, stop any shows which are run in private members clubs, or at private parties. Also they cannot stop any which are for research purposes. So don't worry too much, as there are so many loopholes in the hypnotism laws that there's a way around them all. Remember to check though, as each council has different bye laws and can also add different conditions to your permission to perform if they so wish.

LEGALLY BREAKING THE 1952 HYPNOTISM ACT

This next section will explain how to completely break the 1952 hypnotism act legally. This means, you will be able to perform at places where hypnotism is usually banned, or where they will not grant you permission to perform. The best thing is, you won't be breaking the law, you will, in fact, just be exploiting the loopholes within it. This of course is very useful information to know, however, I accept no responsibility for anyone using this information and anyone doing so, does so at their own risk. If you wish to check the validity of what I say, then please consult your solicitor for more details and show them what I am about to reveal to you.

BREAKING THE GOVERNMENT GUIDELINES 1989

A Read section A, and you will see this is down to commonsense only.

B Section B states, "no person shall be caused, while under the influence of hypnotism, to do, or say anything offensive to the audience which are there." Well this one is a matter of personal taste and censorship. So, for example, if you were doing a family show it would need to be very clean and non racist or sexist etc. However, if you were doing an adults only show, and the posters and advertising stated "stay away if easily offended", then there would be no comeback to be made, as you would have warned people that they were to see a show for broad minded adults only. Also, as it's down to personal taste and censorship, the only problem could be if several people complained who had not been warned what they were about to see.

C Section C, part 1 says: "any experiment involving the age regression of the subject." Well, it's only age regression, if they really regress in their minds back to that age. However, if you tell them, that when they awaken they will "imagine" they are 8 years of age, then they will only imagine it and as such, from a legal view point it is only roleplay and not genuine age regression.

Section C, part 2 states: "the giving of hypnotherapy, or any other treatment." Well, look at section D of the 1952 hypnotism act and you'll notice that nothing in the act shall prevent the demonstration of hypnosis for scientific or research purposes, or for the treatment of mental or physical disease and as such, there is not anything in the act which can stop you. As such, you can carry out hypnosis to stop people smoking etc. which lets be honest, is caused by habit (in the mind), and can cause physical disease, so you are in effect treating both things at once. Therefore you can do hypnotherapy and if you were to stop a couple of people smoking and helped a couple of people loose weight within your show, then essentially your demonstration could be classed as being for the treatment of mental and physical disease. As such, no licence would be needed to do the show, as the act does not stop demonstrations of this kind.

PART THREE: "Any experiment in which the subject is suspended between two supports as in Catalepsy." Well, as I said earlier, if you inform them of what they are to do, and they then agree to take part, they have willingly placed themselves into a position of possible harm. As such, English law states you could not be prosecuted if they are hurt by accident, as they volunteered to take part, in full knowledge of what they were to be made to do. Also it does not stop you "hypnotising" the female partner of your act, then performing the "Catalepsy" upon her, as she too, would have volunteered and as such, it is her responsibility. Or you could get your female assistant to present it and you could self-hypnotise yourself and be the one who is supported across the backs of two chairs, here it was your own personal choice and as such, nothing can be done.

PART FOUR: "The giving of suggestions to the subject that they should perform any act or behave in any manner which is likely to be interpreted as indecent, offensive or harmful, nor that they shall consume any substance which is either noxious or harmful." Well, once again, it comes down to taste and censorship. So if anything some class as "rude" is to be done, then make sure that these types of people are not at the show, by warning them of the shows nature in your advertising, then it will not be considered "rude" by the people at the event. Also, as for the consumption of harmful or noxious stuff is concerned, an onion is part of many peoples every day diet, so it is not noxious or harmful, in fact it is healthy to eat. So making people eat an onion believing it to be an apple is OK. Also, if someone was given a tin of catfood to eat believing it to be jelly, well catfood has to be fit for human consumption, as such, it cannot be noxious. You could, of course, just empty out the tin, wash it and then fill it with meat pate to act as a cat food substitute. So here, it is down to using your own common sense.

PART FIVE: "no persons under 18 shall be placed into trance." Well if both parents are present and it is witnessed by the full audience, and the child is also willing to take part, then as long as the parents agree that their child can partake, it technically is legal and the responsibility then lies with child's parents. However, I would never hypnotise anyone on stage under the age of 16, even with the consent of their parents and to be honest, I wouldn't consider it wise to use under 18 at all. In fact, you'll have so many people wishing to take part, that you'll never need to even consider doing this. If someone under 18 does take part in your show, without parental consent, then your only defence is that you honestly did not know and believed that they were old enough to participate.

SECTION D: Obviously it's common sense to cancel out all suggestions you give the subjects before they leave the building. However, you can give them suggestions to carry out in the interval, even when you are not around, just so long as they are in the building in which the show is taking place at all times. And, of course, if they have been commanded that, should they leave the building for any reason, all suggestions will immediately be cancelled out, then there aren't any problems which can occur.

SECTION E: Have in small letters on the description that you submit to council, "subject to change without notice", then once the permission is granted, you can with the law, do as you so desire.

SECTION F: This speaks for itself, but you can pay people to play along as if hypnotised because they aren't in a real trance.

SECTION G: Once again, use your common sense here, but it's down to censorship, personal taste and obviously where the advertising is to be displayed.

SECTION H: Do exactly as it says, there is no need to ever break this rule.

SECTION I: You can't break this, but there again, if the subjects have volunteered, then they have no legal comeback on you.

SECTION J: There is not need to ever break this rule.

SECTION K: No need to ever break this, but if you're a qualified first aider up to health and safety at work standards, then you could get away with playing that angle. Otherwise, send free tickets to your doctor and get him/her to come along, you will then have given them a free night out and you've kept to the conditions.

SECTION L: No need to ever break this, but as you'll see the 1952 act has more loopholes than may have first thought.

SECTION M: As these are actual law and I don't know the loopholes in them, you had best abide by them 100%.

BREAKING THE 1952 ACT

A. This does not stop shows in private members clubs, or shows of a private nature where the audience are invited guests only.

B. Again, it does not stop shows of a private nature, or shows held in private members clubs, such as social working mens clubs etc.

C. Once again, it may be possible to use under 18's if they consent and consent has been given by both parents. As the act says, a police constable may enter the premises if they feel the act has been broken, however, note these very important points. As you cannot be prosecuted for a crime until it's been carried out, in much the same way, even if you were illegally breaking the act which you don't need to, the police cannot stop it until you've finished, unless the show is pornographic and breaks standard laws of England and Wales. They can enter and stay there until the end of the show, then arrest you for breaking the law, but they cannot stop the show whilst it's occurring, or proof to commencement. As what right have they got to stop a legal show before it starts, as they don't know for certain what you will be doing and whether it will break the law. You can only be prosecuted for a crime if you have committed that crime, you are innocent until proven guilty, remember that. Another point here is, they can't exactly stop the show anyway when the subjects are in trance, as then they would be placing the subjects into a position of potential harm. Because the act only says that police constables may enter the premises, this means that council officials have, in fact, no legal right whatsoever, to come in. In actual fact, as it's up to each venue owner who they allow to enter their premises or not (when you're booked) and when you've hired a venue, it's at your discretion who is admitted to the venue. So if they tried to enter the venue without permission, they would in fact then be breaking the law themselves and would be trespassing. It is only the police who have a legal right to enter when they wish, and even then they must have a justifiable reason to believe that something is being done to break the law.

D. As mentioned earlier, this means you can do hypnotherapy whenever you wish, as long as it's for "research purposes" or purposes of a scientific nature.

E. This means, that if the subjects upon the stage hypnotised themselves and then you just conducted or directed the show, then it could go ahead without permission and would not be breaking the law. So in order that the subjects have legally hypnotised themselves you must not touch them during the process of induction. If you touch them, then you have induced the trance, however, if you don't touch them and say things such as, "I'd like you to allow yourself to relax and allow yourself to go deeper", then when they react they are allowing themselves to do it. As such, it's self hypnosis and as a consequence, the 1952 act has no validity whatsoever. Your show can then go ahead without permission, and also you can perform catalepsy etc., as it does not fall under the act of 1952, as they've hypnotised themselves and volunteered. Lets take this one step further, you could even call yourself a "persuasionist" or "relaxationist", instead of a hypnotist, you could then say you are just going to guide them into a deep relaxation not a trance, not a sleep state and certainly not hypnosis. This then completely blows the 1952 act apart, but you would of course have to be careful to never mention the words sleep or trance within your act. Instead you would just have to use the word relax all the time. This means you're then 100% in the clear to do as you wish, as the act does not stop self induced hypnosis and it certainly does not stop you helping people to relax a little more.

F This section is irrelevant, with what we are dealing with here.

Well I hope you now see just how badly worded the 1952 hypnotism act and 1989 guidelines are, and just how easy it is to exploit the massive loopholes to our own advantage.

So you are booked to do a show, or are promoting a show yourself and either they will not grant you permission to perform, or the council has banned hypnotism shows in that area. What do you do? Well, here are five ways in which you can legally go ahead with your show, even if the council has not, or will not grant any form of permission.

1. If the venue that has booked you, is a private members club, then permission need not ever be applied for. The reason for this being, it's not then classed as a public show. Private members clubs usually include places such as, Labour and Conservative clubs, special interest clubs, working men's clubs etc. So here alone there are more than enough venues at which to earn a living from and they are exempt from the 1952 act.
2. Any show at which the audience are specially invited guests and it's not open to the general public at large. For example, wedding receptions, birthday parties etc.
3. If your show is one open to the public and is to be held in a public venue, such as a pub or theatre etc., then the way round it is this. You advertise that only members of your private fanclub are allowed to enter on the night, this makes the show a private members club performance, as such no permission is needed. You, however, point out that temporary one night memberships to your fan club are available for just £10, or whatever the intended ticket price was to be. So as they are paying for a one night membership to a private members club, and not purchasing a ticket to a public show, then it's legal to perform without permission being granted by the council. As of course full members of your fanclub, which may or may not exist, are admitted free of charge.
4. As we have already discussed, no permission is needed if the show is for research or scientific purposes. So if you were to advertise that the show is for research purposes, this is the loophole. If asked what you are researching, you can say, "I am researching the effects of Hypnosis and Hypnotic suggestions, and who these things affect most." ie, what age group responds best, are men better subjects than women, can people be hypnotised easily in public etc. I'm sure by now you've got the general idea, by saying this it's up to them to prove you were not researching these things and that's practically impossible.
5. The 1952 act does not include hypnotism, mesmerism etc., which is self induced, as such, if you require to perform without a permission then just word your suggestions carefully as earlier detailed and have the people place themselves into the hypnotic state.

So there we have it, you now know how to completely break both the 1952 act and Government guidelines, you are also in a position to perform when you so desire, without applying for a permission to perform. Use this knowledge, like all other knowledge in this course, wisely, also keep it to yourself at all times. If someone else wants to know the details within this course don't tell them, or lend it, you paid hard earned money to find all this out, it's only right that other people should do the same.

To end the subject of laws relating hypnosis, allow me to say this, at the time of going to press, in England you don't need any qualifications to become a hypnotist or hypnotherapist, as such, there is nothing to stop you setting up a show or consulting room. This, however, I feel is a ridiculous situation, as it means there are so many cowboys getting away with giving our misunderstood business a bad name. I will end this chapter, by giving you the criteria which mush be met in order to join the Professional Organisation of Stage Hypnotists and The Association of Complete Mind Therapists.

THE ASSOCIATIONS - (P.O.S.H.) and (A.C.M.T.)

Membership to P.O.S.H. and A.C.M.P. means that you will comply to a code of ethics of the very highest order. All venues and booking agents and councils will know that as a member, you will always present a safe, legal and ethical performance. This means, that permissions to perform, which are applied for, will be granted without any problems. As a member, you will receive a certificate of membership, which is signed. This can be displayed in you consulting rooms, or copied and then sent out to councils to prove that you are indeed, a member when applying for permission to perform.

P.O.S.H. and A.C.M.T. members are encouraged to help each other out in anyway that they can and we promote an equal opportunities scheme. We are neither racist nor sexist. As a member you can obtain professional help and back-up support and advice. Special seminars at discounted rates are organised for members on all areas of the hypnotism industry and related subjects.

Our aim is to professionalise the art of hypnosis on stage and in therapy and with our standards. People will always know that when booking a member they are booking a safe, legal and ethical professional performer, who knows their craft 100%.

All members and students of this course are also invited to join our private members Yahoo Internet News & Chat Group on which you may learn even more about the fascinating art of Hypnosis.

To join simply visit *http://groups.yahoo.com/group/hypnotorious* or simply send us an email request along with your contact details to join at ***hypnotorious@yahoogroups.com***

PART TWELVE

MAKING MONEY FROM STAGE HYPNOSIS

This chapter contains stacks of knowledge, which has been obtained from real life practical experience and can help you make up to £36,000 or more in your first year of trading. If you follow my step by step plan to hypnotic success, then financial freedom can be yours.

This part of the course, is a collection of advice on how to get to the top, quickly and with as little effort or expense as possible. You see I live by an old saying of millionaires, "why work hard, when you can work smart." In order to do this, you must grab every opportunity that comes your way, now don't say you never have opportunities and that you are unlucky, because I will suggest that this is not true. In this life you create your own "luck" and "opportunities". In fact, I truly believe and my own personal life experience shows me, that the only limitations, which we have in life, are those that we psychologically impose upon ourselves. So never forget that positive thinking is a most positive force, as it breeds positive actions and from positive actions come positive success, as it brings you one step closer to your ultimate goals, whatever they may be.

I'll give you another two sayings here, which contain within them the secrets of success. A. "As man thinketh, so he becomes" and B. "How do you eat a big elephant?" Answer: "One spoonful at a time and very slowly, but you'll get there in the end if you don't give up."

Remember, inch by inch, piece by piece, it is possible. You may be thinking that this is all starting to sound like an American Motivational Training Seminar, on how to run your life and the reason for that is, because it is. In the days of Music Hall and like, the motto would have been, "it's 99% show and 1% business" which will open the door of success. Now I'd say, in this modern day, it's "99% business and 1% show", which will give you the income and lifestyle that others only ever dream of.

What I'm saying is, learn your hypnotism, yes. In fact, learn it off by heart, but once it's second nature to you, spend 99% of your time on sales, marketing and publicity. Remember, it doesn't matter what product you are selling, but the way that you sell it is all important. If you are an unknown act, then you want to get famous quickly, as then you'll be in great demand and as the economic laws of supply and demand state, you will then be able to charge more for your shows. And charge even more if you are unique in the style of act you do, as then you have a competitive edge. If you can afford it, get a good Public Relations Agency working for you right from the start. This will cost you a few thousand pounds per year, but they really can make you a star "overnight", and turn you into the countries most publicised and talked about hypnotist. Once you're a household name, you will automatically be earning telephone number style fees for your theatre shows. A public relations company will create a huge nationwide or worldwide demand for you right from day one for your career, if you have the money to invest into your future. After a while, the media, radio and TV will all come and ask you for stories, by which time you'll just be referring them to your personal manager.

Another way to make it, probably the cheapest, is through personal contacts that you know, as, remember the old saying, "it's not what you know, but who you know," is indeed very true.

I will now, also make what some will consider to be a very controversial statement, but I speak here from personal experience. The casting room couch syndrome still exists. Oh yes it does. If you're male and you can hang out in the bars, where the people to meet go. Then if you've got the charm to chat up the females (or males if so inclined) and you are successful. You will also get many perks as a result. For example, I frequented a place called "Stringfellows" in London during March/April 1993, whilst working two shows a night, three nights a week on a weekly basis at the London Bus Emporium Night club, in High Wycombe. Although I only went in once or twice weekly, for four to six weeks, I made several contacts, who are indirectly, or in some cases directly responsible for the position I hold within the Hypnotic industry today. I'm just making the point that, if you want peanuts you associate with monkeys, if you want gold, see the organ grinder.

Remember, each person you establish as a close contact on first name terms should be treated with the very best respect , in return they will ensure you get that TV appearance instead of someone else. I know it sounds horrible, but that's the way this business really is at the top. For example, I once dated a female, who works for a certain television company, and during our relationship I got a lot of TV interviews and offers, it's a case of you scratch my back and I'll scratch yours. It's not that hard, despite what people say, to make it to the top business level (the top of the tree financially). The hard thing, however, is stopping yourself from getting knocked down again, once you're there, or at least, if you do get knocked down, being in a position where you never have to worry about money again before it occurs. Money can make you a sight happier than being on the dole. With money, you can live in the poshest area of town/city, drive a brand new sports car every year, wear suits that cost what an average person earns in a month. In fact, you can do whatever you want when you are financially secure. Setting goals is all important in life and business.

Remember, it must be in the mind first, before it becomes action or reality. It also helps to get mental images of what life will be like when you are in that successful position, act as though it's guaranteed to happen.

Another way, which I use to get work, is to have top quality publicity packs printed on the best quality paper. Then have them distributed to every single agent, venue, manager, show booker/promoter, holiday camp, theatre, in fact, every possible place you could work and could afford to send to. The more people who know of your services and know your name, the more likely you are to get lots of work. It's the law of averages. Have good, in fact, excellent materials for publicity made up first, and if monies are short, send out good quality photocopies from these professional laser copy quality masters.

As soon as you can afford to have a promotional video of your act done, then do so and duplicate many copies of the tape. This tape, with colour laser copy cover, should be sent to all the top people in the business, who can afford to pay the kind of fee which you wish to be earning. So don't start from the bottom, like most people. Keep going, contact all the top people and you yourself should take control, act rich, dress rich, live beyond your means for a few months, go thousands into debt on your plastic cards, lease a flashy sports car and guess what? Yes, you'll owe a whole stack of money, but also you'll start earning huge sums of money, as people always like to give money for anything in life, to those who don't seem to need it. (Don't ask me why, but they do.)

Another way, is to hire shows and self promote shows yourself, not forgetting, of course, to send free tickets to agents, media and TV etc., so that they come and see you working live. Theatres can usually be hired on a straight fee basis or a percentage split of the door take, which means no risk to you except advertising costs etc.

Keep plodding along in this vein, keep phoning the agents you mailed your publicity to and then you'll get given some poor gigs by them to shut you up.

Do an excellent show, even if it means on this one occasion, using loads of stooges, as you can bet your life that a representative from the agency will be in to watch you, so be world class and then you'll get classy work as a result. From there, you may be lucky and get a personal manager, which then means, they do all the marketing, telephone calls etc. You can concentrate on what you do best, which is showing up early at the venues and doing world class shows every night you are booked to perform. Success is then near.

A weekly publication which you should subscribe to, which runs adverts from venues and agents requiring acts for immediate work, is the Stage and Television Today, you can subscribe to it by contacting them directly at:

The Stage and Television Today Newspaper
47 Bermondsey Street
London
SE1 3XT
Tel: +44 (0) 207–403–1818
www.thestage.co.uk

A yearly publication called Showcall, which is sent to all agents, venues and bookers, is well worth running a full page advert in, at a cost of just under £100 for the year, it's a bargain at that small cost. The advert just bears your photo, contact details and notable achievements to date upon it, but please remember, the KISS principle of sales and marketing. Keep It Short and Simple. To place your own personal advert in next years edition of this vital book, contact them directly by sending a S.A.E. for full details to them at:

Showcall Publication
47 Bermondsey Street
London
SE1 3XT
www.showcall.co.uk

Another place in which it is worth running an advert and, believe it or not, the adverts are free of charge. They do produce results, as I have found out.

The White Book International Production Directory
Bank House, Warwick Road,
Coventry, England,
CV1 2EW
Tel: +44 (0) 2476–571171
www.whitebook.co.uk

Incidentally, it's also financially worthwhile to fund a box advert in the "artists" section of the Stage and TV paper. A decent sized advert, the size of a matchbox, costs as little as £10 per week to run and does produce profitable results.

From a marketing and sales point of view, I'd recommend three audio cassette training programmes, which really will help you onto the ladder of success. These are:

1. Unlimited Power by Anthony Robbins (6 cassettes).
2. Unlimited Power. 30 day guide to success (24 tapes and written textbook).
3. Lead the Field by Earl Nightingale (6 cassette programme).

All three of these highly recommended audio training programmes contain the tried, tested and proven to work secrets of success and, I would say, have changed my life. I know it sounds corny, but it's also very true. These audio courses and more are available from:

Nightingale Conant
2 Aspen Units
Aspen Way
Yalberton Industrial Estate
Paignton
Devon
TQ4 7QR
Tel: +44 (0) 803 - 666100
www.nightingale.com

Also a book, which I'd consider essential reading, is The Magic of Show Business by Simon Lovell . This is available from:

Magic Books By Post
29 Hill Avenue,
Bedminster
Bristol, England
BS3 4SN

This company also supply numerous other titles which would be of use to the trainee hypnotists.

The Simon Lovell book is one that I value highly, as it reveals in detail the secrets of getting TV, Radio and Media publicity on a national scale and on a regular basis. How to get work, get an agent and then a personal manager.

To continue, business cards should be carried at all times, and state that you do both stage shows and private hypnotherapy consultations, if this be the case. Hand these out to everyone you meet, people are fascinated by hypnosis, the card will be kept and may result in a show, or therapy session being booked at a later date. It happens more often than you'd think. Remember, that Word of Mouth advertising is, by far, the best on earth, so get in the media as much as possible and do some regular shows of a high standard and very quickly, you'll get a good reputation, both within and outside of the business. Remember the old show business adage, that all publicity is good publicity, just so long as they spell your name correctly. I whole heartedly believe this to be true. As Barnum and Bailey, the American Circus Proprietors, once said, if you have something to sell them, then advertise it, even if it's with your last dollar. But make sure you have a product worth selling first.

Another avenue of work available, is to work the forces bases, this itself, is good in two respects, A. It's good money and B. The people who will see you are more than used to taking orders and as such, will go under very easily.

Most of this work is obtained through Entertainment Agents around the world and a good source of their contact details is the site of ***www.entsweb.co.uk*** and for England you can also look at ***www.yell.com*** and search for Entertainment Agents.

So with these contact details, I leave you to find and explore that field of work, which for many hypnotists has proven to be very successful and financially rewarding.

You may still ask how do I get work? Well simple answer, go out there and find it. Where did you see a hypnotist work? Start there and try to book yourself in at that venue, as they are obviously open to the idea of a stage hypnotist. To convince a venue that has never had a hypnotist on before, say things, such as, "hypnotists are now so popular, I've had to turn people away at recent shows, due to the great public demand. You see, it's a very funny show, it's very popular and of course, your overall profits will be increased." The words, "your profits will be increased," do the trick and bring the greed factor into play. In fact it paints a mental picture in their mind of the financial gain they will make, that's what everyone in business wants, so you stand a damn good chance of closing the sale and getting the contract. It's in situations, as just mentioned, that a knowledge of sales and marketing comes in, as such, I, once again, recommend the audio courses from Nightingale Conat.

Now, a few more important points to cover, firstly agents. Your agent, or venue agent? Do not mix up the two breeds. Yours, theoretically, works for you, in practise, they work for themselves. They often represent a club or forces base, hotel or pub, and as such, you can only get work at that venue through them. They are the agent for that establishment, not for you. Remember, that they will charge you from 10% to 20% of your fee in commission for getting you the show. He/she will book in any hypnotist that they can get at the right price and will not actively seek work for you and you alone. A personal manger, well, they look after you, arrange where you work, when, for how much and in fact, all that's necessary to arrange, they do it and actively seek you work. His or her fee is an arrangement made between you both. It will most certainly be a higher percentage of commission than the agent takes, but then again, you'll be getting more and higher paid work as a result. You work for him on the same basis if you get a job yourself, you will still pay him his normal fee, or he can forbid you to do it because of the contract that you will have signed between you. He may, if you have the money, arrange for a public relations company to sell you to the public in various ways, which is well worth while, and can turn you into a star very quickly. If you get a good reliable manager, or even agent, then they are well worth sticking with, as you can then concentrate on what your best at doing, which is doing shows before audiences who wish to be entertained.

CONTRACTS

Your work as a Hypnotist, will be controlled by contracts, written or not. They stipulate all that both parties must do, by that I mean you and the show's booker. So read them carefully, including all small print and ensure that they are Equity approved. Make sure also, that you understand all that it says fully, as they are binding in law. You will often think the contract is with the venue, when in fact you may find it is with the agent. You see, by law, usually the person who signs the contract is your employer and, as such, is legally the person bound to the agreement by law. So I can only repeat, read them very carefully and if it's for work abroad, then ensure also that it's an Equity approved overseas contract. In fact, as an Equity member, ensure all your contracts are all Equity approved and if in doubt check with a solicitor before signing, better safe than sorry. I have at the end of this chapter included a copy of an example contract which is Equity approved and which is fairly self explanatory. Two copies are done, one signed by the booker is given to you, one signed by you is given to the booker. The legal agreement has then been made. You of course, can have your own contracts designed and extra clauses added. When you have a good reputation within the business, then you can have a clause in the contract which states that you get paid whether or not anyone ends up being placed under hypnosis. In other words, you get paid if you show up to perform and attempt a show whatever the actual outcome may be.

Always photocopy the contract you're given by the booker, leave the original at home and take the copy to the venue with you on the night as proof, should you have any difficulties in getting paid. The reason for the copy is simple, if it gets damaged or torn, then you will still have the original copy at home should you need it for later use in court to claim your money.

VIDEOS

If people want to video your act, unless it's TV etc., then amateur or not, the short answer should be **no.** Otherwise you charge them twice your normal fee for the show and restrict it's showing to no more than 10 persons at one time, for personal viewing only, not for commercial use. As such, it is never to be shown in a place of public or private entertainment. Put all this in writing, signed legally prior to the show and on your contract add a note that videos will not be allowed at the show and send a copy to the venue. Place a notice at the entrance doors to the theatre etc., stating that recording by any means mechanical or electronic is strictly forbidden unless prior written permission has been applied for and granted. If anyone then videos your show without consent, you can sue them and obtain substantial damages, but only if this procedure has been followed to the letter. Remember it's your lively hood which they are trying to steal from you.

CHASING YOUR FEE

If you have not been paid within a reasonable time, you have written asking for your money and you have a legal contract, then do this.

First write to the agent or venue, whoever is paying you and give them seven clear days to send you the money. Date the letter and keep a copy for yourself. This letter, incidentally, is sent by registered post. If, after 10 days have elapsed, you have not got the cash from them, then write again. This time stating that if you have not got the money in full by (give date 7 days later) then you will immediately issue a courts summons upon them in you local small claims court. If the money arrives even a day late, it will be too late, and the court costs will also be added and they will have to pay them once you have placed the matter into the hands of the court, which you will do seven days from date of letter. Again date this letter, take a copy and send by registered mail to them. Then if you do need to go to a small claims court don't worry, as the clerks will help you fill out all the forms to take out a summons. This is fairly cheap to do and you get it all back after the hearing from the agent or shows booker. It is heard by a local judge or registrar, they are most helpful, especially when you have the copy of all letters sent and original contract to show them. A free booklet is available from the court which will tell you in full the details which must be followed when making a claim. If you are and Equity member however, you can get them to do this for you on your behalf and at their expense, just so long as the contract issued was an Equity approved one.

PLACES TO WORK

Hire a theatre, a hall in the summer, either or both in a seaside town. Anywhere large numbers of people go for a holiday. Discount your tickets to the selling agent, tobacco kiosk, newsagents, corner shops, landladies and anywhere that will sell them for you and where the public go on a regular basis, this includes the pubs and hotels. Sometimes, give a very big discount if they buy a set number of tickets at once. Remember that it is much easier and more enjoyable to give a show in a large theatre than in a working mens club or public house. You can hire most theatres, especially on a Sunday night. If you want to hire for the summer season, then apply very early, as demand for the venue will be high. Apply to the local council for your licence long before you give the show, it can take them a long time to agree permission and of course if they don't, you can arrange another plan of action based on this course contents. It is also preferable to get your solicitor to apply for the licence on your behalf.

Telephone and send all your particulars to working men's clubs and similar venues. Most districts have their own club magazine, advertise in this and work will result. Find out all the addresses of forces bases that you can, and mailshot them, marking the letters for the attention of the Entertainment's Officer of the Officers Mess, the Sergeants Mess and the Corporals Mess. Find out the addresses of all the Holiday Camps that are privately run and send them your details also.

Also send your promotion pack to the entertainments officer at Head Office for Butlins, Warner and Haven Holidays etc., as they employ their own agents to supply them with acts. Also go to the travel agent and get loads of cruise brochures and send to the Head Office of each of the cruise companies your details, as this is a most lucrative and pleasurable field of work to be in. In other words, spend money sending your publicity pack everywhere that you could possibly imagine and from whom you might possibly get some work. You must always speculate in order to accumulate.

COMMERCIAL VIDEOS

Make certain that you know the terms of contract, as the video may be sold to anyone. Your show is personal to you and once it's on tape you could be losing money. It is better to forbid all videoing unless it involves substantial financial income to yourself. It's your livelihood they want to sell to others.

NO SOLE AGENT

This means you work for yourself, find your own jobs and do all your own publicity etc., whilst accepting shows off all and any agents who may wish to pass them your way. If you have good sales and marketing skills, then this may be the option for you.

SHOW LENGTH

Most Hypnotists give a club show of around 45 to 60 minutes of duration. A theatre show would be at least two hours, including the interval time and two hours thirty minutes is closer to the norm. Universities and college shows are usually 60 to 90 minutes long, forces bases are from one to two hours long. TV shows as long as they want it, will usually be timed in minutes. Your show length is of course up to you at all times and what the venue wish you to provide for them.

TV SHOWS

On TV you cannot do adult routines prior to 9pm, due to the threshold set down by the I.B.C. Family style hypnotic routines, can be aired at all times, but the full hypnotic induction cannot be shown or heard. Edited highlights, as in the Paul McKenna TV show, can however, be transmitted. On TV interviews always look directly at the interviewer, unless told otherwise.

When it's a live performance that's just being filmed, work as if no cameras are actually there, when being filmed think of the camera as your audience at home who are watching and these would be who you play your act to.

When you put the subject under prior to a TV show or break when live on air, then remember always to use a code word or phrase to control them when you are not around. This code word will also put them back under rapidly in the second half of the show. TV exposure is worth it's weight in gold, whether you are paid for the appearance or not it can ultimately lead to increased popularity in your act and as such, an increase in your performing fee.

INTERPRETERS

When working abroad, you will usually find that it's an English speaking audience you've been booked for, in which case no problem. If you are booked to appear abroad for the natives and you speak their language, then do the act in the foreign tongue. However, there may come a time when you need to work with an interpreter, don't let this scare you one tiny bit. It will work perfectly well if you follow these guidelines. Have a new voice over intro done for your act, which introduces you in the foreign language, by your interpreter, so think carefully what you are to say. For example, I'd take the trouble to learn the foreign pronunciation of the two words sleep and wide awake. You can then, via the interpreter, hypnotise them so that when you say sleep they will go back under and when you say awake they will awaken and do as they have been told by you via the interpreter. They will know you are speaking to them, as you'll place your hand upon their shoulder. Explain that your hand commands must be obeyed (make these up as needed.) At the start of the act appear to hypnotise the interpreter and place them under your control, now this may sound corny, but it must be done, so that you appear to be controlling them in order for the belief and expectancy factor to come into play. When hypnotising them use a method in which you are touching them, such as the falling backwards test, this means that you still get some kind of instant rapport with your subject. Apart from that, proceed as normal, just allowing for the fact that it has to be interpreted before it is acted upon. Oh yes, although you may be working through an interpreter, it's very handy to know enough of the local lingo in order to be able to order food and drink etc.

An excellent way to learn most foreign languages within a week, is with the Paul Daniels language courses that uses a memory system, which is so effective that even I managed to learn French in just a few hours. You can get full details of these by sending an email via the site of ***www.pauldaniels.co.uk***. I believe that the courses still cost around £150 per language to be learnt. This itself is excellent value for money and of course it's tax deductible.

PUBLICITY MATERIALS

Of course, if you are to send out top quality publicity materials to as many potential bookers as possible, then you will need to know from where to purchase them, so here's some leads for you.

STICKY BACK PHOTOS

These are photos of yourself, which are reproduced in different sizes and have a self adhesive back, making them ideal to stick to envelopes, letterheads and small posters etc. For details contact: Sticky Back Photos (Colab Ltd), Herald Way, Coventry, CV3 1BB. ***www.colab.com***

BUSINESS CARDS AND LETTERHEADS

Both are essential, as you'll come into contact with people everyday who potentially could offer you work and in any business you will always need to write letters. Local suppliers of both items can be found in your Yellow Pages. But as a general rule of thumb, for that successful image, always use Conquerer top quality paper for the letterheads and have the cards printed on finest quality cardstock. The place where I personally have all these kind of things printed is: ***www.woodwardprinters.co.uk***

BROCHURES AND POSTERS

Your brochure can of course be printed in black and white upon good quality paper, in which case Speedy Printing can help you. I however prefer full colour photographic brochures, as they look far more impressive and successful, that's the image that you need to create in order to demand big fees. The cheapest and best quality colour printers, I've found in the UK, are UK Flyers, Suite 210, Victory House, Somers Road North, Portsmouth, Hants, PO1 1PJ. Tel: +44 (0) 23 – 9229 – 3050. ***www.ukflyers.com***

PHOTOGRAPHS AND LARGE SHOW POSTERS

You will also require 10 x 8 colour repro photos to send to all potential bookers and agents etc. Also, possibly, postcard size colour photos for autographs etc. These items along with full colour cassette and Compact disc covers are available from **www.woodwardprinters.co.uk** At the time of writing, 10 x 8 colour photos with super gloss finish cost £179 per thousand, including caption, post and VAT. Delivery being free of charge and you also get 1,000 Full colour business cards Free with your order. 1,000 A3 full colour show posters are just £375 including delivery and VAT etc and again you get 1,000 Full colour business cards Free.

GENERAL PUBLICITY MATERIALS

Invoices, receipts, compliment slips, letterheads and in fact almost all printed matter are available, again by mail, order from Cornerstone Print, 1 Cecil Court, Pegrams Road, Staple Tye, Harlow, Essex, England, CM18 7QR. Tel: +44 (0) 1279 – 437851.

GOLD, SILVER FOIL BUSINESS CARDS ETC

For gold and silver metalic foil finish business cards and promotional merchandise, such as key rings, badges, mugs, cards, T-Shirts etc., which you can sell for profit at gigs simply look in the back of Exchange and Mart or search the Internet for a cheap good quality supplier.

PHOTO MASTER COPIES

To have photographic reproductions done by Woodward or UK Flyers, you will of course need a professional shot done in a studio first of all. To find a photographer who has experience of doing sessions for show business acts, look within the pages of The Stage and TV Newspaper. You may have to travel quite a distance, but the expense is well worth it. I can however recommend:

a. Michael on +44 (0) 161 792 5291
b. The Contact Studio on +44 (0) 161 860 4235

All three have experience in this field, for example they did my first ever shots and Michael, I believe, did some shots for Peter Powers (Hypnotist). You should look immaculate on the photo, make up can go a long way to helping achieve this desired effect. A straight 10 x 8 head and shoulders shot is all that you require to send out to agents etc. A full length postcard shot will do for autographs to give your fans after shows. For some reason, all stage hypnotists seem to do weird things with their hands on photo and on posters. Well on posters I think it looks OK and sets the scene, but on photos I think it looks crap and really all the agent wants to know is what you look like. A mirror held up in front of you can help you get the pose you wish the man behind the camera to see through his lens. As a general rule of thumb, I would say never look directly into a camera, unless a last resort.

SOLICITORS

At some time you'll need the services of a good solicitor and it helps to use one that has a sound knowledge of the showbusiness industry and how it works. As an Equity member, you will be put in touch with a suitable solicitor, but one that I personally have found to be excellent is: Flacks Ross Solicitors, 35 Peter Street, Manchester, England M2 5GD. Tel: +44 (0) 161 834 7368.

PROMO VIDEO MASTER

A promo video is a most valuable tool in getting work. As these days many agents and venues wish to see you perform before booking you and by having a video to show them it saves the need for an audition etc. You can have a cheap publicity video made for around £500 with a local company that you can find in Yellow Pages. However a broadcast quality video, shot by professional cameramen, on several cameras and professionally edited etc. will cost between £2000 to £3000, for everything that needs to be done to produce you master tape for you. From this master tape, numerous copies can then be made and sent to potential bookers, agents etc., and clips can even be used by TV companies, should they interview you, that's why you need your video to be of broadcast quality standard. Usually shot with two or three cameras, professionals will know how to make you look like a star. The expense is a once in a lifetime investment. It's tax deductable and if the tape is of broadcast quality you will usually be the first hypnotist chosen to go onto chat shows etc., as they can save both time and money by just paying you some extra money and transmitting material from your tape, instead of filming a hypnotist live at work. So in time, you can actually make a profit on your investment. Many production companies are around that can help you, they advertise in the pages of the Stage and TV

Newspapers. However, for information the company which do all my promotional tapes and teaching tapes etc. is: Prospect House Productions, Prospect House, P.O. Box 12, Huddersfield, England, HD8 9YP.

YOUR OWN PERSONAL REPORTER?

A personal pet reporter can also be invaluable, as they will, whenever they think of a story connected with hypnosis, contact you and feature you in it. A personal reporter is very hard to find and of course an element of trust must exist between you, which can only be created after a long working relationship of a harmonious nature. You will have to hang out where reporters go and buy them drinks, get friendly and then they'll do you favours. One important point I must mention here, is that most feature stories in newspapers only contain 10% or less of actual truth, the rest is untrue. However, the paper itself does not usually know this and only you and the freelance reporter will ever know. My pet freelance reporter has got me a feature spread in a leading ladies magazine, several features in the Sun and much more. You can find contact details for all worldwide TV, Radio, Newspapers, Magazines and Journalists via Internet the site of ***www.mediauk.com***

MAKE UP AND GROOMING

You must always look like a film star, both on and off stage, when you are in the show business industry. Every aspect of your personal grooming should be immaculate, but I'll cover this subject only briefly as it is dealt with in depth in, The Magic of Show business by Simon Lovell, available from Repro Magic. For a quick sun tanned image, use a sun bed for short time each day, use fast tan tanning tablets in conjunction with this.

For stage make up ask in Boots Chemist, available manufactured by Leichner of London at various prices. I, however, personally prefer to use a ladies all day pancake base make up by Max Factor and powder off with a colour toning powder by Yardley or Max Factor. A black eye pencil is used to blacken my eyebrows and to underline my eyes for that sinister and mysterious look. Lastly, some very subtle and lightly coloured lipstick/grease paint is used to pick out my lips slightly. Now let me assure you on stage you do not look effeminate, you just look like a person with a suntan, who appears successful and don't forget, without the make up, under the stage lights, you'd look white like a ghost. To apply the make up is something which you must learn, through practice, until you get it right, advice, however, will be freely given to you by the sales assistant in your local Boots make up department.

To conclude briefly, you must always be clean, remember deodorant and subtle after shave, your hair must be washed and combed and in other words, you should have made every possible effort to look your best in every way. I always wear "Pheromones" on stage, which is a liquid spray "musk" after shave, which contains within it powerful "pheromones." These "pheromones" cannot consciously be smelt by women, but they do have the psychological effect of attracting women towards you. It can also make them more willing to do as you say and they can be purchased for £10 a bottle from any of the companies which advertise in national papers and adult magazines.

COSTUMERS

Here it is just a case of finding a good tailor who can do what you want and have the best hand made clothing that your money can buy. These days, however, it is becoming more and more acceptable to wear off the peg, high class clothing, which although of a similar style to that worn by the general public, is one million times better. For example, theirs is a black shirt and yours is a black shirt encrusted with imitation diamonds upon pure silk material with a designer label. It is most obviously a fashion designers creation, direct from a Paris catwalk show.

FURTHER NLP TRAINING/LIFESKILLS TRAINING

Training, in both neuro-linguistics and in Motivational techniques, is available from McKenna Breen, a company based in London, who also supply a range of excellent self help audio and video tapes. They also supply corporate stress management hypnosis training to large companies. All the details can be found on his site of ***www.paulmckenna.com***

FEMALE/MALE ASSISTANT

For a male performer, a female assistant can be of use and for a female stage hypnotist a male assistant can be of use. She/he can escort people from out of the audience up to the stage, she/he can set props upon the stage ready for the next routine and of course, he/she could be used to participate in the onstage routines with the hypnotised subjects. For example, he/she could be the lovely model that the entranced members of the opposite sex turn down for a blind date and then wish they hadn't when you snap your fingers and they return to reality and see the stunning model before them. So with a little imagination, I am sure you can easily see how a male/female assistant can add much sparkle, polish and professionalism to your on stage show.

MIDNIGHT HYPNOTISM SHOWS

Mr Robert Halphern was the first stage hypnotist to present a show at midnight, the witching hour, this he did at an Edinburgh Festival Show many years ago. Since the Peter Powers and myself have both presented shows at midnight and there are certain advantages to doing this. For example, as a hypnotist show has very little in the way of props etc., to set you can quite easily go into a theatre after the standard evening performance has finished and be set up ready for a show at midnight. As such you can book up a tour of theatres quicker than usual, as they will already be open that night and to stay open a few extra hours will not cost them much more, as such, unlike usual, when you have to book the venue many months in advance, a few months notice can often be given for a midnight show.

The midnight hypnotism show is also a gimmick, which you can use to obtain much free publicity for your shows and it sets as eerie atmosphere for the show. The best nights for such shows are Fridays or Saturdays, as you will then attract the night club style crowd to the show, who are out anyway at that time of night. Incidentally, as Peter Powers has done many times in the past, as you are aiming for the night club clientel, you can do a midnight show and then a 2.30am show. The second show catches all the people as they come out of the night clubs and as strange as it sounds, these shows can be very well attended indeed. The only drawback with such shows, is that the venue usually demands that extra security staff are employed and you must then pay for this cost from your own pocket.

COMBINING MAGIC WITH HYPNOSIS

Magic tricks and illusions can, as I have found with my own stage show, be used within the hypnotic show to make your show different than those the audience may have seen before. Without giving away too many of my ideas, let me just say that it looks better to magically be produced from "nowhere" than just walk on stage at the start of the show. Also it can amaze and shock the audience to see an entranced subject be by hung on a gallows or in an electric chair.

Also, why chance hurting someone by piercing their skin with a real needle, when there is a magical way to achieve such things? Now that I've set your mind thinking on this subject, I will leave you to come to your own conclusions, however many excellent magical props, illusions and effects, which can be combined within your show, are available along with books of plans for illusions etc. from many of the companies who advertise on ***www.magicweek.co.uk***

COMBINING SINGING AND MUSIC WITH HYPNOSIS

In much the same way as magic can be combined with hypnosis, it is also possible to combine vocal songs sung by yourself and the playing of musical instruments into your act. My colleague, The Astounding Anthony "S", has already done this with great success and has established himself as the original "Song and Trance Man." He has the volunteers react to key words within a song he sings by reacting in hilarious and relevant to the song ways. When singing such songs, he also plays the music to accompany himself upon his guitar or other instruments. With a little thought you could adapt this idea to suit your own manner and style.

SOUNDMAN/DRIVER

You will most definitely need to employ someone to operate your music and change the tapes etc. As you will have to pay them for this, I always make sure that I employ a soundman who drives, so that I can just pay the petrol/diesel money and he then also takes me to and from the show as well as acting as my soundman. This means that after the show I can have a drink or two if I desire, I can also go to sleep on the way to and from shows. If your soundman also happens to be on the very muscular side then he can also act as your body guard and intervene should any nasty situations occur. This means that you will then not get hurt during the time it takes from any agro starting to the moment the establishment's bouncers get to you and sort out the situation. This itself is worth it's weight in gold. So how do you find a soundman? Well, simple answer, I just found a well built (bouncer style) guy on the dole, who had a car and wants to earn some money on the quiet. You agree to pay all petrol costs and all they have to do is drive you to and from the venue, help you get your gear in and set up, act as your bodyguard and control the music tapes during your act. For one nights work you will pay them £50.

As for the music cues, it's quite easy. Each piece of music is recorded onto a separate audio tape of the highest quality that you can afford. The name of the routine it's to be used for is then written both onto the cassette and onto the cover. This way, if they get separated you will always know which goes with which. The reason each track of music is recorded onto a separate tape, is because sometimes you might let a routine run three minutes and sometimes only for a minute, dependant upon the audiences response to it.

As a general rule of thumb, I have the track of music recorded five times in a row onto the tape. This usually gives me 5 minutes of continuous music upon each tape, this way you can be 100% sure that the music will never run out during a routine which you are milking for laughs. I have the music recorded onto the tapes, so that it's always on side A, so that the moment it is place into the tape deck and started the music starts to play. You must always have the tapes set in their covers prior to a show so that the right tape is in the right cover, also so that the music will instantly start to play when placed in the tape machine. The tapes, of which I carry around two sets of 45 tapes a case, are transported inside one of those executive style cassette tape holders and are in the order you require. The routines name is written on the edge of the cover so it's visible with the case lid open. For example, the music might be the Bladerunner theme, but upon the cover it say 60 second fast induction music. The Birdie song is used when making them believe they are chickens laying square eggs, so on the cover it just says chicken, on Jailhouse Rock it just says Elvis and on Like A Virgin, it just says Madonna.

Hopefully by now you will have got the general idea of just how easy the music cues will be, as your cue is given automatically within the commands that you give to the onstage volunteers. For example, if you said "in a few moments, when I awake you and the music begins to play, you will be Elvis". Then the soundman just looks for the tape which says Elvis upon it, places it into the tape deck and presses play when you give him a nod, it really is as simple as that. You could of course invest a lot of money and have all your music recorded onto a couple of Digital Audio Tapes (D.A.T.S.), these give CD quality sound and full shows music will fit upon one DAT tape, which can be in the DAT player at all times. You can then, by infra red remote control, start whichever track of music you want from the tape at any time, in just the same way as you can select any track from a CD player.

You could of course convert all your tracks to MP3 and record them onto one Compact Disc which can then easily be used by yourself through your PA using a Remote Control CD Player.

However if using a soundman I personally find that mini discs are my music medium of choice.

Best to have your music recorded on Audio tape, mini disc, Compact disc and DAT as then when you are booked for a venue which has its own PA you will always have the right medium of music with you which will play through their system.

P.A. SYSTEM

At the start of your hypnotic career you'll need a P.A. system consisting of a minimum of a 150 watt amplifier, two speakers, two speaker stands, a double dolby system tape deck (or mini disc player), radio microphone and all the connecting leads. As you'll be working mainly in pubs and clubs to start with, a 150 watt mixer amplifier with four channels minimum, will suffice along with two speakers, which must be capable of handling 75 watts per channel each.

You can buy all your new equipment from local suppliers, who can be found in your Yellow Pages directory, they may even be able to supply you with some good quality second hand equipment. Your local Free Adverts paper is also a good source for second hand equipment, of high quality at cheap prices. You should expect to pay between £500 and £1000 for second hand and from £1000 up to £3000, for a high quality brand new set up with guarantees etc.

You could, of course, hire a P.A. from a local music shop on a nightly basis until you have earned enough to buy your own. However, when you are working a lot, it's much more profitable to own your own, as it can cost from £20 to £40 a night to hire a suitable P.A. system. Anywhere which needs amplification of more than 150 watts will usually have their own P.A. in house system, which you can just connect your radio mike to. You can of course, eventually have in the rider to your contract, a condition stating that the venue is responsible at all times for providing a suitable P.A. at their own cost. This then saves you the aggravation of transporting and setting up your own P.A. Incidentally, by law, all places which have been granted an Entertainment's Licence, are meant to have their own in house P.A. system, although obviously, this is not always reality. The systems are easy to connect up and whoever sells you one will be pleased to demonstrate which leads connects to what socket etc. The speaker stands are used to raise the speakers up into the air to avoid "feedback" as you walk around, I'd advise you to purchase a top of the range sure radio mike so that you don't get interference from taxi cabs etc.

At the time of updating this for release as a Hardback and paperback book a new system has come onto the market called The Peavey Escort. This is a complete systme of 150 Watts in a carry case on wheels, which is the most compact system of its kind I've ever seen. I've been using one now for the past two years when a PA has been required and when you consider you can find places on the Internet selling them for less than £400 including delivery to your door they are a true bargain.

FEMALE STAGE HYPNOTISTS

There is already one by the name of Sapphire and one by the name of Lo Reid and lovely people they are too. So there is definitely an opening in the industry for female stage hypnotists. I feel that it's harder for women to become stage hypnotists because of the stereo typed view that the public at large have of all hypnotists being men, as such, this can affect the belief and expectancy factor. However, I do feel that more females should take up the art and I for one, would give them all the help I possibly can.

DUAL HYPNOTIST ACTS

I believe that I was the first person, certainly in the UK, to do half of a dual hypnotism show, entitled "Battle of The Hypnotists." In it's most basic format, there were two separate halves to the show and two very different hypnotists.

One hypnotist did the first half of the show and then the influence was changed from hypnotist A to hypnotist B, so the subjects would react to the new performer in the second half. To transfer the influence from one hypnotist to another, you would just say, "I'm now talking to each and every person upon the stage. For the rest of this evening, whenever you hear this voice, (hypnotist B then says, sleep and relax). Yes the moment he says (hypnotist B says sleep and relax), you'll instantly react to whatever he says for the rest of tonight's show and carry it out as an automatic reflex action. So you will now only react to this new voice (at this point hypnotist B says sleep and relax and then takes over the act, with the people on stage now reacting to his commands.)

It is very easy to transfer the influence in this way from one hypnotist to another and it looks very impressive to all audiences, whilst also being a good ploy to use in order to obtain much free publicity for all the shows you do.

If one of you was male and the other female, you'd also have the battle of the sexes element coming in play and once again, much free publicity could be obtained. Another advantage with dual hypnotism acts, is that you can apparently hypnotise you partner and then perform such banned stunts as catalepsy across two chairs on them without ever breaking the law. With a little thought on your part, much comedy banter could be devised along the lines that you keep trying to place each other under hypnosis and get one another to do stupid things.

Look in the Stage and TV classifieds for comedy script writers, they would be able to devise original routines and scenarios for you dual hypnotism act.

PROPS

As we have covered in depth already, you can't see hypnosis, but you can see the effects of it upon people. The use of props makes a lot of routines much funnier than they would have been otherwise. The reason being, the audience have more of a visual element to observe and enjoy when props are combined into your shows. Judicious use of props will enhance any show, look around, you will be very surprised what you can use as a prop and with a little thought many ideas will present themselves to you.

Words of advice though, a blow up penis may seem funny, a blow up rubber doll also, but both carry implications of pornography, so please, for your own sake, do not use such items in your show. They may be funny at private parties, or among friends, but never at a public show. No, the audience are not narrow minded, they just laugh at different things in different situations of life. In a club or theatre, that is not the place they will find it funny, obscene yes, funny, no.

COMEDY TECHNIQUE

To learn the art of comedy timing is something which only comes with experience of doing live shows. So the more shows you do and get under your belt, the better you will become. A good book, which I thoroughly recommend on the principles of presenting comedy and the psychology of comedy is, Comedy Techniques For Magic Shows, by Mr Joe Riding, and this book is available for under £20 from:

Mr Bill Thompson
The House of Secrets
12 Claunce Street,
Blackpool
FY1 3Dn
Tel: +44 (0)1253 20902
www.joesmagic.co.uk

YOUR GUIDE TO £36,000 INCOME IN YEAR ONE

Firstly let me point out, the research and development of this course started in 1994, and prices as mentioned were correct at time of writing. Should you be reading this in years to come, the principles will remain the same, but just bring the amounts up to a more realistic figure for your time of reading. So let me start this chunk of the money making chapter by stating that it's much better at the start of your career to do 10 shows at £250 each, instead of 5 shows at £500 each. Now the reason for this is simply that although you'll end up doing double the shows for the same money, you will have gained twice as much practical performing experience with your act. No amount of money can buy you this experience, which will teach you more than any course or book ever could. Once you have polished your act to perfection and have created a demand for your act then you can raise your fee and demand your own price. Even if you only worked pubs, you can have an excellent income and lifestyle. I well remember, that when I did work, then I was rebooked at the same venue every 6 to 8 weeks, that means, that one pub can have you on up to 6 or 7 times a year. Now if you get 16 venues who'll book you every eight weeks then if you book them in staggered and charged just £250 a show you" have 16 venues providing eight shows a year, each which is a total of 144 shows you be doing year. And 144 shows by £250 per show equals and income of £36,000 each year and as all the pubs would be in your local area, most of this would be profit. This itself is a good income by anyone's standards, you'd still have loads of time left to promote your own theatre shows, which could earn you up to £15,000 or more profit a night on each 2,000 seat theatre that you fill at £10 a ticket. So hopefully you can now see that if your act is well planned and presented you really can earn an income and live a lifestyle that others only ever dream of getting. All you need to be in business is, yourself, costume, make-up, small case of props, music tapes, P.A. system and radio mike and your advertising materials.

Even if you're not very good at sales and marketing, you must be able to find 16 venues that will book you every eight weeks in your local area for £250 a night. If this is hard, drop your price to £125 and find 32 venues that will book you each eight weeks, you will then still be on an income of £36,000 a year, you'll just be performing more regularly for it. In your first year of trading this would be a good idea, to perfect your act before taking your show on a theatre tour of England. Charging £250 a show as stated above, you would be working on average three nights a week, at £125 a show you'd be working on average six nights a week, which not many people in show business are doing. You can earn an additional income by doing private hypnotherapy sessions in the daytime at a charge of around £75 an hour, also by selling home hypnotherapy tapes by mail order.

After 12 to 18 months of doing this and saving most of the money, you'll then be in a position to promote your own theatre tour of the UK and start earning up to £15,000 or more profit on a nightly basis. As you have been doing so many shows all over the area, you will have built up a following and your first theatre show should, as a result, be sold out many weeks in advance. So, let's just say only 40 people from each of the 16 regular venues came to your theatre show, that's 640 tickets at £10 each, which would have been sold almost instantly. £10 by 640 people is a total of £6400 cash, which would have been pulled in almost instantly and this alone would bring you into profit on the cost of hiring the theatre and publicity. You'd still have about 1360 seats to sell at £10 each, which when sold, would be another £13.000 cash profit for you after all expenses. So you see in the long term, the really big profits are to be made in promoting your own theatre shows, which can realistically, within a couple of years, turn you into a millionaire, even without having had your own TV series. When you are up to this level and people want to book you for show, you should then be charging an absolute minimum of £500 a night and in fact, I'd say £800 to £1500 is closer to the mark.

Also, remember, that in the hypnotism industry, there are so many avenues of income to be made, some of which include, shows, TV series, hypnotherapy, corporate stress management hypnosis sessions, sale of audio tapes, books and videos of various natures. Training courses, personal appearances, advisor to magazines, TV and films on hypnosis and many, many more avenues, including article writer on hypnosis for magazines etc. etc. In fact, the ways in which hypnosis can be put to use to earn money, are only limited by your own imagination and skills in sales and marketing.

Now I may have made all this sound so easy. But if you have a good act, good sales and marketing skills and can "win friends and influence people" which, incidentally, is the title of a book I highly recommend by Dale Carnegi. Then you truly will be able to "think and grow rich" which is the title of another book I recommend by Napoleon Hill. So you see that income and life style that you have always really dreamed of, is now realistically in your grasp. And the plan I have just outlined will start you earning money from day one and set you on a three to five year plan to financial freedom of the very highest standard.

PART THIRTEEN

COMEDY SKETCH IDEAS

The appeal of a stage hypnotists show to an audience is two fold.

A. They like to witness or experience what they believe to be a great power, and:

B. There is nothing funnier on this planet, than seeing your friends make complete fools of themselves and not be able to stop their own actions, which become automatic.

To conclude the area of stage hypnotism, before we move further into the therapy side, there follows a comprehensive compilation of routines to ensure a successful show.

This chapter contains numerous ideas for sketches which you can use. With a little bit of thought you can adapt the examples I give or come up with brand new ideas, which will then give you your own unique show. How you word the suggestions you give and how you present these scenarios to on stage subjects I will leave you to work out for yourself, as your should by now be armed with more than enough knowledge to do this. I will however, point out that where possible, there must be continuity in your suggestions, so that one routine leads into the next one logically. This will make the whole show look that much more organised and professional and as a result will make it more entertaining for your future audiences.

For example, at the end of a routine where the subjects have been freezing cold and snuggling up to each other in bed, you will be able to logically link it to the next routine by just saying. "It's no longer 7am in the morning and it's no longer freezing cold. In fact, we are in a new time altogether, it's 4pm in the afternoon, it's now lovely and warm and we're all on a sunny Spanish beach."

Another example of how routines can be linked together is that they are cold and told to hug themselves. The moment they do this, their arms are now in the correct position to tell them that they are stuck inside a straight jacket and there is a ferret running around inside it. Music then starts and they become the Saturday Night Fever dancers, extending one arm out into the air whilst one arm remains against their chest.

Can you see how cleanly this makes the routines link together? I hope so, as this is the kind of thing you should be aiming for in your own comedy hypnotism stage show. Another example, they are riding their horses along at a canter, they are John Wayne, out to catch Billy the Kid. Then the music changes and it's now a new time altogether as they are now all jockeys at the grand national races. Can you see now, how the routines can be linked logically, either by words, continuity or an overall underlying theme, which links them?

Enough said on the subject, this is something which you must do for yourself, so that your show becomes unique and personal to you. Another technique to get maximum comedy exposure is a running gag, which carries on for a while and gets funnier in the audience's eyes each time you refer to it. An example of this being that a subject is told to stand at the side of the stage and start counting from one up to three million. At intervals throughout the show you go to the subject, hold the radio mike to his lips and the audience hear that he has indeed gone much higher with his counting. Now this may not sound at all funny, but believe me, in reality, each time you return to him, it becomes funnier. Obviously you must be careful not to milk the gag for too long, as always remember, the old adage, "always leave them wanting more". A final example is that one subject is told they are Madonna and one is to be Elvis. Just as the Madonna girl sits down, the Elvis music starts, so it's instantly into that. This is then done in reverse and repeated a few times, the resulting mania of people diving out of their chairs and being a famous star one minute, then acting as if they have done nothing the next, becomes hilarious to the audience. The comedy hypnotism show is situation comedy at its best. Obviously you must suit the style of routines that you use each night to the venue, audience, age ranges and tastes. Family shows are 100% clean, adult shows a little naughty, but not over the top. Stag and Hen night shows are as blue as you like and you can, as long as it's legal, do whatever you so desire.

Also remember to check if people are allergic to onions before getting them to eat as apples, or check that they are not allergic to feathers before giving them a feather boa to wear and turning them into Shirley Bassey. You must always put the Health and Safety of your on stage subjects first, foremost and last. Also ensure you know clearly what kind of show the person booking you wishes you to present, that way you won't offend anyone and will always get paid. Basically, it's all down to thinking on your feet and using your common sense, so if in doubt about a routine, then leave it out. Remember too, that for someone to try to put their hands up a woman's skirt but being stopped in time is funny. To allow them to do so for real is rude, vulgar and in bad taste and could well get you a smack on the nose from the girl's boyfriend or husband. Things can actually be funnier by letting the subjects only go so far and then leaving the rest to audience's imaginations who will then draw their own conclusions on what would have occurred if you hadn't stopped them.

Also always ensure that the subject has understood the commands which have just given them, a good phrase to use for this is:

"Just nod your head if you understand."
Also ensure that if giving several suggestions to different people one after the other in succession, that each subject knows for sure which one they are meant to act upon, a good phrase to use here is:

"I'm only talking to you if my hand's upon your shoulder."
Obviously if you want everyone to react to the same suggestion at the same time you would just say something like:

"I'm now talking to each and every person upon the stage."
Another way in which to increase the comedy element of the act is to say:

"As soon as the music stops you'll wonder what the hell you're doing."
This means, that they awaken, the music plays and they then do as you have commanded. Then, when the music is stopped unexpectedly you will find that the sincerely puzzled look upon the subject's faces is hilarious in itself. Another very useful phrase to use is:

"In a few moments when I awake you."
This makes sure that they know when to carry out the suggestion and also, ensures that they do not awaken whilst the suggestion is being given to them.

ADAPTABILITY

Being versatile and adaptable is the key to success in the show business industry. When working a stag night with an all men audience, the show must be planned to suit the occasion. By far the best way to make regular money until you've made it big, is to do squeaky clean family style show that will offend no-one and will entertain all. If you are engaged for a cruise, generally the audiences will be made up of the older generation. Ideally try and get any younger ones up to participate, but if required to use the elderly people, then do not give any controversial type commands, only use middle of the road ones. Also bear in mind that running around trying to catch invisible grasshoppers may be funny, but it's not very nice to expect an old person to do this, (they may have heart trouble). Use your common sense and judgement at all times, with an older audience. The guaranteed handclasp test should be used at the start of your act, so that your credentials are immediately established and belief and expectancy sets in to make life easier. Also always flatter the older ones, (don't patronise) as flattery, correctly used, will get you everywhere in life. In smaller social situations act reluctant to give a demonstration for free, then when everyone keeps asking you to, they will then be in the correct state of mind to be placed into hypnosis easily and rapidly. Lastly, before we consider the subject of routine and sketch ideas to get the hypnotised subjects to carry out, lets now discuss the subjects of stage lighting and how it can be used to best effect in our hypnotic show.

Lighting can in itself create different psychological moods and atmospheres, it can also add to the comedy effect of a sketch within your show. For example, you make someone believe they are Elvis and they start dancing to Jail House Rock, here the coloured spotlights on stage should flash on and off in time to the music to create a rock concert effect. Another example, you make a number of men dress up in tights and become the worlds greatest ballerinas, the lights should dim to just blues and reds and then two follow spots should follow the "star" ballet dancers around the stage as they do their stuff.

A quick word here on the subject of costumes for the onstage subjects, a person becoming Madonna can be very funny, it can however be even funnier if it's a man and he is dressed in a wig, bra and Madonna style outfit for the sketch. The subject can be sent offstage to be dressed by the stage crew and is then brought back on at the correct time to do the routine. So give the subject of costumes a thought as well.

Obviously, the use of props and background music helps to enhance any comedy sketch that you do, so use these most effective tools also. Large comedy items of use are available from all novelty supply stores.

Back to lighting. For intro and opening patter) use stage lights on reds and blues and you work under a white follow spot. (As subjects come up to stage) stage lights full up (white) and house lights on too. (Once all subjects upon the stage) turn out all the house lights, but leave the stage lights full up and start induction's etc. (From then onwards) I suggest lights of reds and blues for each test, with a single subject with a spotlight directed upon him/her and stage lights full up for all group routines involving all subjects.

NOTE: You must be followed by a follow spot at all times during the opening patter etc.

When the subjects are made to perform sketches within the show they are then the real stars, not you and as such, either the spotlights are upon them or the stage lights are full up.

ADDITIONAL LIGHTING EFFECT IDEAS

A Have a baby spotlight mounted overhead in the flys, have amber gels upon it and focus it vertically downwards at your special "hypnotic" chair, or have a few over the chairs or different relaxing colours to aid the induction process. Incidentally the idea of a special chair is just pure showmanship and you use it for the best subject to sit in.

B A baby spotlight in the wings, focused at the performers face, with stage lights dimmed, can be very effective when doing an induction and staring at a subject in the eyes. (Try a green gel here).

C A floor lamp behind the subject's chair directed over his shoulder gives an interesting aura effect.

D A double faced mirror on a revolving turntable with a spotlight focused upon it where it is in the wings. As it revolves, it gives (reflects) out flashes of light around the stage and makes a really weird atmospheres, ideal for induction's.

E A revolving mirror globe, fixed over the stage in the flys, with a light focused upon it will send flashing lights throughout the entire theatre, a good effect for when they are entering the theatre at the start of the evening.

EFFECT OF COLOURS

Yellow seems to increase suggestibility, whilst purple, blue and green, all help to induce the hypnotic sleep state. As such, if you have lights in the flys pointing at the subjects, so that the light shines into their eyes as they look up for the P.R.I. eyestrain induction, then the following colour effects can be used to enhance the induction.

1 When commencing the induction (yellow on).
2 (As eyes close) off yellow and into purples.
3 (When sleep and cold day) blues for effect.
4 (When sleep and hot day) reds for effect.

I hope all this has given you an idea of how much effect a few lighting changes can have upon your entire show. Your onstage backdrop, ideally if left blank should be a dark deep colour, such as black, blue or rich wine, so that the subjects clothes make a good contrast and do not blend in. Paul McKenna has a black backdrop with little fibre optic lights all over it, with an opening in the centre shaped like a human eye which he steps through at the start of the show. Peter Powers uses large cut out caricatures of himself, which are then scattered one on each side of the stage, with a large evil looking head caricature set centre stage which he steps out from behind of, to make his appearance at the start of the show. I use a sign of one man making another fall back to the floor with the name "Hypnotic Party Time" on for family shows. This is then fixed to the centre area of the backdrop and I make my entrance from the wings. For entrance, I have the curtains set so I can come on from centre stage out towards the audience, or on big shows I am magically produced from an illusion. Well that should have set your mind thinking on some more important elements, which can make your show that much more professional, now to some ideas for sketches which can be used within your hypnotic show. A good comedy script writer, like the ones who advertise in the Stage and TV, could no doubt come up with some new ideas for you.

ADULT AND FAMILY SHOW COMEDY SKETCH IDEAS

Very cold morning and shivering, snuggle up to the person next to them. In love with the person next to them, getting more and more intimate with the one they love. All relax again and when awoken, one has a sore bum, one man has a funny taste in their mouth and wonder what they've been doing. A women has a smile on her face, doesn't know what she was doing, but knows whatever it was, she enjoyed it a lot. Two are awoken and are paralysed from the neck downwards until you cough they cannot move and two men are awoken, one with his hand on the knee of another he cannot move it for thirty seconds.

Very hot day on the beach and they're sun bathing, so hot they need to rub invisible suntan lotion into their body and the hotter it gets, the quicker it has to be rubbed in. 100 degrees, 150 degrees etc., etc. Now it's so hot all the men's feet are burning and so are all the women's arms, as they rub in the suntan lotion as quickly as possible. Now relax it's cooled down and you'd like nothing more than a lovely delicious ice cream. The moment I give you your ice cream you will start sucking and licking it as quickly as you can. (OK, all relax now, when you awaken sir your hand is covered in dog dirt and you really stink of it and you madam will find your hand is stuck around the ice cream and you cannot remove it from your mouth until I say bananas, bananas. Wide awake. Stare at me again "bananas, bananas". OK now, just put it down please. Go to dog dirt subject. Have you had a bath recently sir? (Then put all others under and awaken after saying). In a few moments when I awaken you, everyone will realise that the man, (here you describe relevant person) really smells and the more I snap my fingers, the worse the smell is going to become, in fact, it's the most horrible thing you've ever smelt. Wide awake. (Snap fingers several times) OK, now everyone, you've just realised it's not that man, it's actually you who smells because you've s... yourself and it's starting to run down your leg and when I awaken you in a moment, you'll make up crazy excuses for why you smell.

Sleep, when you awaken this time you really need a drink of water to take that horrible taste away from your throat. When I give you the glass of water, you sir will find that the water is 100% proof alcohol and you'll get drunk on just a few sips of it. You sir, will find that you cannot get it to yours lips, in fact, your arm will get stuck 4 inches from your mouth and you'll spill it all over yourself. You sir, will find that the moment the glass touches your lips and you take a mouthful, that the liquid will taste like cat pee and everyone else will just get inebriated, as the water becomes 100% proof alcohol. (They are then given a plastic cup each with water in.) Here a couple of people can be told to stand up and walk around in their drunken state which gets laughs. You've all had a wonderful night out on the beer and you've got to get home, now so we'll all drive home in our cars, but we're so drunk, we'll all pretend we are high speed racing drivers, (milk it). Then, OK now, we're no longer high speed racing drivers, we are now all horrible greasy bikers and we're on our Harley Davidsons, rev the bike, make rude signs at the person behind you.

We're now in the Apollo space rocket and preparing for take off, belt yourself in, check the meters, hold on tight, take off, wave at people below. Now we've arrived in space and when I awaken you, upon the moon you will be, there is no gravity, you are lighter than air and you will leap and float around the stage. This time when I awaken you, we are all still in space, the hypnotist is invisible, you cannot see him, but you can see everything which he moves around. To avoid the things, you'll still have to float and bounce around the stage. Then into invisible hypnotist routine, carry objects around, tap them on shoulder etc., then the top half of you is visible and the bottom half invisible, then the bottom half visible and top half is invisible.

Sleep. In a few moments when I awaken you sir, you'll be a Martian from outer space and you speak fluent Martian and can see only through your finger tip. You sir, will also be a Martian, speak fluent Martian and see only through your fingertip and you madam will be a Martian interpreter and you can speak both English and Martian and will interpret for us. Everyone else will have returned back to earth and just be witnessing a live interview with the Martians we have brought back from space. Then ask the Martians various questions via the interpreter. Sleep. You've all been such wonderful volunteers in this the first half of the show, that I'm going to reward you with an apple, it will taste, smell, look and feel like a juicy delicious apple. (They then eat onions as apples), when I awaken you in a minute you'll be eating an apple, you'll just think everyone else is eating an onion, you'll try to stop them (they have argument etc). OK, this time when awoken, you'll realise it's you who's eating the horrible bitter sour onion, you will not be violent and will not hit the hypnotist, but will dispose of apples as quickly as possible. Sleep. All awaken, give invisible water, mouth will taste better. Sleep.

You sir, when awoken will be five years of age, it's your birthday party and you'll be eating your jelly and ice cream. (He's given tin of catfood and spoon to eat,) everyone else will imagine you are five years of age, but you are all being badly behaved, as five year olds would be. (Awaken). Sleep, when awoken, if you lie you will get a red hot tongue and feet. Who did what to who? Everyone just sleep (use half face masks of famous stars here, like politicians, royal family etc.) When awoken and the more outrageous lies you make up the more relaxed you'll be, you are John Major, You're the Queen. Then milk it, asking about the famous people's lives etc. Sleep.

At this point, implant the suggestions that they are to react to during the interval and then to give them a taste of the second half. Make a women fall in love with the hypnotist, the more you ignore her, the more she falls in love and wants to marry you. Then awaken everyone, send them back to audience and take a bow because it's time for the 20 to 30 minute interval section.

During the interval the 12 or more hypnotised subjects will be walking around the theatre carrying out the things you have commanded, so a show within a show will be occurring. For example:

One man will believe that the moment he goes to the toilets, which he will have to do every five minutes because he will be caught short, that a large gorilla will come in after him. He'll run out screaming, look out in the loos fellows, there's a big gorilla. Another man is told that he is a Casanova and will be trying his skills during the interval. A women is told she has lost her pet kitten and will be trying to find it, a man is told he has lost his money and must try to find it.

A woman is told she is a member of that strange cult religion, who worship Harry Corbett and she will walk round trying to convert people to the Harry Corbett religion, who all pray to their God Sooty. (A Sooty hand puppet is placed onto her hand.)

A man will find out that every person in the audience is a long lost relative or friend and he hasn't seen them all for years, so will be greeting them all happily.

A woman believes that in the interval, she is the world's most outrageous gossip and will go around telling stories about audience members to other audience members. A man is given an empty video case and told it's a mercury bomb, which he has to look after, should the case get tipped then the bomb blows up.

Another man is told he has lost their pet duck, Webster, and is given a duck call to try and find it during the interval. The audience is warned not to tell him that it's in the video case, otherwise he'll end up chasing the guy who's got the mercury bomb. Another man is told they will be looking after an invisible lion, that is very visible to him. It's escaped from the zoo and it's a very vicious and ferocious lion, it will be dragging him all over the place and he must stop it from attacking people. One woman is told that every time someone asks her who is the best hypnotist, she will instantly shout out "Alex LeRoy is the greatest hypnotist of them all, Hallalugah."

The final person of the twelve on stage is told that when they hear this noise (Music plays) that they will instantly become the worlds greatest bouncer, they will not be violent and will not hurt people or touch them. But they believe it's their job to get everyone back into the theatre in time for the second half of the show.

Each and every person upon the stage will instantly race back up onto the stage the moment you say, "Come and join the party". They will still be doing the jobs that you give them to do.

When the second half begins you come on, do your opening introduction patter and then say, "come and join the party," at which point everyone rushes back up to the stage to a round of applause. You then spend a few minutes questioning them on the events of the interval. Have they found their money and kitten etc? Then return them to sleep. In a few moments when I awaken you sir, you'll find that the man in the front row has got your money, you'll be furious and you want it back. Wide awake...... Sleep. When you awaken this time sir, you'll find that your money is back in its rightful place, in your pocket. Wide awake. Sleep.

Madam, when I awaken you, you'll find not only has your pet kitten returned, but every time I snap my fingers like this, your kitten will become more adorable. Wide awake. (Click fingers a lot for comedy reaction). Sleep. OK, now everyone, when I awaken you, your hands will be rigid, stuck in the position that I place them and only I will be able to move them around. Wide awake. You then place all their hands above their heads, gags such as, now I'll nick all the stuff out of your pockets and do you trust me lady? Well you shouldn't, are used here. One woman is made to place a finger in her ear and twist it around, being unable to remove it to the line, you understand that I'm not picking on you of course.

Well ladies and gentlemen, now that we've proved that their imagination would put the headline writers of the Sunday Sport to shame, I'd like to try an experiment with you all. Her the guaranteed handclasp routine is done, prior to getting people up and doing the world record high speed hypnosis induction and implanting the suggestion that, when you say goodnight, they will all jump up and shout out, "we all love Alex LeRoy, Hallelujah."

Each and everyone of you, has now got ants all over your body, they are itching, so give them a scratch, in fact guys, you've got ants in your pants and women, you've got fleas on you knees, so scratch them hard. Fellows put your hands down your pants and scratch, then sleep. When all the guys awaken, their hands will be stuck down their trousers. Wide awake.......Sleep.

When all the men awaken this time, you'll all have 48inch boobs, you'll be really happy and show them off. Wide awake. When I cough your left boob falls off fellows, then the right boob. When awoken all the men will find they are giving birth to babies. What's it's name, sex etc? Sleep.

You sir, will use this megaphone and each time the audience laugh, you will think you are the theatre manager and will tell every one to stop laughing, as it's banned in this theatre. You sir will go back to the audience and the moment you sit down, you'll rush back to the stage and ask for some food, because you're hungry. The moment I give you a pie it will go plop, straight into your face, then you'll sit down and each and every time your bum touches the seat, you'll instantly return to the stage and ask for another pie and each time it will go plop, into your face. (Here you use custard pies for comedy.)

You madam, will find that I send you back to the audience and the moment you get down the stairs you will see a hole in the stage and water is flooding in through it, you'll put your finger in the hole to stop the water and save us, each time I ignore you as you shout out Mr LeRoy, help or we will drown, the more I ignore your cries, the more angry you will become.

You sir, will find that when you hear this music, (Rocky Theme) you are the worlds greatest shadow boxer and you'll dive out of your chair and be boxing an invisible opponent. The moment the music stops, you'll knock yourself out, fall to the floor and stay there until the music starts again. At this point, you milk the routines, switching from one to another in quick succession for maximum comedy impact. This will kill about 10 easy minutes of the show. At this point, if running short of time, continue as follows, if there is plenty of time left then add a few fills in here. Sleep. OK, now I'm talking to each and every person upon the stage, when you are awoken you will be the worlds greatest ballet dancers, it's Swan Lake and you are all swans. Here the music starts, they are awoken and react, then say, ladies and gentlemen, please welcome the stars, Rudolph Nurev and his female partner. The two guys who were sent off earlier are now returned, in tights and short ballerina skirts with big cod pieces and wigs, they prance around the stage. We are now all dying swans, dying, as we fall to the floor to sleep.

When awoken, the legs are made of rubber and will try to drag yourself back to the chairs. Wide awake. OK, back to your chairs please. Can't move? What a shame because every time I cough your hands give way under you. Then sleep and all returned to seats. (During this routine a guy has been sent off stage and dressed leather bondage gear, like Madonna.) In a few moments when I awaken you sir, you'll enjoy putting your hand on the guys knee next to you, the more you do it the more you enjoy it. You sir, will enjoy the man next to you placing his hand on your knee and will positively encourage it, you sir, will be upset because you think it should be your knee that is getting rubbed. Wide awake. Milk for a few minutes, then sleep.

In a few moments when I awaken you, it's the last routine of the show and after it all commands will be cancelled out. When awoken, you all are the worlds greatest male and female strippers, the more noise the audience makes, the more clothing you will remove. Now we need some music for this, so invite my very special guest, Madonna, who will interact with all the strippers to prove how erotic she really is. Like a Virgin, begins to play, on comes the man in bondage gear, they all go through a simulated strip routine and interact then. Sleep.

IMPORTANT – When giving suggestions that they will become strippers, ensure you include a phrase such as "......you will become the worlds greatest strippers. You will not remove any articles of clothing past your shirt, jumper etc". If you do not include a safety clause, you may find yourself in trouble with a number of naked subjects on stage.

Gag, if enjoyed me I'm Alex LeRoy, if not Andrew Newton and say goodnight, at which point, loads of people in audience jump up and shout out, we all love Alex LeRoy, Hallelujah.

(POSSIBLE STANDBY ROUTINES FOR EXTRA TIME)

Dogs and rubber bone, fetch bone, heel etc. Both male dogs start to make love to each other.

Shops, dummy and voodoo doll routine, where what happens to the dummy they feel the pain. Dummy is then hit, arm twisted etc and subjects react.

Audience seen in the nude through special glasses, then they are in the nude and have only got very small willies, now six inches bigger than they thought they were.

Invisible razor blade with a bit of cardboard. They believe the cardboard is a razor blade, they can see the blood, feel the pain. You then mutilate yourself.

Two people in a dingy, rowing it, one gets lazy and the other gets fed up. Water starts coming in and they have to empty out with their hands. Sharks start to attack, helicopter flies over and they shout for help, dive out and swim to shore, at which point shark comes back, chases them and then all back to sleep.

ADDITIONAL COMEDY ROUTINES.

When awoken you can't count, think or say the number seven, it no longer exists for you. Then ask how many dwarfs Snow White had? How many wonders of the world were there? How many brides for how many brothers? Then get them to count fingers, they will count, 1,2,3,4,5,6,8.9.10,11 etc.

Your noses are made of rubber, bend stretch them and rub them, it's very pleasurable. Then stretch all their noses out and let them go twang back into their face.

(You place a clean bra in a man's mouth, knickers in another man's mouth and a pair of men's briefs in a woman's hand) When you three awaken, you won't know what you have done, but you know whatever it was, you really enjoyed it.

At end of show, we will all join hands and take a bow, but when we do, a 10,000 volt electric shock will travel through the line and get more powerful and then through the person at the end of the line to the floor.

When you awake, you're the world's most bad tempered sergeant major and you will believe the audience are your recruits and you'll order them around.

(Do this with a stooge) give a man real scissors, tell hem he's Vidal Sassoon and get him to really cut another mans long hair short.

You can have a card on double sided tape and an empty staple gun and appear to staple gun something to someone's back.

Whenever this music plays, (James Bond theme) you will all become James Bond types, with guns in your hand and rolling around the stage to hide from the enemy.

Woman in house watching TV. Audience are people in her house having party, drinking beer from her fridge, being sick, spilling beer and stubbing cigarettes on her new carpet. She can say and do whatever she wants, but cannot hit anyone. Possibly can always only speak Japanese and no one understands her.

You sir, will have a terrible pronounced stutter. You will speak fluent Chinese and you fluent Japanese when I awaken you.

Two people can become ice cream/popcorn sellers, trying to sell their wares to the audience in the interval.

Everyone is in a band playing invisible instruments. One is standing limp wristed, hand on hip bending his knees in time to the music.

All are now teapots and lean over to pour out the tea.

All toothpaste tubes, being squeezed tighter and tighter.

All top female glamour models, pout and blow kisses to the camera.

All goldfish in bowls, swimming around.

All actors, taking part in screen test for comedy/horror/dramatic/sex/erotic/ war and science fiction films.

All now mad professors in their laboratories.

When the music plays, you are the worlds greatest band conductors, here you can give someone a feather duster to use as a baton.

Whenever I awaken you sir and a woman shouts out Tarzan, you will instantly jump out of your chair and do a Tarzan call three times and then realise what you are doing. When you wake up madam, whenever I say there is a man who swings through the jungle and his name is...... you will then instantly jump up into the air and shout Tarzan. All the rest of you, when you hear a man do the Tarzan call three times you will jump out of your chairs and shout, the Russians are coming to kill us. IE There's a man who swings through the jungle and his name is (woman gets up and shouts Tarzan). Then bloke gets up and does Tarzan call three times, then others get up and shout, the Russians are coming to kill us.

Floor is moving like a ship, you keep falling down every time you get up.

Big dog coming down the beach, stopped at you, has urinated on your leg, all over your shorts. Oh get them off now, now it's all over your hands. Oh dear, take your shirt off and use it to clear all the wee off yourself.

It's Monday morning, do what you would be doing at 10.30am.

It's Friday afternoon, do what you'd be doing at 4.30pm.

You are a bull (foam horns on head) you are a matador (give cloak and foam sword). They then have a bull fight simulation.

The worlds greatest musical pianist.

Playing Starwars with the 3D screen images trying to kill you.

Play 3D cowboys and indians with the film image.

Two of your fingers are now totally missing.

When asked their name they shout out a rude word instead.

Invisible fairies routine. Feed them sugar puffs, tickle them under the chin, say hello, what colour are they? What's their name? They are running away, sad and cry for them. Then hypnotist jumps on them and kills them.

High wire circus tightrope walker and proceeds to lay string on floor and do it.

The worlds greatest comedian, or worlds greatest hypnotist and when they tell you to go to sleep they fall to the floor to sleep instead.

When you close your fist the audience disappear, then open your fist and they reappear.

Turn white guy into a black and black guy into a white.

Turn a man into woman and woman into man.

You are deaf, dumb, blind, limp etc.

You've just found £1000 and no-one saw you, now here comes a harassed man asking if you've seen it.

Woman next to you has a see through dress and no bra on underneath. Man next to you has fly undone and has no underwear on.

(Give guy a spanner) During interval, you are a plumber, trying to get odd jobs from the audience, in the toilets etc.

(Give guy a cap) In interval you are Steven Speilberg and all the audience are in your next movie, you need them back in the theatre now to start filming.

Stick all the subjects together in a weird chain hands on peoples bottoms, on their head and generally in strange positions.

When music plays you are Elvis Presley (use an inflatable guitar here, or a broom.)

All on your horses at the grand national races and trying to win the race.

Each time you return to your seat in the audience you will realise that you have forgotten your tie and will return and I'll give you your tie. Every time you return to your seat you immediately come back to get the tie which you have forgotten.

When awoken, you will have an invisible bucket and spade and be building a sandcastle on the steps of the stage, some idiot will keep stepping through it and if they do you will be really angry.

Worlds worst behaved class of six year olds. Ring a ring a roses etc. A velcro rip apart teddy, which they have a fight with.

When woken man/woman in front of you is person of your dreams.

Man made to believe he's a frigid woman wearing a dress and everyone can see up the dress. He's embarrassed about it and gets upset. Has no knickers on.

Two men made to think one is the mother and other is baby that she's breast feeding, changing nappy etc.

Man has invisible basketball, worlds greatest player. Hypnotist and him play with invisible ball, bounces it around, does the fancy tricks, spins it on finger etc. Then you burst the ball and he's upset, then you re-inflate it with an invisible pump.

Bought new sports car, pride and joy. Go for a fast ride, miss trees by inches, tell police to get lost, park up, get pay and display ticket turn around and watch your car explode in front of you.

Two men, one made into woman and they both have a camp conversation.

Are all chickens jumping around, flapping wings and trying to lay square eggs.

M.C. Hammer dancing live at Wembley. Michael Jackson with bendy body and all the flashy dance moves.

Forgotten their name, where they live, how old they are.

When looking through glasses, when you cough they see the people with long giraffes necks, elephants ears and clowns noses.

Women become Mr Muscles and do body building routines to the music. Men become the worlds sexiest female catwalk model.

When I say, bananas, bananas, you will jump out of your chair and shout I believe in fairies and give a big wet kiss to the man nearest to you. (Do with man.)

When hear a certain noise, they all run to bar, shout can we buy you a drink Alex and then argue over who's paying, before kissing and making up etc.

One is given (any object) and told it's worlds most precious antique and must look after it and must not let anyone have it. Another is told that they want the object and will try to get it but each time they touch it they will receive a mild electric shock.

All are now farmyard animals, milk the cow etc.

There are mice on the floor and bees buzzing around you in the air.

You're in your house, it's on fire and you must try to blow it out.

Think you have inherited a million pounds, then find out it's wrong.

Get into bath of beans and wash hair with ketchup, thinking it's clear water and shampoo.

They are worlds leading authority on parrots. (Use stuffed parrot.)

They are bad tempered traffic warden/football referee.

I cough and the person next to you has pinched your bum and angry about it.

They get up to tell you something, as they get to you they forget it. You speak and they say get lost.

On a ship, sun bathe, eat, drink, be sick, relax etc.

On sleigh with reindeers helping Santa to deliver the presents, avoid the trees, do Ho, Ho, Ho, etc. and tickle reindeer under chin, give food etc.

Given a brush and told it's Miss Broom, woman of his dreams, he then proceeds to chat her up before trying to cement the romance.

When awoken will think the guy next to you has just molested you.

You're a man of wisdom, saying wise sayings to the audience, like don't drop a brick on your foot, it hurts, etc.

You're a gospel preacher, trying to convert everyone and the more people ignore you, the more you will try to solve their sins and convert them.

Aerobics teacher with whistle around their neck and they are demonstrating the keep fit moves and trying to get the audience to join in with them.

Guy thinks he's the lounge lizard and every woman in the room wants him very badly.

The glove puppet upon your hand will keep insulting you and you shout at it, hit it etc, but still it insults you and the more angry you become.

Tell them you will touch their skin with a cigarette then touch them with pen top and the burn will still appear.

Find out what their sexual fantasies are and make them live it out in their imagination.

Cigarettes become joints, they stop smoking when you cough, they become reformed non smokers and go around the room putting out everyone cigarettes. They cannot get it to their lips, then smoke it through their elbow and another roars like a dragon as he exhales.

You're Mick Jagger with the handclaps and sticking out bum.

Slow motion football player, miming the game and then playing for real with a balloon as a football.

When awoken all men have got womens names and when asked their name they say it seriously and everyone else's because it's a female name etc. and then it happens to them.

You are washing machines, tumble driers, cheeky little monkeys, pop up toasters, milking a cow etc.

Have now got a big wart on nose, your eyebrows have been shaved off, etc.

Being a strong man, lifting two balloons upon a cane and then another person can't do it.

Deaf traffic warden, just gave you a ticket in your own driveway.

They are typewriters, grandfather clocks etc.

Shoe is now a puppy, tell everyone whilst stroking it.

When hear the ringing noise, the shoe of the person next to you has become your mobile phone and you must answer it.

(To E.T. music). Watching E.T. crying because E.T. is dying, hands on the handlebars and feet on pedals, pedal bike to save him. Ring your bell to let him know you're coming, almost there, wave to let him know you care. Now grab hold of him and place him into the basket at the front of your bike, now pedal faster so we can take him back to his home high in the sky. We're there now, give E.T. one big goodbye kiss and put him back on his planet and wave goodbye. Now chain up your bike, lock the padlock, throw the keys away and sleep.

Scottish dancers in time to music.

Are all contestants of different nationalities in the Eurovision song contest.

(With invisible dog leads from joke shop) Are all exhibiting their dogs at Crufts and getting them to do tricks etc.

They have lost their belly button and the person next to them has got it.

All become tap dancers in a chorus line.

Two become Flamenco dancers, one with dishmop in mouth as rose and one using a tennis racket as guitar.

FINAL NOTE ON COMEDY ROUTINES

I have given you more than enough ideas now to set you thinking on some original ideas of your own, you really are only limited here by your own imagination and with a little adaptability, many adult routines can be cleaned up for family shows and vice versa. For additional ideas go and see several hypnotists performing live and see what they do. Purchase the Paul McKenna and other tapes and you'll see many more routines in action. You will then have far more routines than you will ever need to use. A comedy script writer can also be employed to devise routines, so there will never be a shortage of new ideas.

I will now end this chapter by explaining how to perform several dramatic stunts, some of which are quite rightly banned as they are potentially harmful to the subjects and are included for information purposes only.

THE BRIDGE (HUMAN CATALEPSY)

This is the routine which gave hypnotism a bad name and is on of the reasons why the 1952 hypnotism act was implemented. This stunt is banned by the 1952 act. I would advise any reader not to break the law and not to use this stunt.

For this you need two straight backed chairs, or two small flat top step ladders. Two cushions are also required, as the shoulders and feet rest on the back of the chair.

To perform this in practice, normally a suitable young male subject would have been used, then having entered the hypnotic state whilst standing up by saying, "sleep, you can stand and you have perfect balance at all times." Then the subject was instructed to place their feet together, hands down by their side, which should then take a firm grip of the side of their trousers and pull outwards from the side of their body at all times. Also their head should be tilted well back, they were told to imagine that they are now stiff, rigid as an iron bar and their whole body is stuck in this position. At this point the subject is lifted up by one audience member by placing their hands under the armpits and by another man placing his hands under the mans ankles. The hypnotised subject was then positioned such that his ankles were resting across the back of one chair, whilst the other chair is positioned in line with his shoulder blades on his back. In this position, as his head will be tilted well back and he is pulling outwards on his trousers, his body will be arched upwards in the centre slightly, like a cantilever bridge and just like a cantilever bridge, this means he is able to now support more weight.

An audience member could now be stood upon the subjects chest, positioned so that one foot is flat upon the chest area and the other foot is flat upon the area above the guys knee, (side towards groin). This means that the weight is distributed across the whole surface and in actual fact, most of the weight is taken by the backs of the two chairs and not by the hypnotised subject. If wishing to stand two people upon the subject, one is placed so that they are standing upon the chest area and the other so that they are supported by the upper leg area. This looked very impressive.

THE BED OF NAILS

Another dramatic looking stunt is to make a subject feel no pain, then have them lay upon a bed of six inch nails before a person stands upon their chest in this position. Now believe it or not, this is very safe and is an old circus performers trick. The secret being, that as all the nails are so close together the persons weight is evenly distributed over them and as such they feel no pain.

Full details of how this works and how to make your own bed of nails can be obtained by reading Derek Lever's excellent book, "Stranger Than Fiction", which is available from the Various Magic Companies. Once upon the bed of nails a person can be made to stand upon the hypnotised subject in much the same way as in the catalepsy stunt.

PAINLESS SURGERY

Painless surgery is an old stunt where you place needles through various areas of a subject's body whilst they are in trance and they feel no pain. The secret of this is also in the Derek Lever book.

THE 24 HOUR WINDOW SLEEP STUNT

This stunt, in effect, gives the impression that you place a subject under hypnosis and then leave them resting in a bed in a shop window for 24 hours. Which in turn generates much free publicity for both the shop and your show. Now this is a stunt, which can be easily faked by having identical twins and switching them over in the early hours of the morning when no-one is around on the street outside the shop window which the bed is in. It can however also be done genuinely by placing the hypnotised subject into a comatose state and slowing down their bodily systems slightly. But I do not recommend you try this until you have much more knowledge and experience about the subject of hypnosis.

Several trance deepenings would have to be done and very strong post hypnotic suggestions would have to be used to get the subject deep enough into the deepest level of hypnosis. They are then placed into the bed and left for 24 hours being awoken the next day. This is a very old stunt, which old time hypnotists used to gain publicity for their shows. However more recently in 1993, Mr Peter Powers used the stunt with a slight change, he placed a man under hypnosis and left them in this state for a full eight days without food, water etc., or at least that's how it looked. A wet sponge was upon the subject's head and water cress was grown upon this, to prove that the subject had not moved. In actual fact, the truth was, yes, the person was in the bed for a week. Yes, they were under the hypnotic influence. And yes, they were there for eight days. But they were awoken at intervals of several hours, so that they could go to the loo, have water etc. and of course an experienced medical team was on hand at all times. I'm sure you can think of many ways in which this stunt can be faked, but I have enough knowledge of hypnosis to know that this can be done genuinely and enough respect for Peter Powers to tell you he did this for real. Obviously the post hypnotic used is such, that each time you say sleep they will re-enter trance except this time they will go 100 times deeper. And of course they are awoken and made to re-enter the trance until they are very deep. Then usual trance deepening techniques are used to take them into the comatose state required to perform this stunt genuinely. A good bit of publicity hype (but also serious) used by Peter Powers, was that an audio tape had been given to the medical team containing his voice. This would remove the person from the hypnotic trance, should Peter himself be killed in an accident, or not be present for any unknown reason. This is the kind of stunt, which done correctly, can make you an overnight star, but you must have a far greater experience of hypnosis than you currently have to do this.

OTHER PUBLICITY STUNTS

Other stunts which can be done along the lines of the window sleep, are to place a subject in trance, have them then dress in a garden gnome outfit and they are then placed, fishing rod in hand, upon a toadstool in a large shop window for 24 hours, which also contains a poster for your show. The incentive to the shop being that as the stunt will attract much free publicity, their business will improve as people will flock to the shop to see the person under hypnosis. You could even get them to pay a fee for getting publicity for their shop and of course, posters for your show are displayed throughout the store. Which in an establishment such as Debenhams, would practically guarantee that with the people who would see it your future shows would be sold out in advance of the event. Always remember, you must gain the written permission of the subject and observe proper medical and back-up requirements for stunts such as these.

HYPNOSIS VIA SATELLITE LINK/LETTER/TELEPHONE ETC

As long as a person wishes to be hypnotised and can hear what you say at all times, then they can be hypnotised even if you are not present in person. I was asked to hypnotise someone by satellite for Channel Four's "The Word" show and basically all I would have done, if their plans had not changed at the last moment, to make my spot a studio item, would have been that some subjects in the studio would have been sitting on chairs facing spotlights and the video screen would have been to the side of them. I, via the satellite link, would then have performed a P.R.I., such as the spotlight eyestrain method and people would have entered trance and reacted to all my post hypnotic suggestions, even though I wasn't present. The same goes for over the phone, if a speaker phone is used at the subjects end, so they have nothing to hold onto, then being able to hear your voice, they can be made to enter trance and react to your suggestions.

As for hypnosis by letter, the secret of this is to have secretly hypnotised the person in advance of the publicity stunt and leave within their mind that, when your letter arrives, on a certain date, in a certain coloured envelope, the moment they open it and read the word "sleep" they will instantly re-enter the state of trance until you say otherwise in person. In all three above cases, co-operation is required and the people must want to be hypnotised, but with hypnosis far more is possible than you could possibly imagine. It's all down to belief and expectancy once again.

PART FOURTEEN

SHORTCUTS TO HYPNOTHERAPY AND PSYCHOTHERAPY

Doctors are good at treating people from the neck downwards. Hypnotists are able to help with any problem that originates from the neck upwards, in other words, from the mind.

Over 90% of all reported illness is psychosomatic, caused by the mind and can be treated successfully with hypnosis, of the 10% that isn't, much of this can be helped with hypnosis.

This part of the course is intended as a brief extension to the in depth principals of hypnosis which you have already learned. The end result of the state of hypnosis is the same for both stage and therapy. It is very easy for a stage hypnotist to practise therapy but very difficult for a hypnotherapist to turn to the stage. This is why you have been given most of the theory side in the first part of this course. The methods of induction are sometimes different in so much as for stage work, a rapid induction technique is required whereas in therapy, the best requirement is often for a slower, more relaxed approach.

Should you wish to take your therapy even further than the advanced stages of this course, further training can be obtained from:

Mr Neil French at The Institute of Advanced Hypno-Analysts.

The principals for therapy are as follows:

1 Get rapport
2 Induce the trance
3 Deepen the trance
4 Ego strengthening/confidence boosting
5 Do the necessary therapy
6 Implant the major post-hypnotic suggestion
7 Awaken them from the trance

You will then be able to earn money from treating people, to stop them smoking, help them lose weight, gain confidence, break habits and all other simple problems. You go to the client's house, or they come to your consulting room. You get rapport by being friendly, taking an interest in their problem and the explaining about hypnosis briefly and what will occur during the session. They are then asked to lie down, or sit in a comfortable chair and commanded to close their eyes. In your early days, until you become more experienced, the moment the subjects eyes are closed, you can remove the scripts from your briefcase and literally just read from the page, the induction, trance deepening, ego strengthening, appropriate therapy, post hypnotic suggestion and then the awakening routine. You here, obviously, replace the scripts into your case just prior to having the patient open their eyes again.

Do not think this may seem like cheating. Your main concern is for the benefit of your client and a successful conclusion to the session. When you have treated a number of people, the scripts will have become second nature and you will have no need to refer to your notes. When you feel ready, you can then move into the more complex areas of psychological problems and use your psychotherapy skills to address emotional problems and help overcome fears, phobias, panic attacks, etc.

At this point, you can then earn £35 an hour, or more and unlike suggestion therapy, where you see the patient once and they should then be cured, with analysis you are treating deep seated problems of a highly emotional nature. As such, six to twelve sessions approximately are required on average to make the subject come to a solution of the problem of their own accord. Also to abreact, which as you know from a previous chapter means they will then have off loaded the emotion of a past event which has caused them indirectly to be scared of spiders, water or whatever.

As for example, a young child may be sexually abused and this is then "blocked" out of the mind, so not to trouble them. This cause of problems may then manifest itself by, in later life, making the child allergic to rice pudding, milk and other similar foodstuffs, without there being any logical or psychical reason for the allergy.

Under analysis , the client may reveal that they were made to have oral sex and as crude as it is, the mind has made a connection between semen and items of a similar consistency and that is why the problems occur. As the old saying goes, "when you find the cause of the problem, remove it and it's gone, then the symptoms will disappear." Here they reveal the cause, their abreaction (emotion) releases (removes) it and the symptom, which in this case is allergy of certain things, disappears as it was just an outwards manifestation of an inwards problem.

Read the chapter which details information about abreactions again, this time viewing it in the context of what I've just said and remembering that if it gets locked into the mind with emotion, then emotion is also needed to unlock it. Then you'll have a better understanding of how psycho-analysis under hypnosis does help people greatly in many ways.

Go to your library and obtain books about Sigmund Freud, Carl Jung and Milton Erickson and read about their theories and you will then have a far greater understanding of how analysis works and helps people to come to a realisation of the underlying cause of their problems.

Psychotherapy, as taught on the Neil French course, can be used without hypnosis. Combined however, the relaxation of hypnosis on the body and mind helps off load information more easily. A clear example of this, is that standard psychotherapists take around 100 hours to solve the problem, whereas when hypnosis is used, the problem can usually be solved in no more than twelve one hour sessions.

There are subjects such as transference, counter transference and rationalisation, which should also be studied .

Another advantage you will find of learning psycho analysis and all about personality types etc., is that you will be able to use this information in your everyday life to assess people. You will instantly be able to tell what type of person the subject is and which style of induction would be best to use upon them, which of course can only be of benefit.

One very true piece of advice, if you expect to treat others problems without yours interfering, then you must first go through sessions of hypno-analysis to release all your skeletons in the closet. Only by doing this will you be a successful therapist and help others. Now you may think you have no need for this, but I know that every person on earth would benefit from six to twelve hours of this treatment and I guarantee it would improve their life in many ways.

ADVANCED HYPNOTHERAPY

Never forget the power which hypnosis possess and always treat your clients with respect. Their senses will be enhanced and sometimes altered but the experience will be very enjoyable, providing you observe the correct guidelines.

Self hypnosis has already been mentioned earlier in the course and the audio cassette supplied with your course is more than adequate for personal development. The following methods and applications involve Hetro-hypnosis (hypnotising other people) and with practice you will quickly develop the most suitable method for your own personality.

One of the main "perception" tools to instil into your client on your first meeting is your expertise and knowledge. If you memorise, or even better use a clipboard containing notes, the following information, you will leave no doubt at all in the mind of your client. Incidentally, if you use a clipboard, you will appear more professional and you will be able to take notes for future reference and if you position your seat so as to conceal the note paper, nothing which is written down will be visible to your client.

THE CONSCIOUS MIND

The conscious mind (around 12% of the total) helps us with daily decision making and thinks out new situations where we have to decide what to do and how to do it. It can hold only a limited number of thoughts and ideas at any one time which is why we often memorise numbers in small chunks of three, for example a nine number (684128472) is much easier to remember as 684 then 128 then472. This is because the conscious mind can hold only between five and nine units of information at any one time.

THE UNCONSCIOUS MIND

The unconscious mind (around 88% of the total) is where we become very interested for the use of hypnosis. This contains all your memories, emotions, imaginations, intelligence and controls the autonomic nervous system which regulates breathing, blood circulation, heart beat etc.

All which has ever happened to you and everything you have imagined is stored away in the unconscious mind which acts just like a computer. All the information is stored away and is available to be pulled back at any time.

A good example of this is riding a bike or driving a car. When we are learning to ride or drive, we hit many obstacles. Loosing balance, crunching gears, lack of confidence and Kangaroo petrol! However, as we practice and become familiar with the skills, they automatically become habit and are stored away in the unconscious mind to use at any time in the future. When we become an expert driver or rider, we don't have to think about how to do it, we just do it automatically.

The conscious mind has an automatic resistance to situations. It reasons and rejects certain situations and acts as our defence mechanism and a safety device.

Once the defences of the conscious mind have been closed down, the unconscious mind is accessed and instructions and suggestions are acted upon. It is very important to formulate the suggestions in a specific way to ensure they are accepted. The techniques for this will be explained later.

There are still various myths and misconceptions about hypnosis. Some people are still scared at the thought of the experience because they assume they will become unconscious or helpless, but this is not the case. When hypnotised, you are still aware of everything going on around you and you are still seemingly in control, but you are in a heightened state of awareness and have the overwhelming desire to carry out the suggestions given.

In the hypnotic trance, you experience a change in awareness. Just as everybody experiences life differently, everybody has a different way of experiencing hypnosis.

Whilst in your consulting room or on a home visit, you must develop a trust partnership with your client. Without this it will be very difficult to obtain the maximum co-operation required for success.

A further extension to this is to go through the following checklist with any new client:

1. Have you been hypnotised at any time in the past?
2. You will not be harmed by hypnosis.
3. While hypnotised, you cannot be made to do or say anything against your normal moral principals and beliefs.
4. No crime has been recorded as being committed as a result of hypnosis.
5. Ensure the toilet is not required.

6. Request that your client removes contact lenses, glasses, shoes, releases tight clothing (tie, belt etc.)
7. Emphasise that they do not try too hard. Just listen and follow your instructions.
8. Tell them that they won't feel much different and not to expect anything to happen.
9. Tell them that intelligence, co-operation and concentration always gives the best results.
10. They may be wondering what happens if they don't come round straight away. Tell them it is very unusual for this to happen, although there are ways to deal with it (see earlier) and if it does happen, it is most likely because they are enjoying the sensations so much that they want to prolong it.
11. A lot of people are a little apprehensive before they are hypnotised for the first time, but afterwards, they experience it as being a pleasant, relaxing state leaving them feeling wonderful.
12. They may be surprised to learn that while hypnotised, they will still be aware and still be able to hear everything around them, it just won't bother them.
13. Ask them. "How do you expect me to hypnotise you?"

The answer to the last question has two reasons. Firstly you will establish the depth of trance estimated. (Deeper and quicker if they have been hypnotised before). Secondly, you are introducing the expectancy and acceptance that you **are** going to hypnotise them.

THE MINDCARE MINDRULES

Mindrule One

EACH IDEA OR THOUGHT GIVES A PHYSICAL REACTION

As you will soon come to realise, your thoughts can affect all the functions of your body. Fear, stress, worry and anxiety can all lead to bodily changes

Thoughts with strong emotions almost always reach the unconscious mind and once accepted, these thoughts carry on producing the physical reactions. To reverse this effect, the unconscious mind must be accessed to change the thought pattern.

Mindrule Two

EXPECTANCY IS REALISED

Our brain and nervous system respond to thoughts and images. Our physical health is largely dependant on our mental expectancy. Doctors recognise that if the patient expects to recover quickly, then they are more likely to. On the other hand if they expect their condition to worsen, then it often does. Negative attitudes bring negative results. Positive attitudes bring positive results.

Mindrule Three

SYMPTOMS, INDUCED EMOTIONALLY FOR LONG ENOUGH CAN CAUSE ORGANIC CHANGE

It is believed that in excess of 70% of human ailments are functional rather than organic, ie. The organs of the body are affected by the reaction of the nervous system through negative ideas in the mind. This is not to suggest that everyone with an ailment is neurotic, there is disease causing illness, but if you continue to complain, fear and think about your nervous headaches or tensed up stomach, then organic changes will occur in time.

Mindrule Four

IMAGINATION IS MORE POWERFUL THAN KNOWLEDGE IN THE MIND

This is especially important when using self hypnosis. We often feel superior to people who have been tricked in some way, but we are also blind to the facts of our own unreasonable beliefs. A thought or idea supported by a strong emotion such as anger or hate is often difficult to alter through normal reasoning but easily addressed through hypnosis.

Mindrule Five

AN IDEA REMAINS, UNTIL IT IS REPLACED BY ANOTHER, IN THE UNCONSCIOUS MIND

If an idea is accepted in the unconscious mind, it stays there. The longer it remains, the more it becomes habit and part of our normal daily lives, whether it is good or bad.

To change our actions, we must first change our thoughts. We accept known facts such as 2+2=4 and the sun and moon are up there even though we cannot see them. But we often get programmed into thinking, " I must have a cigarette with my coffee" or "I must eat my lunch at 12.30." These are not actually correct, but have developed into a fixed habit and there will be a conscious resistance to changing them. Changing them unconsciously however, will bring about permanent results.

Mindrule Six

AT THE SAME TIME, OPPOSING IDEAS CANNOT BE HELD

This is not to say that more than one idea cannot be remembered, but means that there will always be a conscious conflict to opposing ideas. If you try to preach one thing while actually practising another, then the nervous system will have a negative response to the conflict.

Mindrule Seven

SUGGESTIONS ACCEPTED CREATE GREATER EASE OF ACCEPTANCE OF FURTHER SUGGESTIONS

Look or think back to your stage training and this principal takes no further explanation.

Mindrule Eight

THE MORE CONSCIOUS EFFORT, THE LESS SUBCONSCIOUS RESPONSE

When dealing with the subconscious mind, do not rush. Work in a methodical manner to develop positive mental expectancy. Do not force anything, just let things happen naturally. The more you "try" the less effective the results will be. Encourage your client to just listen, relax, co-operate etc.

PRE CONDITIONING

If you are happy that your client is willing to commence quickly you can start the induction, but if there is apprehension or you suspect they do not believe they will be hypnotised, any of the previously explained pre-demonstration methods can be used, or the following usually provides adequate proof for therapy.

Take a ring, small weight or key and tie a length of string to it about eight inches long and tie the other end to the end of a pencil. Next, take a sheet of A4 paper and draw a bold straight line on it about six inches long down the middle. Place the paper on your desk or table and tell your client to stand in front of the paper, hold the pencil between the end of their thumb and forefinger, with the ring about one inch above the line, in effect making a miniature fishing rod. Ensure the elbows are not touching the body and start to give instructions as follows:
"As you stand concentrating on the line at all times, allow your mind to focus only on this. Just gaze at the line. Don't think about anything else apart from the line. As you gaze and concentrate, you will soon find that the weight will start to swing backwards and forwards, along the length of the line. Concentrate all your attentions on the line and as you do, you will find the weight will start to swing up and down along the length. The harder you concentrate, the more the weight will swing. Allow your mind to think only of the weight starting to swing up and down the length of the line."

Keep repeating these suggestions and vary them slightly if you wish until the weight starts to swing. Your client will be amazed by the apparent power you are demonstrating. (Try this experiment on yourself by using the focus of your imagination to get the weight swinging).

While the weight is swinging, you can then start suggesting that if an ellipse or circle is imagined, the weight will follow these shapes. Just keep repeating in a confident manner until it happens.

It is important that you encourage a positive response from your client because if thoughts such as "I don't think it will work for me" or "It is not moving" will probably result in the weight staying put as both the conscious and unconscious mind will have accepted negative thoughts.

With success in this, you will have surprised your client how quickly you can exert your "power" and they will be ready to co-operate for hypnosis.

An alternative to this could be to lock your clients eyes closed within a matter of seconds. This method has been touched on before, but a suitable routine and narration for the consulting room would be as follows:

Ask your client to sit comfortably in a chair and stand in front and slightly to the side of them. Explain in a confident manner that you are now going to demonstrate how you are going to simply and quickly lock their eyes closed so that they will not be able to open them until you say so. Take a pencil and starting around six inches centrally in front of their face, instruct them to follow the pencil wherever it goes without moving their head. Now move the pencil slowly from side to side, gradually increasing the distance you move it. Tell them to try and watch the pencil, even when it goes out of sight. After moving from side to side four or five times, alter the movement to up and down and again, gradually increase the distance you move the pencil. Tell them to try and follow it, even when it goes out of sight above or below the field of vision. This will have a slightly disorientating effect and lead you on to the next stage.

When you have completed this routine, tell your client to close their eyes normally and let them relax for a few moments. Then with your finger, touch the point on their forehead which is mid way between the eyebrows and half way up the forehead i.e. the exact point where you would imagine the third eye to be. Instruct your client to leave their eyelids closed and at the same time, try to look at the point on their forehead which you are touching (you should be able to see the eyes under the eyelids move upwards). Now, with an authoritative tone, instruct them to continue to try and look at the point on the forehead and focus their attention there. Repeat these suggestions and ensure their eyes are still in that position (don't leave this too long as it may become uncomfortable) and then say in a confident and positive manner. "Now you can not open your eyes! You can **not** open your eyes. Continue to look at the spot and however hard you try, you can not open your eyes. The harder you try to open your eyes, the tighter they will stick together. You will not be able to open your eyes until I tell you that you can."

This method, if used correctly, will work every time because of the muscle arrangements around the eyes.

At this point you can either tell them to relax and stop concentrating on the spot and then they will be able to open their eyes, or leave them in this state and start the induction directly from here. (You should of course tell them to relax their eyes, stop looking at the spot and let them remain closed)

There are many favourable conditions for your consulting room which will prove beneficial. First and foremost, a reclining chair or couch should be used. When preparing for your induction, it is best to ask your client for their preference on how they feel most comfortable. You may be surprised that some (especially female, if you are male) feel a little vulnerable if reclined fully back in a chair. The best advice is to let them decide, then there will be a minimum of resistance from them.

Ensure the room is warm and as quiet as possible (although noises can be used to your advantage later – refer to the therapy video cassette). Avoid any bright lights shining directly on your clients face. Some people prefer to work in a dimmed room with a light bulb of 15 to 20 watts, but this is down to personal preference.

What is a major asset however to therapy is blue light. This has already been mentioned for stage work, but for the consulting room, both the décor and the lighting have positive influential effects when used around the theme of blue. It is perfectly adequate to obtain a number of blue light bulbs from your local DIY store and replace the existing ones, - bear in mind however that even a 60 watt blue bulb will provide very little actual light and you may need a number of them in a larger room – if you are using a spare room in the house, you may prefer to set up your own "hypnotising light arrangement" on a portable stand with two or three bulbs arranged on it. This can then be placed to the side of your client as and when required.

Soft relaxing music in the background will help with the induction routine. The shadow tape included with your package will work well, even better if you record one of your own with your own voice. If you prefer however, audio cassettes and CD's are available from libraries and High Street shops. A little forward planning is required here though, as the length of the tracks may only be four or five minutes and you will be needing (especially in the early stages) possibly twenty to thirty minutes of continuous music. It is much better to copy a number of suitable tracks onto one side of a C90 cassette without breaks (watch out for copyright laws) and use this for your induction sessions. You can vary your choice of music and build up a selection to use with different types of clients, but always ensure the music is of a soft and relaxing nature and play it at a lower volume than the level of your voice.

Your preparation aim is to influence as many of the senses as possible. You have now addressed the sense of sight (blue light), touch (warm room and limited movement) and hearing (soft music). There is little you can do about the sense of taste at this stage but the sense of smell can have an immense influence.

The art of Aromatherapy is based on the sense of smell, influencing the Olfactory Nervous System and now proves so successful that the therapy is being introduced into intensive care units of hospitals. The natural oils have different effects on the frame of mind and can be stimulating, sedative, rejuvenating, warming, refreshing or relaxing. For this reason, a blend of Lavender and Frankincense in a small oil burner within the room will be invaluable. Lavender is well known for it's relaxing and sedative properties while Frankincense encourages deeper breathing.

To repeat again, as it is vitally important for therapy also, the manner in which you speak is very important. Use a quite but firm tone of voice which leaves no doubt at all in your client's mind that you are fully confident and know what you are doing. While making your suggestions, there should be a minimum of pauses and your delivery should flow smoothly. Postcard sized cards can be used to refer to. Don't worry about your client seeing the cards as they will have their eyes closed, simply conceal them from view until they are no longer open.

Before you start, ask if the toilet is required, make sure a comfortable seating or lying arrangement has been taken and release any tight or restrictive clothing (untie or remove shoes, slacken belt, loosen any clothing around the neck etc.)

HYPNOTISING FOR THERAPY

The numerous methods for inducing hypnosis on stage which have been detailed earlier can be used as described or adapted for use in the consulting room. However, if you prefer, a more detailed description of four methods which are ideal for therapy follow. The first method is probably best for the beginner, but any can be used to vary the approaches as you develop your skills later. Once you have mastered the techniques, you can modify or combine them to suit your own individual preference and personality.

The four methods which follow will take most clients into a light state of trance where little or no reaction to suggestion will be obtained. To obtain maximum response, it is necessary to deepen the state and this is covered a little later.

FIXED GAZE INDUCTION

With your client seated comfortably take a pencil or something similar with a shiny end. Instruct your client to take a number or deep breaths and on inhaling totally, hold the breath for a few moments, then release slowly and fully. Repeat three or four times. Hold the shiny end of the pencil slightly higher than the level of the gaze and about ten inches away from the face and ask your client to gaze and concentrate constantly at the end of the pencil. As the elevated position of the eyes is maintained for a period, the muscles will tire. This is because the eyes are pulled inwards and upwards and are not accustomed to the strained position. The tiring of the eyes is a psychological process and you should anticipate, by observing, when the eye muscles are becoming tired. When this appears to be starting to happen you start your suggestions by saying something similar to: "Your eyes will soon begin to feel heavy. Your eyes will feel tired. Your eyelids will feel heavy and tired. Your eyes are now felling more and more tired. Your eyelids will feel so heavy, they will want to close. You are getting sleepier as you gaze at the pencil. Your eyes are now feeling so heavy, they will want to close down". If you observe any blinking of the eyelids say

"You will find your eyelids starting to blink and as they do, your eyes will feel even more heavy and tired."

Keep repeating suggestions of heaviness, sleepiness, tiredness of the eyes etc. until your client's eyes close down. When the eyes are closed **YOU HAVE HYPNOTISED YOUR CLIENT!** You have closed their eyes with the power of suggestion. Simple as that. This maybe true, but you have only guided your client into a light hypnotic trance at this stage. You must now go through the process of deepening the state to ensure the post hypnotic suggestions are as effective as possible.

A number of other techniques now follow and to avoid repetition, as with the above method, the explanation will be only to this light stage, as fuller and more detailed instructions for deepening the state are given later and are common to each light trance induction.

VISUALISATION METHOD

Assuming your subject is comfortably seated and has gone through the deep breathing routine, say something similar to "Now just close your eyes. That's right, allow your eyes to close down and let yourself relax, let yourself feel comfortable, let all the tensions in your body start to fade away. Now with your eyes closed at all times, I want you to visualise the letter O or zero in your mind. See the circle in your imagination and now put it on a flat piece of wood in front of you. Now take an imaginary pen and draw another circle, a little smaller this time on top of the first one so you now have the figure of 8. You will now see the figure of 8 which is the small circle on top of the large circle. Now, take your pen again and fill in the centres of the two circles so now have two circular discs or wheels. Take the small one off the top of the large one and place it carefully on the piece of wood at the side it. Now take a small paint brush with the bristles loaded with white paint and draw a spiral on each circular disc so both look like the end of a swiss roll. Now, tilt the piece of wood slightly to your right and watch them swirl along the piece of wood right to the end, the piece of wood can be as long as you like, watch them swirling away to your right. When they reach the end of the wood they will stop. Now tilt the shelf to your left and watch them swirling off to your left. See them as they come whirling and spinning to your left. From your left now, with the wood tilted slightly to your right, watch them come spinning back. Just to the centre from where they started and...... stop. Now take a rubber and rub out the middle of the discs so you are left with the two original circles and place the small one on top of the large one and you will have the figure of 8 back. Now let the small circle on top start to disintegrate into dust and disappear. Totally disappear. You are now left with nothing at all so just let yourself relax and let your mind go blank. As all the images and pictures disappear let all the sounds fade away into the distance. Just relax, let your body start to feel heavy. Feeling sleepy. Sleep deeply. Pay no attention at all to any sounds, apart from the sound of my voice. All the other sounds fade away into the distance. Feeling drowsy and sleepier. Just listening to the sound of my voice. You're sinking further and further down. With every breath you take you're drifting down dee-per and dee-per. All of your muscles releasing and letting go completely. Your mind and body letting go completely, everything letting go and feeling very relaxed --- heavy --- comfortable. Nothing at all will disturb you sinking down still deeper.

Commence deepening routines.

FOCUS OF CONCENTRATION METHOD

Assuming your subject is comfortably seated and has gone through the deep breathing routine say "For the next few moments just let your arms rest comfortably on the chair arms or on your thighs. Let them relax and go limp. Let them feel heavy. Let all the muscles in your arms relax. In a moment I will place my hand in front of your face and I want you to concentrate on my middle finger." Place your hand in front of your client's face with your middle finger above the line of vision and about eight inches away. Hold this position for a few moments then continue "In a few moments I will bring my hand down in front of your face and when I do, just follow my middle finger downwards which will cause your eyes to close. Follow my finger downwards and close your eyes. Now, keep your eyes focused on my middle finger and follow it down as it passes in front of your face and let your eyelids close down." Pass your hand slowly down in front of your client's face until their eyes close down then continue "Now your eyes are comfortably closed down, let all the little muscles around them relax. Let all the tiny muscles around your eyes let go. Let them feel heavy and even more relaxed. Let them release all the tensions to such a point as they would not work at all even if you wanted them to. When you have let them relax to such a point and not before, that they would not work even if you wanted them to, test them. When you have let them relax so much that they will not work, you have been completely successful. Re---lax. Re—l—ax. Well done, now stop trying and let the whole of your body relax in the same way. Your whole body relaxing and feeling heavier. I will now take your hand and lift your arm slightly into the air. As I lift it, let the muscles release and let go even more, so your hand and arm hang loose and limp. Then when I let go, let it fall like a heavy weight of lead. When your hand touches your body I want you to send a surging wave of relaxation right from the top of your head all the way down to the very tips of your toes. This will double your level of relaxation and make you feel twice as comfortable." Take the hand and continue "I'm raising your hand now. Just let it hang loose. Let it feel heavy and limp. Let all the muscles let go.

That's right, that's fine. Now when I drop it, let it fall like a heavy weight of lead to your body. When it touches your body feel the surging wave of relaxation move from the top of your head to the tips of your toes." Let the hand go and direct it to fall onto the upper legs and when it touches emphasise the relaxation by saying "Waves of relaxation sweeping through your body" or something similar. Then repeat the process with your clients other hand.

Continue with deepening routines.

THE COUNTING METHOD

Assuming your client is comfortably seated and has gone through the deep breathing routine. Arrange a low wattage blue light bulb or a blue disc which you can illuminate in a position which is easy for your client to gaze at. Ensure the rest of the room is in subdued light. Now tell your subject to fix all attentions and concentrations on the light or illuminated disc and follow your instructions. Then say that when you count "one" they should close their eyes and when you say "two" they should open them, when you count "three" they will close them and when you count "four" they will open them. Tell your client that you will continue to count and with every odd number they will close their eyes and with every even number they will open them. Then say "As I continue to count, you will find that your eyelids start to feel drowsy, your eyes will become heavier and heavier with every number. As I count further you will experience an increasing resistance to open your eyes which will grown stronger with every number. Your eyes will soon become so heavy and tired and the resistance to open them will be such that you will not be able to open them any more. When you find you are unable to open them, do not worry, just let them stay comfortably closed and relax and continue listening to me."

It is not necessary to indicate how long this will take but you could say for example, that by the time you reach twenty the eyelids will feeling heavy. This will be down to your judgement based on your previous tests.

As you start to count, make the pause after the odd numbers be progressively longer than the pause after the even numbers. Do not make this too obvious at first, but lead into it gradually. The result of this is that your client's eyes are closed for a longer period than they are open. Keep a smooth rhythm which will avoid any tenseness or uncertainty which you must avoid. As you reach the number twenty, observe what is happening. If it appears your client's eyes are starting to close voluntarily then continue counting. If there appears to be resistance, then amplify the suggestions by saying something like, "20 -- 21 you are feeling very relaxed. 22 -- 23 you are resting very comfortably in the chair. 24 -- 25 your eyes are becoming heavier and heavier. 26 -- 27 you are resting pleasantly and quietly. 28 -- 29 your eyelids are becoming heavier and heavier. 30 -- 31 it is now becoming too much of an effort to keep your eyes open. 32 -- 33 they are getting so heavy and tired, it's too much of an effort and your eyes want to stay closed. 34 -- 35 it's much more pleasant to sit resting with your eyes closed as they are so heavy. 36 -- 37 your eyes are so heavy and all you want to do is rest quietly and peacefully."

Make sure that you comment on the odd numbers while the eyes are closed and when they stay closed continue with the deepening routine given later.

DEEPENING THE HYPNOTIC TRANCE

You should now be proficient at inducing a light trance in your client which is a state little different to the normal waking state. To ensure your suggestions have maximum results, you must go through a number of procedures to deepen the hypnotic trance progressively. Each routine takes your client deeper every time and influences the next one. It is only a matter of guiding by talking patiently and observing the responses. When you get a little further through the routines, you will be able to awaken your client and return them into a deeper trance by simply saying the word "sleep."

A number of observations should be noted as you go through your deepening routines as these will provide you with a guide. It is always difficult to gauge the actual depth of hypnosis but as you become more experienced you will notice these reactions and be able to assess the depth.

- The face often changes in appearance and turns to a slightly wax like shade.
- Reflex actions start, such as: swallowing, twitching fingers, breathing deepens.
- Spasmodic movements start, such as: frowns, rolling of the eyes under the eyelids.
- The head often falls to one side or forwards.
- The lower jaw often falls open a little.
- There is an appearance of total muscle relaxation in the whole body.
- There is an apparent total reluctance to move.

Remember the senses mentioned earlier (sight, hearing, touch, smell and taste) as these are very important now. The more senses you are able to bring into the induction, the more effective it will be. An excellent example would be: "As you lie on the soft golden sand you can feel the warm summer sun beating down on your body. You may be able to hear the birds singing in the distance and smell the sweet scents of the flowers drifting over the cliffs. You can see the leaves of the palm trees gently rustling in the warm breeze and hear the sound of the sea, gently lapping up the coastline." Sentences such as these are very expressive and use descriptive words to make it easy for your client to visualise. This is exactly what you want.

Below is an example of what to say to start the deepening procedure. It has been purposely kept quite long to give you a good idea of the style and repetitiveness required. You can either use a copy of this or devise your own, but always remember to use a monotonous tone. As you become more experienced you will find that a shortened version of this will only be required. This speech should be started when your client has closed their eyes and spoken in a slow, methodical manner and you could start your music at this point for extra effect. Emphasise the words in italics, but not too obviously. The aim is to guide your subject into a deep state of physical and mental relaxation which will then close down the conscious mind and allow you direct access to the unconscious.

It is assumed your client is sitting in a chair. If however, they are lying down, amend your suggestions to suit.

"As you sit peacefully in the chair (or lie on the bed or couch) I want you to remain *comfortable* and allow your eyes to remain closed and just listen to my voice. Just *let go* of all the tensions and *enjoy* the feeling of being relaxed. *Now,* as you sit comfortably relaxed, let all your thoughts drift away. Don't think about anything apart from what I am saying and think only of that. *Now,* I want you to think for a few moments and think about -------- (slight pause) *weightlessness.* Just think about *weightlessness.* What it must feel like to be weightless. You may have thought about it before or seen it on a film. Think about becoming weightless. Your whole body feeling lighter than air and *relaxing* even more. Weightlessness. It's just as if you're floating away on a cushion of air which moulds itself perfectly to all the contours of your body and supports it. Feeling lighter than air and *weightless.* Now beginning to float and drift away to anywhere you like. And you can now start to relax your whole body even more, drifting *deeper* into comfortable relaxation and continuing just to rest peacefully. Your whole body continuing to relax even more, starting with your feet. Just imagine for a moment, imagine in your minds eye, imagine your toes and all the little muscles round them. See them in your mind and *feel* them relaxing. Let them go limp. Let them go heavy. Feel all the tensions just fading away. Limp and heavy. Now your feet, both feet. Feel them relaxing. Going heavy, feeling just like lead. Both feet, totally relaxing, getting *heavier* and *heavier.* Now starting to move up your legs, moving up both legs, all the way up to your knees. *Relaxing.* Your calf muscles, *relaxing,* feeling heavy, all the tensions just fading away. Now moving further up your legs, up both legs, to you thighs, *relaxing,* feeling *heavy.* Now just ask yourself if there is any tension at all left in your feet and legs ----------- and if there is, let it *smooth* away. Calmly let it smooth away and your legs will become even heavier. Now slowly moving further up you body, through your stomach, right up through your chest, *relaxing,* all the way up to your neck, *relaxing.* Your stomach, your chest, all the way up to your neck, *relaxing.* Feeling *heavier* and *heavier.* All the tensions, *completely* fading away. All the muscles letting go completely. Now you back, your whole back, right from your thighs to your neck, all the muscles in your back, *relaxing,* feeling heavy. As your back relaxes even more, enjoy the feelings and now let your shoulders *relax,* your shoulders relaxing and feeling heavy. All the muscles in your back and your shoulders, *relaxing,* going limp and *heavy.* Now your arms, moving down both arms, to your elbows, *relaxing,* further down your arms, right into your hands and flowing through your fingers and thumbs, *relaxing,* feeling heavier and heavier. With every breath you take and with every word you hear, you are sinking *down* further and further into deep relaxation. Your shoulders now relaxing even more and starting to droop as they feel even *heavier.* Your whole body feeling heavy and relaxed, with no effort at all. Now, as you rest feeling wonderfully calm and peaceful, just think for a few moments about your breathing. Allow your thoughts to dwell on your breathing, because when we're asleep we don't have to think about our breathing, our body does it for us. So do that now, think about your breathing and be aware of your breathing, but just let it happen naturally. Focus upon it and be aware of your body taking in just the right amount of air. As you breathe out, you are breathing out tension and as you breathe in you are becoming more and more relaxed. Every time you breathe in, you are becoming more and more relaxed and every time you breath out you are releasing more and more tension from your body. You don't need to make any effort at all, just let it happen and let it happen naturally. Your whole body now relaxed and now moving up you neck. Moving up your neck and the back of your head, *relaxing.* Up the back of your head and over the top of your head. *Relaxing*, feeling *heavy.* Now down over your forehead, all the little muscles in your forehead, *relaxing.* Now round your eyes. All the tiny little muscles round your eyes and your eyelids, *relaxing,* feeling heavier and *heavier.* Even your nose, your ears, your cheeks, relaxing. Your lips and your jaw, feeling heavy. Even your tongue inside your mouth, *relaxing.* You will find, with every breath you take, you are drifting down deeper and *deeper* and getting sleepier and sleepier. Now as I count from ten to one, you will find yourself drifting down even deeper to sleep and feel even heavier. *Ten*, relaxing more with every number I count. *Nine*, feeling heavier. *Eight*, heavier and heavier with every number. *Seven,* getting sleepier. *Six,* drifting deeper to sleep with every number. *Five*, feeling yourself being dragged down even deeper. *Four,* sleepier and sleepier. *Three,* heavier and heavier. *Two,* almost there, feeling so heavy and sleepy and *One,* so deeply relaxed now feeling wonderfully calm, peaceful and tranquil. Sleeping deeply where nothing at all will disturb you."

At this stage, your client should be in a deeper state of hypnosis and will probably respond to further suggestions but you should continue with the deepening routine and include visualisation techniques explained below until you become a little more experienced. Remember, your client is still aware of everything which is being said and done so don't rush anything:

"You're sitting comfortably in the chair doing nothing at all but resting. You can hear my voice speaking to you all the time, but it won't disturb you at all. Nothing at all will disturb you. You will find, as you sit there, that your mind is becoming sleepier and sleepier. You won't try to think about what I'm saying, but you will hear everything. As I talk, you will find that your heavy, limp body will start to relax even more and with every breath you take you will find yourself sinking further and further d-o-w-n deeper and deeper getting sleepier and sleepier with every breath. One part of your mind is now already asleep, but you will continue to hear everything I say. Your mind is now at quiet peacefully rest. You will soon find the whole of your body will start to have sensations of tingling. Pleasant tingling sensations throughout your entire body. Tingling, more and more feeling good. It won't disturb you at all and it won't make you feel uneasy, it will feel wonderful and you will enjoy the feelings which will help you to drift down even deeper and deeper to a really deep sound sleep. All you want to do is just go on sinking further and further d-o-w-n, drifting d-e-e-p-e-r with every easy breath you take. You're resting quietly and peacefully and nothing will disturb you. You will find this feeling of rest, of being sleepy and drowsy, becomes more and more pleasant as time goes by. It's just as though you're swirling d-o-w-n, being dragged deeper and deeper, floating peacefully into a deep sound sleep, where nothing at all will disturb you and nothing will worry you and all you'll want to do is just go on resting, getting sleepier and drifting deeper. You will soon find that your breathing will become deeper. Breathing deeper." (Notice at this point how your client's breathing deepens and time your words to match it.) "Deep easy breaths, in -------- and --------- out. Take no notice of this and just continue to rest, breathing deeply and drifting d-o-w-n. Any noises you hear will seem such a long, long way off, they will not interest you at all, you won't be interested in anything at all except drifting deeper and deeper to sleep."

(If any noises do occur, you can use these to your advantage by saying something like. "As you hear the sound of the dog barking" or "as you hear the sounds of the cars passing outside, they are now meaningless and just help you to drift even further and further down. All the noises seem such a long, long way off." This will be an advantage if any unforeseen noises do occur.)

"You have learned now how to let go completely. Just let go completely and sink down further getting heavier and heavier. Soon you will start to feel even more comfortable and warm, feeling too tired to bother about anything at all. You may feel a little dizzy or dreamy while I'm talking, or my voice may seem to drift away at times, but take no notice of this, for steadily and quietly you are sinking further and further down even deeper, all the time."

Providing you have followed the correct guidelines without rushing, your client should now be in a deep enough state of hypnosis to respond to further suggestions which will deepen the state even further. Any number of the following routines can be included or you can formulate your own to suit particular individuals. Avoid at all costs, any suggestions which your client would have a fear or resistance to, for example, imagining the sound of the sea if there is a fear of water or having the sunshine beating down on the body if your client burns very easily. It is far better to use ideas which your client would normally find pleasant.

"I will now count from ten to one and as I count I want you to imagine you are walking down a staircase. Any staircase. One step with each number. With every step you take, you will find yourself being dragged even deeper to sleep and becoming heavier. Ten, starting to walk down the staircase. Nine, getting heavier with every step. Eight, falling deeper and deeper with each step you take. Seven, sleepier and sleepier as you walk down the staircase. Six, drifting deeper and deeper. Five, heavier and heavier. Four, sleepier and sleepier. Three, almost at the bottom. Two, relaxing even deeper and One, deeply sound asleep. Now you've reached the bottom of the staircase and in front of you is another. You will walk down this staircase and this time, as you walk down, with every step you take, you will fall twice as deeply to sleep and double your relaxation, with every step. Ten, doubling your relaxation with every step. Nine, falling twice as deeply asleep with every step." Etc. etc.

The staircase routine can be repeated as many times as you wish as it will help to deepen the trance, but do not allow it to become too boring.

Once you have taken your subject down the flights of stairs, it is a good opportunity to expand on this by explaining that at the bottom of the last flight there is a door which is to be approached and opened. As they open the door you continue with: "Now you have opened the door and in front of you there is your own private place of paradise. It is the place of your dreams and the place you have longed to visit. This is now your very own private place where there is nobody else and you have total freedom to do anything you like. Then continue. "As you enter your own private place of paradise you feel totally at ease, you can feel the soft golden sand on your feet and between your toes. The warm summer sun is beating down on your body and it feels wonderful. The leaves of the palm trees are gently rustling in the warm summer breeze and the birds are singing in the distance. The sweet fragrances of the flowers are drifting over the cliffs and you can hear the sound of the sea gently licking and lapping up and down the shoreline." Continue with suggestions similar to these and observe the reactions. It is then a suitable time to start your suggestion therapy explained later.

When you have deepened the trance partially (to the point where your client is entering the paradise beach), you should change your music (the ideal way is to use a twin cassette deck) to the subliminal sounds cassette. As I have already mentioned, the more senses you bring into operation the better and you will now see the benefits of the "outside influences", for example the trance will be deepened even further when you say: "as you walk along the golden sand etc...hear the birds singing...... smell the sweet fragrances of the summer flowers......hear the sound of the sea gently licking and lapping up the shoreline...." Your client will indeed associate the warmth of the room with summer, they could imagine birds singing on the subliminal tape, they will smell the Lavender and Frankincense as summer flower fragrances and definitely hear the sound of the sea. Take as long as you feel necessary for this part, it is extremely enjoyable for the hypnotised person.

Always remember to give safety device instructions before you start by saying "Before we start the session, if for any reason during the therapy, your immediate attention is required, you will instantly become wide awake and alert to deal with any situation presented to you."

Do not actually state colours, types of birds or actual fragrances as this may cause conflict and confusion in their mind if they are thinking about something else eg. You say red roses when they may be thinking of highly scented honeysuckle. – Leave it open ended and entirely up to their own imagination.

Time your talking and breathing to coincide with theirs. Use the words "deeper, relaxing, sleepier, heavier etc" on their out breath and stretch them out and don't forget that counting down helps relaxation while counting up tends to help awaken.

Your client should now be in a suitable state to accept suggestions. Look for the physical indications explained earlier.

There now follows four examples of suitable suggestion therapy for clients with some of the most popular complaints, smoking (this can be easily adapted for other habits), weight loss, confidence with other people and skin complaints. The suggestions should be given when your client has been taken into the deepened state.

STOPPING SMOKING

"All the outside sounds will continue, but they are not important now and you will take no notice of anything except the sound of my voice. Just centre your attentions on the suggestions which I will give you. Nothing can distract you and nothing will disturb you while you are listening. Peacefully and feeling wonderfully calm and relaxed in your own private place of paradise. All the time drifting deeper and deeper while you listen to the sound of my voice. All the suggestions will help you, they are for your benefit. No one is **making** you stop smoking, you are stopping because **you** want to and you know it makes sense. Some people resent having to stop smoking and feel irritable, this is because they don't really want to stop or they don't think that they should. But you are different, because you have now decided that you really do want to stop and you now have the will and desire to stop smoking with no feelings of resentment or irritability. In fact, you will feel much, much better for stopping. You will feel cleaner and healthier. You feel very happy and glad you have made up your own mind to stop smoking. You feel relieved to be free of a weed and you are proud of the fact that you are no longer a slave to the drug of nicotine. You are now released from the grip of cigarettes for ever and you feel a wonderful sense of personal achievement. Now that you are an adult, you know that you don't have to prove to anybody that you are an adult by smoking as you may have done in the past as a child. You no longer need to prove that you are a man/woman by smoking, in fact people will now respect you more for not smoking and really admire you for stopping. You may have used to smoke because it seemed to give satisfaction, but it has not been very satisfactory at all, has it (slight pause). The smell and taste of tobacco is unpleasant and if you get smoke in your eyes it stings and causes tears to come. If you enter a room where many people are smoking, your eyes sting and your clothes and hair absorb the nasty smell. You may also find that you cough as a result of tobacco smoke. All these unpleasant side effects will now disappear because you have stopped and your lungs will start to recover. This makes you feel even more proud of yourself. If you have tried to stop smoking before, you may have had withdrawal symptoms and found it unpleasant to stop or were continually thinking of how you wanted a cigarette. You now know that you are doing this in an entirely different way. You have stopped smoking altogether by using hypnosis and the very powerful help of your subconscious mind. Your subconscious mind is your inbuilt computer and is accepting all the helpful suggestions to store and use in the future. This part of your mind knows that it is bad for you to smoke. That is why you have stopped. You are now a very proud non smoker. Another reason you have decided to stop is to save money. If you smoke 20 cigarettes a day for 40 years it will cost you £40 000. Just think what you could spend that money on. You will now save all that money for yourself and your family. It is a great relief to know that you no longer smell of tobacco, that your breath is fresh, that your clothes are clean and free of the smell and ash, your fingers are unstained and your teeth are whiter. You will also taste your food much better and your skin tone will improve. You will have more energy and be able to sleep better. Now, with every deep breath you take, drifting even deeper, you are becoming more and more determined not to let tobacco get hold of you again. With every day that passes, you will become more and more determined to remain a non smoker and be proud of it. Now that you are a non smoker and your food will taste better, you will be aware of this, but will be careful to eat properly. You will only eat enough food to give you the amount of energy that you require and no more that you eat now. Your appetite is fully satisfied with the same amount of food as before. Now (name of client), you will leave here as a non smoker and we are both very, very confident that you will have no need to smoke ever again. You will have no reason or desire ever again. Never, never at any point, will you have the desire to smoke because you will have an extremely positive attitude. You will have no negative thoughts, they will all be positive and further strengthen your resolve. Sometimes, when people attempt to give up without help, they tend to think "oh dear, suppose I get withdrawal symptoms, or suppose I miss smoking," That is a negative attitude, it is just in the mind. Your mind can create any symptoms it wants and negative attitudes can be thought in the imagination. You will have a very positive attitude which will help you. Now (name of client), I want you to go even deeper now, relaxing further , five, deeper, four, deeper and deeper, three, that's right, doing very well even deeper, two relaxing deeper, and one, so deep, very well done. I now want you to imagine that someone in the room has lit a cigarette. See that cigarette, long, white, with filter tip and see the smoke rising from the lighted end. You know that if the smoke got into your nose, you would hate it, it would sting and be uncomfortable. Now (name of client), that cigarette is under your nose, you can smell it, you can sense it when you breathe, you will feel stinging and unpleasant smells from the smoke and you don't like it. If ever you are tempted to smoke again you will remember this and you will know it will make you feel uneasy and perhaps sickly. To get rid of this nasty smoke I want you to say these words quietly to yourself, under your breath for only you to hear. REPEAT. "I never want to smoke again, I want clean fresh air." Repeat this to yourself and the feelings will go away and you will feel fine. See how much better that feels now. You feel good again now and you like yourself and are proud of yourself. You like yourself because you have done this for yourself. You brought yourself here and you are happy that you did. You feel really special. You are going to leave here with a positive attitude and your mind will not create withdrawal symptoms, but will just help you to remain peaceful and calm. This will enhance and reinforce your determination. You are co-operating very well, you are doing excellent, allowing the access to your subconscious mind where there is no resistance. All the time you are helping to increase your determination to remain a non smoker. You are now feeling really very good about yourself, just as if a heavy weight has been lifted off your shoulders and you can start a new healthier life with your family. You will not miss or pine for cigarettes and you won't feel deprived. Cigarettes are not worth missing or worth caring about. That's why you feel good and pleased with yourself. You have not lost anything but you have gained a great deal. You will have more money, your children will be happier and safer, you will not have nicotine stained fingers, your house will smell better and your breath will be fresher. When you see someone else smoking it will not give you the desire to smoke. It will have opposite effect on you and will strengthen your resolve. You will feel sorry for that person who is smoking and will want to help them, but you can't, they've got to help themselves, just as you have done by coming here. You will be glad that you are not doing to yourself what they are doing and what you used to do to yourself. You are now looking forward very much to the rest of today as a non smoker and your husband/wife will notice this too. They will be full of admiration of you and tomorrow when you wake up to a whole new day when all thoughts of smoking will be dismissed totally out of your mind you will feel wonderful as a non smoker. You won't want to even think about smoking, you will prove to your family and friends that it is easy with the help of hypnotherapy. You just want to breath pure healthy air. And any time you like, you can close your eyes and remember your own special phrase which you say under your breath to yourself which is: "I never want to smoke again, clean fresh air." Say it to yourself again. You have now successfully broken the habit and you are well and truly a non smoker. You do not smoke any more. So soon I am going to wake you up and when I do you will feel an overwhelming feeling of being very, very healthy. You will be determined never to smoke again, you will be glad you are now a non smoker and proud of the fact. You will never again smoke another cigarette. When you wake up you will have an overwhelming feeling of being very, very healthy. You will be determined never to smoke. You will be happy and feel fine, alert and full of energy and vitality.

One – Determined never to smoke again.
Two – Feel very healthy and starting to wake up
Three – Waking up further feeling happy and confident
Four – Feeling full of energy, vitality
Five – Wide awake feeling fine.

WEIGHT LOSS

"All the outside sounds continue around you and you are still in your place of paradise but the outside sounds are not important now. Just centre your attention on these suggestions which will help you. Nothing can distract you or disturb you while you are listening to my voice. Drift deeper and deeper while you are listening. These suggestions will help you. They are for your benefit. No one is making you loose weight, you are doing it for yourself. You really want to loose weight and you will do it with a positive attitude which you now have. You are now ready to let go of the excess pounds which you no longer want or need. You are letting go of the excess weight easily and effortlessly. Your appetite is getting smaller and smaller. It is just as if your stomach has shrunk a little and simply cannot take in as much food as it used to. You feel lighter and freer with every day, loosing the excess pounds one by one and it's so easy. You only eat modest portions of food and you are satisfied, completely satisfied. You do not eat between meals, you never eat between meals and you can already see yourself in front of the full length mirror, wearing those clothes which you longed to be able to get into and you look wonderful. Just see yourself there. It fits you perfectly. You look great, light and free. If ever you are tempted to overeat you will close your eyes, take a deep breath and say the words, slim and trim, slim and trim. Repeat these words to yourself now, under your breath. Slim and Trim. Whenever you are tempted to overeat you will close your eyes, take a deep breath and say slim and trim. You will concentrate on your food, notice the colours, notice the textures, you will eat each piece slowly, chew each mouthful slowly and thoroughly, think about what you are eating. You do not eat fatty food. You do not like fatty food. You eat only lean, healthy food and eat it slowly and deliberately. See yourself as slim and healthy. You are becoming more vibrant as your eating habits become healthier. You eat your food slowly. Chew slowly. Enjoying your food. Enjoying the different textures, the clean fresh taste of healthy food. You slowly eat your food and see yourself as vibrant and healthy. You are learning to eat only healthy food and you are becoming pleased with yourself. You like the new slimmer person that you are becoming. You are beginning to loose weight and you are aware that other people are starting to see you as trim and attractive. This makes you feel happy and even more determined to carry on eating only good healthy food. Each day as you loose pounds and inches, your interest in life becomes greater. The more you enjoy life, the healthier and happier you become. You only eat the food you need and you will not eat more than your body needs. You will not eat between meals. As your body burns up the excess fat, your skin becomes clearer and more youthful looking. Your body fat is melting away, leaving you looking and feeling younger and firmer and more dynamic. If you go out for a meal, you choose food which is only low in fat. You eat slowly and only as much as your body needs. As your body fat melts away you are becoming more interesting as a person. People like to meet you and you are enjoying the new attention you are drawing amongst others. This makes you happy and more determined to eat less and burn up even more body fat. You will loose weight regularly every week until you are at your desired body weight and you will like yourself. You like the new slim trim body that is developing with your new eating habits. You have totally lost the desire to eat snacks between meals. Your 2 or 3 small meals a day are sufficient for your body's needs and you look good. The new slim trim figure you are developing is healthy, firm, vibrant and full of energy. You will never again eat more than you need. You have lost all the desire to eat stodgy, fatty foods. You have lost all desire to eat unhealthy foods. You have lost all desire to eat between meals. The new slim you is emerging like a butterfly from a chrysalis becoming firm, healthy and full of energy. You will stay firm, trim and full of energy. You will never again overeat. You will start your new eating habits from today. From today you will restructure your life and start your new eating habits You will not let yourself or anyone else down. You will stick strictly to your reduced food intake. You will enjoy the wonderful adventure of getting slimmer and slimmer and seeing the scales going down every week. Just see yourself on those scales now with them registering your ideal weight and see and feel how good it feels. You will get down to your own target weight in a positive manner and you will enjoy feeling good about it. Now see yourself in a full length mirror at your ideal weight and wearing your ideal clothes which you want to wear, maybe in your swimwear or the glamorous dress you long to wear. See yourself there and feel how good it is. Each week that goes by you will become slimmer and slimmer. You will find that your appetite gets smaller and smaller and that you are satisfied with far less food than you used to be. In a few moments I will wake you up and when I do you will feel an overwhelming desire to carry out all the suggestions which have been made. When you wake up you will be absolutely determined to loose the weight and you will feel happy and confident about it. I will wake you up by counting from 1 to 5 and when I do you will feel very refreshed, confident, happy full of vitality and determined.

One – Starting to wake
Two – Feeling refreshed, confident
Three – Eyes opening, feeling happy, full of vitality
Four – Waking up feeling confident about loosing weight
Five – Wide awake feeling fine.

SKIN PROBLEMS

Now (name of client) I want you to go to your own private place of paradise, where the birds are singing beautiful songs, the wonderful scent of summer flowers fill the air. There are palm trees with their leaves gently rustling in the warm breeze. You can see and hear the sea gently licking and lapping up the coastline. You will walk down 5 steps to your place of paradise and then along the soft warm golden sand. Walk down the steps and count yourself down going deeper all the time. Walk along the beach without a care in the world. You are totally safe because there is no one else around for miles. Feel the soft sand on your feet and between your toes and enjoy it. You are now free from the rest of the world and you have no cares or worries. See yourself there. See yourself in the warm sunshine. There is not a cloud in the sky, there is nobody about, you can hear the birds singing, smell the beautiful flowers, hear the sea, the palm trees are around you with their leaves gently rustling above. You are there and you can see yourself with soft, healthy, clear skin. There is not a blemish on your body and you feel good, you feel happy and confident. You feel really good and proud of yourself without a blemish on your body. Tell me what you are doing now.

Tell me what you are wearing.

You are hearing subliminal messages to your subconscious mind which will help you beat your stress and worry. You will have healthy, clear skin as you are now determined to overcome the psoriasis which used to upset you but does not any more. You have now learned to remove your stress by allowing your body to heal it for you. You know you are a very special person and very important. To heal your psoriasis all you have to do is relax, take a deep breath and say to yourself " I am healing myself" REPEAT

When you say these words you will feel your whole body tingling which is the sign that your adrenaline and beneficial chemicals are being released and starting to attack and destroy your psoriasis. Keep saying these words to yourself and feel the pleasant tingling in your whole body starting to move to all the areas of your psoriasis and destroy it. You can already feel it reducing. The more you say these words to yourself the stronger the attack on the psoriasis will become until it has no further resistance and gives in and disappears altogether. All through this you will feel pleasantly happy that the psoriasis is being removed. You will remain totally calm and relaxed throughout the process. Keep saying to yourself "I am healing myself" REPEAT and feel the wonderful sensations. You may be wondering when your psoriasis will go altogether, but it will. You will remain happy, calm and relaxed throughout. You will remember this place of paradise and every day you will be able to relax and count from 10 to 1 and say to yourself. "I am healing myself" REPEAT until the tingling starts and moves to attack the areas of psoriasis. You are calm and happy throughout this. You will easily be able to remember this place of paradise always, but when you relax yourself and count backwards from 10 to 1 you will be there and feel very good. And as you say your special phrase to yourself "I am healing myself" and keep repeating it, the tingling will start and then move through your body to attack and remove you psoriasis. And you will feel wonderful. In a few moments I will wake you up by counting from 1 to 5 and when I do you will have an overwhelming feeling of well being in body and mind, you will feel refreshed and alert. You will be very very positive and confident about hypnotherapy and will be very eager to experience them for your benefit and speed up the clearing of your skin very soon and these feelings will stay with you.

I will wake you up by counting from 1 to 5

One – Feeling an overwhelming sense of well being in both body and mind
Two – Feeling very positive and confident about hypnotherapy.
Three – Wanting to speed up clearing your skin
Four – Waking up further starting to feel refreshed and alert
Five – Wide awake feeling wonderful and happy.

The above script should be suitably modified for the individual concerned. Encourage your client to use the self hypnosis techniques and listen regularly to the audio cassette you provide. The levels of physical and mental relaxation involved sometimes will result in cure themselves.

CONFIDENCE BUILDING WITH OTHER PEOPLE

"All the outside sounds continue, but they are not important now. You won't be interested in anything except drifting down, even deeper, while listening to my voice. All the suggestions will help you. They are for your benefit. No one is forcing you to tackle and your problems. You have now decided that you are doing it for yourself and with the immense power of your unconscious mind, you will easily be able to beat the memories and negative thoughts you were holding. You are now going about this in a totally different way with only positive thoughts and a confident approach and you know this will help you succeed. This new adventure in your life will reap tremendous rewards. From now on, and with every day that passes, you will be filled with confidence and have a very positive attitude with every new challenge in front of you. Each and every time you meet new people, whether they are male or female, you will have a warm comforting feeling inside of supreme self confidence. You will remain calm and relaxed at all times, just as you are now and you will not allow your mind to play tricks on you. You will have no negative thoughts at all. All your thoughts will be positive and satisfying. You will remain calm and relaxed whenever you are due to meet new people. The negative thoughts and memories you used to have will be totally dismissed and your new, positive way of thinking will carry you through with pride and self satisfaction. The negative thoughts and memories you once had will be totally dismissed, as that is all they are – memories – and they don't matter any more. The only thing which matters now is moving forward and a positive, confident manner. Your unconscious mind is there to help you and it will help you in the future. It will allow you to dismiss, from this day forward, all negative past memories and replace them with wonderful positive thoughts and desires. At any time in the future, you will be able to engage the help of your unconscious mind to help you in any situation or any circumstance. At any time in the future, you will be able to simply close your eyes, take a deep breath and say these words to yourself: Calm, peaceful, tranquil. Calm, peaceful, tranquil. Repeat these words to yourself now and see how good it feels, filling your entire body and mind with a warm confidence. As you keep repeating these words to yourself, you will feel a pleasant warm sensation which calms your whole body and mind and you will feel much better and full of new confidence. You will be able to speak normally, in a calm and reassuring way. You will remain in full control of any situation and will be so calm and positive that people will notice this. People will like and admire you. You will also be proud of yourself and like yourself. People will associate and communicate with you better because they will like your conduct and attitude. They will see you as calm and relaxed and they will appreciate these new qualities. At any time in the future, you will be able to close your eyes, take a deep breath and say the words: Calm, peaceful, tranquil. Calm, peaceful, tranquil. Now repeat these words again to yourself until the warm comforting feelings of confidence move through your body even more. Now just for a moment, imagine yourself in a situation where you are about to meet someone new, but this time you have a totally different approach. You have made your preparations with your keywords and you are totally at ease."

At this point, take your client, in detail, through a suitable situation in their imagination while meeting a new person, but with the new feeling of confidence and calmness (this is a very powerful technique).

Now, in a few moments I am going to wake you up and when you wake up, you will remember all the positive suggestions I have given you and you will also remember the wonderful feelings of warm self confidence inside. You will remember all this and keep it to use at any time in the future. When you wake up, you will also feel happy, confident, refreshed, revitalised and relaxed. You will be looking forward to the rest of today and even more so to tomorrow and each further day that passes as your confidence will grow stronger and stronger.

One – Full of confidence, getting stronger and stronger.
Two – Feeling positive, relaxed and happy
Three – Feeling revitalised and waking a little more.
Four – Determined to continue building, eyes starting to open
And Five – Wide awake, feeling fine.

HYPNO-ANALYSYS

Hypno-analysis is used to help clients with various problems and can sometimes uncover the reasons behind certain fears and phobias.

The technique is relatively simple. You induce the state of hypnosis by which ever method you prefer then suggest to them that "We are going on a journey back in time etc." You can be as inventive as you wish in this and with time and experience will decide which suits you best.

You can simply say "I want you to think back to your childhood. I want you to remember something, anything that happened when you were very young." Do not put ideas or suggestions into their mind by saying something like "Somebody touched you". That would be leading their own thinking process. Just ask your client to think back to their childhood days. (You will realise by the end of this course that the majority of neuroses have their roots in childhood and this is why therapists are so interested in the formative years.)

Another way of helping a client to trace their thoughts back, is to say, "Think about your final year at school. Think of your teacher's name, think of some of your fellow pupils name." This will almost always awaken a few memories. Then move to the last but one year at school and repeat the technique. Carry on going back through the years as far as you can (unless some important memories come out through the journey backwards) In some cases, a new and possibly startling unpleasant memory may pop out from the unconscious mind giving you material to work on later (this is covered later in psychotherapy).

A further alternative would be to ask your client to free-associate. For this you just tell them to say the first thing that comes into their mind, then the next thing and the next and so on. Instruct your client firmly, not to be selective and not to overlook a thought if they think it may be irrelevant. They must tell you every thought that comes into their mind. Getting a person to freely associate is quite difficult because they usually feel self conscious about it. This is where your previous work with rapport will help.

If you achieve an abreaction in your client, they will probably go into a panic state, but don't let that put you off. They will come to no harm if you show that you are in control. Should your client become distressed in any way you should do the following:

Tell them to relax and assure them that everything is all right and that they are not really in this situation or period in time. They are looking at an image on a large screen, as if at the cinema, and they are totally safe, with you, in the consulting room. All they are doing is acting as an observer of what they are seeing on the screen, they are totally safe and just telling you what they see and hear.

The reason some therapists use Hypno-analysis is establish a point in time which could be relevant to a problem in their present life. For example, someone with a fear of water may in the past have experienced an unpleasant situation with water years ago but are unable to remember anything about it. This is because the memory may have been repressed into the subconscious mind. Hypno-analysis can sometimes be used to take the client back to this point in time and then come to realise what the root cause of the problem is, which can then be part of the cure as they realise why.

Once the situation or problem has been uncovered some clients may be cured immediately. Others will require discussions and counselling sessions to help them come to terms with the outcome.

Never leave the opened can of worms unattended with anyone who is not cured as this can be just as psychologically damaging as not treating the problem in the first place.

The principal of Hypno-analysis can be combined with suggestion therapy for smoking, nail biting etc by taking the client back to the point in time when they did not smoke etc. and letting them experience how much healthier they felt.

CREATIVE VISUALISATION

Creative visualisation can be an excellent supplement to suggestion therapy with cases where there are physical symptoms or depression and stress are present. The treatment consists of putting your client into hypnosis and then using the powerful visualisation technique to increase or decrease the symptoms.

Instruct your client to imagine a large side control in front of them set in the middle (similar to a volume slide control adjuster) and that when the control is pushed upwards, the symptoms or pain increases and when it is pushed down they decrease. Tell your client to push the control upwards slowly to a point where the symptoms or pain become almost unbearable. Then tell them to slide the control downwards until the pain or symptoms improve or disappear. This should be practised every day for two weeks and each time the control be moved further downwards until the symptoms disappear completely. If the symptoms should then ever appear again in the future, they should go through the self hypnosis routine and progressively slide the control downwards until improvement is obtained.

ADVANCED HYPNOTHERAPY

With the knowledge you have so far, you should be more than capable of treating the more simple problems such as smoking, confidence, weight loss, nail biting etc. as these lend themselves well to straightforward suggestion therapy. This should be adequate for treating up to 90% of your clients, but as a competent practitioner, you should be able to deal also with the more lasting and deep seated problems.

This involves the principal of psychotherapy and requires the art of counselling and often a great deal of patience. You should, at all times, carry your own belief into your practice that you can help, if not totally cure, any condition which is presented to you. It is much better to hold too positive rather than negative attitude.

Never at any time though claim you can cure things which the medical doctors cannot. This course does not teach the skills of a medical practitioner and you should not attempt to make people believe you are. You will gain more respect both from clients and members of the medical world by portraying yourself as a "Complementary Therapist" rather than an "Alternative Therapist". This way you will be seen as an asset rather than a rival as a "Holistic Practitioner".

The next part of the course deals with Psychotherapy and the more complex problems which you are likely to encounter.

PART FIFTEEN

PSYCHOTHERAPY

A wise man once said, "It's not so much the psychological knowledge that you have, as quality of respect and empathy that you afford your client, which brings about healing".

When Chad Vera founded the Samaritans, he set up at an office in a church and people would go along and tell him all their troubles and worries. As the word got round, more and more people started to come and see him. He then enrolled some helpers to make tea and coffee for his clients while they waited to see him.

Gradually, he started to notice that his demand of clients was reducing and as further weeks went by he decided to investigate. To his surprise (although very pleased) he found that the people were not intentionally turning their backs on him, but instead were finding just as much help from the tea and coffee makers! These helpers had no training, so they could do little more than listen and unintentionally were giving what the people needed...... a sympathetic ear, their attention and their time. They were providing these "sufferers" with their greatest need.....another human being to listen and care. From this point onwards, Chad Vera developed the phrase, "Don't just do something, sit there."

During you hypnotherapy and psychotherapy sessions, you will need to make your client feel important and worthwhile enough to want to change and to gain their inner permission to stop hurting themselves. You will never be able to make your client change but you can give them the tool of self value and explain that what has happened in earlier life which may have an effect now, is not their fault. With you ability to use hypnosis also, you will be able to direct these facts easily into your client's mind.

Like all mammals, the human being enters the world from the perfect environment – the womb. In the womb there is warmth, sustenance and usually harmony. There is no strange world of anxiety or confrontation.

It is very important for therapists to be aware of the child's way of coping with the world form the very start, as this is where the personality begins to form and also the thinking pattern which may contribute towards a neurosis later in life.. For example, the child may become resentful and angry about being handled roughly for crying and so may develop the idea that the world is an uncharitable place from where you get no favours and you have to look after yourself by whatever means you can. Similarly, if the young child is left alone for long periods, it may well develop a very jaundiced view of the world. Not only is human contact vital for a feeling of safety, but it also contributes towards a well balanced personality and thought pattern.

This may appear a little far fetched, but believe me, it is often the way the thought patterns and personality can begin to form. The vital formative years of a human are estimated as being up to the age of seven, therefore there are other factors to be taken into account when you try to asses the client in front of you in your consulting room. As a "therapist of the mind" is very similar to being a detective and you should have enough knowledge to start picking up the clues.

Self perception, as I have detailed earlier, is important. The social philosophers, G. H. Mead and C. H. Cooley claimed that a person's view of their own identity comes about as a result of the way which they are regarded by others. We use our imagination to get from others, a perception of ourselves. When you go into your own practice, you will start to meet people who have a rather distorted view of both themselves and their value.

It isn't true that Freud "discovered" the unconscious, but he did develop the focus of the belief that the unconscious controls much of the way we behave because of the dynamic power it possesses. He then went on to call it the "Dynamic Unconscious". The theory he proposed, which is still observed today, was that unpleasant or traumatic events which took place in earlier life (the formative years) are repressed into the unconscious mind, only to express themselves later on in life, often in disguise and sometimes as symptoms of neuroses.

When you think about how vulnerable the human infant really is and consider the fact that at only two or three days old, they are working out methods of how to deal or react to situations, then you will understand why I say that the young child will often repress any painful, frightening or depressing memory. They do not forget these situations, but simply cast them out of the conscious mind and away into the unconscious.

To complicate matters further, as you will find both on stage and in therapy, there is no concept of time in the unconscious. If a repression goes in , say at the age of two, it will stay that age. I ask you to think about that for a little while...... A two year old's emotion hitting a person in their twenties or thirties or forties.... No wonder they become ashamed of their neuroses! Add to that, until they have received therapy they don't know where this feeling is coming from and it seems to be attacking them from thin air, I'm sure you'll agree, it's not difficult to appreciate that they think they are literally going out of their mind. What else can they possibly think if they don't know or understand or if it has not been explained to them. It is vital that you explain these things to them, but I believe this is not the final cure.

Some schools of thought argue that to only discover the cause of a neurotic problem is to cure it. I will here and now state that this is definitely **not the case**. I and a number of fellow therapists would suggest to you that to carry such a belief to your client who is desperately needing your help would do more harm than good and could be dangerous. To discover the cause of a neurotic problem is a very good starting point, but you must then explain to your client what you have learned through this section of the course. The cause of the repression, the way the imagination works, how helpless the young human child is, how confusing the world is to us when we are born, how powerful and influential the parents are, repression – how and why it works - All these facts must be driven home (hypnosis can help here) until they become an accepted part of the daily way of thinking. Always remember though, at the same time, your job is to be "a good listener".

All this may seem a little daunting at this moment, but believe me, when you have successfully completed this course in Complete Mind Therapy you will have so many different assets and abilities, you will impress your clients and fellow therapists who will realise that you have had extensive training and get referrals and recommendations form sources unable to help. Also, at conferences or professional gatherings, you will be in no way left out of touch or out of your depth. Many therapists in practice today have been taught only by narrow one line methods, but you will be head and shoulders in front of them.

The successful hypnotherapist is a masterful psychotherapist, as well as being an efficient craftsman. You should know life, people, society and always try to notice these with one eye on improving your own skills and understanding (this is the point I have been making since early on in the course), then you will be able to make an even greater contribution towards the curing of the client in front of you.

Hypnotherapy and psychotherapy are very valuable aids to the treatment of cases that have not responded well to ordinary medication. I personally feel with my experience, that they will play an ever increasing role in curing both physical and metal conditions and relieve a great deal of human suffering.

We have here, a powerful curing agent. An elderly wise colleague of mine, who had many years experience, once referred to it as "a powerful drug which you can't put in a bottle" and he often said to his clients, "The genie really is now out of the lamp!" How right he was. As you will now becoming to realise, many seemingly "organic" ailments are physical results of a neurosis which can be helped or cured when the mental conflict is resolved. Medical GP's, whether it be consciously or unconsciously, use suggestion in their practice, so why don't we use it in a more organised and methodical manner as a speciality? Well WE do. And very well too.

For example, the trained nurse knows the importance of all the psychological factors in medicine and realises that the mind must be treated as well as the body. This is done by trying to introduce confidence into the patient and providing a cheerful atmosphere. The road to recovery is also treated with positive anticipation. Problems sometimes arise however when the patient visits their Doctor who is desperately short of valuable time to spend with each individual and sends them off with some pills when the root cause of the problem is in the mind. This is where Private Practitioners – and this includes you – are very successful, by giving the client the time they require, even though they are paying private fees for the service. A point here is that, unless you are running an advertisement campaign, it is not a good idea to give anyone free consultations. The reason being is that if they think they are having to pay for the service, there is a far greater success rate (this has been covered earlier).

If you remember the principal of the repressed memories coming out later in life you can compare it to a clock which has stopped ticking and in this case you know there is something wrong internally. Using hypnosis and psychotherapy, you can relatively quickly, uncover the neurotic defence mechanism and then effect the cure. In all cases, you need to remove the cause of the anxiety and give your client an insight into the unconscious reasons which are responsible for the symptoms. The sooner your client faces up to the anxiety and fear, the quicker the cure will be.

The audio cassettes which accompany this course will give you a greater in depth understanding of the subject, so I will now cover the most common phobia's and then give you idea's of suitable suggestive therapy given for treatment and ultimate removal. Phobia's are *exaggerated* fears and as such, can be broken down into almost meaningless confusions of the thought patterns. They can usually be seen as rather foolish by the adult after they have been uncovered.

The phobia's are considered to be *exaggerated* fears because they go beyond what we would think of as "reasonable concern" and a "normal sense of precaution". As a rule they are self induced into the unconscious, as explained earlier and as I will show you later, they can easily be removed.

Agoraphobia	Fear of Open Spaces
Claustrophobia	Fear of Enclosed Spaces
Nosophobia	Fear of Disease
Pathophobia	Fear of Suffering
Astraphobia	Fear of Thunder
Monophobia	Fear of Loneliness
Misophobia	Fear of Dirt and Germs
Acrophobia	Fear of Heights (causing vertigo)
Hematophobia	Fear of Blood
Ochlophobia	Fear of Crowds
Erythrophobia	Fear of Blushing
Zoophobia	Fear of Animals
Xenophobia	Fear of Strangers/Foreigners
Insectophobia	Fear of Insects (mostly spiders)
Nyctophobia	Fear or the Dark
Aichmaphobia	Fear of Knives
Hamartophobia	Fear of Failure

Every phobia is simply a state of mind and when you have removed the thoughts of fear, you will then also be able to move on to further processes. Overcoming stammering, hesitation, sowing the seeds of success, ambitions etc.

Please remember the phrase on a bottle of pills, "If symptoms persist, consult your doctor." Should you find that the phobic symptoms continue after therapy, you should refer your client for medical or psychiatric advice. There are sometimes (although a very small percentage) cases where there are physical problems and chemical imbalances in the brain which require medical attention. I remember a case of a young woman in her twenties who was pregnant where, because of this, hypnosis was not wise. She had previously been on medication for "depression" and came for therapy as a last resort. (This incidentally is often the case. People often try many, many different methods before they turn to us for a permanent cure). She had an unexplainable inner belief of total mistrust of her husband and was convinced that every other woman was a potential threat to her. She was constantly checking up on him, even at his work which started to get him into trouble. Many of their friends were lost over quite a short period as her accusations started to spread to anyone and everyone. As time went by during the Counselling and Psychotherapy sessions and speaking independently to her husband, it became clear that there was something else which was not quite right. To cut a long story short, after recommending she sought further medical advice, it turned out that the "depression" was actually "acute paranoia" which was caused by chemical deficiencies. A new medication was prescribed which improved the situation no end.

The above factual example is just to show you that each case should be treated on it's own merit, but the majority will respond exceptionally well to your therapy.

Imagine for a moment, a child being forced by it's parents to sleep alone in a bedroom while there is a violent thunderstorm outside. In later life, whenever there is a thunderstorm, the adult mind goes back straight away to the terrifying time in that bedroom, all alone, frightened and the fear is relived all over again.

Again, in the early years, a child may have been bitten by a dog or scratched by a cat. In later life there can be a fear of dogs or cats, to have them near would be unbearable and to stroke a cat or fuss a dog would be unthinkable. Both animals could bring back, through association of ideas, the terrifying experience of former years.

As with the thunderstorm and the animals, the relevant phobias set in.

This is why you must discover the basic reason for the problem. This as I have mentioned before, is the abreaction – the reacting of an unpleasant experience in order to discover and accept the origin.

To give you some examples of how to tackle phobia's, the following guidelines will be helpful. You should obviously use your own common sense and always use the principals of what you have learned so far in the course. The sessions are in a more traditional approach and it is up to you whether you use these methods or the much quicker "30 minute fast phobia cure" method explained later. Both methods are in your course to ensure you have the widest possible knowledge of the subject and as such will be far ahead of many of your future colleagues.

FEAR OF OPEN SPACES

Recall

Were you alone in a large field with a bull? Was there a wind blowing? Were you approached by a stranger? Had you lost your parents? Were you soaking wet in the rain? Did you feel frightened and lonely? Were you lost? Did you become frightened to venture into open spaces? Or were you out in the crowds and become fearful in the busy streets? Did you loose your way? Did anybody frighten or harass you?

These sample questions will start to help your client remember part thoughts until suddenly, the truth will dawn and they will recall the reason that made them fearful of open spaces. There is now apparently a very good reason for being afraid.

Repair

Tell your client what happened then will not happen again in the same way. They are no longer a child. They will not get lost. The wide open spaces and the countryside are wonderful places to be and the trees, grass, flowers, expanses of blue sky are beautiful. When alone in these places, they need have no fear. In crowded streets they are surrounded by many others who are only on their daily business, just as they are. Strangers will not accost them. They are no longer afraid of people walking beside, in front, or behind them or going in and out of shops. They are not afraid of each other. They like the sounds and are no longer afraid of anyone because there is now no reason to be.

FEAR OF ENCLOSED SPACES

Recall

Were you once shut up in a cupboard or other confined space on purpose or by accident? Did you become locked in somewhere and could not get out? Were you frightened somewhere, like the underground with lots of people and felt you could not get out? Were you ever lost in a wood or somewhere similar surrounded by tall trees and could not find your way out? Were you ever trapped in a lift and unable to get help to be released? Have you ever been travelling in a car at high speed and thought you may be in an accident?

These types of questions will alert the past negative experiences which may have contributed to feeling suffocating, closed in or frightening.

Repair

Tell your client that these are only memories of the past. They will never again be locked in and unable to get out. When travelling on the underground, yes, they are surrounded by other people, but they are friendly and they too will feel hot and bothered, but they are talking to each other and they are not afraid. There is no reason why they should be afraid. There is plenty of air. If they are in a fast travelling car, they can open the windows and let air in. The driver is friendly and knows what he/she is doing. It's best to sit back, relax and enjoy the countryside as soon the journey will be over.

FEAR OF HEIGHTS

Recall

Was there a time, in your childhood or youth, when you looked down from a great height and it felt absolutely dreadful? As if you had the feeling you were going to throw yourself down to the ground? Did you have to pull back quickly, as the world started to swim around before your very eyes and you felt you were loosing your balance? Or, perhaps when on holiday or out walking at the weekend, you may have been climbing a hill and looking down, those dreadful feelings of vertigo came over you? Then, if you could not have grabbed a handrail or a tree, the dizziness may have made you fall and plunge to the bottom? Even if you haven't had this actual experience, you may have still got an automatic fear of heights and be unable to get to them without having an attack of vertigo or even worse, feeling you may fall or throw yourself off the ledge or hilltop?

Any number of past memories may be relevant here. Even recalling a horror film.

Repair

Tell your client that this phobia is not only a matter of the mind. It's also a question of the sense of balance dictating to the brain what they see and hear which are connected. Use the Creative Visualisation technique to take your client through the experience, but this time with a new approach and full confidence in a relaxed manner. Keep instilling into them that they can not and will not fall. They have no desire to throw themselves off. Walk away slightly from the edge and take deep regular breaths until they feel much better.

FEAR OF BLOOD

Recall

Was your first sight of blood that of your own or somebody else's? How did you react at the sight of your own blood? Did it happen as a result of an accident or injury or having a blood test? Did it make you feel faint? Did it cause you to pass out in childhood? If it was the sight of another person's blood because of an accident or an attack, did it make you shudder? Did you have to turn away from the sight? Were you or did you feel sick? Did you find the sight of blood repulsive? If you saw an accident with an animal, did it make you feel the same? Do you now feel frightened of cutting or grazing yourself in case you draw blood? Would you shudder at the thought of having a blood transfusion in hospital? Would you be unable to give blood as a donor? From the types of questions above, I am sure you will very quickly see how this particular phobia starts.

Repair

Tell your client that blood is the life force of every living human and animal. They may fear the sight of it because it is red which is the colour of anger, war and conflict. They are lucky to have healthy blood and they are not anaemic. Without blood they would not be alive and healthy. Without blood, the people they know and love would not be alive. They should not turn away from the sight of blood at an accident, but they can and must steel their nerves if it means they can help someone who is suffering from blood loss. If, at some time in the future, they require a blood transfusion, they should welcome it, because some donor has given them the chance of life. If they are required to give blood in an emergency, they will feel happy that they are in the privileged position of being able to help save someone's life. If they see an animal in distress, loosing blood, they will do all in their power to help and not turn away in weakness or disgust. If they injure themselves, they will not faint at the sight of their own blood, but will take all necessary steps to remain calm and stem the bloodflow without becoming squeamish.

You will now appreciate that, with the power of hypnosis and the correct way of approaching and phrasing things it is quite easy to re-program the negative thought patterns,

The remaining phobia's can all be dealt with in a similar manner for a lasting cure.

EIGHT NEGATIVE STATES OF MIND

COVERSION NEUROSIS
A worry turned into an illness

OBSESSIONS
Fixed ideas that cannot be dismissed by common sense.

INFANTILISM
A childish attitude to problems in order to escape finding a solution.

INHIBITIONS
Mental brakes put on normal everyday actions.

COMPULSIONS
Fixed feelings that certain actions must be taken, otherwise you will be in danger or things will go wrong.

ANXIETY NEUROSIS
Unreasonable worry about ordinary things, circumstances and situations.

INTROVERSION
The desire to withdraw from life, from society and family. To always be looking back instead of forward. Living in the past instead of the present and not looking to the future with positive hope.

SCHIZOPHRENIA
The "Jekyll and Hyde" condition. A serious mental illness in advanced cases but, in ordinary everyday ways, a general sense of moodiness and temperament. An up and down outlook which is disconcerting and upsetting.

FURTHER PROBLEMS TO TACKLE AT ADVANCED LEVEL

ACUTE DEPRESSION

Acute depression can strike at any time of life and on any person, but it is more common in women. The reasons for it occurring are too numerous to mention but include repressed memories form childhood, social, domestic or professional problems and even the pressures and pollution of life itself. One thing for sure, is that when this problem presents itself to you, you should treat it with urgency because it is unlikely to improve of its own accord and the consequences could become serious.

Exactly the same principals are used as you have learned, by getting to the root cause of the problem and then breaking the behavioural loop. When this has been established, you should instil feelings of confidence, self worth, esteem and ego as explained earlier. Often an audio cassette provided to use at home gives added benefits.

SEXUAL PROBLEMS

This is an area which could be developed into a full time practice in it's own right and you could be a pioneer of this therapy in your own particular area of the country. The one thing to observe here though, is to keep yourself at a sensible distance from your client/s. (On this subject you will often find that you have both the male and female members of the relationship for consultations either at the same or different times). You are **not** a marriage guidance counsellor, you are a therapist and as such should not let yourself become involved in the relationship or even worse, start giving advice on whether one partner should leave the other etc. If you get involved in this, there will always be one side of the relationship which will see you as "wrong" and there will be a come-back which will damage your reputation. It is simply not worth it.

Impotence in the male is relatively easy to deal with, but frigidity in the female can be more deep seated and often requires a little more patient progress.

The Male

In most cases, the failure to achieve and/or retain an erection is only psychological and is exactly the same as the patterns which I have explained earlier. The chances are, that at some time in the past, for whatever reason, the man has failed (as far as he is concerned) to perform satisfactorily due to outside influences such as stress, worry, overwork etc. This then stays with him or reappears later as a fear of failure during sexual intercourse. This is compounded by thinking that he will fail again and again and so he enters the viscous circle. Assuming that he was able before this and has no medical reason why he cannot, then the treatment pattern should follow confidence building and creative visualisation techniques.

While in hypnosis take him through the process in a relaxed, confident manner. Tell him to imagine that he is now the greatest lover. He will be performing so well that everything is perfect and he is giving his partner immense pleasure and satisfaction. His erection will be strong and long lasting and he will be the tentative lover throughout the session. He will be able to make the session last as long as he desires.

All through these suggestions, keep your phrases vibrant and positive which will describe in detail how good things will be for both of them.

There is an important intermediate stage for sexual therapy in the form of counselling advice. This should be aimed at both the male and female and is designed to be psychologically rewarding by denial! This may seem strange to you at the moment, but believe me, the more people are denied of things, the more they want them. This is especially true with the natural human desire of sex.

Tell the couple to specifically put aside a two month period where they should "go back to basics". They should put aside a little time each week to spend with each other wherever and whenever the time suits them. They should start doing the things they used to do. A glass of wine in front of the fire, the lights dimmed down low for a change, a romantic film, taking a bath together and absolutely anything else which takes their fancy. They should kiss, cuddle and caress each other, even to the point of foreplay, but no sexual intercourse. The reason for this is to relieve the pressure on the man and put his mind at rest that from the start, nothing is expected of him sexually. If they observe your recommendations of keeping to this for two months, then they will, almost certainly be soon be enjoying revitalised lovemaking within days of the end of the period.

The Female

Frigidity in the female requires your skills as an all round therapist to effect a cure. The first thing to establish is whether there is a deep seated fear or phobia about sex. You have now learned how to uncover these and how to deal with them. Involve the male partner to enlist his help (for his partner) and thus developing an association and double barrelled attack on the problem.

If you establish that there is no real deep seated problem which is contributing to the situation, you should advise a similar pattern as the treatment of the male, but for a slightly longer period, say an extra three to four weeks.

REGRESSION

Regression is sometimes a little controversial as people can sometimes relive or "remember" false memories and although it has been used on many occasions successfully it should be treated with caution. It is a method of taking people back into "past lives" and letting them explain when and where things were happening. Imagine the scene from years ago when you were engrossed in a film or a book and actually felt part of the situation. Then think of how powerful the subconscious mind is and that the memories are stored away in there. Now put yourself into the position of being in some way associated with a ***similar*** situation and imagine how easy it is to truly believe that you have knowledge of something from the past. This is how easy mistakes can be made.

The subject of regression in depth would warrant a whole course such as this one and therefore the principals only are included to give you a complement to your therapy knowledge. Use it with extreme caution, if at all, and be prepared for unpleasant possible reactions.

The procedure for regression is simply to take your client into the deepened hypnotic trance and then give the following instructions:

"I am now going to take you back in time a little at a time until you reach the point in time you want to reach. You will travel back in time past the point of your birth and into a past life. Don't try too hard, but let it just happen naturally, as I take you back. Just let your mind drift back through time and you will become more and more relaxed. In a moment, I will click my fingers and each time I do, you will travel back in time a little further. One or two years backwards in time with each click of my fingers. Easily and gently you will drift back in time with every click of my fingers. (Click) Going back, back, easily and gently. (Click) Moving further back through the years. (Click) Year by year, drifting backwards through time......." Continue along these lines and then say. "Is it night or day? Are you inside or outside? Are you with others or alone? What is your name? What are you wearing? Who are your friends? Who are your enemies? Are you married or single? Do you have any children? What are their names?

You can be as creative as you like when using regression and gradually build up a picture of where the person is. Recording the session or taking notes will enable you to cross check any information disclosed. If you have an interest in this subject, you will find actual documented accounts of people disclosing accurate information using regression of past lives from various text books available.

Should your client start to become distressed, you should use the same methods described earlier to calm the situation.

SHADOWING TAPES

The "Shadowing Tape" supplied with your package will prove successful for many or indeed all your hypnotic inductions.

A shadowing tape played at the same time as your hypnotic induction will add to the relaxation, confusion, disorientation and attention of your client and so enhance the effects. It can also be used successfully for stage work.

The principal behind this is that the "attention" is the act of concentration on one or more physical functions or pieces of information which are hitting the senses. When attending to just one piece of information we are being selective, but when we give our attention to more than one source, we are demonstrating divided attention. Some functions need all our attention, while others need only part of our concentrations. Things which we have not properly learned call for a higher level of thought and concentration than routines which we perform as automatic reflex actions. Think back to the riding a bike or driving a car routines I explained earlier.

When we go through familiar routines, we are able to do and say other things at the same time and give only limited or divided attention to the task in hand. It follows therefore, that when your client is being guided into hypnosis, spoken words on a lower level to do with relaxation and sleep will help with the process.

The principal is straightforward. Just record onto an audio cassette simple keywords which are associated with relaxation, sleep, going deeper, feeling heavier, drifting down, feeling comfortable, totally at ease etc. etc. If you like, you can also mix some suitable music at the same time. As you start your induction, you then play this audio cassette at a lower volume than your spoken voice and your client will be picking up these commands to reinforce what you are saying. The example provided is for an induction, but you can record any number for use with different problems and use them as required. Smoking, for example, would have different keywords and would be played during your suggestion therapy.

PART SIXTEEN

SHORTCUTS TO ALTERNATIVE MEDICINE

This section of the course is purposely presented in a hap-hazard way, so that you have to re read what I say and think about it, so you discover the truths within. As always you can only fully understand and discover all the truths when you put what you have learnt into action. Although the information below is meant to be used in conjunction with your standard therapy in order to speed up the process, some people, I'm sure, could see how the knowledge could be used on the phone to convince a potential client to come and see you instead of a different style of Complementary or Alternative Therapist. Of course, you show them the way to treat themselves for free with the other methods, but suggest to them it will be even better for them if they had a session or two with you.

EXPERIENCE IS THE BEST TEACHER IN LIFE

OBSERVATION AND EXPANSION OF KNOWLEDGE IS THE SECOND BEST

ALWAYS LEARN FROM OTHER'S MISTAKES SO YOU DON'T MAKE THEM

SPIRITUAL DEVELOPMENT IS PURE INTELLIGENCE

WE TREAT FROM THE EYES UP AND DOCTORS TREAT FROM THE EYES DOWN

OVER 90% OF ALL REPORTED ILLNESS IS PSYCHOSOMATIC

OF THE 10% THAT ISN'T, MOST CAN BE HELPED WITH HYPNOSIS

PROBABLY ALL UNREPORTED ILLNESSES ARE PSYCHOSOMATIC

THE HUMAN MIND IS BY FAR THE MOST POWERFUL COMPUTER EVER CREATED

JUST LIKE A COMPUTER, THE PROGRAMMES IN IT CAN BE CHANGED

AROMATHERAPY

The shortcut to aromatherapy is to surround yourself with fresh flowers of the season, the smell (aroma) will naturally get into the air of your house and their bright visible colours will cheer you up. Also surround yourself with plants, by doing this you are returning your body to nature and as such, it will feel better. Also as plants take in the carbon dioxide which we breathe out and in turn give out fresh oxygen, in turn the air in your home will be cleaner and this too will protect your health and make you feel better. Should you wish to actually use the essential oils of the plants, it couldn't be easier, just go to the Body Shop and get the Tisserand leaflet on the oils, this tells you how to use them and what each oil does. The leaflet costs nothing, I recommend the use of the flowers and plants in conjunction with a vaporiser ring and an oil suited to the specific complaint, this is the easiest and I've found, most effective way to use aromatherapy.

REFLEXOLOGY

The shortcut to reflexology is to simply walk around at home barefoot. It is unnatural for our feet to be covered with shoes, which store up a huge electrical charge and as such, knock the body out of balance. If we were to return to nature then we would walk barefoot. Well today it is only safe to do this at home, so do it whenever you are at home and naturally all the points will be stimulated automatically and without effort. The other way, is to massage the whole area of your own or your partners foot and in that way you have got to feel better as a result, as the whole correct point will be massaged.

HERBALISM

As with all the examples I am going to give, return to nature, buy lots of different herbs from the Herbalist and on them it will tell you what food each herb can be added to. If you are adding the herbs to your cooking on a daily basis then it will become unnecessary to use any other form of herbal treatment, as it's natural and automatic. Should you wish to proceed further and make up actual remedies, get a copy of Potters new encyclopaedia of botanical drugs and preparations, with this you can check up which herbs should be used for what problem. Then the general rules of thumb to follow are as follows: If the herb is on sale to be added to food then it should be safe for use. You give the patient a one month course of treatment for each year they have had the problem. You use one ounce of herb to one pint of boiling hot natural spring water. The contents are placed in a teapot and stirred up and left for about 10 minutes to stand. The liquid is then poured into a strainer and into a bottle for dosage so it's then clear liquid but has the goodness of the herbs within it.

This pint of liquid is to be consumed over the period of one day, so half a pint is drunk the same morning and half a pint that night. It must be used the same day, as no preservative has been added to the mixture, this is called an infusion. If you can't find a strainer, a silk stocking, which has not been dyed, will do the same job if the liquid is poured through it.

Some people add brandy to the mixture so it lasts longer as it acts as a preservative, but I'd advise as above. The other way of preparation is a decoction, this is used with root herbs, such as garlic etc., it's put into a pan with the water and boiled for about the same time as above and then strained, this is the way to get the goodness out of root herbs. By the way, half a pint is basically the amount an average household coffee mug holds, so if you have no jug you could use that as a measure. Lastly, if you use a mixture of 8 herbs, of course one eighth of an ounce of each is used so the total herb total is 1 ounce to 1 pint, then you can't go wrong.

HYPNOTISM

In a suggestion form, any suggestion you wish to make to yourself out loud three times a day, will, if you have faith and belief in it, become genuine and happen. In other words, it's positive thinking or self hypnosis.

MASSAGE

Regular sex is the best form of massage and relaxation there is, if you do it correctly. Also, by telling your partner what you like and don't it can be fun and beneficial to experiment with your own amateur massage. The art of massage goes back thousands of years and providing you keep to the more gentle strokes, no harm will be done. The golden rule is, **JUST FOLLOW YOUR INSTINCTS**, but please don't use essential oils in any "sensitive areas".

NATUROPATHY

The basis of this therapy is to return to nature and eliminate any unnatural habits from the patients life. They may just need more light or more of a kind of food, they may not have a good posture.

By studying your patient and questioning them, common sense will lead you to a correct solution and as in analysis, if you remove the cause of the problem all the symptoms will vanish. For example a friend kept getting corns on her toes, so I knew extra weight must be putting onto her toes. I asked her what she did, any sport? No. Did she have to reach up to high shelves at work? No. Then I asked if she danced. She said she did up until a year or two ago. This explained it. She didn't wear high heels, so I knew that wasn't the cause of the problem. As it turned out, I got her to walk around a bit and without realising it, she was putting more weight onto her toes. I asked what kind of dancing. She said ballroom and then the problem was solved, she had loved ballroom dancing and as it required moving on her toes and her mind had connected this with enjoyment it had become habitual. She then, for a week or two consciously thought of how she was walking and then it became habit not to do this and she has not been troubled with her feet since. So you see it's rather like psycho analysis find the cause of the problem, remove it and the symptoms vanish.

Someone with a bad back usually does office work and no gardening. Nature designed the body to plant things, so if they did some gardening the joints in their body would loosen up. Arthritis is more likely to be usual in people who have used the joints of their body in a repetitive way. (Tai Chi exercises will help stop arthritis.)

HOW TO HELP WITH MEMORY LOSS DISEASES.

If you have any aluminium pans or cooking utensils, throw them away, as, if you keep using them, later in life you are likely to get a mind disease. Aluminium, is highly toxic, but has a coating on it to stop such effects, but once a metal spoon has accidentally scratched this surface off and made the pan or utensil shiny, then the toxic part can get into the food as it's cooked and you then eat the food and as you can see, it's a vicious circle. If you are going to have metal pans and utensils then please have stainless steel. By throwing out items of an aluminium nature of someone with a mind disease already it could help stop the problem getting much worse.

HOW TO HELP WITH LONG AND SHORT SIGHTEDNESS

Both long and short sightedness are, in some cases a conditioned problem and as such, a cure of conditioning can be used to help them. If short sighted, these people have probably been used to sitting near the TV and always looked at things close up, or without the correct light etc. If long sighted, then they have probably looked at things from a distance for much of the time. In both cases it has become a conditioned response and by reversing things and conditioning themselves to do the opposite they will very quickly have no need for glasses. Another way to help as well as reversing their habits and acting in a more natural way, is for them to stand outside at night and look at their thumb, (which is near) for a minute and then to look at the sunset (which is far) for a minute and to repeat this at least five times, (takes 10 minutes). Done each day in conjunction with the reversal of their wrong habits, their vision will rapidly improve.

HOW MIRACLES ARE WORKED

There are no miracles and yet there seems to be in the bible and in everyday life, well, I think they omit some of the facts. For example, "he caught loads of fish in a short time", well most people don't know that fish get hungry at sunset so your more likely to catch them then. A man stands in a field, he utters a strange command and suddenly about 100 birds land at his feet, coming from nowhere. Well, you are stunned, what you didn't see were the three months of effort that went into making this possible. Each day for the past three months at the same time in the same place, rain or shine, that man has gone with three loaves of bread and fed the birds. This time he takes no food, but they see him, it's the right time of day and so they assume food is on the way and all fly down to his feet leaving you to think it was a miracle. Well as I see it, here the real miracle was the effort put in here to engineer the effect. Some psychics say it would be possible to walk on water, but would take 20 years of study, I say why waste 20 years when the next boat will take you across in 10 minutes time.

Women seem to have periods at different times, this is because artificial lighting has had an unnatural effect on their bodies. If you take these women and put them in prison where they are all subjected to the same conditions and lighting etc., then within a short time they will all commence together, at the same time, as that is how nature intended it.

So I hope you now see the secret behind miracles is TIMING, PREPERATION and the creation of a NATURAL environment.

I hope you realise this section has been included in order to make you think and as a result hopefully open your eyes up to nature more and start to realise what has been under your nose all the time.

As it says in the bible, "His divine power HAS given us everything we NEED for life". Now it's up to us to realise it's there and use it in our every day lives then there would automatically be less illness.

If the body was conditioned to the climate it's in, as nature intended, then like a friend I have, you'd never need the heating on, would have more money and would never get the common cold or other ailments. Heating etc., is unnatural and man made, so it has to be man broken.

For back pain, sleeping on the floor each night will solve the problem quickly.

WE ARE NOTHING ON THIS EARTH

YES, WE ARE NOTHING, NO PHYSICAL THING

WE ARE NOT A PHYSICAL THING, SO WE MUST BE INTELLIGENCE

THIS MEANS THE INTELLIGENCE RULES THE BODY AND NOT VICE VERSA

AND ONCE YOU REALISE THAT, well my dear friend when asked who are you? The best reply would be Pure Intelligence. For that is what you are, so it's wise to expand your intelligence all the time and then your quality of life will improve and once you have faith in knowing who you are, everyday illness will be a thing of the past and will not bother you. Until you have faith in that you are stuck in Hell because we create our own Heaven or Hell.

Spiritual yogis take years in temples to find themselves and then are only allowed to leave when they know and have faith in the fact they are nothing. You are pure intelligence and once you know that and realise that is too valuable to destroy, then you will know you are immortal. You will know you will live again and as such, have lived many times before. Knowing this, all worries will leave you, you have all the time in the world and if you don't complete your tasks in this life don't be surprised if you do next time.

You'll also find the things you're really good at now are probably what you did in a previous life and that would explain how you can have child prodigies etc. The body is just a shell and you will get another shell when you leave this one.

Anyway that's the end of this section, I hope it has given you some food for real deep thought, for within it really are many keys which can be used to unlock the doors which may be blocking your success in life.

So observe and expand your knowledge. Know you will be a success and you will be. Again, as the bible says, "As a man thinketh so a man becomes."

So I hope you now realise you really are in charge of your own life and that luck is engineered by you.

INCREASING YOUR HYPNOTHERAPY BUSINESS AND INCOME

Below are some keys to increasing your clients and as such, your income. An easy way to get more work is through TV, radio and press publicity and best of all, these can be got for free. To do so, come up with a gimmick, like a novel headline saying The TRANCE of a lifetime, for hypnotist Alex or whatever. The headline must be catchy and preferably humorous, this increases your chances of the story getting into print. The press release should be typed in double space format on to single sheets of white A4 paper. You stand a better chance of getting the story in print if you supply a few matt finish black and white photos with the story, as papers prefer to print a story if it has a photo with it. This is what helps to sell papers and make them look more interesting. The release should be short and to the point and of public interest if at all possible. Or you can tie the story in with some event that's in the news etc. and ride on its success.

For example, it hits the news that people are dying of cancer and you offer discount treatment to local people who have cancer and to stop people smoking, as the story is in the news it's topical and up to date and as such, will get in print. This will get you a large, free write up with a photo and on the advert will be the number at which you can be contacted. This will get you many, many clients. I had a write up on noesitherapy in a local paper and offered "free sessions" the article got me 107 enquiries within 24 hours of the paper coming out and of them I converted 87 into clients who paid me, YES, they paid me and it was legal. When they called I explained that they would need about four sessions and half would be free. But so they had to make a commitment they paid for the first two sessions at £25 each and got the second two free. After that would be at a discounted rate of £15 per session. As I say, 87 of the 107 who called were delighted with the offer and it not only earned me much money, but gave me loads of experience within a short space of time. If I really had given the treatment totally for free and not just partly for free then all of them would have come. To do that near national no smoking day, say to the local paper if they pay you a fee they can then offer readers free sessions of smoking cessation therapy and this will help their papers and get them much goodwill and new readers. They then pay you £100 per day for 8 hours of your time (treating 32 clients within that eight hours by doing them in groups of four). The reason for doing it so cheap, is that each person will buy a tape off you at £6.95 to continue the therapy and some may come back again for a paid session. But most important the paper will run two stories, one prior to the event and one after, both giving details of how to contact you and as such, you get loads of clients, plus the "free" clients become walking adverts. Any stunt of this kind should be included in the FREE local paper as more homes will get this and more people see it. When you've done a few things for the paper and got on good terms with them, then it will get to the point where they call you and ask for a story as they are running short of news that week. Each week after such an article you should have a classified wordage advertisement in the paper, giving brief details of your service and contact number. I find I get best results when this goes under the personal column, as more people read this than do the health column. These adverts should appear each week and that way your name stays on their mind and they will come to you first

To get on radio tell them the TV company have shown an interest and they should get in first. To get on TV, tell them a bigger TV production group has shown an interest and they should get in first. It's a competitive business and this trickery will work many more times than you'd think.

My classified produces at least 20 calls a week. Why? And, oh yes, about 18 of them will become paid clients. The advert below is what I include and you would do the same with your own name and number. When they call I explain as above, that one or two sessions are free, this way you are not breaking any laws and they become clients. Isn't business a lot easier than you thought? Being qualified in marketing, finance and management and having been in show business 20 years plus, I know all the tricks and pass them on to others.

The advert I used was worded as follows, with the underlined words being printed in bold print. By the way, FREE, is the most powerful and effective word that you can ever use in an advertisement.

FREE HYPNOTHERAPY, Psycho Analysis, Psychotherapy and Past Life Regression, available from professional of many years experience call, Heywood Hypnotherapy Centre, on XXXX XXXXXX and ask for Jonathan.

The above advert cost me about £10 a week to run in the busiest local paper on the busiest day of the week and it worked wonders. I found that I also got extra business and more word of mouth advertising by offering a small discount in fees to students, unemployed and pensioners.

You don't have to advertise of course, but done properly, it is a very good investment and with every one of your clients being a potential source of further business it makes good sense.

There are many other ways of getting yourself known than the ones I have explained so far and a good pointer is to look at your "opposition". Do regard other therapists in your area as opposition. Each client that your opposition treats is a blow to your business.

Look in your copy of Yellow Pages under Hypnotherapists and asses how your own advertisement would look against the others. Yellow pages can be a little expensive compared to other publications, but it does come up with the results. People tend to look here first when seeking therapy of any kind. An advertisement in Yellow Pages also gives you a professional perception. People see it as carrying bonafide advertisers (although this is not strictly true).

If you decide to choose Yellow Pages, you will notice that they cover many different sizes. If you can stretch to it, you will do much better with a quarter column including your own photograph, or at least some type of picture. People warm and respond much better to a human face in an advertisement, especially so with therapy. In this publication, you also get over the principal of having to be visible time after time, before someone responds.

If you are in a rural area, the local church or village magazine can give good results for very little outlay.

As an extension to actual therapy, with what you have learned in this course, you have more than enough information to give talks, lectures and seminars to countless numbers of groups and organisations. Start with the local women's institute and prepare yourself for lots of bookings and enquiries.

Small cards in local shops are inexpensive and although do not give high numbers, they do help to get your name established.

Strangely enough, dependant on his or her views, your own and surrounding Doctors centres may see you as an asset. Especially if you write a professional letter explaining that you can provide private counselling and psychotherapy.

The last piece of advice in this section will leave your mind racing and your body reaching for a pen to write down all the other potentials which will be stimulated. Design a poster or write out a card carrying your speciality subject as CURING FLYING PHOBIA'S. Pop down to your local travel agent and they will almost pay you to display it!!!!!

Well you now have all the keys you need for success, so now go and use them to open up the doors of opportunity.

PART SEVENTEEN

HOW TO EARN MONEY FROM STRESS MANAGEMENT AND MOTIVATIONAL TRAINING.

It is estimated that in the UK at least 40 million working days are lost each year due to the effects of stress. It is hardly surprising therefore, that practically everyone has heard of stress management training. It has become so common that the majority of middle to large size companies have at some time or another arranged stress management training for their employees, whilst most colleges run part time stress management classes.

Anyone who is a good communicator and able to manage their own stress responses can capitalise on the growing market for good quality stress management training. It is remarkably easy to obtain lucrative contracts to deliver stress management training, in both industrial and academic environments.

Contrary to most people's belief, no qualifications are required to teach adults, either in the work place or at colleges and other adult education centres. In fact, most part time and adult evening class tutors have absolutely no teaching qualifications. Furthermore, in subjects like stress management, which are non skills specific, it is somewhat of a rarity to find tutors or trainers who hold qualifications in the subject itself.

Instead of qualifications, certain personal qualities are needed to become successful in stress management training. Primarily, these are:

1. Communication skills – the ability to organise your thoughts and ideas in a logical way and to present them clearly and concisely to others, whilst stimulating their appetite for further learning.
2. A belief in the power of the mind to produce physiological effects in the body. A basic understanding of the relationship between mind and body.
3. The ability to get on well with people and to relate to both individuals and groups in a totally non-judgemental way.
4. Patience, understanding and tolerance.
5. The ability to generally control and manage one's own responses to stress provoking situations.

If you feel reasonably confident that you possess each of these qualities and are capable of reading and learning from the wealth of material which exist concerning stress and stress management related topics, there is absolutely no reason why you would not be able to earn a very good income from providing stress management training.

Once you become a regular adult tutor at a college or other adult education centre, you will be offered the opportunity to undertake some part time training, which if successfully completed, provides you with a qualification. An example of such a course and qualification is the City and Guilds Further and Adult Education Teaching Certificate, (F.A.E.T.C.). Whilst stressing again that a qualification is NOT necessary in order for you to teach adults, the F.A.E.T.C. is a very desirable and useful qualification to obtain and the course will provide all that you need to know to become a first class adult education tutor.

Whilst qualifications and actual training experience are not essential, it helps if your background includes some supervision, management, sales or interviewing experience. Any experience which involved working with groups of people such as chairing meetings, youth work, community work or entertainment's management would also be extremely useful. Once again though, none of these backgrounds is essential and there are many, very successful stress management trainers who have no relevant background.

Perhaps the easiest way to prove this point, is to describe what stress management consists of. When you have read through the typical course overview which commences in the next paragraph, you will fully appreciate that what is involved could easily be taught by any good communicator, regardless of their background and experience.

Stress Management Course Overview.

1. The nature and causes of stress.
   The "fight or flight" response.
   The Physiology of stress.

2. Stress response choices.
3. Sources of stress – personality, lifestyle, environmental and chemical
4. Recognising stress symptoms.
5. The nature and power of the unconscious mind.
6. Relaxation techniques.
7. Self Hypnosis.
8. Goal setting.
9. The role of diet and exercise in stress control

A course programme composed of the above topics would appeal to both adult education centres and employers alike. Before describing some very effective techniques and strategies for marketing and presenting such a course to employers and colleges, I will explain each of the topics in more detail. At the end of this part, I provide you with information about where to obtain sufficient knowledge of your subject so that you can teach it to other people.

The Nature and Causes of Stress

To understand what causes stress and what is happening to us when we experience the symptoms of stress, we need to take a look at the original purpose of stress responses in primitive man.

Flight or Fight Response

In primitive times, a constant stream of life threatening dangers presented themselves and two responses were vitally important for survival. These were the response of flight and the response of fight. Hunting ferocious beasts one day and taking part in a bloody tribal battle the next, primitive man had to respond in either of these two ways if he was going to survive. Running for his life to escape an aggressor who was stronger, or fighting to overcome a lesser opponent. The choice was a simple one and totally appropriate to those times.

Nowadays neither response is appropriate to most of challenges we face in everyday life. Instead, civilisation has brought with it many new and highly complex demands to replace most of the truly life threatening ones.

Everyday we are faced with some sort of challenge – "out of the ordinary demands", if you like. Because our autonomic system cannot differentiate between the various sources of arousal, being stuck in a 20th century traffic jam can produce exactly the same bodily responses as being chased by a woolly mammoth or sabre tooth tiger would have done in our ancestors.

In other words, our primitive response mechanism still works in exactly the same way as it has always done whilst the responses themselves have become less and less appropriate.

Fighting your employer when he refuses to promote you is probably going to get you into more trouble than running away from him, but neither response is suitable or sensible.

If we cannot respond to challenges in the way we were designed or programmed to do, some conflict is bound to result.

A definition of stress is: The state of arousal with which the body responds to out of the ordinary demands. Or challenges which are imposed upon us.

The Physiology of Stress

The process is an extremely prompt, speedy and efficient one which starts the instant we perceive the challenge. Note the word perceive, because it doesn't have to be a "real" challenge – merely a perceived one. The challenge, or out of the ordinary demand, sets off a chain reaction of bodily processes which produce an upsurge in strength and energy, the two things we need for the flight or fight responses, of course. But that same surge of energy has no outlet when the chains of civilisation restrain us from fleeing or fighting and as a result we are filled with the all too familiar sensations of frustration and pent up anxiety. We find ourselves unable to run and unable to fight, yet at the same time having to deal with the very same chemical reactions that gave our ancestors the strength to fight and the energy to take flight.

We only need to IMAGINE an out of the ordinary demand to place our system on "stress alert." Some inner impatience, anger or anxiety is enough to produce the same chain reaction of body chemistry. This makes it perfectly possible to create a vicious circle of producing stress from – AN ANXIETY ABOUT STRESS.

Stress Response Choices

We do however have some other choices which are appropriate to 20th century living. We have several in fact, but some are unhealthy choices which in the long term cause far more problems than they solve. Examples of unhealthy choices are smoking, alcohol abuse, over eating, drug misuse etc.

Examples of healthy choices are, relaxation and exercise, because with these we are disconnecting and recharging our systems instead of allowing the energy to build up and overload the system. We must either use up the energy or turn it off.

In fact the whole art of stress management is about learning how to control our responses to stress. We cannot remove stress or remove ourselves from all the sources of stress. But stress only becomes harmful when it is uncontrolled, so learning how to control or manage stress is all that we need to concern ourselves with anyway.

The recognition of this fact is the first step towards reducing the harmful effects of stress in your life.

Sources of Stress.

The second step is to recognise the various sources of stress. They can be divided into four main groups:

- Personality
- Lifestyle
- Environmental
- Chemical

The personality factors are those which arise from our values, beliefs and behaviour patterns. Your value system is the deepest level of your personality, and from them beliefs are formed which in turn produce behaviour patterns. Trying to alter behaviour without understanding or changing your values and beliefs is doomed to failure.

Real change comes from making changes at the deeper levels of your personality. For example low self esteem is formed from certain values and beliefs we hold about ourselves and our world and low self esteem produces stress. To tackle this source of stress we need to learn more about the underlying values and belief which are producing the loss of self esteem and where appropriate, reconstruct them. Stress management explores various techniques for doing this.

Lifestyle as a source of stress concerns the stressful events which are provoked by the way we live. Research by two American doctors, Holme and Rahe, produced a scale of life events, which were valued according to the amount of adjustment needed to cope with them.

Death of a spouse or child came out top, followed by divorce, separation and imprisonment. At the other end of the scale, the two doctors listed changes in eating habits, taking a vacation and even Christmas.

Environmental sources of stress are things like inadequate housing, unpleasant or unhealthy working conditions, crowded public transport and that sort of thing. What is not quite so obvious and easy to recognise about some of them is that we sometimes pretend to actually enjoy them.

For example, some commuters get a buzz out of the mad rush and the crowded trains. It becomes a way of life to boast about, giving a sense of pride at ones ability to "take it" and cope with it all. Underneath this superficial level of enjoyment, the stress factors are still operating and taking their toll. The person who recognises them and learns to manage the stress responses will be OK, but the person who goes on ignoring them, pretending they do not exist, is undoubtedly heading for trouble.

Chemical sources of stress are substances which act upon our central nervous system to produce the symptoms of stress and anxiety. Many such substances are harmless or even beneficial when taken in relatively small doses.

Examples are:

Caffeine: which is in coffee, coca cola and in tea, is a stimulant which boosts the output of stress hormones. Initially it will make you more alert but later, especially when consumed in large quantities, it will produce symptoms of irritability and cause sleeplessness.

Salt: which increases nervous tension.

Sugar: too much sugar can decrease blood sugar, causing fatigue and irritability.

Nicotine: far from being the relaxing drug smokers often claim it to be, nicotine is actually a stimulant which stimulates the adrenal glands, causing full stress response.

Alcohol: which is a depressant when taken in excess, although it relaxes when drunk in moderation.

Recognising Stress Symptoms

Becoming aware of your own stress responses is not quite as it sounds. Stress distorts perception. We do not notice what is happening as we keep driving ourselves harder. The more stressed we are, the less chance we have of noticing it.

Psychologists sometimes talk about different personality types in relation to stress response. One type is very ambitious, competitive, hard working, impatient and aggressive, actually thrive on stress, getting a "high" from a stress hormone known as noradrenalin. Such a personality can become hooked on this substance and they seem to produce it in greater quantities than other personality types.

Another type of person, often labelled "the over achiever" is equally at risk. This type of person gives the impression of always calmly coping with everything life throws at them. Being tough, proud of being able to withstand the pressure. They will deny the dangers of stress and disapprove of others who "give in", considering that to be a sign of weakness. They are generally unable to admit to any personal limitations of vulnerability.

In reality, pure examples of these character types are rare, most people combining and exhibiting the different qualities according to changing circumstances.

Nevertheless, the beliefs that, "stress is something which doesn't affect me" or "something I just have to grin and bear", illustrated by both of these personality types, are extremely widespread.

Stress Symptoms

These can be physical, psychological, or behavioural. Here are some common physical stress symptoms:

Chronic stomach upsets, ulcers, bowel disorders, blood pressure, skin rashes, irregular breathing, impotency, insomnia, fatigue, irritable bowel syndrome.

Some examples of *psychological* symptoms are:

Irritability, impatience, restlessness, frustration, hostility, anger, loss of control, apathy, boredom, guilt, shame, helplessness, hopelessness, depression, mood swings.

Examples of *behavioural* symptoms are:

Leaving important things undone, panicking, allowing insufficient time to get to work or to appointments, talking too fast, arguing for the sake of arguing, losing your sense of humour, over reacting with emotional outbursts, suspicions, difficulty with decision making, memory loss, inability to concentrate, loss of discriminatory power, poor judgement, erratic or uncharacteristic behaviour.

The Unconscious Mind

The unconscious is so much wiser and more powerful than the conscious mind. And so it should be, because it holds all of our past experiences, all of our fantasies and all of our future possibilities. All of the things we might recognise are there as well as the things we are capable of having, as well as those we have already thought.

The power of the unconscious mind can work, both for us and against us. The unconscious cannot differentiate between what is real and what is believes is real.

An example, which proves this to be the case, occurred in 1964, when a man was found dead in a refrigeration unit. He had become trapped and his body revealed all the correct signs consistent with someone who had frozen to death. That's what you'd expect after being locked inside a refrigeration unit, isn't it?

It's certainly what that man expected and it's exactly what he told his unconscious mind to believe, because if he hadn't he would have lived. The refrigeration unit wasn't switched on and the temperature inside was well above freezing point.

Such is the power of the unconscious mind to work in a negative fashion, but what of its power to work for us? In the USA, research is currently going on to establish exactly how it is, that a significant proportion of terminally ill people are still alive several years after they should have died. The diagnosis for these patients, their circumstances and condition was identical to patients who died within six months of the diagnosis, yet seven or more years later they are still living. The research is still incomplete, but enough is already know to tell us that these patients are using the power of their unconscious mind to create a life giving belief system to overcome the physical effects of their illness.

So, if the power of your unconscious mind is on the one hand capable of killing you and on the other hand, capable of saving you from certain death situations, it is obviously a good idea to harness its power for your well being. What that really means, is learning to make it create positive thoughts and thereby produce positive energy for you.

Relaxation Techniques

Relaxation is just about the most natural thing that anyone could experience. It is also an experience which by definition requires the absence of any effort. Because of its essentially natural and effortless nature, it seems almost paradoxical to suggest that relaxation is a skill that can be acquired and developed through regular practice.

Practising the art of relaxation in order to become more proficient at it, is however no more paradoxical than practising any other art or skill. You should be prepared to practice at least twice a week.

To start with, you probably only need five to ten minutes per session. But when you have successfully completed the preliminary exercises, the second stage sessions will require you to devote something like twenty minutes per session.

This is what you do. Simply lie back on whatever you have decided to relax upon, ensure that you are completely comfortable.

Allow your eyes to focus on some spot just above your forehead and simply let your mind and body slow down. Do not try to make anything happen or do anything other than allow yourself to rest comfortably with your arms laying loose by your sides and your hands open. If your eyes begin to feel tired or watery, just let them close, but if they are more comfortable remaining open, then allow them to do so.

Your only objective at this stage, is to let your mind and body slow down and that will occur automatically, without you trying to make it happen.

You'll probably start to notice sensations of tiredness of which you were not previously conscious. Explore these feelings and begin to experience where they are situated. Feel the sensations in the various muscle groups of the arms, legs, neck, shoulders, back and stomach.

After a little while of allowing yourself to experience the sensations in this fairly general way, start to focus your attention on one area of your body at a time.

Start with one of your hands. Focus your attention on this hand and concentrate on whatever sensations you can sense there for about ten seconds. Then shift your attention to the other hand and do the same. Next, carry out the same observation of the sensations in your feet, spending about ten seconds on one foot before shifting your attention to the other. After this transfer your attention to gain a similar awareness of the sensations in the various sets of muscles of your face. Consider the ones in your cheeks and the tiny ones surrounding your eyes. Continue by shifting your attention to the muscles of your jaw and the ones surrounding your mouth. Whilst you concentrate on each of these sets of muscles, let them remain as still as possible.

By focusing your attention on specific areas in this way, you will find that the remaining areas of your body lose their tension automatically, whilst your mind learns how to forget that they even exist at all.

Repeat the cycle of hands, feet and facial muscles, three more times, dealing with any lapses of concentration in the gentle, detached way I have already described. You have all the time in the world and learning to be really patient with yourself is an essential part of the skill which you are developing.

You will begin to notice how tension that was present when you first started the cycle of awareness of each area, melts away with each successive round. The sensations, which were present when you commenced the exercise, are replaced with other sensations and you will become more adept at tuning yourself into the subtle variations with repeated sessions.

Follow the same procedure in subsequent sessions but extend the cycle of areas on which to focus your attention to include the upper arms, the thighs, the calves, the shoulders, the neck and the abdominal region. Eventually, the restlessness and mind wandering which was a feature of your initial attempts will start to disappear and a greater feeling of comfort will be experienced in all areas of your body.

An indication of how near you have come to achieving the objectives of the first stage, preliminary exercises is the degree to which you have now developed the ability to distinguish between the very different and distinct characteristic sensations of tension and relaxation.

Further evidence of your progress is the way in which you are now able to direct attention and focus concentration of awareness on any part of your body, whilst all the remaining parts feel as though they have ceased to exist.

Whereas five to ten minutes was all that was required for the first stage exercises, you will probably need about twenty minutes for each session of the stage exercises.

Proceed exactly as you did for the preliminary exercises, but now you are actually going to deliberately induce tension into various areas of your body.

Start with one of your arms. With the rest of your body relaxed, focus your attention on the arm and slowly raise it about six inches above its resting position. Introduce a little more tension into the arm, concentrating your entire awareness on how it feels as you allow it to stiffen and become very straight. Explore the sensations in your fingers and follow them through the rest of your hand, up your forearm, through your elbow and into your upper arm. Switch attention to your other arm and repeat the process.

When you have been right through the process with each arm and fully recognised the subtleties of the varying sensations of tension and relaxation in each, go right through the whole exercise again, but this time without raising your arms.

Instead of using the physical process of raising, stiffening and straightening your arms to induce tension, induce the tension and letting go by mentally giving yourself suggestions. Keeping the suggestions at the level of unspoken thoughts, silently say to yourself: "My muscles are tensing. They are becoming more and more tense." Repeat this suggestion a number of times whilst focusing your attention on the arm which is being tensed.

When you are ready to move into the relaxation phase, say something like: "Let go – my arm is relaxing now." Followed by: "I'm letting go completely." And: "All of the tension is melting away." Repeat these suggestions as you continue to focus your attention upon the resting arm letting go of its tension and becoming more and more relaxed.

Induce and relieve tension in the legs in exactly the same way. Physically at first, then mentally, by silently issuing suitable suggestions.

After you have completed the leg muscle exercises, explore the sensations of tension and the absence of tension in the small of your back. This is carried out physically by slightly arching your back, holding the muscles tense, then drawing in the stomach muscles.

Finally, produce and relieve the tension mentally, using similar suggestions to those used during the previous exercises.

Go through the same procedure with the muscles of your face, head, and neck. Focus all of your attention on the experiences and feelings you receive.

Carried out properly, these relaxation exercises will produce some extremely pleasant, almost euphoric moments of mental detachment during the periods of rest.

Self Hypnosis

Self hypnosis is a completely safe, natural, everyday phenomena, experienced by all of us in one way or another. It may be accurately defined as: "A state of relaxation and concentration at one with a state of heightened awareness, induced by suggestion."

There is no special skill or knowledge needed to practise self hypnosis. It is merely a natural extension of the relaxation techniques, described earlier. Having become deeply relaxed, counting down from five to zero and focusing on the idea of each count being a step deeper into relaxation and calm, is all that is required to achieve the state we call hypnosis.

From that point on, self hypnosis is all about giving yourself positive suggestions aimed at the subconscious mind. Because you are using self hypnosis to help manage stress the suggestions will be about stress coping skills. For example: "I feel calm and assertive when I am criticised at work."

There are many books available about self hypnosis and the power of auto suggestions. The distance learning package, "Positive Changes", is particularly recommended.

Setting Goals

Stress occurs when we feel that events control us, instead of us being in control of events. Having clearly defined goals helps to create a sense of being in control. Changes cannot occur, successes cannot be achieved, habits cannot be overcome and improvements cannot be made, unless goals are specifically and clearly defined at the outset.

The best way to set goals is to sit down with a pen and some paper and brainstorm for as long as it takes you to come up with some really clear and totally compelling goals. The best goals are those which are not only specific but are also inspirational.

Having listed in precise details, the goals you wish to set yourself, you will next need to draw up a blueprint which plans the route between where your now and where you will be when you achieve your goals. The way to do this is to start with the ultimate long term goals and to break down into ever increasing detail, describing the various stages of action that will have to be accomplished on route if you are to reach your final destination. This process will involve quantifying things, making each outcome measurable and allocating specific periods of time for the completion of each stage.

It is also essential that the targets you set yourself are realistic and obtainable. The achievement of one small step towards a goal has a snow balling effect which makes each of the subsequent steps become easier and easier as you progress. Making that step a little too steep can have the opposite effect, causing a negative spiral of mini failures and deflated ego to develop. This prevents the ultimate goals from ever being achieved.

The way to ensure that you really do attain your goals is to regularly rehearse achieving them. You can actually rehearse attaining goals with the help of self hypnosis. Visualise yourself carrying out your plan and accomplishing the things you have set out to accomplish.

The *Relationship Between Stress and Diet*

The relationship between stress diet has been affected by the developments of our sophisticated lifestyle. In primitive man, an automatic balance of energy input and energy output was sustained for most of a man's life. He burnt the right amount of calories to fuel his body for warmth and physical exertion. Today, it is not like that. Physical work is becoming the exception rather than the norm and even for those of us who are still engaged for most of our time in physically demanding work, the nature of the tasks we perform are quite unlike the exertions of our hunter, gatherer ancestor.

On the other side of the equation, foods, especially rich, fattening ones, are plentiful. Twentieth century man can no longer expect nature to provide an automatic balance between diet and exercise. It's up to us to take the appropriate action to introduce the balance ourselves.

It's easy enough to find out what to do. There's a multi-million pound industry of diet plans, exercise programmes, books, tapes and video information on the subject. There are many good diet plans, but whatever one you choose, make sure that it includes fresh fruit, vegetables and fibre.

The other thing to ensure is that you eat regularly and peacefully. Stop for meals. Put away your work. Relax. Put that book down. Don't answer the telephone. Just sit down and really relax to savour every mouthful of whatever it is you choose to eat.

Stress and Exercise

Motivate yourself to start taking enjoyable, regular exercise. Exercise has an immediate effect on anxiety. It is also an ideal outlet for tension, bottled up aggression or frustrations.

Other benefits are:

Improved sleep
Fewer stress related aches and pains
Greater inner calm
Improved mental clarity
Better powers of concentration

Exercise releases brain chemicals:

Endorphins = happiness and euphoria – thereby dispelling anxiety and depression.

There are basically six types of exercise to choose from. Deciding which ones to include in your personal exercise programme is a case of checking out which types satisfy your specific needs. The exercise you choose has to be enjoyable, forcing yourself to do exercises you don't enjoy is going to be a pretty stressful thing to do.

Types of Exercise

1 **Aerobic dance**
Requires approximately 2 hours a week
Increases flexibility of movement
Strengthens abdominal and leg muscles
Excellent for cardiovascular endurance

2 **Aerobic exercise**
Can be jogging, hill walking, cycling or swimming
Requires 10 – 15 minutes daily
Promotes flexibility if preceded by simple warm up exercise
Strengthens leg muscles.
Swimming also increases upper body strength
Second to none for strengthening heart and lungs and improving overall stamina.

3 **Calisthenics**
Requires 30 minutes daily
Stretching exercises particularly useful for improving all over flexibility.
Can improve cardiovascular endurance but best results achieved when supplemented by aerobic exercise

4 **Yoga**
Requires 30 minutes per day and a regular class
Excellent stress reliever and muscle tension relaxer
Improves flexibility in all parts of the body
Offers only minimal cardiovascular improvement

5 **Weight Training**
Requires approximately 30 minutes, three times weekly, in a suitably equipped fitness club
Excellent for strength building
Improves flexibility if correctly executed
Offers only minimal cardiovascular improvement

6 **Martial Arts**
Requires twice weekly attendance at 1 – 2 hour class
Stretching exercises and high kicks are excellent for improving flexibility.
Push ups and sit ups are usually a main part of training and these help to build strength.
Cardiovascular endurance is improved considerably through most martial arts, with the possible exception of Tai Chi.

Other Stress Management Topics

Here is an alternative list of stress management training topics for you to consider. Perhaps you will need to read up on a few more of the topics but there is a wealth of information available about all of them:

Managing Change:

- Relationship between Stress and Change
- Accepting Personal Responsibility for Change
- Identifying aspects of behaviour which can be modified to accommodate change
- Making our responses to changing circumstances a positive experience.

Time Management

Compiling and Using Positive Affirmations
Creative Visualisation

How to make a Proposal to Colleges

When approaching a college or adult education centre, you will need to submit a proposal in a form which shows that you are organised and have carefully planned the design and delivery of your training. Here is an example.

Stress Management Course Overall Course Objectives

1. To enable students to examine and understand the causes and effects of stress.
2. To provide them with techniques and strategies for reducing the levels of stress in their lives and for effectively managing responses to potentially stressful situations.
3. To demonstrate the power that is contained in every person's mind and to teach students how to tap this inner resource and utilise its positive energy.

Day One – Two Hours

Session 1: Introductions. Overview and aims of course.

Objectives:

1. To "break the ice" and help students to feel relaxed in group setting
2. To ensure course content matches students' expectations and if not, to resolve any misunderstandings etc.

Session 2: "What is Stress?"

Objectives

1. To offer a definition of stress
2. To enable students to understand the physiology of stress
3. To enable students to understand the "fight or flight" response.
4. To examine the sources of stress, personality, lifestyle, environmental and chemical.

Session 3: "How stressed are you? Part one"

Objectives

1. To complete a "self assessment" exercise

Day Two – Two Hours

Session 1: "How stressed are you? Part two"

Objectives

1. To help students recognise their stress responses
2. To understand stress symptoms and signals
3. Review of self assessment exercise

Session 2: The Unconscious Mind

Objectives

1. To enable students to understand the nature and power of the unconscious mind
2. To show that this power can be controlled for positive benefits or can be left uncontrolled to work negatively on occasion.

Day Three – Two Hours

Session 1: Relaxation

Objectives

1. Students will learn and practice the techniques of deep relaxation

Day Four – Two Hours

Session 1: What is Self Hypnosis?

Objectives:

1. To reveal the nature of hypnosis
2. To establish its value as a practical tool with which the unconscious mind can be programmed for beneficial effect.

Day Five – Two Hours

Session 1: Other Stress Management Strategies

Objectives

1 To provide background material explaining the role of diet and exercise in stress control
2 To introduce students to the concept of meditation
3 To briefly describe other popular aids to stress proofing. (e.g. aromatherapy, nutrition and massage.)

Session 2: Course Evaluation

Objectives

1 To check students understanding of course material
2 To answer unresolved questions
3 To help students consider ways of maintaining and further developing strategies to manage stress in the future.

Having prepared a course outline, showing the learning objectives for each session, similar to the example above, you will need to send it with a covering letter to colleges and other adult education providers in your area.

Adult part time courses start mainly in January and September and it is a good idea to time your approach well in advance of these months. Write a letter modelled on the example below and enclose your proposed course outline with it.

Mr………..
Adult Education Tutor
………..Adult Education Centre

Dear Mr …………

I am writing to introduce myself and offer to teach Stress Management at your centre.

I have an extensive knowledge of my subject and believe that I am an effective communicator, in both group and one to one situations. (Mention here any relevant experience or qualifications that you have.)

The enclosed example of a course outline is based upon ……. Hours tuition, spaced over ………weeks. It can however be adapted to fit other lengths of time and I would be delighted to meet with you to discuss how best to tailor the proposal to suit your centre's actual requirements.

I would appreciate it if you could telephone me at the above number when you have had sufficient time to consider the proposal.

Yours sincerely

Fees from Adult Education Work

Colleges are fairly consistent in their payment to adult education tutors who are employed on a sessional basis. At the time of writing, all colleges in my own county pay £14 per hour. A neighbouring county is paying £16. This may not sound like a lot of money if you are doing only one, two hour evening class per week, but there is no reason why you should not be able to teach at different centres four nights per week and possibly do a two hour Saturday morning session as well. Your income from adult education work could therefore total as much as £160 per week.

How to Market Stress Management to Employers

It is unusual to find employers who employ less than one hundred people interested in running stress management courses. Rather than waste your time and resources in approaching these smaller companies therefore, it is better to concentrate on reaching those who employ over 150 employees and who have a heavy concentration of technical, administrative, sales and managerial occupations.

You can discover who these employers are within the geographical area in which you decide to operate, by referring to the detailed records held by the local chamber of commerce or public library.

Initially, it is best to aim for a "mailing list" comprising of fifty to one hundred employers. You will need to research the name of the personnel and training director or manager. If the company does not employ one, obtain the name of managing director or most appropriate decision maker. If this information isn't readily available, a simple telephone enquiry to the company is usually sufficient to ascertain it.

When your initial list is complete, prepare a letter similar to the one set out below.

Dear……… (Training and Personnel Director if Possible)

It is estimated that in the UK at least 40 million working days are lost each year due to the effects of stress. But the cost to industry doesn't end there, because the figure only relates to actual absences from work. Stress produces several other effects. Over-stressed employees at any level of a company, are inefficient employees. At clerical and operative level, stress might reveal itself in carelessness, poor timekeeping and absenteeism. Whilst at more senior levels, creativity, judgement and decision making skills are affected.

It would be unrealistic to talk about eliminating stress. On the other hand, learning how to manage stress is something that everybody can do and benefit enormously from, which is why I offer Stress Management Training for people at work.

My training helps people to recognise stress symptoms, discover and understand its root causes, use "good" stress to their advantage and to deal with "bad" stress by adopting appropriate coping skills.

Your employees will come back from their course of Stress Management refreshed, confident and relaxed. But more importantly, permanent effects can be achieved with everyone who follows our simple programme of post course practice. To help to ensure that course participants continue to progress and develop their skills, I like to arrange a follow-up session six months after the course. The increased efficiency of the employees you have selected for training will repay their course fees many times over, whilst the personal benefits which each individual experiences from attending a course promotes a sense of appreciation that they are employed by a caring employer.

I appreciate that you may need to consult with other personnel before deciding whether you would like to meet with me and discuss the details of what the training has to offer your company. With your permission, therefore, I propose to telephone you two weeks from now to enquire whether you have been able to consider the contents of this letter.

Yours sincerely

Another idea is to produce a brochure which describes the training you are offering. This is posted out with a slightly shorter sales letter which draws attention to the contents of the brochure. You would still conclude with your proposal to follow up by a telephone call and in either case, it is important that you do in fact make the call at the time you have specified.

The telephone call would go something like this:

Hello, is that Mr Jones, the Personnel Director?

My name is……… And I wrote to you a couple of weeks ago about stress management training. Do you recall the letter? Having read the material I sent you, when would be a good time for me to meet you and explain exactly what the training consists of and how your company could benefit from it. Would next Thursday be convenient or would you prefer some other day?

How much to Charge

Although you will come across some competition, it is important that you do not try to sell your stress management training on price. Point out to the employer that you are a specialist – A Stress Management Consultant, as opposed to a run of the mill training company who offer training in a wide range of subjects.

If you give the employer the idea that your training is cheap, he will also assume it's not worth having. If you present yourself as a specialist, offering quality training which can be customised to suit the requirements of the particular company, you can actually get away with making it more expensive than your competitors. Do some research of your own first and find out what your competitors are offering and what their fees are. As mentioned earlier, rates in excess of £500 per day are not at all uncommon.

A guideline base figure for you to consider might be in the region of £30 per day per trainee. A group of between ten and fifteen trainees is about the right size for stress management training, so a one day training course, based on this rate, would give you an income of between £300 and £450.

Appendix

Suggested Background Reading and Further Study

1. Courses Covering Most of the Topics of Stress Management

Dr. Wilf Archer of *www.mindskills.co.uk*
He markets a CDROM Course which is the best training in Corporate Stress Management and Human resources training I have ever seen, he also offers

telephone coaching to teach new therapists how to break into this lucrative field.

Positive Changes Personal Development Distance Learning Course
Available from:
Positive Changes
47 Duncombe Close
Luton
Beds, England
LU3 2HR

The Professional Stress Consultants Course.
The Advanced Stress Consultants Course
Both available from:
Associated Stress Consultants
The Old Vicarage
Clawton
Nr Holdsworthy
Devon, England
EX22 6PS

Professional Hypnotherapy Courses are available from:

The International Association of Hypno-Analysts
P O Box 180
Bournemouth, England
BH8 8NH

British Hypnosis Research
8 Paston Place
Brighton,
England
BN2 1HA

2. Teaching Adults

Adult Learning Adult Teaching
An excellent publication available only from:
The Publications Officer
Publications Unit
Department of Adult Education
"C" Block
Cherry Tree Buildings
University Park
Nottingham, England, NG7 2RD

3. Books on Stress Management Related Topics

Stress Control Through Self Hypnosis by Dr Arthur Jackson
Awaken the Giant Within by Anthony Robbins
Relax and Live by Dr Jack Gibson
Stress Management for Wellness by W Schafer

All of the above books can be obtained from:

The Anglo American Book Company
Underwood, St Clears
Carmarthen
Dyfed, Wales
SA33 4NE
Tel: 01994 230400

No More Fears by Dr Douglas Hunt – Useful information about the nutritional approach to stress management.
Creative Visualisation by Ronald Shone
Stress Busters by Robert Holden
Burnout by Ken Powell
Introducing Neuro-Linguistic Programming by Joseph O'Connor an John Seymour

All of the above books can be obtained from:

Thorsons Mail Order
Harper Collins Publishers Ltd
Westerhill Road
Bishopbriggs
Glasgow, Scotland
G64 2QT

The Book of Stress Survival by A Kirsta/Publisher: Guild.

Now I'm sure you'll agree the previous pages on "How to make money from stress management training" by myself, a professional therapist, are both highly informative and also contain information which can earn you back the entire cost of this training course many times over.

From my own personal point of view the only things I can add on the subject of stress management training are as follows:

1. Read all books you can by Anthony Robbins i.e. Unlimited Power, Awaken the Giant Within and also purchase all his audio courses. Do this and not only will you have all the knowledge required to earn from stress management but you'd also be able to run motivational training sessions also, which can also be highly profitable. One other book on stress management which I'd highly recommend is "Stress Management Techniques", subtitled "Managing people for healthy profits" by Dr Vernon Coleman. It's by Mercury Bodis, 44 Hill Street, London W1X 8LB and order number is 1SBN 1 85251 0366.
2. Don't forget also that not only is the "Positive Changes" distance learning course as detailed in this chapter useful reading material. But it is also a highly profitable business venture in itself which can earn you a high income indeed. For full details contact, Positive Changes as stated earlier in the chapter.

I will now end this chapter with an example sales letter of my own for Stress Management and Motivational Sales Training. Incidentally, as you offer a 100% confidential service, you aren't allowed to tell customers which media stars you've motivated in the past.

STRESS IN THE WORKPLACE?

Ignore this at your peril. Already companies are in court paying out thousands and thousands in compensation for under estimating this serious issue.

Individual company reports carried out, also lectures given. Our counsellors are qualified with over 20 years experience in this industry.

We use only the most up to date, tried, tested and proven to work techniques to effect positive change in your company's workforce.

40 million working days per year are being lost to employers as a result of stress related absences. Our services will prove that prevention is better than cure and will save your company thousands of pounds in lost manpower and revenue.

Unlike most other personal development training consultants, Alex himself is a successful professional hypnotherapist, psychotherapist and psychological counsellor with a vast experience of dealing with Major Blue Chip Companies and Organisations.

Personal support and guidance is provided in response to individuals needs as well as group motivational training and stress management sessions being held to enable your workforce to operate at peak performance consistently.

As one director was heard to say after a Leroy training session:

"My job as the boss is to provide the right atmosphere in the "greenhouse" of our company, so that people can constantly grow. Alex Leroy's training sessions provide that environment."

ABOUT YOUR TUTOR

Now considered to be one of Britains most dynamic personal development consultants, sales advisors and motivational trainers, Alex Leroy is also an accomplished stress management consultant and shares his experiences and techniques in a highly effective and entertaining down to earth style.

LIFE CHANGES

Now for the first time, you can hear and experience for yourself, his techniques for confident communication and personal improvement in his "Lifechange" seminars.

Lifechanges is a genuine product and a unique service which is of invaluable use to all company managers, self employed people and in fact, every human who wishes to effect positive and lasting change in their lifestyles.

YOU WILL LEARN

"Powerful communication skills for business and winning solutions for life."

SO DON'T FORGET

"Innovative business leaders are measured by results and not by efforts."

And

"People don't plan to fail, but many do fail to plan."

THE SOLUTION

Well as Henry David Thoreau said, "Things do not change, we change." Alex Leroy's Lifechanges seminars and lectures teach you and your workforce how to take immediate control of your mental, emotional, physical and financial destiny.

Through inspirational anecdotes, case studies personalised self help tests and a program that anyone can follow, Alex Leroy teaches the lessons in destine that lead to success through self mastery.

The only limitations we have in life, are those which we impose upon our own minds. So take control of your life and allow Alex Leroy to make you a no limits person.

DREAMS DO COME TRUE

"The only way to discover the limits of the possible is to go beyond them into the impossible" Arthur C Clarke

And as it states in the Holy Bible
"As a Man thinketh so he becomes."

Lifechanges seminars can program your mind and guarantee you the success you so richly deserve and as Mark Twain so correctly said.

"There is nothing training cannot do, nothing is above its reach, it can turn bad morals to good, it can destroy bad principles and recreate good ones, it can lift men to angelship."

THE LAST WORD

Our courses can be tailored to suit your individual or company needs and have in the past taught self hypnosis, creative visualisation, neuro linguistic programming, subliminal communication and many other highly effective techniques to numerous satisfied customers to achieve self improvement, stress management, business skills, self awareness, personal growth, career development, habit cessation, increased performance and much more.

Whatever your problem is, Lifechanges can solve it for you.

Our courses are an exciting voyage of self discovery which guide you across an ocean to a new world of opportunity and success.

To put your company back onto the track of guaranteed success, increased performance from your workforce and ultimately higher profits give me a call today.

HOTLINE NUMBER

(XXXX) XXXXXX

Top television Hypnotist Alex Leroy has already used his pioneering techniques to help famous media and sporting stars to effect positive change and increased performance in their careers and lifestyles. Major household name blue chip companies, have also benefited enormously from Leroy's confidential service. So remember, if you don't contact Lifechanges, then your competitors will.

SUCCESS CAN BE YOURS – RING NOW

A. Stress costs your company over £1000 per employee per year.
B. So if your company employs 100 people then stress costs the company over £400 per day.
C. If your company employs 1000 people, then stress costs the company over £1,000000 a year.
D. In an average lifetime, the average employee loses one and a half years from work because of stress induced illness.
E. Whatever else you try, and however much you spend on high technology equipment, nothing will improve your company's efficiency and profitability more than taking care of your employees. Reducing their exposure to stress and learning how to get the best out of them. Your company's biggest hidden asset is the people it employs.
F. In Alex Leroy's "Lifechanges" seminars, Alex explains exactly how, why and when stress causes problems. More importantly, he also explains how you can control and minimise the amount of stress in your company to consequently have staff perform at their peak performance and to increase the profitability of your company.

If you follow the above principals, you will soon be in control of your own Stress Management Consultancy.

PART EIGHTEEN

THE FAST PHOBIA CURE TREATMENT KNOWN AS NEURO ASSOCIATIVE CONDITIONING (NAC)

Welcome to part eighteen, which will teach you the treatment developed and pioneered by top American motivationalist Anthony Robbins. His treatment is known as Neuro Associative Conditioning or N.A.C. for short. Full details of this treatment can be obtained free of charge by borrowing Mr Anthony Robbin's book "Awaken the Giant Within", from your local library. I believe Mr Robbins entitled his treatment N.A.C as it works rapidly, just as Neuro Linguistic Programming techniques do, but with this treatment a strong neurological change is effected within the patient's body by the thoughts instilled into their minds. It is this change in their neurological behaviour as a result of the original thoughts in their mind, which makes the treatment so successful.

In this part, I will introduce you to the subject, so that you can put it to immediate use, in a similar fashion as was demonstrated on Paul McKenna's Network First programme, which was broadcast on ITV during Spring 1995. On this 60 minute documentary, we were clearly shown that after a therapy session of between 30 to 60 minutes maximum, a female patient, once scared of flying, not only flew in an aeroplane, but was relaxed and happy whilst doing so. A man once scared of spiders was happy to let a furry looking tarantula spider walk all over his palms. And a woman, once scared of heights, successfully completed a bungee jump from a great height after only one treatment session.

The same week on Central TV's Friday Night late show "Central Weekend Live", we were treated to a discussion on this treatment method and the network first programme. Live on TV we saw another man, once petrified of spiders, now able to handle a tarantula after just a brief treatment session with the therapist responsible for all these dramatic sounding case studies, Mr Michael Breen, a good friend of Mr Paul McKenna, who made the Network First programme.

The McKenna documentary also showed step by step, how and why the treatment worked, so if you can obtain a copy of the broadcast shown as I say in Spring 1995, then you will be shown with the aid of visual and verbal tuition the basics of how and why this treatment works.

The treatment shown on the McKenna show has a huge similarity with N.A.C., as taught by Anthony Robbins, so read Awaken the Giant Within and you too can achieve such dramatic results as those I've just mentioned. Now you know what is possible with this unique treatment, which I call "The thirty minute fast phobia cure", because it's a fast phobia cure and the one session the patient will require, will take approximately thirty minutes. Sometimes as long as an hour, but usually an average, somewhere in between. In Mr Robbins book, he details how using this N.A.C. treatment, he has also stopped people from smoking, over eating and other bad habits as well as curing fears and phobias. It seems obvious from all I've seen, that this is the treatment of the future, enabling you to solve most patient's problems in the space of just one session of one hours duration (maximum).

Imagine this, if you used noesitherapy for pain control and N.A.C. for fears, phobias and bad habits, then you'd instantly be able to set up in practice and treat most all clients for most all problems in just one session of no more than one hours duration. Earning a fee of £35 to £50 an hour, (minimum) you could treat 40 clients a week on a 9am to 5pm five day basis and that should bring you an income of between £1400 and £2000 per week. That's a possible income of £104,000 per year which by anyone's standards is a good income and as you could treat clients in their own homes you wouldn't even need an office or expensive equipment. So you'd practically be in profit and earning big money from day one.

Now down to a little theory, so that you can then put this treatment into practice. Firstly consult the illustration which is the last page of this chapter. It shows exactly how N.A.C., Neuro Associative Conditioning, (the master system) and the psychology of change works. You will see a diagram of the human mind, showing that the mind bases everything in life on how much pain or pleasure it causes the person to do or not to do that particular thing. So for example, if a person's mind has stored memories which make smoking seem pleasurable, e.g. the person has stored associations between smoking and relaxing etc. and as such, it becomes hard to stop smoking due to the pleasurable, neurological associations the person has made in their mind and body with direct regards to the action of smoking.

So obviously, if enough painful neurological associations were to be programmed into their mind and body with regards to smoking then it will become an automatic reflex action NOT to smoke, as it would be too painful to the person to smoke due to the neurological associations made between the patient's mind and body by N.A.C. treatment. The basic principle behind how the treatment works is the same whatever it is you are intending to treat. So to stop over-eating you'd have to create enough neurological links between the patients mind and body to make it painful for them to overeat and very pleasurable for them not to eat. Whereas their present behavioural patterns show they are associating pain with not eating and pleasurable associations with eating.

So to put it bluntly, it would seem that if a patient wants to stop a habit or stop some form of behaviour which is inappropriate, e.g. fears and phobias, then neurological associations between their mind and body must be made to make it painful to do this, to carry on the habit or to have that fear or phobia and you must also make it pleasurable not to do these things or to react in these ways. If a patient wishes to be able to do something, achieve something (i.e. improved sports performance, more energy, more confidence etc.) then you must create a strong painful neurological association between their mind and body not to do these things and strong associations of pleasure to be connected with both doing and achieving these things.

Put another way, the strong pleasurable associations must always be used to achieve the patients goals, hence it says "towards values" on the picture and strong painful associations must always be connected to the behaviour or habits which they do not wish to continue with, hence it the picture it says, states of pain = away values. Knowing this, once the patient has set their goal and for the following example we'll use a fear of spiders. You just need to follow the six master steps to change as shown on the picture and then success will be yours.

SIX MASTER STEPS TO CHANGE

1. Decide what you really want and what's preventing you from having it now. Eg. You want a relaxed life full of confidence in all you do. But your fear of spiders prevents you from having it now.
2. Get leverage = Associate massive pain to not changing this behaviour now and massive pleasure to the experience of changing now. Eg The pain of not changing now would be panic attacks each time you saw a spider. Feelings of inferiority and a lack of confidence etc. Whereas the pleasurable points of changing now are that you'd have no fear of spiders, increased confidence, feelings of great happiness and a sense of great achievement in all that you do. Which of course would be a far more appropriate form of behaviour for you to have.

3. Interrupt the limiting pattern. Eg. Once in the hypnotic state which will increase the success of this six step process, although it can and often is as successful without the use of hypnosis, you then interrupt the limiting pattern through the use of visualisation. As shown on Paul McKenna's network first broadcast, for a fear of spiders you'd visualise the tarantula spider talking with a squeaky voice, wearing a funny party hat, with welly boots on eight feet and a big red clowns nose. In other words, you change that mental image of a spider from something that scares you to something you find hilarious. In fact, to the point where you physically laugh at the thought that anyone could be scared of this strange and silly image in your mind. At this point the neurological limiting pattern will have been broken and mentally you are not scared of this image you have created.
4. Create a new, empowering alternative. Eg. Here again through mental visualisation you'd see in your minds eye that each and every time in the future when you see a spider you will instantly bring the stupid and silly mental image you have created to mind. And as such, will feel calm, relaxed, happy and in fact, a little jovial in this, a situation which once bothered you. See yourself in your minds eye feeling proud, happy and confident with your new behaviour and you will then have created a new, empowering alternative.
5. Condition the new pattern until it's consistent. Eg Where you'd have several mental rehearsals, where you'd rehearse reacting to the sight of a spider with the comical mental image and calm confident behaviour. So in your minds eye, imagine seeing a spider, then rehearse reacting in your new calm and confident manner, now no longer scared of spiders due to the new neurological associations you will have made.
6. TEST IT. Eg. Quite simply, what it says, once all the other five steps have been made, pain has been associated with not achieving your goal, pleasure with achieving it and the limiting pattern has been interrupted, you will then be ready to test your new behaviour in a real life situation. In other words, now is when you confront what were once your worst fears to prove 100% to yourself that they are no longer things that bother you. An ideal test would be to allow a tarantula to be placed on your palms, as shown on the Network First show. Once you have it on your palm, allow the comical mental image to resurface, notice how calm and confident you feel. Then the treatment will be complete and your belief and expectancy would be 100% total and your new behavioural patterns will be set for life.

Here, let me say, to have seen a video of a past patient confronting their fears after this N.A.C. treatment would instil extra belief into you prior to the treatment, which would help ensure success in one session only.

SUMMING UP

Follow the six master steps to change, as outlined in this chapter and follow the other rules as outlined in this chapter and success with N.A.C. will be yours. In this chapter you have learnt all you need to know to, with a little common sense, adapt what I have taught you, so that you can treat practically any patient for any fear, phobia, habit or nervous disorder. Further details can be obtained from Mr Robbin's book, Awaken the Giant Within. And of course, I'd recommend you obtain a copy of the McKenna broadcast and even The Hypnotic World of Paul McKenna book, which contains Mr McKenna's own experiences and thoughts on this treatment. Many psychologists take weeks to do what you can now do in under one hour using N.A.C. treatment. All I need to mention once again, is the importance of facing up to your fear as step six of the treatment. So that when you survive it with no ill effects it concrete's the new mental images in your mind and ensures that you never fear that subject matter again.

With the case of habits etc., time is the test here, so here don't light up a cigarette to prove it makes you feel sick. Do, however, dispose of all ashtrays, tobacco, lighters etc., so that no temptations exist for you.

This six step plan correctly followed will ensure success and achieve the patients goals. Remember also, that they are first placed under hypnosis and this will ensure that the new comical mental images, as in this example, will always spring to mind, when that once fearful event occurs, in order to ensure you are calm and relaxed. You can also, prior to removing them from trance, implant a major post hypnotic suggestion along the lines of that if ever they do feel the slightest bit of fear in such a situation, then by just taking 3 deep breaths in and then out, the patient will instantly feel calm, confident and relaxed. This gives the power of N.A.C. treatment combined with a powerful post hypnotic suggestion and as such, the old behaviours will be out and the new ones in.

I'll end this chapter, by saying this. Treatment alone can change peoples lives for the better and at the same time earn you an income and lifestyle others only dream of.

PART NINETEEN

MORE SHORTCUTS TO HYPNO AND PSYCHOTHERAPY OR HOW TO EARN AS YOU LEARN

A BRIEF EXPLANATION OF THE THERAPIES

A professional and ethical therapist will always discharge each and every client from treatment at the earliest possible moment, consistent with that clients good care and will also offer the client the style of treatment which ultimately will be most beneficial for them and not necessarily the most profitable for you. The reason for this being, not only is it ethical practice, but in this way, you will only end up with happy clients, who will go off and sing your praises to other people and as word of mouth advertising is by far, the most profitable and effective you will ultimately benefit more in this way.

The therapist undertakes to respect a client's confidentiality at all times and would not even disclose to a spouse or parent that they were undergoing treatment. The ethical therapist will also ensure that any hypnotic (or post hypnotic) suggestion given to any client will be so worded, that any effects can only be beneficial to the client. He/she will have a clear understanding of the concept of symptom substitution, (which, without being too technical, means the possibility of switching from say, agoraphobia to claustrophobia) and in consequence, will only use what is popularly termed "suggestion therapy" for the more minor problems, where the probable substitution can be foreseen and thus controlled. (Eg anti smoking therapy would contain suggestions to avoid over eating.)

In therapeutic circumstances there is no question of being controlled or manipulated or even induced into a deep trance state. A person in hypnosis (often referred to conscious hypnosis) is not "asleep", they are often more aware of what is taking place than usual and their senses function more efficiently than normal. In normal therapeutic circumstances, nobody could be made to do or say anything they would not want to. Everyone (except the truly mentally sub normal, very young boys and inebriates) can enter the hypnotic state. People who say or think, "nobody could get me under" or "I wouldn't want anyone controlling my mind", or "I might blurt my secrets out", are really demonstrating that they have a total misconception of what hypnosis really is. The state of hypnosis, a totally natural phenomenon, is most pleasant and particularly relaxing and a person can converse quite easily whilst within the state. It is inconceivable that any harm could befall them. Indeed the centuries old technique of hypnosis is being used increasingly as an adjunct to orthodox medicine where it is proving a valuable alternative to drugs for anaesthesia, to accelerate healing, relieve stress and control pain. A good definition of hypnosis is "a state of relaxation and concentration at one with a state of heightened awareness induced by pure verbal suggestion." The therapist uses his or her voice to induce you into the state of hypnosis and although you are unlikely to feel "hypnotised" as such, you will most probably experience a feeling of mental and physical relaxation and your memory may well be enhanced. You will find that the therapist is a caring professional person, totally devoid of any mystical or magical powers. No flowing robes or swinging watches, just a reassuring manner to put you at ease and the expertise to help with you problem. There are two entirely different treatments using conscious hypnosis and these are as follows:

Suggestion Therapy – Which is used for simpler problems, such as smoking, nail biting, pre test nerves, slimming, relaxation, confidence boosting etc., which require one or two sessions, with perhaps a booster session, several months on. Usually the client receives one session of therapy and prior to being awoken is given the major post hypnotic suggestion, that each time they listen to the audio tape you give them it will have just the same effect with them as if you were in the room with them. They are awoken and for the next few days they listen to the tape which strengthens the suggestions in their mind for the type of therapy of habit cessation they've had.

Analytical Therapy – This is used to discover causes of psychological problems (and of course, one does mix the two forms of therapies at times.) Hypno analysis can be summarised briefly as the doctrine of "cause and effect". Every effect (the symptom) must have a cause. Hypno analysis reveals and thus removes the cause, (see section in course on Abreactions), consequently relieves the symptoms.

As mentioned earlier in the course the cause of the problem has been "repressed" with emotion and now from an adult view point the therapy is used to release it with emotion. You see emotional problems respond particularly well to conscious "hypno analysis". The object of analysis is to bring the patient to "a moment of surprising and liberating enlightenment" and one can be fairly confident that a release will be obtained usually within six to twelve sessions of analysis. With these cases we are talking about a complete and lasting release, by finding and removing originating causes, as opposed to mere control of symptoms by suggestions. There is no reason why anyone should put up with something "inside themselves, but outside their control". Providing they are prepared to devote time, money, effort and self discipline to be free of their problem. The use of conscious hypnosis dramatically speeds up analysis, and similar results can be achieved in a few weeks, which take mainstream psychologists much longer with conventional 100 hour analysis. A question often asked is, can normal people be psycho analysed? I'd reply, not only can they be, but they should be. For an insight into yourself, it has no equal and as a professional therapist to be, is not only wise to remove any neurosis you yourself may have prior to treating others, but it is also an excellent way to learn the procedures of psycho analysis through the experience of having it done on yourself.

The process used is to get rapport with the client, induce the trance and then deepen the trance. (Details of these in earlier chapters) Next it's time for the process of free association, which will be explained more fully in a few moments. The next step is to give the patient some ego strengthening therapy, the major post hypnotic suggestion is then given, that at the next session the patient will instantly and deeply enter trance being able to recall events and memories freely and easily. Lastly, of course, the client is awoken from the trance in the same way as they would be on stage. So, for psycho analysis, the seven step guide to success and release of the patient's problem is:

SEVEN STEPS TO ANALYSIS SUCCESS

1. Get Rapport
2. Induce The Trance
3. Deepen The Trance
4. Process of Free Association
5. Ego Strengthening Therapy
6. Major Post Hypnotic Suggestion
7. Awaken From The Trance

Whereas in suggestion therapy the seven point guide to success is:

SEVEN STEPS TO SUGGESTION SUCCESS

1. Get Rapport
2. Induce The Trance
3. Deepen The Trance
4. Ego Strengthening Therapy
5. Do Necessary Suggestion Therapy
6. Major Post Hypnotic Suggestion
7. Awaken Patient from Trance

So basically, for both analysis and suggestion success, all you need to know has been taught earlier on in this course. So I leave it to you to find out from within these pages. Ego Strengthening is quite literally what it says to make the patient feel good and confident about themselves by the use of positive suggestions.

As for the necessary suggestion therapy, I have told you earlier in the course the ways to phrase these.

If a client wants to do something they aren't doing, then suggestions would be given that they can and will achieve or do this. When they are doing something they don't want to, you must give suggestions that they will not and can no longer do that thing in question. Lastly, the last few main things you need to know are with regards to hypno analysis and are the subjects of:

1. Transference
2. Counter Transference
3. Rationalisation
4. Free Association

I will explain briefly what each of these four things are.

Transference

To cut quite a long story short, this is the phenomenon often experienced by a client in analysis. As they off load memories from the past and numerous emotions surface within them, the patient will often come to regard you as the only person who seems to care about them and this can and often does result in romantic interest from the patient (whether male or female). You as an ethical therapist must not take advantage of this for two reasons.

A. It would be unethical, and
B. As emotions are unsettled in the client and this is just a side effect of analysis. If you were to take advantage of the situation to gain sex,

which will sometimes be on offer, not only would it be unethical, but as emotions are unsettled in the client, you once having done something, could find yourself being accused of rape by a client whose mind is slightly in a twirl at the time. This has as you'll have seen in the media, occurred to several therapists in the past.

Counter Transference

This is the phenomenon of a therapist starting to feel emotions towards his clients of a sexual or unhealthy for a therapist/client relationship nature. This usually occurs after a client has demonstrated that they are experiencing transference for you the therapist, so be careful you don't fall victim to this, as it can be dangerous for the same reasons as detailed for transference.

Rationalisation

This is, to put it briefly, the process whereby a patient in analysis tries to rationalise with themselves why they are experiencing certain emotions and certain feelings which they at that time, may not want to or may be scared of feeling. It is done out of a fear of finding a solution to the problem as the patient starts to worry that the cause might be something they can't handle. Well, the truth is now from an adult viewpoint, once they come across the memory that triggers off the abreaction and thus the emotional release of the cause to their problem, then not only will the symptoms vanish, but also they, looking at the cause from an older logical adult viewpoint, will see it wasn't their fault and they need not blame themselves for the way they felt at the time.

Free Association

This is the process, whereby once in the hypnotic state, the patient is allowed to freely associate one memory to another in their mind and at the same time tell you what is popping into their minds. Once under hypnosis, you'd tell the patient to just relax and tell you the very first thing that pops into their mind and then to link and connect this to another memory which they must tell you. And so they must go on linking and connecting all memories to other memories which pop into their mind, however unconnected or illogical those memories may seem at the time of recollection to the patient. So the key phrase here is, "link and connect." You, as the therapist take notes of the things said and quite often you'll see a pattern occurring which often indicates to you what the cause of the problem is even before the client has realised and has their moment of enlightening emotional release which ends their problems. It is merely a matter of time before all the memories recalled start to have a lot in common and then soon after an abreaction will occur and the problem will be released with emotion. At this time it is very useful to have a box of tissues handy in your consulting room.

If based on what you have learnt in this course, you feel sooner than spend £500 on the Neil French course to learn the in depth secrets of analysis, you feel you have enough confidence to start doing analysis now and learn from experience in order to save money. Then I say, although I'd recommend you earn as you learn by doing suggestion therapy first and as you earn study the Neil French Course. I would say if you decide to do this, then an excellent book to buy which will teach you all the rest you need to know about analysis prior to you treating a patient and costs under £10 is the book "A Laymans Guide to Psychiatry and Psycho Analysis," by Doctor Eric Berne. He is also the author of Games People Play and I believe this is published by Penguin and available from the psychology section of your local bookstore.

PART TWENTY

LEROYS BIZARRE

A mixture of information introducing you to the subjects of past life regression shows and therapy sessions, U.F.O. and police forensic style investigative hypnosis and ideas for getting rich in the hypnotic industry.

In these next few pages, we shall be exploring a mix of information on several areas of the hypnotic industry which are often never mentioned in training courses such as this. Firstly lets cover the subject of police forensic style hypnosis, which was featured on Paul McKennas Network First documentary during Spring 1995 on ITV. The subject was also covered in The Hypnotists Bible, a book written by my mentor and tutor, Delavar, a respected stage hypnotist and hypnotherapist of over 60 years extensive experience.

The comprehensive book is available through The Mindcare Organisation via Delavar himself. Anyway to get down to basics, in the USA, several police forces as was shown on the McKenna show have brought in hypnotherapists in order to uncover the identity of a victims attacker in cases such as rape or assault. The reason that hypnosis can be so useful in circumstances such as these is that being raped or assaulted can be so traumatic to the victim that it becomes too "hot" for the mind to handle. In order to instantly come to terms with things, the memories of the event are repressed into the subconscious mind and as with standard psychotherapy you can make the client relive the event which has been repressed, except this time, as they are under hypnosis they can do it without any emotional or psychological attachment as if they are just watching the event happen as a movie on the TV screen within their minds eye, which of course, is what you instruct them to do. The only difference between police forensic hypnosis and most psychotherapy is that usually you know there's a problem, but not what it is and as such, it takes several sessions, whereas with forensic hypnosis you know when the event took place, what happened etc. and where, so you are able to just place the person into a trance and once under hypnosis and having instructed them to experience all they are to remember as just a movie and TV screen in their minds eye, so that they are emotionally unattached from the memory of events, you literally just have to instruct them to go back in their mind, through their memories to the time, place etc. that the event took place and recall everything as a crystal clear technicolour image in their minds eye. You then just take down the details they give and ask questions to clarify on small points. Eg. Was it a big nose or a small nose? Remembering of course to always ask open ended questions, so that it cannot accidentally be taken by the person under hypnosis to answer in a certain way. As a therapist doing analysis or regression, you must always be careful to ask only open ended questions and never to suggest things that could have happened, either indirectly or directly. For example, if you said, did he put his penis in your mouth? Even if this hadn't taken place, the patient under hypnosis would think that as you had asked the question, it is possible it could have occurred and as such, false memory syndrome could come into play and the patient could recall memories which far from being true, are in fact, the product of direct and/or indirect suggestions made by the therapist. So the rule of thumb in all cases of this nature is the therapist has two ears and one mouth, so should use his ears twice as much to listen. In other words, under analysis you need only say "now link and connect" to the next memory etc. until you become well versed in the subject, be cautious at all times to say anything else to extract information from the hypnotic client. The collected information on the attackers identity, is then used to form a photo fit picture, which can then be used to find the criminal responsible.

Those who have seen the Paul McKenna TV Documentary, will have seen police forensic style hypnosis in action and as such, will know just how successful it is and just how similar the criminals caught who admitted to the offences looked to the pictures compiled from the descriptions given by the victims under hypnosis. So yes, this does work remarkably well.

The last thing I will add here is, that a police artist can be in the room at the same time as was done on the McKenna documentary to compile a sketch drawing of the attacker as the session takes place, the victim is then awoken from trance and when they confirm the picture looks like their attacker, this can be used by the police to find the criminal. Incidentally, I am led to believe, several UK police forces have used this forensic hypnosis method, but as of yet are keeping very quiet about it.

U.F.O. investigative hypnosis is much the same in many ways. Again you must never suggest anything to the client, they must be the ones to offer up information to you and as mostly they will believe they have been abducted by aliens in a U.F.O. you know what event you are regressing them to and as such, you proceed in the same way as getting a victim to recall their attackers identity and let the patient offer up all the information, which of course is recorded by you, so that the client has it to refer to when they are awoken from the trance. There are several U.F.O. societies in the UK and even more in US. Join one of these and you'll meet lots of potential clients for your new services as well as meeting other hypnotists who do U.F.O investigative hypnosis and as such, you can learn tricks of the trade from the horses mouth, so to speak.

The next subject I will discuss, is past life regression shows, which were pioneered by a stage hypnotist Mr Julian Caruso of Stoke on Trent. (He can be contacted via Stoke on Trent Yellow Pages.) Should you contact Mr Caruso and discover where his next show is, then you can go and see him in action, which will teach you far more about the format of a past life regression show than anything I could write within these pages. As a past life regression show can be presented quite legitimately for scientific research purposes, no licenses are required and comedy can be injected into the show by you the hypnotist using one liners that relate to the situations the on stage subjects are reliving. These shows are both enjoyable, entertaining and educational. As such, they are well attended by the public and can be very lucrative.

The basic course of events is much the same as a normal stage hypnosis show, except that once under, instead of comedy routines you get the on stage subjects to regress to 8 years of age, then to being a baby, then to the birth experience. Next to the womb, then to a past life etc. Each time getting them to relive the memories which they tell you. (Here a microphone is held near to their mouth so audience hear too.) You can then inject comedy lines also to make the evenings events funny and basically that's what the show is made up of. After the show is a great time to get clients for one to one personal past life regression sessions and make even more money out of the shows. So next you need to know how to conduct personal one to one past life regression sessions, which of course, is what I'll be discussing next.

The basics have been covered earlier in the course, basically, you get the client under hypnosis, set the tape recorder running to record any events they recall and then regress them in much the same way as detailed above. Although several patients I have regressed in the past have been featured on TV shows and in magazines, I have very little experience in this area and as such, would advise anyone wishing to conduct regression sessions to go have your own past life regression done by another hypnotist, as you'll learn an awful lot from this. I'd also recommend a book by Mr Richard Webster, entitled "Making Money from Past Life Regression." It's available from Magic Books by Post in Bristol (address earlier in course.) and contains a complete induction script and full instructions on how to conduct a successful past life regression session. For just £30 including postage and packing, this book is a bargain as you'll earn this back many times over in treating clients at around £30 to £45 per one hour session. As a patient could have had more than one past life, they may wish to explore several of them and so each new client is a potential goldmine in monetary terms. Incidentally, master copies bearing blank spaces for your details are included in the book for publicity materials to promote your new past life regression services. New age shops are ideal places to site your advertising leaflets and with the weekly feature about regressions recently shown on ITV's Sunday evening show "Schofields Quest" interest in the subject has never been so high and regressions alone could earn you a huge weekly income. To cut a long story short, it is believed that if you have a weak wrist in this life, under regression you might recover memories showing that in a past lifetime you were in a sword fight and your hand was chopped off. When awoken from trance, knowing this information, your injury in this lifetime could disappear and your wrist could be returned to normal strength. The Bridey Murphy case is the most famous case investigated and a book by the same name is available. Incidentally, the investigation carried out on Schofields Quest TV show, proved beyond a doubt, that there's truth in the belief that we have all lived before and retain these memories in our sub conscious forever. The leading expert on past life regression is in the industry generally regarded to be Miss Ursula Marcum, who has written several excellent books on the subject all of which are available from your local library or bookstore. Anyway, I hope to have given you enough information on the subject so that should you decide regressions are for you then you'll be able to earn as you learn and source all the reference materials you need very quickly.

The next area of the industry I will discuss is the huge income that can be earned from increased sports performance and motivational training. (Both hypnotic and non hypnotic.) With regards to these subjects I say just read Unlimited Power and Awaken the Giant Within, by Anthony Robbins and you will have all the knowledge you need to start offering these services and earning from them. Basically though, under hypnosis, you strengthen their egos, make them feel confident and have them carry out "mental rehearsals" in their mind, in which they see themselves successfully achieving their goals and performing at an increased level. Having done things several times in their minds, the persons subconscious will believe that they have already done this successfully, several times and so will be confident enough to now achieve it in reality.

PART TWENTY ONE

COMPLETE MIND THERAPY (CMT)

Well my dear student, our time together is almost at an end, and your initial education in all areas of hypnosis is almost complete.

Now the reason I say "initial" education is because you will learn far more from the university of life and through the medium of hands on practical experience than any training course could ever teach you.

That is not to say that your academic study should end. Indeed at the rear of this, the final manual you will find a recommended reading list which you are advised to follow in order to further your studies as you also put the contents of this course to use and therefore start to earn as you learn.

This course in Complete Mind Therapy will without doubt, through its unique combination of audio tape, video tape and printed instructional material have taught you more about the stage hypnotism and mind therapies industry than many, if not most all so called established stage performers and therapists will ever know about the subject, so I assure you that you may proceed with the greatest of confidence in your new found skills at all times.

Prior to teaching you the concept and operation of a Complete Mind Therapy session, I would urge you to consider the very true fact that personal hands on training with an experienced expert of their craft is by far the easiest and most effective way of learning a new skill and hypnosis is no exception.

As detailed in the rear of the course prospectus as a student of the Complete Mind Therapy Course, discounted personal one to one training courses with me your head tutor, Dr. Jonathan Royle are available in order that you can learn through hands on demonstrations, exercises and experience.

Those of you seriously wishing to pursue a career in stage hypnosis and/or hypnotherapy are without doubt advised that eight hours in my company (from 10am until 6pm) on the day of your choice would not only be the learning experience of a lifetime but would also be an excellent chance to ask me any questions you may have.

Now without further ado, I shall explain the concept of Complete Mind Therapy. As I do, please bear in mind that whilst the printed content of this course may seem to have been heavily dominated with Stage Hypnotism training, in fact, each and every method, ploy and technique you have learned throughout this course is of use both on stage and within a therapeutic context. So please remember this most important point at all times.

What follows is the structure of a one hour complete mind therapy session, which when followed in this order will produce excellent results at all times.

Use this format for all your one hour long Complete Mind Therapy sessions and due to it's unique structure you will be able to treat any and all problems presented to you with just one single one hour session and the audio tape which you give the client on completion of their session.

THE COMPLETE MIND THERAPY SESSION STRUCTURE

1 Advertise to obtain your clients
2 Client shows up for session
3 Get the relevant fee off them now
4 Obtain rapport over a cup of tea
5 Obtain total belief and expectancy by your professional office and personal appearance
6 Ask the client to answer all pre – session questions
7 Do follow your thumb with your eyes, suggestibility test and anchor the cure to successful completion of this test
8 Induce trance via physical relaxation method and then counting backwards from 300 method
9 Deepen trance via staircase of relaxation
10 Deepen further by image of bed/sleep
11 Deepen further by dream/blackboard method
12 Ego strengthening therapy

13 The Necessary therapy

- **A. Anchor good time of life feelings to finger and thumb action**
- **B.** Ruler to 100% confidence
- **C. Ruler to 100% willpower**
- **D.** Ruler to 100% self image/esteem
- **E. Ruler to 100% relevant to actual problem the client has**
- **F.** T.V set get rid of the past visualisation
- **G. Mirror stare to instil new feelings and behaviour as reality**
- **H.** Direct suggestion therapy
- **I. Pain and pleasure suggestions**
- **J.** Repeat of direct suggestion therapy

14 Implant major post hypnotic suggestion
15 Awaken the client from trance
16 Give them their tape and any other information
17 Say goodbye to them and prepare for your next client to arrive

These are the 17 sections which go together to make the whole, which is a Complete Mind Therapy session. The structure is such that we have combined together the most effective elements of counselling skills, psychotherapy, suggestion therapy, aversion therapy, creative visualisation, noesitherapy, sports psychology and in fact all 14 areas which this course teaches are combined with an emphasis on neuro linguistic programming or as it is sometimes called neuro associative conditioning (N.A.C.), to give us a one hour long approximately session, which is so effective, that in my personal experience, only one session is necessary to cure the clients problem forever. If they do need some back up therapy later, they can then of course just listen to the audio tape which you have given them. I shall now explore each of these 17 separate sections which make up the whole and explain how to carry them out for greatest success.

ADVERTISE TO GET CLIENTS

Advertising has been touched on before but here is some further advice.

By far the most effective way to obtain clients is by word of mouth advertising, which will be generated for you at no charge by past clients which you have successfully treated, but of course you need some clients first for word of mouth advertising to start happening.

Upon passing the exam which leads to you receiving your diplomas for this course, you are advised to obtain a black and white matt finish photograph of yourself, apparently hypnotising someone in the usual cliched stage hypnotist manner. This is then sent along with a press release typed in double spaced format on single sided white A4 paper, explaining that after a comprehensive course of study, with the Mindcare Organisation UK, you have passed exams and have now been accepted as a member of both The Association of Professional Hypnotherapists and Psychotherapists and The Professional Organisation of Stage Hypnotists. Whilst now being the ONLY Complete Mind Therapist in your local area able to help people with all their habits, fears, phobias, emotional problems, pain control and other areas. This photograph and press release bearing your contact details are sent to the features editors and news editors of all your local and regional newspapers and magazines, often leading to a large write up promoting your business, which costs you nothing whilst generating lots of clients. This approach can also be used with local and regional radio and TV stations, leading to feature interviews on their news and entertainment shows, which costs you nothing and leads to more clients. Those who are ambitious can do this on a national level with TV radio and press, leading to stardom, appearance fees and more clients for your business. Talk shows such as Kilroy, Vanessa, This Morning and many others are always looking for interesting guests and subjects to feature and this may as well be you.

The general rule of thumb, is that on a local/regional level you do all TV, radio and media interviews for free. Whilst those on a national level will always involve all your out of pocket and travel expenses being paid, along with an appearance and/or interview fee being paid to you also.

The next best way to get clients at NO cost, is to offer FREE lecture demonstrations of your hypnotic skills to local women's groups, lions clubs, Masonic lodges and other special social clubs of these kinds. Doing these FREE lecture demonstrations costs you nothing and will usually lead to many sales of your audio hypnotherapy tapes on the night and also to bookings for your sessions in person.

Another excellent way to get started at NO cost, is to offer some local venues a FREE stage hypnotism show, which both gives you a chance to rehearse your new stage show and the show itself will lead to paid bookings for other shows, sales of your hypnotherapy tapes on the night and of course, bookings for personal one to one sessions.

Handing your business card to each and every person you meet by way of introduction will rapidly get your name circulated around the community and ultimately lead to many bookings. With business cards available as cheaply as £25 for 1000, from companies advertising in Exchange and Mart, this also is a practically no cost way to get your business kicked off.

Other low cost and effective ways to obtain clients, include having some A5 size leaflets advertising your services printed, then visit all your local libraries and place a folded up leaflet into each and every book on the shelves of the self help, psychology and health sections. People borrowing these kinds of books tend to have problems and/or health complaints they wish to sort out and as such, are red hot leads for you to target, very often leading to bookings.

A classified advert in your local and regional papers, whilst being very cheap to run, can generate 100's of clients, especially if the advert is worded as follows:

FREE HYPNOTHERAPY AND PSYCHOTHERAPY, AVAILABLE FROM ESTABLISHED PROFESSIONAL MIND THERAPIST. FOR FREE SESSION CALL XXXXX XXXXXX. SINCERE HELP FOR ALL PROBLEMS.

This advert of 20 words is placed under the Personal Services section of the Classified adverts. As the advert offers the reader a free session, you will get loads of calls and when the potential client calls you explain that most therapists take around three sessions to treat people at an average of £40 per session, which would cost them around £120 at least. However, as a special offer, if they book now, they can have a FREE session of Complete Mind Therapy, which is so powerful and effective that only one session is needed, which immediately saves them around £80 at least. On top of this instant saving, you'll give them the session FREE of charge, just so long as they purchase the back up audio "Hypnotheratape" for the special price of just £39.95. This means you end up getting just 5p less than the normal cost of your sessions anyway and most all callers will book, as they think they are saving lots of money, getting something for FREE and getting a discount on the back up tape. Which means all in all, they feel they are getting a bargain and so book there and then. Believe me, this classified advert offering FREE sessions will generate you your income of a substantial nature on a weekly basis. Each advert placed will pay for itself many times over, so the more local and regional papers you advertise in, the more money you'll make in the shortest space of time possible. As mentioned before, in the long term, it's worth having a display advert in your local areas Yellow Pages. This display advert, should be as big as those which other therapists are running and there are a few things which will ensure you get all the business. These are, to have a photo of yourself upon the advert as it adds a personal human touch, mention upon the advert your Professional Association memberships, state that you offer FREE Complete Mind Therapy sessions for ALL problems and offer them a FREEPHONE number to call you on. People will always call a freephone number first before paying for a call, especially if it's on the advert offering FREE therapy sessions, which of course, yours will. The final thing to improve your advert response, is to name you business something such as, ABC Hypnotherapy, so that your business appears at the top of the alphabetical list and so is seen first. You are also advised to obtain your FREE lineage entries in both you local Thompson Local Directories, and within the Yellow Pages, as again, this costs nothing for a lineage ad and it does generate some extra enquiries.

It's also worth writing to your regional head office of both B.U.P.A. and your areas N.H.S area healthcare authority, requesting that you are granted a B.U.P.A. and N.H.S. provider number respectively. They will send you all necessary forms and there is no charge to obtain your provider numbers, which once obtained and listed on all promotional materials, helps to attract more clients, as B.U.P.A members will know they can claim on their healthcare insurance to pay for the session. Also doctors will know they can refer people to you on the N.H.S. as you have the N.H.S. provider number. Bearing this in mind, once you have obtained both provider numbers, which costs nothing, it is worthwhile sending a letter of introduction, along with your advertising leaflets, to all the doctors and dentists surgeries in your area, who may then refer clients to you and so increase your business.

A little common sense will reveal numerous other no cost or low cost advertising methods, which do lead to 100's of clients. A last few examples to set you thinking on the right track are as follows:

- Place cards on supermarkets "For Sale" boards, using the FREE sessions ploy detailed earlier.
- Place cards on newsagents notice boards all over your local area, again using the FREE ploy.
- Send leaflets advertising driving test nerves therapy, to all the driving schools and instructors in your area, offering to wholesale them audio hypnotherapy tapes, which they can then sell on at a profit to their clients, thus also helping to increase the level of their pass 1st time success rate, as the students will not be nervous during the test.
- Leaflets sent to travel agents, offering cure your fear of flying sessions, with a cover letter pointing out that any clients they obtain for you will cure their fear and so will want to go on a holiday which involves flying, which means the holiday will cost more and so as the travel agent, they will get more commission on the deal which means by being your unpaid salesman they are increasing their own profits.

These are just a few examples of ways to get clients at little or no cost to yourself. But with a little imagination and common sense, 100's of other ways of obtaining clients at little, or no cost to yourself will present themselves to you, if you think along the lines I've already illustrated.

To sum up on advertising, in the rare event of potential clients replying to your adverts and then not booking there and then on the phone, I would suggest you take their name and address and send them your advertising leaflet, by first class post, as quite often, when they receive this, it's enough to spur them into action, so that they do call back and book a session rather than never hearing from them again. One last point is, that by contacting you in the first place, the client has admitted to themselves they have a problem and so are now making a commitment to change things for the better and so they are already 95% of the way to a solution and just need a trigger to success and that is where we therapists come in. We give the client permission to heal themselves and through the therapy, motivate them to a successful outcome. This combined with the large element of the placebo effect coming into play, as quite simply if they book a session with you, they obviously believe you can help them and expect it to work, or why else would they contact you? Upon taking the booking off the client, take their name, address and telephone number and inform them that if they have to cancel, for any reason, they must give you at least 24 hours notice, or else the full fee will be payable anyway, just like going to the dentist. This stops timewasters and compounds the belief in the clients mind that you're a busy and successful professional. Should they not show up for the session, send them an invoice on a letterhead, headed "Litigation Department", demanding the £39.95 fee and without doubt, you'll get payment by return of post.

1 CLIENT SHOWS UP FOR SESSION

AND

2 GET THE RELEVANT FEE OFF THEM

AND

3 OBTAIN RAPPORT OVER A CUP OF TEA

AND

4 OBTAIN 100% TOTAL BELIEF/EXPECTANCY

Having booked their session, the client showing up is an important point in their treatment, as they have then made a real commitment to solve their problem. You greet them at your office door and shake them firmly by the hand, whilst looking them directly in the eye, which both gets instant rapport and puts you in control. They see you dressed smartly and professionally which compounds their belief and expectancy levels in your ability to cure them. Having got the client to sit down you say, "Just as when you go to a gypsy, they say cross my palm with silver, well I've got to say cross my palm with £39.95, please, as none of us like talking about money and by getting it all out of the way now, it means we can then concentrate on what's most important today, which is YOU and us solving your problem today."

This both puts them at ease as they perceive your main priority is them and also, it means you've already been paid, which is both a lovely feeling and also a most powerful part of the therapy itself. You see, when the client parts with the money, it's really serious commitment to their own success and concrete's their belief and expectancy levels to a height such that success is 100% guaranteed, as they must believe you can help them and they must expect the treatment to work as why else would they either contact you, book a session, show up and/or pay the fee up front, unless they expect to get the end result of being cured. Bearing this in mind and the power of the placebo effect, combined with the therapeutic power of your caring bedside manner it would almost matter little what treatment you actually gave them now, as the end beneficial result of them being cured would no doubt be the same anyway, however, the CMT session, which they receive, is so powerful and effective in its therapeutic content, that success is 100% guaranteed, if the clients belief and expectancy levels are total.

The diplomas they see hanging on your office wall, together with the book shelf of impressive looking psychology books, all compound the belief and expectancy thing even further. Your office should contain a black leather reclining chair for the client to lie in, a black directors chair for you to sit in at your desk, upon which should be a desk lamp. Your diplomas are displayed, framed upon the wall and you have 2 tape recorders, one of which is positioned behind the clients chair will play the relaxation music for the session later, whilst at the same time, the one upon your desk, to which is connected a microphone, records the entire session from the point of asking the client to close their eyes and starting the induction, until having awoken the client, which should be 45 minutes maximum, so one side of a 90 minute tape will be sufficient and as your voice and background music are picked up by the microphone the end result is a tape which bears your voice over the top of the relaxation music which will be highly effective when listened to. Giving the client a cup of tea instantly puts them at ease and helps relax them and then you can answer their general questions prior to moving onto asking them the pre-session questionnaire, which follows:

5 ASK CLIENT LIST OF 16 PRE-SESSION QUESTIONS

What follows are the 16 questions which you ask the client to answer, honestly, directly and in detail, before you start the actual hypnotic induction process. The answers given will help you carry out the session with the greatest of success for the reasons detailed after each listed question that follows. The fact you use their answers, which are personal to them, as part of the therapy makes the session seem far more personal to them, especially as you try to use their name a lot, as a persons name is, to them, the sweetest thing in the entire English language. It also means that as you feed the personal information they have given to us by the questions asked back to them as part of the therapy as it is personal to them and they can relate to it so well this explains why the concept of Complete Mind Therapy is so successful. The 16 questions to ask are as follows:

1) What is your name?
This is so we can call them by their first name throughout the session

2) Your address please?
This is just for future reference, as in future you may wish to contact clients to see if they will participate in TV and/or radio show broadcasts.

3) Your telephone number?
Again just for reference as in question 2

4) Your date of birth?
By knowing this, we can work out the clients age. (Never ask their age outright).

5) What's their problem?
Obviously asked so we know what we're treating

6) How long have you had this problem?
Using this piece of information and the clients D.O.B. we can work out what age the client was when the problem started

7) How do you feel this problem started?
Whilst the way they feel the problem started may not exactly be correct, just so long as it's what they at this time consciously believe to be correct, then we can use this information to erase connections with the past during therapy.

8) What do you feel I need to do for you today to permanently cure this problem?
Again the answer they give, however daft, will when acted upon, provide the ideal way to cure the patient. This is because, if they feel doing XYZ would cure

them, then they believe that if you did XYZ they would be cured. So by doing XYZ they will be cured, as this is what they have convinced themselves needs to be done for a cure to be achieved.

9) What is the final outcome you wish to achieve from today?
Whilst you may think, for example, that a smoker would say to stop smoking in reply to this question, this is not always the case. They could just as easily say that by stopping smoking today they wish to become healthier and be able to go swimming again like they used to. In other words, the answer to this question very often reveals something we can feed back to them later as an incentive to achieve their goals.

10) What was the best experience of you entire life, a time you felt confident, proud, loved and on top of the world?
Their answer is later used for the finger and thumb good times feeling connection technique.

11) What was the worst and most emotionally painful experience of your entire life?
This answer can be used later in the pain/pleasure section of therapy by having them imagine how they felt then etc. and linking it to the thought that any continuance of past actions will make them feel just as bad as they did then whereas avoidance of past actions makes them feel as good as, if not better as their reply to question 10

12) Who's the one person you love most in the entire world?
By getting the persons name, you can refer to them directly during the pain/pleasure section of the therapy by way of having the client imagine how upsetting it would be to this named person they love so much if they were to have continued smoking and killing themselves. Until they saw each other no more or indeed if the habit/problem had continued making them so stressed and anxious that the person they loved so much feels driven away from them and grows to hate them. As the client loves this person so much there will be strong emotional connection with any thoughts about this person and needless to say the client will wish to avoid upsetting them at all costs and because of the scenario just given to them, the only way to avoid upsetting them as far as their subconscious mind is concerned is by ending their habit/problem etc. once and for all.

13) Are you on any medication for this problem?
Here, a copy of the medical reference book PIMMS is useful, as you can look up the drugs name, revealing exactly what the drug is prescribed for, what its side effects are and indeed, by having prescribed it, what the clients medical GP

seems to think the real problem is, which may not always be the same as that being presented to us by the client and so we can ensure our therapy targets the correct problem as well as the clients perceived problem if necessary.

14) Is there a history of this problem within your direct family?
This really just gives us more of an idea why this client has got this particular problem in the first place

15) Have you tried any other alternative therapies to cure this problem before?
If they answer yes, ask which and then make it clear to the client that the treatment you will give them is the most powerful and effective of its kind. Hence it's called Complete Mind Therapy. This is done to remove any doubts they may have instilled in them due to past failures and helps to concrete their belief and expectancy levels in the treatment working 100%

16) Have you got any questions for me before we begin?
Should the client have any questions, it's just a matter of using your common sense to answer in a manner which puts their mind at ease and ensures they totally believe this treatment will change their life.

Then you get the client to sign and date the bottom of the questionnaire below a printed statement, which says:

I (THEIR NAME HERE) OF (THEIR ADDRESS) DO HEREBY DECLARE I AM OVER 18 YEARS OF AGE AND CONSENT TO (YOUR NAME) TREATING ME WITH HYPNOSIS AND COMPLETE MIND THERAPY.

Once the client has signed such a statement it will be far harder for any legal claims to be made against you for malpractice. Where wishing to treat children and/or those under the age of 18 you must have their parent sign a statement saying:

I (THEIR NAME) OF (THEIR ADDRESS) DO HEREBY DECLARE I AM THE LEGAL PARENT/GARDIAN OF (CLIENTS NAME) AND DO HEREBY GIVE MY CONSENT FOR (YOUR NAME) TO TREAT THEM WITH HYPNOSIS AND COMPLETE MIND THERAPY.

Again this is done to cover you 100% legally, as without proof of parent or guardians consent it is illegal to hypnotise these people under 18 years.

6 DO FOLLOW YOUR THUMB WITH EYES TEST AND ANCHOR THE CURE TO SUCCESSFUL COMPLETION

Here, you get the client to stand upright, feet together, left arm down by their side, right arm stretched out in front of them and right hand clenched into a fist, with their right thumb stuck up directly into the air. You tell the client that on the count of 3 you want them to move their right arm around in a clockwise direction as far as they comfortably can, without moving their feet from the position they are currently in. They are told to stare at their thumb at all times, whilst doing this and indeed should tell you when they have reached the point where it becomes uncomfortable to move any further. You then count to 3 and the client does as they've been told and when they reach the point where they can move no further, you ask them to stare past their thumb and tell you what they can see in the background in line with their thumb, which can act as a marker to how far they got this first time. The client is then told to resume their original position and then told to close their eyes and keep their arm exactly where it is until you say otherwise. You ask the clients to imagine in their minds eye as 100% total reality, that they are once again rotating their body from the hips in a clockwise direction whilst staring at their thumb just like before. However, as anything is possible in their imagination, you want them to imagine being able to move considerably further than before, both without discomfort and with the greatest of ease and they are told to tell you when they have gone further in their minds eye than they previously did in reality. The client is then told something such as:

"Well (their name) that's excellent, you have just achieved something which was once so difficult in a way which has proved so ridiculously easy, thanks to the power of your mind. Now, (their name), believe it or not, if you've used your powers of intelligence, imagination and concentration effectively, then for you this will have become 100% total reality. So on the count of 3 I'd like you to re-open your eyes and repeat the test by rotating your body as far as you comfortably can in a clockwise manner and as you do so, on the count of 3, notice how as those imagined thoughts of but a few seconds ago become a reality for you, how your goal of solving (their problem) which you once thought would be difficult to achieve will also prove to be so ridiculously easy."

You then count to 3, they repeat it again for real and I guarantee you that without fail, the client will be able to move considerably further this time than they did the first time around and as they see with their own eyes, their thoughts of but a few seconds ago become a physical reality, so they come to believe as 100% total reality that the treatment you are about to give them will work and so they are now 99% of the way to solving their problem.

7 INDUCE TRANCE VIA PHYSICAL RELAXATION AND COUNTING BACKWORDS FROM 300 METHOD

It's now time to get the client to sit down, to close their eyes and to begin breathing deeply and regularly in through their nose and then out through their mouth, as they continue to relax etc., etc. At this point the relaxation music is turned on and you start to record the session, thus making their "back-up" therapy tape as the session continues. You explain to the client that you will mention areas of their body and that upon doing so, you want them to physically tense up all the muscle groups in that body area, whilst at the same time in their minds eye, imagining 2 pieces of rope tied together in knots and that these knots represent the stresses, tensions, fears, and upsets of days and weeks gone by, which are stored in the muscle groups they are physically tensing. Then the client is told you will count from 3 to 1 and that on 1 when you snap your fingers like this (do it as example) they are to instantly relax the muscle groups they were tensing, whilst at the same time imagining as 100% total reality, in their minds eye, that with your click of the fingers the 2 ropes in their minds eye instantly separate. As they instantly untie, so as they become separate pieces of rope, so in reality all muscles in their body becoming so limp, so loose, so relaxed, so heavy and so tired. They are then asked to nod their head if they understand. Then you proceed to do as just stated for the following muscle groups in this order:

A The feet and ankles
B Lower leg area and knees
C Upper leg area and hips
D Stomach and abdomen
E Chest area
F The back and spine
G Finger tips to wrists
H Every muscle from wrist to elbows to shoulders
I The shoulders and shoulder blades
J The neck area
K The jaw and cheek muscles
L The eyelids and forehead

When you've gone through this list and the client, who is listening both to your voice and the background music, has physically tensed up and then physically relaxed all these muscle groups from head to toe, they will, I assure you, feel genuinely relaxed in a physical way, especially as your office will be nice and warm and the room will be dimly lit by only your desk lamp at this point. On top of this the visual imagery of the knots untying helps them to achieve psychological relaxation also, and with both a relaxed mind and body, they are in an ideal state for the therapy to be 100% successful. As you go through the 12 point list of muscle groups, you can link from one group to the next with a phrase such as, "with every breath you take, every noise you hear and every word I say, you relax even more. With each second that passes by." This, along with the "standard phrases" as detailed in the induction's chapter earlier in this course, both help to link nicely from one muscle group to the next and also help to deepen both the physical and psychological levels of the clients relaxation. It can also be good to suggest to them that as each muscle group relaxes, so a feeling of warmth and total relaxation floods their entire body. Having gone through their entire body's muscle groups, you then immediately ask them to start counting backwards from 300 in their minds eye, as you continue to suggest things to them and then link into the induction method as explained in the verbal psychology section, being that of a "subliminal" nature.

8 DEEPEN VIA STAIRCASE

After continuing with the "subliminal" induction, it's time to deepen the level of trance, here we use the staircase of relaxation as detailed earlier in the course. The client being told that as you count backwards from 10 down to 1, so in their minds eye they will take another step down the staircase they can now see and as this is a staircase of relaxation, they will sink 100 times deeper with each step down they take. Then using the "standard phrases" whilst counting backwards from 10 down to 1 the trance is deepened.

9 DEEPEN FURTHER BY IMAGE OF BED

Upon reaching the count of 1 with the staircase deepening, it is suggested to the client that at the bottom of the staircase is a beautifully relaxing and comfortable bed into which they are to climb, snuggle up and go fast to sleep, allowing their mind to wander free, allowing your voice to become but a distant sound as they go deeper and deeper to sleep.

10 DEEPEN FURTHER BY BLACKBOARD

Now tell the client:

"Your now so deeply relaxed and so deeply asleep, that whatever I tell you to do, you would do for your own good and whatever I tell you will happen, will happen again for your own good. However, in order that the work we do together today will be 100% successful in every way, we need your subconscious mind to take you to a level of deep satisfying relaxation, of both mind and body, which will be right for you. Just as your subconscious can be trusted to circulate the blood around your body 24 hours a day, so it can be trusted to take you to a level of relaxation which is going to be for you 100% successful in every way. So I'd like you to…."

You then get the client to imagine that as they've gone to sleep in the bed, they will start dreaming and as they do, they are to dream they are in a classroom, in which is a large blackboard, upon which their name is written in chalk. They are told that in dreamland, when the blackboard is blank they are instantly taken to a depth of relaxation where they can achieve anything and then they are told to imagine rubbing their name out from the blackboard, so that each chalk letter, one by one, is rubbed out and as each letter disappears, so their level of relaxation doubles in every way, until they rub out the last letter. When they relax so completely that your work together today will prove 100% successful as an automatic reflex action.

11 EGO STRENGTHENING THERAPY

This is where, as detailed in an earlier section of the course, we praise the clients ego, make them feel good about the work you are about to do together and make them believe they are such a wonderful client, with such good powers of intelligence, imagination and concentration, that their success in achieving their goals and aims is 100% assured.

12 THE NECESSARY THERAPY

A GOOD FEELINGS FINGER AND THUMB ANCHOR

This technique is to remind the client of the most special and pleasurable time of their life. (See answers to 16 pre-session questions). Tell them then to push the tip of their right forefinger against the tip of their right thumb, thus making a ring, a ring of confidence. As they continue to push their finger and thumb firmly together, they are to notice how confident they feel at that past time, they are to notice how calm and relaxed they feel, how full of will power and ability to achieve anything they are and how, in fact, life seemed so wonderful at the time. They are then told to let go of the image as they separate their finger and thumb. You then tell them that any time from this moment forward, when they feel a little unsure about continuing in their new life as (opposite of what their problem was) they just need to press their finger and thumb together to make the ring of confidence. This will immediately flood their mind and body with all those positive, pleasurable feelings of the past that continuing with their goal will become so ridiculously easy. This incidentally, is called anchoring, as we have "anchored" a thought to a physical action

B RULER TO 100% CONFIDENCE
C RULER TO 100% WILLPOWER
D RULER TO 100% SELF IMAGE/ESTEEM
E RULER TO 100% RELEVANT TO PROBLEM

The ruler technique is to have the client imagine a ruler in their minds eye and that upon this are the numbers from 1 to 100%. With 100% being the most desirable level to be at in order to achieve everything and anything. It is if you like a measuring stick of confidence or of willpower or of self esteem, or whichever is relevant at the time. But for this example we'll use confidence, you tell them it's a measuring stick of confidence and that it's filled with liquid mercury, just like a thermometer is and that if they take a closer look, they can see then tell us at what level from between 1 to 100% their confidence levels are now at, as this is where the mercury level will be. When they have answered with a percentage, we tell them that they need to be at 100% to achieve their aim with 100% success. So they are to imagine heating up the mercury with a very hot lighter flame, until it's become so hot that it has rapidly risen to 100%, at which point they should indicate by saying yes. You then have them imagine taking a hammer and a nail and hammering the nail through the mercury mark at 100% and through the measuring stick, so that their confidence levels are now permanently locked in place at 100% and can never again fall below this level. Once they've done this you tell them to think of the next ruler, which represents their levels of willpower, then the next ruler, which represents their self-image/esteem and how they feel about themselves. Finally the ruler which, using your common sense, you make 100% relevant to each client's particular problem. In all 4 cases, however, the bizarre mental images are used to get the levels to 100% so that 100% success can be achieved. Don't forget that the more bizarre a mental image is, the more effectively it will be acted upon. Lastly, with reference to the ruler relevant to each client's personal problem, use your common sense, but for example, people wishing to pass their driving test, could have a ruler of nerves control, which means that when it's at 100% they are 100% in control of their nerves and so can pass the test.

F TV SET GET RID OF PAST VISUALISATION

Here, we get the client to imagine watching a TV set in their minds eye, upon which they are watching themselves as they once were. The volume is still very loud, the colour is very bright and all in all, it's very much a reminder of how they once were, which they no longer need. So first, they are to imagine turning the colour down so low that they can no longer see the picture of themselves as they once were. Then they are to turn the volume down, so much that they can no longer hear how they once were. Now that they can neither see nor hear how they once were, they are to turn the TV set off and once switched off, they are to unplug it from the wall, so it can no longer be fed any power to survive as it once was and lastly as they can no longer see, hear or be as they once were, they are to destroy the TV set in their minds eye, by blowing it up with a huge bomb. As they imagine the TV set blowing up, they are to wave goodbye to how they once felt, how they once acted and what they once did, which is no longer part of their everyday reality.

G MIRROR STARE TO INSTIL NEW FEELINGS/FUTURE AS REALITY

Having got rid of the past, we now need to instil the future and the clients new reality. They are to imagine staring into a full length mirror, in which they can see themselves as they now are, as a (here insert what they wished to achieve). They are to notice how good they feel within themselves, they are to notice how proud they are feeling as they have now achieved their goal and ambition. They are to notice how much better they look, how much better they feel now they are a confident, happy, healthy, calm and relaxed person with bags of willpower, who has now become a (here what it was they wish to achieve). They are then to imagine turning a key in the frame of the mirror, which freezes the reflection in place forever and just so long as this image remains frozen in place so they will continue to be a (here what the aim is).

H DIRECT SUGGESTION THERAPY

Here common sense is used, the direct suggestions must suggest clearly that the client has achieved their aim. Examples of direct suggestions are contained within the script outlines given within the advanced hypnotherapy chapter. But in short, clients who want to stop doing something they do now, must be told that they have stopped doing it. Whereas clients who wish to do something they don't currently do, must be told they have started to do it, with the greatest of ease.

I PAIN AND PLEASURE SUGGESTIONS

Here the principle is to reverse the pain and pleasure connectors in the clients mind. So that by so doing, their behaviour is reversed to that they desire and because the cause of the problem which is the pain and pleasure circuit in their mind relevant to their problem has been reversed. The cause of the problem has effectively been removed and so a cure achieved without the need for long sessions of psychotherapy treatment. Thus getting the same end results within one 1 hour session. Also, as the cause has indirectly been dealt with and removed, there is no chance of symptom substitution, so the client you've stopped smoking has no debris left in his/her mind, which could for example, then cause them to start biting their nails instead.

The 3 steps of pain/pleasure therapy are

1. Get the client to imagine how they were when they had the problem and in their mind connect this to the most awful experience of their life, in order that it becomes painful for the client to think about or continue being as they once were, because it now has painful associations with this awful real life event of the past. (See their answers to questions.)

2. Get the client to imagine how they are now, without the problems of the past and in their mind get them to connect this with the most pleasurable experience of their entire life, so it becomes pleasurable to continue with their new behaviour pattern. Because as they continue with the new behaviour pattern, they are always reminded of this very pleasurable past event and feel just as they did then.

3. Have them think of the person they said they loved most and use the example I gave earlier, of how if they had continued with their problem, they would have ended up dead and/or pushing this loved one away. Either way, the idea is to make it so upsetting to continue with past behaviour, as by doing so, it would remind them that it would upset the one they love so dearly in a way they wish to avoid and so a strong emotional motivating link is made here.

J REPEAT DIRECT SUGGESTIONS

Prior to implanting post hypnotic suggestion the direct suggestions are repeated to the client once more.

13 MAJOR POST HYPNOTIC

Here it is suggested to the client, that everything you have said to them, will remain with them for the rest of their lives and will grow stronger with each second that passes by, from this moment forward. Also they will find that each and every time they listen to the audio tape you will give them, it will be just as, if not more effective, than if you were with them in the room in person at the time of listening to it.

14 AWAKEN CLIENT FROM TRANCE

Here counting up from 1 to 10, you awaken the client, an ideal therapy awakening is:

On 1 – everything I've suggested to you, growing stronger with each second of each minute of each day of each week of each month and of each year for the rest of your life.

On 2 – from this moment forward you will continue with you new desirable lifestyle as an automatic reflex action as 100% total reality.

As on 3 – from this day forward, you will awaken with an inner warm glow of confidence, a renewed optimism to life and by far a more positive attitude to get things done, whilst also continuing in your new lifestyle, as a confident, happy, healthy, calm and relaxed (their aim here)

As on 4 – finding that each day you have a huge inner reservoir of willpower which can be drawn upon when ever needed and which in fact, you will draw upon as an automatic reflex action whenever that little extra help is needed.

As on 5 – every day in every way, things are getting better and better.

As on 6 – something you once thought would be so difficult to achieve has turned out to be so ridiculously easy.

As on 7 – almost as though each and every muscle group in your body is being filled with energy, vitality, confidence and optimism.

As on 8 – almost as though your whole body is being washed in cool refreshing spring water.

As on 9 – lighter and brighter, coming on up out of it.

And on 10 – wakey, wakey rise and shine.

15 GIVE THEM TAPE ETC.

They are now awake and so you give them the audio tape of the session, along with an instruction sheet, clearly stating that to ensure 100% guaranteed success, they must listen, (but not whilst driving) to the tape every other day, for the next 28 days. In other words, the day after the session they don't, the next day they do and then it's do a day and miss a day for the next 28 days, as it takes 28 days for new habits to be formed and concreted into the human mind. This also puts the onus on them to commit time to their own success and seems to attach so much importance to the tape that A. they will listen to it as instructed and B. the tape will prove to be just as effective as if you were there with them in person.

16 SAY GOODBYE TO THEM

It's then time to say goodbye to them and await arrival of next client.

This format is followed 100% to the letter for all problems presented to you, with the only minor changes being as follows.

FOR;

**** Habits, emotional problems, general nervous complaints etc.***

These kinds of problems are such that the CMT session is conducted 100% to the letter as per example given.

**** Fears and Phobias***

Here, instead of using direct suggestions twice, the first time you get the client to imagine what they used to be scared of and then you have them make it an object of ridicule. So that the thought of what once scared them now makes them think humorous thoughts making them laugh and as laughter leads to relaxation, they will then feel relaxed when presented with what once scared them. The more ridiculous and bizarre the mental image is that you get them to imagine in order to make the original fear trigger an object of ridicule, by far the more powerful it will be. For example, a person once scared of spiders is told to dress them in wellies, put a silly party hat on it, a big clowns red nose, a bright silly coat and so on, until the image which was once the trigger to their fear becomes so ridiculous, that all that image can now trigger is laughter and/or relaxation. The rest of the session remains the same.

**** Sports psychology/peak performance***

Where the first set of direct suggestions normally go, we instead have the client run through a successful mental rehearsal of the increased success they wish to achieve in their sport and/or work. For example, mentally we would take a football player through the full match in a matter of a few minutes and as we did, we would have him imagine as reality scoring more goals than ever before. We would have him feel how it feels to be an achiever and we would make him believe in his mind that he had already successfully achieved his aim and so to do it again would be easy. This works and to illustrate, think of Roger Bannister, who first ran the four minute mile, until then no one had got close, but Roger believed he could do it and so he made it his reality and guess what? Once other athletes had seen Roger achieve something they once believed to be impossible, they knew it could be done and within days of Roger having done it athletes the world over found themselves able to run the four minute mile. Such is the power of belief and mental rehearsals.

**** Pain control***

Again the only change is that instead of direct suggestion, you instead run through instilling the saliva leads to no pain trigger as detailed in the Noesitherapy Course which we market. With it here being done whilst the client is in trance and then at the end of the session, the client is reminded to get saliva on their tongue and make the affirmations whenever they need instant pain control in the future. You can download Dr. Angel Escudero's book teaching Noesitherapy and Noesiology his original creations for just Five Euros from: ***www.iglobal.es/escudero/ntheng.htm***

**** Illness and disease***

Instead of direct suggestion number one, the client is told to visualise a rabbit in their minds eye in a field filled with 1000's of carrots. These carrots are cancer carrots, AIDS carrots or whatever their illness is carrots. They are to imagine the rabbit is so hungry and never loses his appetite and he is rapidly eating up all the carrots, one by one and with each carrot the rabbit eats, so in turn as 100% total reality, the cancer, AIDS virus or whatever, is growing weaker and so in turn they are becoming healthier and healthier.

**** Stress Management***

Instead of direct suggestions twice, the first time the client is told to visualise the burning fire within them, that has got too hot to handle. Then they must imagine connecting a hose to a tap and aiming it at the fire so to keep it cool. Although it continues to burn it will be at a level where the client will be able to deal with challenges which may arise. Or you can the Noesitherapy fight/flight saliva method. Not for pain control, but rather for stress control and instant relaxation.

**** Allergies***

Instead of direct suggestion on two occasions, the first time get your client to visualise a Perspex screen across the room and see a clone of themselves becoming "one".

A SUMMARY OF THE KEY POINTS

1. The more bizarre the images, the more effective they will be.
2. The subconscious is abstract and is best reprogrammed through images and not just words.
3. Phrasing suggestions to the subject (are they a visual, auditory, sensual person) helps.

4 Using their name helps a lot.
5 Pain/Pleasure and Fight/Flight is the secret.
6 The CMT session combines all the major areas of hypno/psycho related subjects.
7 Give them a tape at the end of the session.

Well, there you have it.

THE COURSE IN COMPLETE MIND THERAPY

Congratulations in getting to the end and may you have all the luck in the world with your new venture.

To become a member of The Association of Complete Mind Therapists and The Professional Organisation of Stage Hypnotists and receive your Diploma's simply contact us to get an exam paper for, complete it and then return for marking. We will do the rest.

Please also observe the recommended reading list.

Unless otherwise stated, all books on the following recommended reading list are available mail order from:

The A.A. Book Co. Ltd.
Crown Buildings
Bancyfelin
Carmarthen
Dyfed, Wales
SA33 5ND
Tel. 01267 211880

OR

The Tao of Books
Station Warehouse
Station Road
Pulham Market
Norfolk, England
IP21 4XF
Tel. 01379 676000

OR

Via most specialist bookstores.

Stage Hypnotism

New Encyclopaedia of Stage Hypnotism by Ormond McGill £29.99

Hypnotherapy

Hypnotherapy by Dave Elman £23.50

Transforming Therapy by Gil Boyne £27.50

Trance Formations by Richard Bandler and John Grinder £9.95

Psychotherapy/Hypno Analysis

A Guide for Beginning Psychotherapists by Joan S. Zaro and others £13.95

The Book of Hypnosis by Davis Lesser £10.95
Hypnotherapy Explained by David Lesser £10.95

NLP

Frogs into Princes (Bandler and Grinder) £9.95

Reframing (Bandler and Grinder) £9.95

Hypnotic Realities (Erickson and Rossi) £26.00

Using Your Brain for a Change (R. Bandler) £11.99

Past Life Regression

Other Lives, Other Selves by Roger J. Woolger £10.50

Cashing in on Past Life Regression by Richard Webster £29.99
From Magic Books by Post, 29 Hill Avenue, Bedminster, Bristol, BS1

Motivation/Stress Management

Awaken the Giant Within by Anthony Robbins £12.95

Unlimited Power by Anthony Robbins £9.95

Business Side

The Hypnotherapy Resources and Career Guide by Morris Berg and Michael O'Sullivan £17.50 inc p&p.
To – "M. L. Berg" Box BCM 3695 London WC1N 3XX

Consumer Guide to Hypnosis by Christine Kirtley £2.95

Noesitherapy

The Simple Secrets to the Power to Heal by John Howard £12.99
C/O 19 – 20 St. George's Avenue, Northampton, NN2 6JA
Tel. 01604 716817

Heal Yourself with Noesitherapy by Brian Howard £19.95
11 Strawberry Close, Birchwood, Warrington.

Sports Psychology

Hypnotic World of Paul McKenna £5.99

Paul McKenna's Hypnotic Secrets £8.99

Creative Visualisation/Self Hypnosis

Self Hypnosis by Charles Tebbetts £5.99

The Magic of Mind Power by Duncan McColl £10.00
D. P. McColl, Pilgrim Tapes, P.O. Box 107, Shrewsbury, SY1 1ZZ

Stage Work Marketing Advice

The Magic of Showbusiness by Simon Lovell £19.95
Magic Books by Post, 29 Hill Avenue, Bedminster, Bristol, BS1

Therapeutic Marketing Advice

Manual of Publicity and Exploitation by Nelson R £19.95
Magic Books by Post, 29 Hill Avenue, Bedminster, Bristol, BS1.

(All prices subject to change)

You Could also Source many of these from *www.amazon.com*

CHAPTER TWENTY - TWO

NON SPECIFIC TREATMENT SCRIPT

PROCEED AS FOLLOWS:

1. Use the Progressive Relaxation Induction (PRI) as detailed in CMT course and mentioned again in chapter 21 of CMT course!
2. Towards the end of this Induction say the "Post Hypnotic" of **"AND JUST SLEEP NOW!"**
3. Deepen the trance via the staircase visualization method as detailed in chapter 21 of CMT.
4. Deepen further using get into bed and go to sleep visualization, again detailed in chapter 21.
5. Further deepen using having a dream and wiping your name off the blackboard method as per chapter 21.
6. Say the "Post Hypnotic" again of **"AND JUST SLEEP NOW"**

Then its time for step 7 – Ego Strengthening Therapy:

As you relax more completely with every breath that you take, every noise that you hear, every word that I say and every second that passes by, You are now so deeply relaxed, so deeply asleep, that whatever I tell you to do, you WILL do for your own good. And whatever I tell you WILL happen, WILL happen for your own good. Because from this moment forward I am talking directly to your subconscious mind and as you relax more deeply with each word I say and every thought that you think, so in turn every suggestion that I give you, WILL for your own good become 100% Total Reality. You have made a promise to yourself and as you relax more deeply with each second that passes by, so you realize that whilst on the odd occasion it may be OK to break a promise to a friend, that in reality you can NEVER break a promise to yourself. In fact your subconscious mind WILL NOT allow you to break a promise to yourself, you can have 100% faith that your subconscious mind will enable you to achieve everything that I am suggesting to you with the greatest of ease. And as you go deeper and deeper, you notice that the deeper you go, the better you feel and the better you feel, the deeper you will go as you realize now that you can trust your subconscious mind, for just as it makes you breath automatically without any conscious effort, and just as it pumps the blood around your body and keeps you alive, so you can be certain that from this very moment forward your subconscious mind will ensure that every single thing I suggest to you, WILL become your new reality as an automatic reflex action, with the greatest of ease. In fact you will find that something you once thought may be so difficult to achieve will now become so ridiculously easy, as you realize that from this moment forward, you can equal the greatest achievements of life's greatest achievers and that for you, your innermost dreams can and have now become your 100% total reality. Noticing now that with every breath that you take, every noise that you hear and every word that I say, that all the stresses, tensions, worries, fears and apprehensions of days and weeks gone by are leaving your mind and leaving your body NOW!

7. *NOW TIME FOR THERAPY SPECIFIC TO PROBLEM*

Realizing now that from this moment forward, each morning you will awaken with an inner warm glow of confidence, a renewed optimism to life, a more positive attitude to get things done. You will notice that every day in every way you find it so much easier to deal with events and situations, which once would have bothered you greatly. Realizing now that from this moment forward within you is a large inner reservoir of willpower, self-confidence and self-esteem, which you may draw upon as an automatic reflex action whenever you need to, enabling you to deal with everything and anything there and then, the very moment it happens, you no longer need, want, crave or desire for stressful situations and as such from this moment forward with every breath that you take, you will be able to handle everything and anything that life presents to you with the greatest of ease. Nothing bothers you as it once did and in fact you now realize that just as all of the stresses, tensions, Worries, fears and apprehensions of days, weeks, months and years gone by are leaving your body and leaving your mind NOW! So you realize also that every day in every way your life is getting better and better, your approach and attitude to life is getting more relaxed, more positive and more constructive and in turn your approach, attitude and response to other people, especially those you care for, those you respect and those close to you, WILL BECOME far more positive, far more relaxed and far more friendly and appreciative in every way, shape and form. You realize now as 100% Total

Reality that your life is now like a mirror, and whatever you give out to others in life is now reflected back towards you tenfold. So from this moment forward as an automatic reflex action you will find that you will send out positive, peaceful, constructive and loving thoughts, actions and words to all those around you and in turn these things will positively and beneficially be reflected back to you tenfold with each second that passes by. Notice how good it feels to realize that these improvements in your daily life have now taken place and will continue to grow stronger and more positive each and every day. Realizing now that just as you can and WILL now equal the greatest achievements of life's greatest achievers, so in turn you now realize that no one person ever did it all alone and so from this moment forward you will eagerly, happily and positively encourage those around you to help in your aims, actions & desires. You no longer resent or feel shy or in any way negative about accepting help, advice and assistance from others, in fact it makes you happy and proud to know that you can enabling you to achieve whatever you wish to achieve with the greatest of ease. Just as you yourself are a wonderful, valuable and worthy person so you now WILL realize from this moment forward, that the opinions of others, especially those of people you respect, people you love and those close to you are worth listening and responding to in a positive manner, just as your opinions and thoughts WILL NOW BECOME and will remain equally Honest, positive, constructive and worthwhile as all the stresses, tensions, worries, fears and apprehensions of every day situations which once would have bothered you have now become and will continue to be but distant memories and things of the past, as from this moment forward you will awaken each morning with an inner warm glow of confidence, a renewed optimism to life, a more positive attitude to get things done and every day in every way you will now realize that you have within you a large inner reservoir of willpower, self-confidence, self-esteem and patience which you can and you will draw upon as a 100% Total Reality automatic reflex action whenever you find yourself in a situation which once would have bothered you. Realizing now that you reap what you sow in life and as such from this moment forward all the stresses, tensions, worries, fears, apprehensions and obsessions which once may have bothered you are now but distant memories and things of the past as you now continue your life as the Confident, Happy, Healthy, Relaxed Stress free positive minded, Loving, caring, considerate individual that you have now become and will continue to be for the rest of your life, with each and every suggestion growing stronger each second of each minute of each hour of each day from this moment forward, you now realize how short life is and how valuable every second of it has now become to you. You no longer need, want, crave or desire to waste a single moment of your now positively Happy, Healthy, Calm and relaxed lifestyle, instead you now wish to and as a result WILL savor every moment, you now notice more closely how enjoyable it is to be in the company of friends, those you respect, Loved ones and others close to you. Their company, their opinions, their honesty, their help, assistance, advice, love and encouragement are all invaluable to you and as a result you WILL RESPOND to them with the same Honesty, Openness, Positiveness, Warmth, Encouragement and Love in all that you do and at all times you spend together. Your greatest achievement in life now being that you have now become one of those rare few, but very talented and perceptive people who is able to admit their own faults and by so doing grow stronger and happier as an individual and as part of a Loving partnership, in short from this moment forward to you the Past is the Past and what you now find is most important to you is The Future, your positive, happy, healthy, confident, relaxed Future made even more enjoyable, positive and beneficial by those around you who are friends, those who Love you, those who respect you and those who care about you which in turn you will reflect back to them as you continue now to live your life like a mirror and reflect to others the way you wish to be Loved for, Cared for, Respected and assisted in your every day life, which from this moment forward is that of a confident, peaceful, happy, healthy, relaxed, stress free, positive thinking, Loving, caring and considerate worthwhile individual.

8. *FINGER & THUMB RING OF CONFIDENCE*

Noticing now that the deeper you go, the better you feel and the better you feel the deeper you will go with every breath that you take, every noise that you hear and every word that I say, as you now allow your mind to wander free as you continue to go deeper down into the world of your dreams and the world of your imagination I want you to imagine and remember that one time in your life when you felt more Happy, more confident, more proud and on top of the world than you have ever done before. It could have been a time when you won an award or just a time on Holiday when you felt you could achieve anything, it matters not just so long as YOU NOW FEEL Happy, Healthy, Relaxed, Calm, Confident & Loving to yourself and to others in everyday life enabling you to live a 100% fulfilling and stress free lifestyle. Now I just want to notice how good it feels to experience these positive and beneficial states of mind and body and as you do realize now that whenever you need to renter this special place in your every day life, whenever you are confronted with the unexpected or those things which once would have bothered or concerned you then now as an automatic reflex action all you need do is push together the tip of your forefinger of the right hand together with the tip of your thumb and instantly this will make your ring of confidence, your ring of willpower, your ring of self-esteem and your ring of patience that will instantly enable you to remain as the Calm, Confident, Happy, Healthy, Relaxed and Loving individual that you have now become and will continue to be from this moment forward. Remembering that your subconscious will remind you as an automatic reflex action to make this ring of confidence with your finger and thumb as and when you need that little extra help in every day life. As you relax deeper and deeper with each second that passes by and every word that I say.

9 *RULERS OF CONFIDENCE, WILLPOWER, SELF-IMAGE/ ESTEEM, PATIENCE & TRUST.*

Realizing now that the personal attributes of self-confidence, Willpower, Positive Self-esteem, Patience and Trust are the only attributes that any individual needs in every day life to remain as a Confident, Happy, Healthy, Relaxed and Loving person, Just as you have now become and continue to be as you live your stress free lifestyle every day in every way getting better and better. So I'd Like you to imagine a thermometer in your minds eye with the numbers from 0 to 100% on it and within this thermometer the level at which the mercury is indicates the level at which your personal levels of self-confidence, Will Power, self-esteem, Patience and Trust are currently at. As you relax more completely with each second that passes by I want you to notice the level that the mercury is currently at and then realize that if we raise the level to 100% then any and all problems you may once have had in your life will no longer ever be able to bother you or effect you and as you realize this as 100% Total Reality I'd like you to imagine heating up the mercury in the thermometer with a lighter or a hot flaming candle so that the mercury gets hotter and hotter, so hot in fact that it starts to rise up inside the thermometer. Up past 30%, up past 40 & 50%, all the way up and past 80% and then notice and just realize in your minds eye that the mercury has now reached 100% and as you notice this realize how much more confident you feel, how you realize now your Willpower is also at a 100%, your self-esteem is higher than it ever has been at 100% and your Patience and trust both of yourself and others is now also at 100% making you a much happier, healthier, relaxed, calm and loving person in every way as you continue to live a stressfree lifestyle. Realizing now that in order to feel this confident forever we need to fix the mercury in place at 100% so imagine now in your minds eye that you have a hammer and a nail and that you are now hammering the nail through the thermometer and through the mercury at the 100% level and rather than leaking out the mercury is now being fixed, solidly, permanently in place so that from this moment forward your levels of self-confidence, Will Power, self-esteem, Patience and Trust are now fixed at 100% enabling you to live your life as the Happy, healthy, Confident, Relaxed, Calm, Loving & trusting individual that you have become and now continue to be as all areas of your life benefit immensely from these improvements every day in every way.

10 *TV SET GET RID OF PAST*

As you relax and go deeper, so the deeper you go the better you will feel and the better you feel the deeper you will go as you now imagine in your minds eye a TV set upon which you can see an image of how you once were, just see it clearly on the TV screen the person you once were, notice all those things about yourself that both you and others disliked which are no longer part of you and realize now these things have become and must now remain part of the past. And as you realize this its time to turn down the volume on the TV so imagine doing this now, then just imagine turning down the Colour and contrast so that the image of how you once were disappears completely and now as we realize that image has gone forever, we no longer need the TV set switched on so imagine turning it off, yes that's perfect and now as you relax more just imagine unplugging the TV set from the wall and as you do realizing that you yourself have now said goodbye completely to the past and how you once were as finally just imagine blowing up the TV set with a large bomb, go on that's it just see it being blown up and realize now that these things can Never, ever bother you again now or any time in the future as you relax more with each second that passes by and every breath that you take.

11 *MIRROR TO INSTALL NEW FUTURE*

Just imagine now as you relax more completely a full length mirror in your minds eye and imagine that you are standing in front of this full length mirror but rather than seeing the image of how you once were, you are now seeing the image of how you wish to be. Notice how happy and confident you feel about yourself, notice how good it feels to look in the mirror and see yourself exactly as you have on many occasions dreamed yourself to be, notice how much happier you now feel about yourself and as a result how much happier you feel around those you love and how easy it has now become to be open, honest and candid about those things which once bothered you before you became this image of beauty, happiness, confidence and contentment that you now see before you in your minds eye and then as you continue to breath deeply and regularly realising now that this is no longer a dream, this is in fact 100% Total Reality, it is in fact your New reality and is indeed the person you have now become and will continue to be from this moment forward, as you go deeper, the better you feel the deeper you go and the deeper you go the better you will feel.

12 *PAIN & PLEASURE SUGGESTIONS*

Realising now as you relax further that from this moment forward you find and get the greatest pleasure from making yourself and others happy, from making yourself and others feel Loved, wanted, Needed and appreciated in all that they say and do and that from this moment forward you no longer need, want, crave or desire any manner of painful situation in your life as you continue to be the Confident, Happy, Healthy, Calm, Relaxed and Loving person that you have now become and will continue to be every day in every way. Making others happy makes you happy and seeing others sad makes you sad as you now live your life like a mirror and give out that which you want reflected back to you.

13 *MAJOR POST HYPNOTIC SUGGESTIONS*

In a few moments time when I awaken you, everything I have suggested to you and everything that you have suggested to yourself will remain with you in every way and will grow stronger and more positive for you each second, of each minute of each hour for the rest of your life. Each and every time you consent for me to help you renter this relaxing and beneficial state you will re-enter this state with the greatest of ease and the very moment that I say **"AND SLEEP NOW"** that very moment that I say **"AND SLEEP NOW"** you will instantly and rapidly reenter this state, and each and every time you reenter this state it will be 100 times more relaxing, deeper and enjoyable for you in every way, shape and form. As you relax deeper realising also that whenever you hear my voice on an audio cassette whether consciously or whilst asleep the effect of my positive suggestions upon you will grow stronger in every way enabling you to realize that something you once thought would be so difficult to achieve has in fact proved so ridiculously easy.

14 *AWAKEN FROM TRANCE (IF DAY) OR SEND OFF TO SLEEP IF ON TAPE AT NIGHT.*

I'm now going to count from 1 to 10 and on the count of ten everything I have suggested will remain with you at a subconscious level and will grow stronger every second of each day enabling you to continue being the Confident, Happy, healthy, Relaxed, Calm and Loving individual that you have now become and will continue to be from this moment forward….

On 1, Everything I have suggested remaining with you and growing stronger in every way.

On 2, Realising now that you will awaken in the morning with an inner warm glow of confidence, a renewed optimism to life and a more positive attitude to get things done as you now realize that you have a large inner reservoir of self-confidence, Willpower, self-esteem, Patience, Trust and Honesty within you that you can draw upon whenever necessary as an automatic reflex action.

On 3, Realising now how much better you feel, how proud you feel about yourself for allowing yourself to come to terms with the problems you once had that no longer bother you.

On 4, It's almost as thought every muscle in your body is now being washed with pure spring water removing all negativity from your mind, from your body and from your life forever,

On 5, Lighter and brighter almost as though you now realize that a huge weight has now been lifted off your shoulders and you are now free to live your life happily the way you once thought may only ever be a dream, but the way which is now for you your 100% Total Personal Reality.

On 6, Normal feelings now returning to each and every muscle group in your body as everything I have suggested is now permanently burnt deep into your subconscious mind

On 7, Realising now that at a conscious Level only, when you awaken in a few moments time you will remember to forget and forget to remember everything that has been suggested to you, instead allowing it all to be stored to your subconscious mind who will ensure that you act upon it all as an automatic reflex action in your every day life.

On 8, Lighter and brighter now, coming on up out of it, feeling better than you have done in weeks, perhaps even in months, feeling so happy. Healthy, Calm and relaxed

As on 9, Coming on up out of it, Lighter and brighter

And on 10, Open your eyes wakey wakey rise and shine.

END OF PERSONAL SESSION WHICH IS SUITABLE FOR TREATING 99% OF PHOBIAS, HABITS, PROBLEMS ETC

PART TWENTY-THREE

MAKE A MILLION FROM HYPNOSIS

The sad, but true fact of life is that 95% of people spend at least 40 years of their life, working 40 hours a week and then end up retiring on 40% of their original income which they found it hard to live on in the first place!

It is also true to say that around 95% of the wealth in the world is owned by just 5% of the people!

Research has shown that if all the wealth in the world was split equally between every Human Being, then each and every person would instantly be able to live like a Millionaire!

However it has also been shown that within a very small space of time most all of this wealth would have made its way back to that small 5% of people, meaning that once again 95% of the worlds wealth would once again be owned by those original 5% of people!

In short it would appear that the idea of making serious amounts of money for very little effort is but a distant dream for many people, especially a Professional Hypnotherapist or similar Complimentary Health Practitioner.

DREAMS CAN COME TRUE!

In early 2002, a British Company called Practice Builders Ltd appeared to be offering an answer to this problem by way of a four day training course at the cost of around Five Thousand Pounds (£5K).

By way of their four day training course Practice Builders claimed to show you how to make £50-£100K per year, working 1-2 days per week as a Hypnotherapist with 2-3 Months holiday a year!

This may seem a very bold claim on their part, but it is one that I know that they have lived up to consistently.

In this chapter it is my intention to set you on the correct path to achieve exactly what Practice Builders would have charged you over £5K to find out and put into action!

Furthermore I intend to reveal tried, tested & proven to work marketing techniques for your business which produce maximum profits for minimum costs and are in our opinion way more cost effective than what Practice Builders were teaching!

THERE ARE THREE STEPS TO SUCCESS

There are three simple steps to financial success as a Mind Therapist and these three steps are what formed the basis of Practice Builders Prospectus and also form the Keys to Success as revealed by Top American Therapist Don Mottin which can be found on his excellent site of **www.donmottin.com** and these are:

01) Obtain expert training and Professional Certification.
02) Implement a proven marketing system.
03) Follow an effective Practice Management System.

We will now examine these three elements in a little more detail in order to make things that whole lot clearer and easier to understand:

01) OBTAIN EXPERT TRAINING & PROFESSIONAL CERTIFICATION

The point of step one is twofold, firstly if you're not trained by a master you will never become a master and as the old Chinese proverb correctly states "It is better to spend years looking for the right teacher than it is to spend years studying under the wrong teacher!"

Obviously the key-point here is that you must be a good Mind Therapist, in otherwords you must have a good product to sell to the Public and as you and your skills are in essence the product, you must therefore be a confident and competent Hypnotist!

Professional Certification is required, as it is a powerful marketing and treatment tool!

From a marketing point of view, you could for example qualify for the professional Diplomas & Certification that I issue:

01) Diploma in Hypnotherapy & Psychotherapy (DHP)
02) Diploma in Advanced Stage-Hypnosis (DASH)
03) Diploma in Complete Mind Therapy (DCMT)

All three of these diplomas would be signed by me your "Course Tutor" and issued by ***THE MINDCARE ORGANISATION UK.***

This would also give you Certificates of Membership to the following Professional Associations:

04) Member of The Royle Institute of Hypnotherapy & Psychotherapy (RIHP) incorporating The Association of Complete Mind Therapists (ACMT).
05) Member of The Professional Organisation of Stage Hypnotists (POSH) incorporating The Association of Professional Stage Hypnotists (APSH).

And then using these three (3) recently obtained & recently dated diplomas and the two (2) recently obtained & recently dated Certificates of Membership you can approach your local newspapers, magazines, TV & Radio stations etc and you have a ready made Local News Story (explained more fully later) with which you can quite easily obtain Thousands of Pounds worth of **FREE** Media Publicity to kick start your business and have clients knocking on your door ready to part with their cash!

Even if you have been a Mind Therapist for years you can still use this technique, but just from a slightly different angle:

EXAMPLE ONE – (New To Therapy)

"Local Man Qualifies As Master Mind Therapist!"

EXAMPLE TWO – (Established Therapist)

"Local Therapist Qualifies in Powerful New Technique!"

These are just brief examples and the subject of obtaining **FREE** Media Publicity for your practice will be dealt with more fully later.

Secondly these letters after your name and memberships to professional bodies are perceptively proof to your clients of your expertise and your ability to help them.

In truth there are currently (2002) no Legally and/or Government recognised Qualifications for Hypnotherapy or related techniques anywhere in England, however from the publics point of view seeing those impressive looking letters after your name and seeing those diplomas & certificates neatly framed and displayed in your consulting room concrete's into the clients mind that you are a Professional, that you know what you are doing and that you can indeed help them!

And once the client believes that ***YOU CAN HELP THEM*** then in short ***YOU CAN HELP THEM*** as the Placebo effect comes into play in a big, big way which is explained in detail in chapter one of this book.

02) IMPLEMENT A PROVEN MARKETING SYSTEM.

However good you are as a Therapist, your skills alone will not make you rich, not unless you market yourself effectively!

On top of this as there are only so many hours in the day you need to charge a fee that reflects your skills and what you are offering the client in return of their financial investment.

A good principle to remember in marketing is to make every penny that you spend on advertising and promotion count.

In my opinion and that of many other experts, you need to be getting £10 back for every £1 you invest into marketing.

With this principle in mind, where once the idea of spending £250 on a Large (approx. Half Page) one off display advert in your Local Paper may have seemed expensive, wouldn't it suddenly seem a much better idea if you knew that you'd get back at least £2500 (10 times as much) from your original investment?

Indeed if you knew that for every £250 you spent on a weekly basis on advertising that you'd get back at least £2500 (10 times as much) on a weekly basis then wouldn't you keep on doing this every week??

OF COURSE YOU WOULD!

And now imagine this, if you were charging your clients £250 per hour and they were prepared to pay this, then you'd only need to get 10 clients and invest only 10 hours of your time to make the £2500 figure which we spoke of earlier.

This would give you a clear £2250 profit on your original £250 Investment, and after the cost of hiring an office, telephone, brochures etc (all covered in more detail later) ***YOU WOULD HAVE MADE AN ABSOLUTE MINIMUM OF £2000+ FOR JUST TEN HOURS WORK!***

Let's say you see just five clients each day working from 12pm until 5pm and do this for two days each week, making a total of 10 clients seen each week and suddenly it becomes clear how easy it is to achieve what Practice Builders Ltd claimed to be teaching people doesn't it?

Using this very simple formulae for success you can easily be earning more money than you ever dreamed possible from your Mind Therapy Business and indeed if you follow a practical 3 to 5 year Financial Success Plan as will be discussed later, then it is realistic to say that within 3 to 5 years ***YOU COULD BECOME A TRUE MILLIONAIRE FROM YOUR THERAPY BUSINESS!***

Also consider this an hourly fee of £250 an hour may seem expensive, but this kind of financial commitment on the part of the client, combined with the Placebo effect, combined with the true value of your Therapeutic skills will make your Success Rate soar through the roof, and with such a high success rate you can safely offer a **GUARANTEE** to back up your work in all the advertising that you do!

In otherwords the key to success as a therapist is in getting a constant stream of paying clients and the key to getting clients is in the first place the effective use of marketing and publicity techniques, such as those that will be explained within this manual.

03) FOLLOW AN EFFECTIVE PRACTICE MANAGEMENT SYSTEM

OK so your advertising has been placed and people are responding to your adverts and other marketing ploys, now you need to get them booked into your diary and turn their initial enquiry into Cash!

You would think here that effective telephone sales skills would be a must, but as we will discuss later this is not actually the case as other easier options are open to you!

Most people can be booked into your diary there and then, however for the few who don't seem able to instantly make up their mind you will need a powerful information sales brochure which you can then send them the same day they ring by first class mail and most times this will convert them into a client.

Along with this powerful information brochure, they are also sent an information and therapeutic ***FREE AUDIOTAPE – WORTH £20-00!***

If after a week these people have not rung back and booked a session then we would send them a friendly sales letter, another copy of our colour sales brochure and a gift certificate entitling them to 20% (£50) off the usual £250 cost if they call and book their session within seven days.

By now most of the people who enquired should have been converted into paying clients, however details of those that have not are kept and once every two months we would send them out a letter and a gift certificate offering them a ***MASSIVE 60% DISCOUNT*** (£150 off the original £250) making it just £100 for the one hour session if they book within 72 Hours!

I will refer to this multi-stage marketing plan in more detail later and explain why it is so effective and how it makes you maximum money for minimum time and effort, even with the clients who end up getting the 60% Discount and pay only £100 for their one hour session!

Each and every client that you treat is also a powerful marketing tool in themselves and this is where personal and Doctor's referral marketing systems come into play as will be discussed later.

And Lastly this key to success refers to running the business side of your Practice in such a manner that you are able to make maximum profits for minimum investment of time and/or money!

Later in this manual we will also reveal how to structure your business so that it is virtually on auto-pilot and runs itself even if you are away on Holiday at the time!

WHERE TO CONCENTRATE YOUR EFFORTS

Of all the truly Successful Professional Mind Therapists that I know and by Successful I mean those earning a £1000 or more each day on a regular basis, they all seem to have something in common and this is worth noting before you start spending money on advertising your business.

In all cases when questioned they have revealed to me that when they have looked at the bookings in their diaries over the past three year period, their clients fall into the following categories:

01) Around 80% for Smoking Cessation Sessions.
02) Around 10% for Weight Loss Sessions.
03) Around 5% for Confidence Related Problems.
04) Around 5% for Stress, Phobias & Other Problems.

The logical conclusion from these facts is that we spend our entire advertising budget on attracting clients for Smoking Cessation Therapy, as this is where at least 80% of the income for most all truly successful Mind Therapists lies!

Having reached this conclusion we can use a simple concept called Target Marketing which will be explained more fully later to increase the profits we make for every pound that we invest into advertising to an even greater extent!

MONEY FOR NOTHING?

By the time you have read this unique manual, assuming that you put these methods into action, then and only then you should be able to attract so many clients that you will end up having to refer some to other Hypnotherapists in your area who will then pay you a substantial referral fee, quite simply because they cannot provide enough clients for themselves!

So in otherwords you will get paid for the clients you see and you will even be getting income from the clients you don't see!

K.I.S.S = KEEP IT SIMPLE STUPID

There are literally 100's of different Mind Therapy Courses on the market, everything from Hypnotherapy and NLP on the one hand to Psycho-Analysis on the other, so which course do you choose? Which route is the best one to follow?

Well over the years I have realised that if I wanted to be regarded as one of the best in the business at helping people to create the changes they want in their life then the system I used to help them achieve this would have to be:

01) Quick 02) Easy 03) Permanent and 04) Fun!

My years of research and practical experience testing out almost every conceivable method for Psychological change led me to develop my own unique system of Complete Mind Therapy (CMT).

This is a tried, tested and proven to work structured system for successfully treating most any problem that could ever be presented to you by a client with a single approx. one hour session of treatment.

My approach of Complete Mind Therapy (CMT) is an approach that ensures that you are able to Hypnotise every client, every time and that the client will Believe they have been Hypnotised, which ultimately means they will respond to all of your suggestions after the session has ended leading them to the change they desired!

The name of my unique approach "Complete Mind Therapy" (CMT) is also in itself a key to your success as some people are scared by the thought of being Hypnotised and with the CMT approach they are led to believe it is just Deep Relaxation (which is what Hypnosis really is) and Creative Visualisation combined with the most effective techniques of NLP and other Human Change Technologies.

As a Hypnotherapist you may be in competition with lots of others in your area, but as a Complete Mind Therapist, which in our opinion sounds more Professional and attractive to the public (your potential clients) you will have little or no competition.

The fact that my technique enables you to advertise that you can and will treat any problem (Especially Smoking) with just one approx. one hour session is attractive in itself as it shows how confident you are in your abilities to help your clients.

In short my system of Complete Mind Therapy works with virtually any problem and with virtually all of the people all of the time!

STARTING WITH NO INVESTMENT?

Given that most all Local Newspapers will allow you to book display advertising space and instantly give you 30 days credit from the date the advert appears means that you can get started without even having the money to pay for the adverts!

After all if your advert is placed in a Local daily paper, as it will be a large half page (or thereabouts) display advert costing around £250 - £500 (depending on whether you wish to have to attract one or two clients to recoup the cost of advertising, bearing in mind that you will be charging £250 an hour!) you should have had the majority of the phone enquiries that you will get within 72 hours of the paper going on sale.

However if your advert is in a Local Weekly paper, it may take up to 10 days for the advert to produce all of the enquiries that it will on that occasion produce.

In either case it means however that you will have had your enquiries and have time to convert them into paying clients ***LONG BEFORE THE NEWSPAPER BILL IS DUE TO BE PAID!***

And considering that you only need to generate one paying client at £250 to recoup the cost of a £250 advert, or indeed just two clients to recoup the cost of a £500 advert, it is logical that with an advert of this size (around half page or bigger) which is designed in a good manner **YOUR ADVERT WILL GET NOTICED** and this will lead to enquiries which eventually leads to paying clients as we will discuss further in a few moments.

It is not good enough to run any advert (whether display or classified) on a once only basis, in truth experience has shown me that you need to run an advert at least on three consecutive (weekly) occasions for it to get its maximum potential response rate.

The logic behind this is that the first time the advert appears, some people may be weary of contacting you however good the advert is as they have never seen you advertising before.

These people will wait until the advert appears again (a week later) and then they may contact you as having seen the advert again it makes them believe that you are not a here today and gone tomorrow business and that Psychologically to be able to afford running such a large advert twice ***YOU MUST BE GOOD AT WHAT YOU DO & MUST BE MAKING GOOD MONEY!***

This convinces them further that you are the right person to Stop them Smoking (or whatever) and so they make that call and end up being a paying client.

Then the advert is run for a third week as it raises interest further and gets your business and name firmly embedded into the minds of the readers of that newspaper, this will of course produce more clients, but also means that whenever the readers decide at any time in the future to Stop Smoking, it is your name that will pop into their head, and as you will be listed in the Local Telephone Directory they will be able to make contact with you easily!

Having such large adverts initially running also establishes your credibility with Doctors & Medical Professionals in the readership area of that publication, so when they receive an information pack from you (we cover this later) then they will be far more receptive when reading it and are far more likely to refer some of their patients to you for Smoking Cessation, Weight-Loss and similar problems!

Booking such a big advert, also gives you room to negotiate to get some additional editorial coverage in that publication on top of that you will obtain using the Press Release angle detailed later!

In all cases you will have obtained 30 days credit for the adverts when booking them so it is easy to recoup your investment as this example illustrates:

ADVERT COSTS £250 A WEEK BY THREE = £750.

As you will be charging £250 per hour session, this means that you need only three clients to recoup the cost of the three (one per week) half page (or bigger) Local Press Adverts. And don't forget you have 30 days from the date of the first advert appearing to get enough clients (3 by £250) to pay for the entire three week worth of advertising!

ADVERT COSTS £500 A WEEK BY THREE = £1500.

Again you have thirty days from the first advert appearing to get enough clients in to cover the cost of the adverts before the bill needs to be paid with the newspaper and you still only need Six Clients at £250 to cover the entire bill of £1500 for the three week period! And lets face it to convert six of the numerous enquiries you will get from such an advertising approach into paying clients sounds realistic dosen't it?

Well indeed it should as using the phone scripts, follow up brochures and other techniques described in this manual, I would expect you to be converting the majority of the enquiries you get into actual paying customers!

A WIDER CATCHMENT AREA

So bearing in mind what we have just learnt from the previous examples, consider what would happen if you spent £500 a week on placing two display adverts (as big as possible) into two different Local Area papers (each advert costing £250) for the three week period!

Well if you choose your two publications carefully so that they both covered different readership areas, you would end up reaching a wider catchment area, would end up with more enquiries and Ultimately **MORE CLIENTS!**

And with this example you would still need only 6 enquiries to turn into paying clients to recoup enough to pay for the adverts when the Invoice becomes due for payment 30 days after the first advert appears!

And best of all to see six clients only takes up **SIX HOURS** of your valuable time, and indeed these six clients could all be booked in to see you on the same day so that you only need to hire an office for one day (discussed later) to recoup the cost of the three week advertising campaign!

ALWAYS ASK WHAT IS YOUR R.O.I?

The question you should always ask yourself before spending any money on any form of advertising or marketing is quite simply what will you R.O.I be?

R.O.I stands for Return on investment and is a phrase you should remember at all times in order to ensure that your advertising and marketing budgets are spent wisely!

The examples I have just given of how to obtain large display advertising in Local Newspapers & Magazines etc provides a good potential Return on Investment whereby the law of averages are in your favour of making enough money back within 30 days to pay for the adverts when the invoice becomes payable.

As in this example we are charging £250 an hour, it also does not take up much of our time to earn the cost of placing the adverts back by actually seeing clients.

And has been logically illustrated an advertising action plan such as this, when combined with all the other techniques within this manual, will we are sure have your phone ringing with a huge number of enquiries which when handled as we will later describe in fuller detail should ultimately lead to more paying clients than you actually have time to see!

And that's the point when you start referring clients to other Local Hypnotherapists in the manner we will discuss later.

THAT'S THE JIGSAW NOW LETS LOOK AT THE PIECES!

What has just been described is essentially the overview of a complete marketing plan, which when followed has the potential to make you more money than you ever dreamed of.

However so that you understand how this "Jigsaw" of things fits together we shall now look at each step separately in a little more detail so that you will have a full understanding of how to increase the number of enquiries you get, how to increase the number of these enquiries you convert into paying clients and ultimately how to set yourself on the path, whereby you could realistically turn yourself into a true Millionaire within a 3 to 5 year period!

WHAT PRODUCT ARE YOU ADVERTISING?

The concept of "Target Marketing" is basically that your marketing concentrates on one specific product at a time.

Now as we have identified that the bulk of clients that most all successful therapists see are for Smoking Cessation, it makes logical sense to spend the majority of our advertising and marketing budgets on promoting the fact that we are the best person in the area at Stopping People from Smoking!

This is not to say that other valuable income cannot be produced from doing other things, because it can, however we will discuss much cheaper ways of promoting these other things such as Weight-Loss, Confidence Problems, Phobias etc later in this manual, for now we will concentrate on Smoking Cessation!

Once you have identified the product then you need to move onto the next step, which is:

SETTING THE CORRECT PRICE FOR YOUR PRODUCT!

Once you have decided on the product to promote you then need to decide on the price to market the product at which will gain you the maximum number of sales and make you the maximum amount of profit for the minimum amount of time, effort and financial investment!

So lets look at the Smoking habit, most of the smokers who come to see you will be smoking somewhere between 20 to 40 Cigarettes a day at an average cost of around £4-25 per pack of 20 at time of writing this which is October 2002.

Therefore we can calculate what the average smokers spends on their habit on a weekly, monthly and yearly basis giving us the following answers:

THE TWENTY A DAY SMOKER

A 20 a day smoker paying an average of £4-25 a pack, will be spending an average of £29-75 over a seven day period! This means that they will be spending around £1547+ over a one year period and that calculates to them spending an average of £128-92 each Calendar month! So charging them £250 to Stop Them Smoking is less than they would on average spend in two months if they were still a smoker and in my book that means that they only need to remain a non smoker for two months and they have their investment back, after that they are into clear profit! This means that within 5 years they will have saved an average of Over £7735+ and over 10 years will have saved an average of £15,470+. Indeed over 20 years they would have saved at least £30,940+ and that's based on what Cigarettes cost now (Oct 2002) in truth they will have saved far more as the cost of Cigarettes continues to rise on a yearly basis!

THE THIRTY A DAY SMOKER

A 30 a day smoker paying an average of £4-25 a pack, will be spending an average of £44.62 over a seven day period! This means that they will be spending around £2320-50+ over a one year period and that calculates to them spending an average of £193.38 each Calendar month! So charging them £250 to Stop Them Smoking is less than they would on average spend in Six Weeks if they were still a smoker and in my book that means that they only need to remain a non smoker for Six Weeks and they have their investment back, after that they are into clear profit! This means that within 5 years they will have saved an average of Over £11,601-20p+ and over 10 years will have saved an average of £23,202-40p+. Indeed over 20 years they would have saved at least £46,404.80p– and that's based on what Cigarettes cost now (Oct 2002) in truth they will have saved far more as the cost of Cigarettes continues to rise on a yearly basis!

THE FOURTY A DAY SMOKER

A 40 a day smoker paying an average of £4-25 a pack, will be spending an average of £59-50 over a seven day period! This means that they will be spending around £3094+ over a one year period and that calculates to them spending an average of £257.83 each Calendar month! So charging them £250 to Stop Them Smoking is less than they would on average spend in One month if they were still a smoker and in my book that means that they only need to remain a non smoker for One month and they have their investment back, after that they are into clear profit! This means that within 5 years they will have saved an average of Over £15,470+ and over 10 years will have saved an average of £30,940+. Indeed over 20 years they would have saved at least £61,880+ and that's based on what Cigarettes cost now (Oct 2002) in truth they will have saved far more as the cost of Cigarettes continues to rise on a yearly basis!

OUR CONCLUSIONS

So this shows us that if we charge people £250 for a one hour session to Stop them Smoking that a 20 a day smoker will have recouped their investment in Less than Two Months!

A Thirty a day smoker will have recouped their investment in Six weeks or less and the Fourty a day smoker will have recouped the cost of our time to treat them in less than one month!

Not only is this positive factual information which can be used to our advantage in advertising brochures to illustrate what excellent value for money our services provide, but also it brings us to the logical conclusion that charging £250 per Stop Smoking session is a good, fair figure to charge our clients!

It is also a proven fact in Sales & Marketing that customers take more seriously and appreciate or value more products & services which have a relatively high purchase price.

This means that by charging £250 it also ensures that all of our clients are those people who 100% Seriously & genuinely want to Stop Smoking and as we know it is only these kind of people who are literally guaranteed to achieve success in their desires.

Ultimately this means we make more money for working less hours and into the bargain we also increase our success rate, which in turn will in the long term increase our professional standing and reputation in the area and as a result lead to past clients becoming our unpaid salesmen and promoting us by word of mouth to everyone they meet who is a Smoker!

Also bear in mind that the majority of people with the desire to Stop Smoking because of Health Problems will usually fall into the 30 to 40+ a day Smokers category and you can see how "cheap" an option this actually is at only £250 for them to become a confident, happy, healthy, relaxed non smoker!

Incidentally when you have written to BUPA and asked for a BUPA provider number and also to the NHS and obtained an NHS provider number, both of which you can obtain at no charge, you will then be in a position to have Doctors refer their patients to you whereby the NHS or BUPA picks up the tab as opposed to the client themselves!

Assuming that all this makes sense to you, as indeed it should, I will now move on to discuss the issue of us being able to offer a guarantee for the unique treatment and service which we shall be providing to our clients.

WHY & HOW TO OFFER A GUARANTEE ON YOUR WORK!

By offering a Guarantee on your work people who see your adverts or enquire about your services will be far more likely to book a session and spend their money with you as they will then feel that they have nothing to lose and everything to gain as that is what state of mind the word 'guarantee" puts people into.

It also implies that you are so confident of the service that you offer in Stopping People Smoking (or whatever) that this is the reason you are offering a guarantee and this in turn makes the potential client **BELIEVE** in your ability to help them even further, so that before they even attend at your consulting room they are placing themselves into the correct Psychological state of mind for the session to be a complete success.

Although we offer a guarantee, it must not be a Money Back Guarantee as doing this would create a secondary gain syndrome, whereby the suggestion is there that at a later time when perhaps the client becomes short of money, they may revert back to their smoking habit in order to claim back the money they paid for their session.

Instead what we offer is a compelling guarantee whereby it is made clear that we are so confident that they will stop smoking after the one off one hour session, that in the most unlikely event that they do not, then we will give them another session of treatment at no extra charge.

As people in sales & marketing know, it is the minority of people who take advantage of a guarantee of this type (non money back) so it's a win – win situation most of the time as by offering to guarantee your work in this manner will gain you more clients and it will be very rare that you ever need to spend another hour of your time giving the person a free back up session as quite simply the majority of people prepared to pay £250 will be so serious about stopping that they will not smoke again and most of the very few (and I do mean few) people who do start smoking again will not even bother to call you back to claim their free back up session which was offered to them under the terms of the guarantee.

Although it would never happen, it would not really matter if you got ten clients a week and all of them claimed the free back up session, you would have still created an income of £2500 (based on £250 per session) its just that you would have ended up doing 20 hours work for this money instead of 10, but even that's not bad at all is it when you look at things logically?

Your advertisements in Newspapers, Magazines and other media must therefore state clearly that your work is ***GUARANTEED!***

This must of course be done in a Legal manner, which does not break the laws set out by The Advertising Standards Authority (ASA) and we would therefore suggest that you use wording and ploys as we will explain now:

EXAMPLE WORDING FOR YOUR ADVERT

STOP-SMOKING
IN ONE HOUR -GUARANTEED*

Celebrity Mind Therapist Jonathan Royle now offers you the chance to become a confident, happy, healthy, relaxed non-smoker in just one hour without the usual side effects and with the greatest of:

ELIMINATE the

ADDICTION to

SMOKING for

EVER!

Tel: 07050-377579. Email: hypno@hypnotorious.com
FOR YOUR EXCITING FREE INFORMATION PACK CALL NOW!
***Terms & Conditions May Apply!**

WHAT THIS EXAMPLE ADVERT DOES FOR YOU!

Well that's the example wording, just a few extra points to note regarding the layout of the advert are as follows:

*In the top Left Hand Corner would go a small clear black and white photograph of yourself (head & Shoulders shot only).

*In the top right hand corner would be placed a duplicate of this small black and white head & shoulders photograph so as to make things look well balanced and symmetrical.

*In the middle right section which is where all the blank space is next to the four short lines of text which make up the word **E.A.S.E** would be printed 3 black and white line drawings which you can get a local art student (phone local University) to draw for you very cheaply and from left to right these would be as follows:

01) The first picture (on left hand side) would be a cartoon caricature of someone who looked stressed out and unhappy whilst smoking a cigarette and just above it would be the word "BEFORE" in underlined bold print.

02) The middle picture would be of a clock face whereby the hands on the clock are cigarettes and then there is a bold diagonal line across the clock face just like there is on a No-Smoking sign in shops! This would visually communicate the message of Stop Smoking in One Hour!

03) The picture on the right would be a caricature of the same person, but this time showing them looking happy, healthy & energetic with no cigarettes in site and this would have the caption "AFTER" printed above it in bold underlined print.

Take a minute to print out the page of this manual containing the example advert and draw a rough sketch of these things in place, located where I have advised and you will get an instant idea of how eye catching and effective this advert will be and therefore just how successful it will be in getting you lots & lots of serious enquiries for your services!

This advert covers you legally regarding the nature of the guarantee as next to the word guaranteed is a small * symbol and then at the bottom of the advert in small print so it doesn't stand out to much is the phrase *Terms & Conditions May Apply!

The small * symbol alerting them legally that this is relevant to the nature of the guarantee which you are offering.

This example advert was formulated using the advertising maxim of ***A.I.D.A.***, which stands for Attention, Interest, Desire & Action!
These are the four key elements to any successful advert and have all been included as follows:

01) ATTENTION = The fact the advert will be a large display advert and contains a balanced combination of words and pictures, including two comical cartoon type caricatures means that this immediately helps the Ad to stand out and gain the attention of the readers.

02) INTEREST = The Bold heading of "Stop Smoking in One Hour – Guaranteed" will then draw the readers attention and also their Interest and so they will read further and become even more Interested by the idea of Stopping Smoking in one hour with E.A.S.E without any of the usual side effects.

03) DESIRE = By this time those who are even just slightly Interested in the idea of becoming a non smoker will have the desire to find out more and then its time for:

04) ACTION = We spur the reader into immediate action by offering them the incentive of an "Exciting FREE Information Pack!" and once they read this, they also read the fact that they need to CALL NOW to claim their exciting FREE information pack which spurs them into immediate action and gets your phone ringing or your email box full of enquiries.

Although this example has covered the structure of an effective advert for your Smoking Cessation services, don't forget that this basis principle of A.I.D.A can and indeed should be used whenever constructing display advertisements and/or advertising brochures of any kind and for any service or product, as it is attention to small techniques and details like this that make the difference between adverts that get some response and those which draw huge responses!

SELL THE SIZZLE & NOT THE SAUSAGE!

One of the other most important secrets of the advertising and marketing world is summed up in the simple phrase "Sell the Sizzle and Not the Sausage!"

What this means is quite simple really, imagine this scenario, there are loads of different brands of Sausages on sale at the supermarket and they are displayed in a cabinet right next to various brands of Beef Burgers and other meat products.

Our Potential customer is walking down this shopping aisle and is overwhelmed with choices!

Should they pick Sausages, Burgers or some other type of meat?

And then when they have for example decided on Sausages, next they must decide which brand they would prefer to buy!

If they have never eaten a Sausage before in their life, then they will probably be drawn to the brand with the nicest looking packaging or the brand available at the cheapest price!

Having said that a large proportion of people will be drawn to the most expensive brand, just so long as it has nice packaging as well

The logic behind their decision being that the packaging looks nice and professional and as they are the most expensive, they must therefore be the best brand of Sausages available!

Also the fact that the picture on the box makes them look very juicy and tasty will influence them to make the decision of buying the most expensive brand as they will have decided that they must also be the tastiest Sausages available!

And that is why sales people always remember the phrase "Sell the sizzle and not the Sausage!" as it is the benefits of what a product or service will do for the customer that makes them come to the decision of buying one thing rather than another.

This means that when formulating an advertising campaign for any product or service you should always put yourself into your potential customer's shoes and looking at things from their point of view ask yourself the question:

"What can this product or service do for me, and why should I buy this product/service rather than a similar one?"

The answers that you produce will bring you many valuable ideas and sales points to formulate your advertising and marketing campaigns from.

SCRIPT FOR THE SALES AUDIO TAPE!

What follows is my suggested structure for the script which you should use when recording the audio tape master, which will then be duplicated and sent out to those people who respond to your media advertising etc!

This suggested script also illustrates the principle of selling the sizzle and not the sausage in so much as it clearly gets across to the listener what the benefits are for them and what is in it for them so to speak!

I am sure you will agree that this is a very powerful and persuasive sales pitch indeed and the beauty of it is, that because it is recorded on one side of the audio tape which you send out to enquirers you are automatically saved the need to spend time doing a long sales pitch on the telephone.

After all once they have received the tape and listened to it, along with reading the enclosed colour sales brochure you can be sure that when they ring you back (on a different number) it will be for one reason only and that reason will be to book a session, part with their cash and become a non-smoker.

On the reverse side of this audio sales tape would be recorded a simple suggestion therapy relaxation session, which they are led to believe by side A of the tape is usually sold at £20 a time, but has been sent to them as their ***FREE GIFT*** for simply taking the time to find out more about how they can change their life forever.

Perceptively the fact that you have sent them an apparently "Free Gift" makes them view you as a genuine, sincere and generous person, in otherwords it makes them feel good about you!

And the truth is that when people feel good about you they are then far more likely to deal with you on both a business and/or personal level, in otherwords this simple action of apparently sending them a free gift, which is actually a powerful sales tool, has the result of creating Instant Rapport with them despite the fact you have not met each other yet!

So here is the basic layout of the script I'd suggest for side A of the sales tape, as for the script for side B this can easily be formulated using the information which we supply in our complete training course "The Professional Art of Stage-Hypnosis, Hypnotherapy & Complete Mind Therapy!"

I will give you extra advice regarding the sales tape after you have read the script...

SALES TAPE FOR SMOKING CESSATION

Good morning, Good Afternoon or Good Evening, depending on when you actually decide to listen to this amazing recording, which can quite literally change your life for the better with the greatest of ***E.A.S.E!***

Allow me to introduce myself, my name is Jonathan Royle and I am a fully qualified and professionally trained member of The Association of Professional Hypnotherapists & Psychotherapists as well as being the President of The Association of Complete Mind Therapists!

On this side of the tape it is my intention to explain to you, how, using Complete Mind Therapy I can quite literally help you to Eliminate the Addiction to Smoking Forever in just a single one hour session.

And on side B of this tape I have sent you an amazing ***FREE GIFT*** (pause) a recording of our self-hypnosis stress relief and relaxation therapy training.

We usually charge our clients around £20 for this information alone, but we are sending it to you ***FREE*** as our way of saying thank you for responding to our advertisement and also as our way of congratulating you for taking that first step on the intelligent path towards becoming a confident, happy, healthy, relaxed, non-smoker.

You can listen to side B of this tape whenever you are experiencing stress in your life and feel that a little more relaxation time would be of benefit to you, but please don't try listening to side B of this tape when driving or operating machinery as the powerful relaxation ***YOU WILL EXPERIENCE*** could prove dangerous whilst carrying out such tasks, as we are sure you will appreciate!

So I'm sure you've got loads of questions you want answering and that's what this side of the tape is all about, so lets start right at the beginning with the question of:

WHAT ARE THE BENEFITS OF BECOMING A NON-SMOKER?

There are three main ways in which you will benefit by becoming a happy, healthy, relaxed, confident non-smoker and these are quite simply as follows:

01) You will ***SAVE*** your ***HEALTH.***
02) You will ***SAVE TIME.***
03) You will ***SAVE MONEY.***

We will now examine each of these three areas in a little more detail:

WHAT ARE THE HEALTH BENEFITS?

Smokers like you are quite literally playing a very dangerous game of Russian Roulette each and every time they light up a cigarette!

Continue with your smoking habit and you are placing yourself at risk in all of the following ways:

- There are over 120,000+ smoking related deaths in the UK alone on a yearly basis!
- That's equivalent to at least 330 smoking related deaths each and every day.
- It has been shown that at least 50% of all regular smokers will die early because of their deadly habit.
- Smokers in their 30's and 40's have five times as many Heart Attacks as non smokers in the same age group.
- Smoking can be the cause of bad breath, makes your clothes, home, car and furniture stink and can be a major turn off for members of the opposite sex!
- Rather than relaxing you as many people think, smoking actually makes you more stressed and as a result this can often lead to any number of stress related illnesses and diseases, which themselves can often prove to be deadly.
- By the way your sense of taste and smell will improve dramatically when you become a non smoker, in fact you will find that food tastes far better than it may have done in years, so what are you waiting for?
- And that's just the tip of the iceberg when it comes to health matters, we haven't even mentioned Cancer.

However the good news is that by becoming a confident, happy, healthy and relaxed non smoker nearly all of the time you can reverse the damage done to yourself relatively quickly, but only if you stop sooner, rather than later!

When you consider that nicotine can leave your body within 24 hours of becoming a non smoker and when you consider that this means you will also have stopped killing yourself slowly on a daily basis, isn't it obvious that the intelligent choice is to book a session of Complete Mind Therapy today and give yourself a whole new lease of life?

WHAT ARE THE TIME BENEFITS?

There are several ways that you will benefit enormously from the point of view of "Time" by becoming a confident, happy, healthy and relaxed non-smoker and these include the facts that:

- A two pack, 40 a day smoker spends around one million 460,000 minutes of their lifetime smoking. That's equivalent to 24,320 hours or indeed 1,000 days!
- Imagine it, that's equivalent to throwing away 2 and ¾ years of your life out of every 20 years that you remain on this mortal coil. That's well over five years that the average smoker reading this stands to waste if they continue smoking!
- That's like subjecting yourself to a five-year jail sentence, just because, until now you have allowed yourself to become a slave to smoking.
- Most people who give up smoking can, on average increase their life span by at least five years, and don't forget those will be five happier, healthier and more relaxed years, during which you will have far more money available to spend on the good things in life!
- So in most all cases by becoming a non smoker you will have added around five years to your life span, add to that the five years you would have wasted whilst actually smoking the cigarettes and you will have gained ***TEN EXTRA YEARS OF HEALTH, HAPPINESS & FREEDOM!***
- Best of all using our unique system of Complete Mind Therapy (CMT) you can become a confident, happy, healthy, relaxed non smoker within just one session which takes only one hour of your most valuable time!

WHAT ARE THE FINANCIAL BENEFITS?

Consider these eye-opening facts and we are sure that you will realise that the most intelligent decision you will ever make is that of becoming a confident, happy, healthy, relaxed non-smoker by calling us and booking an appointment today!

- Those who smoke between 20 to 40 Cigarettes a day will save around £2,500 per year by becoming a non-smoker.
- That means you could save well over £100K Thousand pounds during your lifetime by simply becoming a non-smoker!
- The current cost of a Complete Mind Therapy (CMT) session to help you stop smoking with ***E.A.S.E*** (**E**liminate the **A**ddiction to **S**moking **F**orever!) costs just £275-00, making it by far the best financial investment you will ever make.
- Consider this, place £275 into a bank or building society account for a year and even if you were getting say 5% interest, this would only make you a profit of £13-75p for the year on your original investment.
- However take this same £275 and invest it into yourself by way of becoming a non-smoker and in around one month you will have recouped your original investment and you will then continue to profit for the rest of your life!
- That means that in the same one year period, your investment of £250, would by becoming a non-smoker have made you a 1,000%+ Tax Free return by way of the money you will save in one year by not buying Cigarettes!
- No other form of investment can bring you such a large financial return for such a low investment in such a short space of time, and don't forget you keep on saving money and thereby getting a huge return on your original investment of £250 for the rest of your life!
- Best of all as we offer a ***"LIFETIME GUARANTEE"*** which entitles you to one ***FREE*** back up session (in the rare event that you ever need it) you can be sure that this is the Lowest Risk, yet by far Highest Return Investment that you will ever make in your life, so don't delay call and book your session today on 07050-377579.

WHY DOES IT COST £275 FOR A CMT SESSION?

Although it may sound like a lot of money, the truth is that the majority of smokers will recoup their investment of £275 in little over a month of being a non-smoker from the cash they save by not buying cigarettes!

Also you must remember that whether you see end up seeing me in person or you are referred to one of my experienced colleagues, you will be receiving treatment from professionals who are at the top of their industry and have spent many years and many thousands of pounds to become expert in this field and therefore expert at enabling you to achieve what you want to achieve with the greatest of ***E.A.S.E***

Its true to say that if you ring around the Hypnotherapists listed for your area in the Yellow Pages that many of them may offer to help you become a non-

Smoker for far less than £275, but you must at all times remember the old saying that "If you pay peanuts you will get monkeys!"

And don't forget we don't just hypnotise you and do part of the job, we use Complete Mind Therapy and do a ***COMPLETE JOB***, which is why we are able to offer our unique Lifetime Guarantee!

Remember becoming a non-smoker is the best investment and indeed by far the most profitable investment that you will ever make into yourself, so don't you owe it to yourself to consult with an expert at the height of their field rather than one of their less knowledgeable, experienced or qualified competitors?

WHY STOP SMOKING USING COMPLETE MIND THERAPY – (CMT)?

The answer to this question is quite simply that by booking a session of Complete Mind Therapy you are choosing the easiest and most effective way to become a confident, happy, healthy, relaxed non-smoker with ***E.A.S.E!***

With ***C.M.T*** we are only interested in helping you to achieve positive and permanent change in the easiest and most enjoyable way possible!

Consider this, in January 1968 an article appeared in "The American Journal of Clinical Hypnosis" entitled "The use of Hypnosis and 1,000 cases of Tobacco maniacs!"

This article detailed the results of a clinical study carried out on 1,000 smokers who were all given a session of Hypnosis to help them stop smoking and the results were amazing.

All 1,000 people treated with Hypnosis to permanently remove their smoking habit were contacted again on a regular basis for the next 18 months and it was found that 94% of these people had remained non-smokers throughout this 18 month period thanks to the power of Hypnosis!

This is good news for you, as our unique approach of Complete Mind Therapy combines the most effective elements of Hypnosis, Neuro-Linguistic Programming and numerous other cutting edge human change technologies, making our approach even more effective than mere Hypnosis alone!

In short we can easily help you to achieve what you want to achieve and ask yourself this, would we offer you a Lifetime Guarantee if we didn't think that Complete Mind Therapy would work for you?

And best of all, as was proven by a 1996 Government Investigation into Hypnosis it is 100% safe, something which can not be said about many of the alternative ways some people use in an attempt to become a non-smoker!

SO WHATS IT FEEL LIKE?

Essentially when you take part in a session of Complete Mind Therapy on the one hand you may be more alert than normal, being able to taste, smell, see, feel and hear everything better than usual, but on the other hand you will feel relaxed both Mentally and Physically to a level that makes instant subconscious change as easy as one, two, three!

Although it is true to say that just as each and every person is different, so each and every person experiences a session of Complete Mind Therapy in a different way, it is also true to say that at the end of our one hour session together ***YOU WILL FEEL DIFFERENT*** and ***YOU WILL KNOW*** within yourself that positive changes within you ***HAVE BEEN MADE!***

Because of the fact that smoking is a habit, it is controlled by the subconscious mind which is the area of our minds that deals with all automatic tasks such as circulating the blood around our bodies, breathing at night without the need for any conscious thought and any number of good or indeed bad habits we may have such as Smoking!

Therefore, since Complete Mind Therapy, Hypnosis and NLP work directly with the subconscious mind this is the only method to Stop Smoking which actually makes any logical sense!

The Human Mind is like having our own Personal Neck Top computer and indeed it works in much the same way as a computer, which is why an experienced Mind Therapist such as myself need only erase the file in your mind which makes you smoke and then simply replace it with one that ensures that you remain a Confident, happy, healthy, relaxed non-smoker for the rest of your life.

WHAT ARE THE ALTERNATIVES TO COMPLETE MIND THERAPY?

There are many products on the market and available from your Local GP to help you become a non-smoker and these include Nicotine Patches, Inhalers, Nicotine Gums and Zyban the stop smoking drug, amongst many others!

Unfortunately products such as Patches, Gums and Inhalers can cause many negative side effects such as nightmares, nausea, indigestion, skin irritation and even long term skin damage amongst many others!

And as for the so-called wonder drug "Zyban" it has been shown by many to be ineffective unless it is combined with some form of Psychological help as well.

In fact one in 1,000 users of Zyban could experience convulsions which could lead to ***DEATH!***

To quote a section from a report published by Glaxo-Wellcome, the company who produce Zyban it states:

"There is a long list of potential side effects, the biggest of which appears to be that when combined with other drugs it could become ***LETHAL!***"

So yes it is true to say that there are alternatives to Complete Mind Therapy in your quest to become a non-smoker, but not only is our method of C.M.T by far the most effective, but it is also one of the rare options which is 100% safe and has no side effects whatsoever when carried out by an experienced trained Mind Therapist such as Jonathan Royle.

To quote the results of the largest clinical study ever done involving 72,000 smokers, which were published in "The New Scientist" in October 1992:

"Nicotine Gum had only just over a 10% success rate, our results have shown us that Hypnosis is ***THE MOST EFFECTIVE*** way to become a non-smoker!"

And its precisely because Hypnosis has been proven to be so effective in helping people like you to become non-smokers with ***E.A.S.E*** that our unique approach of Complete Mind Therapy combines the most powerful Hypnotic Techniques with other cutting edge technologies to form, what many have found to be the most reliable treatment method available to Stop Smoking Permanently!

WHAT ABOUT YOUR DOCTOR?

Many people have asked their Doctor for advice, help and guidance in their quest to become a non-smoker, but as we have explained already there is currently no way a Doctor can help you in such an effective manner as a Hypnotherapist or indeed a Complete Mind Therapist when it comes to Smoking Cessation.

This fact is clearly illustrated by the findings of a detailed report in "New Scientist" magazine which discovered that only 6% of the people who seek advice from their Doctors to stop smoking actually end up becoming non-smokers as a result of their GP's advice!

This is in stark contrast to the 94% of people who have been found to Stop Smoking after just one session of Hypnosis in other clinical studies!

CAN IT REALLY BE SO SIMPLE TO STOP?

So we now know that there are absolutely no good reasons to continue smoking, and we also know that there are many logical, desirable and beneficial reasons to become a confident, happy, healthy, relaxed non-smoker using Complete Mind Therapy and the proven power of Hypnosis!

But we hear you cry, if such a simple solution to the smoking habit is available then why do so many people who say they sincerely want to stop, carry on smoking?

Well in our experience, we have found that for 99% of people the answer always comes down to the same thing....***FEAR!***

- ***FEAR*** that you'll never be able to continue your life as a non-smoker completely free of the craving for Nicotine!
- ***FEAR*** that you'll put on weight when you stop or start biting your fingernails instead as a substitute to your damaging smoking habit.
- ***FEAR*** that you'll have to give up the pleasurable crutch that your smoking habit seems to give you, and that as a result you may become a lesser person.
- ***FEAR*** that in order to become a non-smoker you will have to go through some kind of terrible trauma or painful feelings.
- ***FEAR*** that when you have become a non-smoker you may find that you are unable to enjoy life or handle stress!
- ***FEAR*** of failure in your attempts to become a non-smoker.

All of these examples of fear are simply potential symptoms of the one simple reason that until now you have not been able to stop smoking and this main reason is yet another ***FEAR........***

THE FEAR THAT IT WILL PROVE TO BE FAR TOO DIFFICULT AND FAR TOO PAINFUL WHEN YOU ATTEMPT TO STOP SMOKING!

The truth is that Hypnosis and Complete Mind Therapy actually make the process of becoming a non-smoker so simple and straightforward, that something you once thought would be so difficult to achieve actually becomes so ridiculously ***EASY!***

In fact our tried, tested and proven to work technique of Complete Mind Therapy makes it so easy for you to quit the nicotine habit, that by the end of only one hour, ***YOU WILL BE*** a confident, happy, healthy, relaxed non-smoker!

We will help you to make instant and positive changes deep in your subconscious mind, which not only enable you to become a non-smoker instantly, but also give you enough will power to ensure that just so long as you follow our simple instructions, you ***WILL*** remain a non-smoker for the rest of your life.

When you leave our office you will not feel deprived, you will not feel any pain whatsoever and in no way will you feel that you have made any form of sacrifice!

In fact because of the way we transfer the pleasure you currently get from smoking to some other healthier habit such as doing more exercise, relaxing more or having a glass of water instead, our approach of Complete Mind Therapy makes it highly enjoyable and pleasurable to become a confident, happy, healthy, relaxed non-smoker!

Its also because of this that with our method of Complete Mind Therapy there is ***NO*** unwanted weight gain, ***NO*** sudden nail biting or other habit will appear and you ***WILL BECOME*** far more relaxed and stress free in your every day life than you have ever been before, which means that you won't be getting grumpy and irritable with your loved ones, friends or work colleagues!

In fact the morning after you attend our offices, you will awaken with an inner warm glow of confidence, a renewed optimism to life and a more positive attitude to get things done as you realise that something you once thought would be so difficult to achieve has in fact proved to be so ridiculously easy.

From the very moment that you leave our office you ***WILL BE*** a confident, happy, healthy, relaxed non-smoker who feels proud to say "No Thank You I don't Smoke!" and the only side effects that you will ever experience are a positive and beneficial increase in your Health, Wealth and Financial Freedom!

All you have to do is make an appointment, attend at our office and then sit back in a nice comfortable chair, close your eyes, relax and follow our simple step by step instructions to the letter and one hour later you will be a non-smoker!

It doesn't get any easier than that, so what are you waiting for??

As you can appreciate demand for our services is high so we can only see people on a strictly first come, first served basis, this truly is a once in a lifetime opportunity to change ***YOUR LIFE FOR THE BETTER!***

The consultation fee of £275 includes the personal one hour treatment session with one of our highly trained expert therapists and also includes your full back up support pack containing a self-help guide and a valuable home treatment tape which alone have a value of over £25!

Consultation fees can be paid in either cash or by way of any major Visa or MasterCard, but please be aware that any appointments which are not attended or are cancelled with less than 24hrs notice, will result in a 50% cancellation fee becoming payable!

So if you are serious about becoming a non smoker with E.A.S.E, then pick up the phone ***NOW*** and ***CALL*** 07050-377579, that number again is 07050-377579 and take your first step to a Happier, Healthier and Richer Cigarette Free Life!

Oh yes and one last thing before I go, please check the envelope this tape was sent to you in, because if you were one of the first 40 people to respond to our advertisement, then as a reward for being so quick in replying we will have sent you a valuable "Gift Certificate" entitling you to a £25-00 discount off our usual consultation and treatment fees!

If you are one of the lucky 40 with such a "Gift Certificate" sent to you, then its even more important that you call us now on 07050-377579 and book your session of Complete Mind Therapy to end your smoking habit now, as your "Gift Certificate" will expire and become invalid in seven days time!

Please enjoy side B of this tape and we look forward to hearing from you today!

That's the wording I use for the sales tape which they get in their ***FREE*** information package, which is sent out to them when they phone you in response to your newspaper advert.

Incidentally if you contact recording studios in your area and explain that you have a narrative script which you wish to make an audio master of and that this should only take two hours maximum to record, you should be able to arrange to book what they call "Dead Time" when the studio is usually doing nothing and this means that you can then get your master tape recording of both sides A and B produced at a greatly reduced cost in a 100% professional sounding manner!

As we mentioned earlier, along with this sales tape which would have your name and contact telephone number printed on either side of it, they would also receive a colour information brochure and an introductory letter thanking them for their enquiry, so now lets consider these two items a little further.

THE INTRODUCTORY LETTER

The cheapest way to produce a quality looking Introductory letter is to purchase a ream (500 sheets) of Conqueror (or similar) quality white "laid" paper from your local discount stationers such as Staples.

You can then quite simply design a nice looking letterhead on your computer and print this letterhead out, complete with the letter on it and you have your end product at a very low cost, whereby you need only print them out on an "as need" basis!

The telephone number on this letter, the colour brochure and indeed on the side of the sales tape (and in the taped narration) would be different than the contact number which is printed on your newspaper adverts and in other advertising mediums.

The idea behind this being, that in the first instance the number they call is always answered by a telephone answering machine upon which they hear the following message:

"Thank you for calling The Complete Mind Therapy Clinic, all of our consultants are busy treating people at the moment, so if you would please leave your name and address after the tone we will be happy to send you an exciting FREE information pack and a FREE gift worth £20-00 which will explain fully our unique smoking cessation treatment, we look forward to helping you become a non-smoker in the near future!"

This saves you talking to any of the people who respond to your adverts until such time as they have left their name and address, you have sent them their information package, they have studied it and decided to invest £250 and then they will be calling you back on a different telephone number, namely the number which is on the Introductory letter, the colour brochure and on the tape itself!

This means that when the other phone line rings you will not have to get involved in a long telephone sales pitch as all of their questions should have been answered by the information package which you sent out to them.

Should they still have questions to ask, just respond as follows:

"In order to help you fully can I just ask you how long you have been smoking and how many cigarettes you smoke each day?"

Whatever their answer is you respond by saying:

"Well the good news is that I can confirm that with just one session of Complete Mind Therapy we can reduce the amount you smoke to Zero, there will be no side effects and as it states in the information package we sent you, our work with you is guaranteed for life"

You then continue:

"So when would you like to come along and become a non-smoker, would Monday or Tuesday suit you best?"

This gives them a choice, but both choices are to book an appointment, so once they have chosen the day you then give them a choice between two times as follows:

"And would 10-30 in the morning or 1-00 in the afternoon suit you best?"

They again have two choices, but either choice results in a booking,

"So let me just confirm that's (for example) 1-00pm on Tuesday afternoon isn't it Sir?"

Here they respond yes and you continue:

"And if I can just take your name, address and telephone number for our records"

Here you jot their details down and book them into your diary

"Well thank you very much for calling Sir, our expert consultant Jonathan Royle will look forward to seeing you at 1-00pm on Tuesday afternoon and helping you to become a non-smoker with ***E.A.S.E!***'

By doing things in the manner I have just explained you are keeping things as simple as possible and also handling things in a manner which seems very professional and business like indeed, which is what people would expect when they are about to spend £250-00 on something!

Right back to the Introductory Letter, mine is headed:

THE COMPLETE MIND THERAPY CLINIC
Tel: 07050-377579. Mob: 07932-975297.
****Appointments cancelled without 24hrs notice will result in a 50% cancellation fee!***
*Our guarantee applies to personal one to one consultations only.

Then the text of the Introductory letter follows and my office address is then printed at the rear of the page as per this example:

Huddersfield C.M.T Clinic, Prospect House, PO Box 12, Huddersfield, England, HD8 9YP.

The actual body of the letter is short, sweet, simple and to the point, the wording I use is as follows:

Dear (here you insert their name prior to printing the letter out from your PC)

Congratulations on taking the first step to becoming a Confident, happy, healthy, relaxed non-smoker.

Please find enclosed an information brochure and an audio-tape, side A of which will explain everything to you about our unique treatment method of Complete Mind Therapy and how using it, we can help you to stop smoking with E.A.S.E with just a single one hour session.

On side B of the tape you will find a ***FREE GIFT*** as our way of thanking you for responding to our advertisement.

This side of the tape contains a self-hypnosis treatment session to help you relax more and control the stresses of your every day life!

We normally charge our clients £20 or more for this powerful relaxation aid, which can be listened to whenever you want to chill out and relax completely, but obviously not when operating machinery or driving as that could prove dangerous!

In the first instance we would urge you to listen to side A of the tape and read the enclosed leaflet which we are sure will leave you with no doubts that a session of Complete Mind Therapy is the intelligent choice to become a non-smoker!

As all our treatments have a Lifetime Guarantee, details of which are on side A of the tape, demand for our expert consultants services are high and therefore we would advise you to listen to the tape and then book an appointment by contacting us on ***07050-377579*** as a matter of priority!

Many thanks for your initial enquiry and we look forward to ending your smoking habit for you in the very near future,

Yours truly,

Jonathan Royle

Well that's the wording for the Introductory letter which convinces them to waste no time in listening to side A of the tape which will then convince them what a good idea it is to invest £275 into becoming a non-smoker.

Then when they call you on the number on the tape, letter and brochure you simply have to use the example script given to book them into your diary with EASE!

And should you be fully booked, or unable to fit them into your diary at a time which is mutually convenient for the pair of you then you would book them in to see one of your "expert colleagues" or to put it another way you refer them to someone else and then take a big commission from that therapist for passing lucrative and valuable work his/her direction!

So with reference to the initial enquiry pack that we send out that just leaves the subject of the colour information brochure, which we will now cover:

THE COLOUR INFORMATION BROCHURE

Once again the cheapest way by far to produce your colour information brochures is on an "as need" basis by designing them on your home computer and then printing them out on your colour printer as and when you need them!

I would suggest that you print the brochures out on nice glossy paper stock, which obviously must be compatible for use in your printer, the stuff I use is actually photo quality paper which is quite thick and I currently obtain a pack of 20 A4 sheets for £6-00, which equates to just 30p per sheet.

This may sound rather expensive, but the advantage is that you need only invest a small amount and have enough materials in to produce 20 brochures at a time, rather than having to buy big reams of this quality paper which would require a much bigger initial investment, despite the fact that the unit price of each sheet would be dramatically reduced.

As a matter of interest I currently obtain all of my computer supplies, including this photo paper (£6-00 for 20 sheets), Blank CDROMS with plastic trays (£5-00 for 10), Printer Ink Cartridges (2 Colour and 2 Black for just £10-00) and lots of other value for money items from the Tobacconist/Newsagents which is situated on Yorkshire Street in Rochdale, Lancashire.

Bear in mind at the time of typing this information up it is August 2002, but hopefully that should give you a good idea of how cheaply, if you shop around you can produce the items you need on an "as need" basis!

My brochures are produced so that they are made up of four A5 size pages which means that they can be printed onto a single double sided A4 sheet and then folded down the centre making the end product into a four page A5 Colour Booklet.

The front page of the brochure is an A5 colour reproduction of the advert that I suggested you use in the newspapers earlier in this manual, the only main difference being that the telephone number on the brochure version is different than the one which appears on the newspaper adverts as it is the number they are to call when they want to speak to someone in person and actually book a session with you!

Also the cartoon pictures on the brochure version would be in full colour, as would be the head and shoulders photographs which appear on the advert of you.

This front page would be printed so that when the brochure is held like a book would be, the front page will appear to have been printed on its side, or to put it another way they will have to hold the brochure in Landscape style in order to read the advert in the manner it would appear in a newspaper.

Pages two and three of the brochure (inside pages) and page four (back page) would all be laid out and printed in normal book style format so that they can be read holding the brochure in a normal portrait (book) style manner.

I will now give details of what information should appear on each of the inside pages and the rear cover.

PAGE TWO

CAN I REALLY STOP IN ONE HOUR?

If such a simple solution to the smoking habit is available then why do so many people who say they sincerely want to stop, carry on smoking?

Well in our experience, we have found that for 99% of people the answer always comes down to the same thing....***FEAR!***

- ***FEAR*** that you'll never be able to continue your life as a non-smoker completely free of the craving for Nicotine!
- ***FEAR*** that you'll put on weight when you stop or start biting your fingernails instead as a substitute to your damaging smoking habit.
- ***FEAR*** that you'll have to give up the pleasurable crutch that your smoking habit seems to give you, and that as a result you may become a lesser person.

- ***FEAR*** that in order to become a non-smoker you will have to go through some kind of terrible trauma or painful feelings.
- ***FEAR*** that when you have become a non-smoker you may find that you are unable to enjoy life or handle stress!
- ***FEAR*** of failure in your attempts to become a non-smoker.

All of these examples of fear are simply potential symptoms of the one simple reason that until now you have not been able to stop smoking and this main reason is yet another ***FEAR……..***

THE FEAR THAT IT WILL PROVE TO BE FAR TOO DIFFICULT AND FAR TOO PAINFUL WHEN YOU ATTEMPT TO STOP SMOKING!

PAGE THREE

WHAT ARE THE FINANCIAL BENEFITS?

Consider these eye-opening facts and we are sure that you will realise that the most intelligent decision you will ever make is that of becoming a confident, happy, healthy, relaxed non-smoker by calling us and booking an appointment today!

- Those who smoke between 20 to 40 Cigarettes a day will save around £2,500 per year by becoming a non-smoker.
- That means you could save well over £100K Thousand pounds during your lifetime by simply becoming a non-smoker!
- The current cost of a Complete Mind Therapy (CMT) session to help you stop smoking with ***E.A.S.E*** (**E**liminate the **A**ddiction to **S**moking **F**orever!) costs just £275-00, making it by far the best financial investment you will ever make.
- Consider this, place £275 into a bank or building society account for a year and even if you were getting say 5% interest, this would only make you a profit of £13-75p for the year on your original investment.
- However take this same £275 and invest it into yourself by way of becoming a non-smoker and in around one month you will have recouped your original investment and you will then continue to profit for the rest of your life!
- That means that in the same one year period, your investment of £275, would by becoming a non-smoker have made you a 1,000%+ Tax Free return by way of the money you will save in one year by not buying Cigarettes!

- *No other form of investment can bring you such a large financial return for such a low investment in such a short space of time, and don't forget you keep on saving money and thereby getting a huge return on your original investment of £275 for the rest of your life!
- Best of all as we offer a ***"LIFETIME GUARANTEE"*** which entitles you to one ***FREE*** back up session (in the rare event that you ever need it) you can be sure that this is the Lowest Risk, yet by far Highest Return Investment that you will ever make in your life, so don't delay call and book your session today on 07050-377579.

PAGE FOUR

TAKE ACTION NOW!

Our tried, tested and proven to work technique of Complete Mind Therapy makes it so easy for you to quit the nicotine habit, that by the end of only one hour, ***YOU WILL BE*** a confident, happy, healthy, relaxed non-smoker!

We will help you to make instant and positive changes deep in your subconscious mind, which not only enable you to become a non-smoker instantly, but also give you enough will power to ensure that just so long as you follow our simple instructions, you ***WILL*** remain a non-smoker for the rest of your life.

When you leave our office you will not feel deprived, you will not feel any pain whatsoever and in no way will you feel that you have made any form of sacrifice!

In fact because of the way we transfer the pleasure you currently get from smoking to some other healthier habit such as doing more exercise, relaxing more or having a glass of water instead, our approach of Complete Mind Therapy makes it highly enjoyable and pleasurable to become a confident, happy, healthy, relaxed non-smoker!

Its also because of this that with our method of Complete Mind Therapy there is ***NO*** unwanted weight gain, ***NO*** sudden nail biting or other habit will appear and you ***WILL BECOME*** far more relaxed and stress free in your every day life than you have ever been before, which means that you won't be getting grumpy and irritable with your loved ones, friends or work colleagues!

All you have to do is make an appointment, attend at our office and then sit back in a nice comfortable chair, close your eyes, relax and follow our simple step by step instructions to the letter and one hour later you will be a non-smoker!

It doesn't get any easier than that, so what are you waiting for??

TEL: 07050-377579 MOB: 07932-975297
(Cash, Visa & Mastercard's Accepted)
****Appointments cancelled without 24hrs notice will result in a 50% cancellation fee!***
*****Our Guarantee applies only to personal one to one consultations Huddersfield C.M.T Clinic, Propsect House, PO Box 12, Huddersfield, England, HD8 9YP***

PLEASE LISTEN TO SIDE A OF TAPE BEFORE BOOKING

THE £25-00 OFF DISCOUNT – "GIFT CERTIFICATE!"

As you may of guessed by now every single person who responds to our media advertisements is sent a "Gift Certificate" in their information pack which is apparently worth £25-00 off the cost of their CMT session if they book their session within Seven Days!

The idea of this is to act as an incentive to them to book their session within a seven day period of getting the information pack, as this will mean that they can claim a £25 discount and thus end up paying only £250 for their session, which oddly enough is all we wanted to charge them in the first place as discussed earlier!

Phrased in the manner it is on the sales tape, finding this "Gift Certificate" inside their information pack also makes them feel lucky and good about themselves as they will think they have been one of just 40 lucky people to receive such a £25 off discount "Gift Certificate".

And as people in the world of sales know when people feel that they are getting a discount, especially if they feel they are privileged in doing so, then they are far more likely to buy the product in the first place, even if they don't really want it!

The "Gift Certificate" is again easily designed and printed on your home PC and should be A5 Landscape format, which means that you can fit two of them onto one A4 sheet when printing them out and then just cut the sheet in half giving you two gift certificates.

Their should be a fancy border around the sides of the certificate so that it stands out like a kind of Certificate or Award would do, and my advice is to print the certificate onto a nice thin bright yellow coloured card so that it stands out a mile when it is removed from the envelope!

The wording on this should be as follows:

"GIFT CERTIFICATE"

Congratulations, you were one of the first 40 people to respond to our advertisement and therefore ***YOU ARE ONE OF OUR LUCKY WINNER'S!***

To claim your ***£25-00 Prize**** simply book your session of Complete Mind Therapy to end your smoking habit within the next seven days and we will deduct £25-00 off the usual consultation and treatment fee of £275-00!

YOUR SESSION THEN COSTS ONLY £250!

This certificate is valid for seven days only until _______________ therefore you must book your session before this date to qualify for your ***£25-00 DISCOUNT***

TEL: 07050-377579 – TO BOOK YOUR SESSION TODAY!

***No Cash Alternative Can Be Claimed For this Certificate and it may not be used in conjunction with any other offers which may currently be available.**

The wording of this is such as to make them want to claim their £25 discount and as this means they have to respond and book a session within seven days, this gift certificate marketing ploy helps you to convert your enquiries into actual fee paying clients in the shortest space of time possible!

Incidentally you will also need a date stamp like those used in libraries to enter the return date of your books! This can then easily be set for a date nine days after the day you are sending their information pack out to them.

This allows two days for the package to arrive with them (this allows for second class post and saves you cash as the package will cost over 40p to send anyway!) and then it gives the person receiving it a clear seven days in which to respond and claim their £25 discount, thus paying only £250 for their session of CMT!

As you will of realised, each part of the initial package sent to them compliments each other, each item contains your contact number, so that if they lose one item they can still easily get in touch with you, and indeed each items concrete's in to their minds that the usual fee is £275 and therefore they will really believe that if they reply within seven days that they will make a genuine saving of £25, when in truth we only wanted £250 a session anyway!

Obviously you keep a dated record of every telephone request you get for more information, the reason for this being if for some reason they don't respond and book a session within seven days, then we would leave them alone for a further seven days to see if they call and book a session and if they don't then it is time for a phase two attack!

THE PHASE TWO MARKETING ATTACK!

When you have sent someone an information pack and they have failed to book a session within 14 days of receiving the package, then we would send them another sales information package, which this time contains:

01) A short "Introductory Letter"
02) A copy of the same Colour Brochure they got last time
03) A new Gift Certificate, this time worth £75-00 off their session!

The colour brochure they are sent is identical to the one they received last time, however the Introductory Letter and Gift Certificate are just ever so slightly different in their wording as follows:

THE 2nd INTRODUCTORY LETTER

Dear (here you insert their name)

A little over two weeks ago you contacted us expressing your interest in becoming a Confident, Happy, Healthy, relaxed non-smoker.......

Our records show that you were one of the first 40 lucky people to respond to our advertisement, and yet you have failed to take advantage of the discount "Gift Certificate" we sent you as a reward!

Those who did contact us and book a session during the past two weeks, have now seen their dreams come true and realised that something they once thought would be so difficult to achieve, has with our help, become so ridiculously easy!

We know that you are serious about becoming a non-smoker, and we are certainly serious about helping you to achieve this with ***E.A.S.E***

(**E**liminate the **A**ddiction to **S**moking for **E**ver)

Therefore we have selected you as one of only a handful of people to receive treatment at a dramatically ***DISCOUNTED PRICE!***

To this end, please find enclosed a "Gift Certificate" which is valid for the next seven days only entitling you to a massive £75-00 off the cost of becoming a non-smoker using Complete Mind Therapy!

This means that if you book your session within the next seven days you pay only £200 to become a confident, happy, healthy, relaxed non-smoker and you will still benefit from our unique lifetime guarantee.

Please listen to the tape we sent you two weeks ago, read the enclosed brochure and then call us on 07050-377579 to book your discounted session ***NOW!***

Yours truly,

JONATHAN ROYLE

THE 2nd STAGE GIFT CERTIFICATE

"GIFT CERTIFICATE"

Congratulations, as you were one of the first 40 people to respond to our original advertisement ***YOU HAVE BEEN SELECTED AS ONE OF OURLUCKY WINNER'S!***

To claim your ***£75-00 Prize**** simply book your session of Complete Mind Therapy to end your smoking habit within the next seven days and we will deduct £75-00 off the usual consultation and treatment fee of £275-00!

YOUR SESSION THEN COSTS ONLY £200!

This certificate is valid for seven days only until _______________ therefore you must book your session before this date to qualify for your ***£75-00 DISCOUNT***

TEL: 07050-377579 – TO BOOK YOUR SESSION TODAY!

****No Cash Alternative Can Be Claimed***
For this Certificate and it may not be used in conjunction with any other offers which may currently be available.

This should help convert a large percentage of the people who have not yet booked a session into fee-paying clients, but there are still two more avenues available should they not respond at this stage!

THE PHASE THREE MARKETING ATTACK!

Any people who do not reply to the phase two marketing attack are then added to your list of people to contact with the phase three approach!

The idea behind this being that we are about to offer them a session of Complete Mind Therapy to become a non-smoker for the once in a lifetime bargain price of only £75-00!

Treating them at just £75-00 a time can at this stage still prove highly profitable as we will not be offering them individual one to one therapy, but rather will be offering them the chance to participate in a group "Stop-Smoking" session.

To get them to part with their £75-00 they would be sent:

01) Another copy of the audiotape just in case they have lost the other!
02) A special Introductory Letter.
03) A copy of the Colour sales brochure.
04) A special £200 discount gift certificate!

The audiotape is identical to the one they were sent in the first place, but it is sent out just in case they have lost the other one.

The colour brochure is identical to the one they have now already received on two occasions.

However the Introductory letter and gift certificate are slightly different as follows:

THE PHASE THREE INTRODUCTORY LETTER!

Dear (insert their name here)
Some time ago you expressed an interest in becoming a confident, happy, healthy, relaxed non-smoker, but for some reason we have heard nothing more from you!!

CONGRATULATIONS
THIS IS YOUR LUCKY DAY

As some people have recently told us that getting together £275 to pay out in one lump sum can prove rather difficult, we have thought long and hard and come up with the perfect solution!

On the evening of Monday 25th November 2002, starting at 8pm prompt, we shall we holding a mass non-smoking clinic at The Rochdale Transport Club, Baron Street, Rochdale, Lancashire!

You will have the chance to become a non-smoker with ***E.A.S.E*** in the company of other people like yourself who want to change their life's for the better!

Seating for this Exclusive Event is Strictly Limited and is available only on a first come first served basis,

So contact us today on 07050-377579 and book your chance to become a non-smoker for just £75-00!*

Yours truly

JONATHAN ROYLE
*Our Unique Lifetime Guarantee does not apply to this mass stop-smoking event!

PHASE THREE GIFT CERTIFIACTE

"GIFT CERTIFICATE"

Congratulations, you were one of the first 40 people to respond to our original advertisement and therefore ***YOU ARE ONE OF OUR LUCKY WINNER'S!***

To claim your ***£200-00 Prize**** simply book your seat for our mass Complete Mind Therapy Treatment Event to end your smoking habit within the next seven days and we will deduct £200-00 off the usual consultation and treatment fee of £275-00!

YOUR SESSION THEN COSTS ONLY £75!*

This certificate is valid for our mass CMT treatment event on Monday 25th November 2002 at Rochdale Transport Club (Baron Street) and therefore you must book your seat for this event now to claim your ***£200-00 DISCOUNT***

TEL: 07050-377579 – TO BOOK YOUR PLACE TODAY!

***No Cash Alternative Can Be Claimed For this Certificate and it may not be used in conjunction with any other offers which may currently be available.**
****Our Unique Guarantee applies only to personal one to one sessions.**

As you will notice the original colour brochure is worded so that it states that our guarantee is only valid for personal one to one sessions and this point is also made on this "phase three" introductory letter and gift certificate!

This means we are covered legally in not giving such a guarantee on our mass group sessions, however by now the people receiving these packages will have seen our materials so often that they will assume the guarantee still applies, which of course works in our favours!

Obviously the date, time and location of the event will be altered on your materials depending on where you decide to hold it.

I like the function rooms in Working Men's Clubs as they already have a stage and a P.A. System which we can use and they also seat at least a 100 people or more, which gives you enough capacity to potentially earn £7500 in one night (100 by £75) or maybe even more!

Best of all these function rooms can usually be hired on a midweek basis for less than £50, which means you really can make maximum money for minimum investment.

At such an event, I would spend about 45 minutes demonstrating the power of Hypnosis and Complete Mind Therapy in an entertaining manner, using the techniques explained in my publications "Hypnotricks" and "The Professional Art of Stage Hypnosis, Hypnotherapy & Complete Mind Therapy!" both available from **www.hypnotorious.com**

We would then have a 20 minute Interval, during which people can get a drink from the bar and are told to ***SMOKE THEIR LAST EVER CIGARETTE!***

Then in the second half, I would start by demanding that everyone disposes of their cigarettes, lighters and other smoking materials into the containers placed at the front of the stage!

This both looks dramatic and psychologically brings them to a point where it will be easy to make them a non-smoker.

Everyone is them told to sit in their chairs, get comfortable and close their eyes and then we simply do a session of Complete Mind Therapy on the whole room at once.

Read my course and watch my video or DVD "Secrets of Professional Hypnotherapy" and all the scripts, techniques and information you will need to successfully pull off such a mass stop-smoking event will be revealed to you in great detail.

At the end of the evening, everyone who attends is given the same support pack (audio and leaflet) that they would of got if attending a personal one to one session.

And in the rare event that some names are left on your mailing list at this point who have not responded to phase 1,2, or 3 approaches then you could consider option 4 before removing their name from your lists!

PHASE FOUR MARKETING APPROACH!

At this stage you could simply write to them and offer to sell them a self-help stop-smoking tape, the same tape that we give people after our personal consultations.

Tell them that whilst this is obviously not as effective as a personal one to one consultation, that in around 75% of cases it will make people non-smokers with EASE and in most all other cases it will drastically help them to reduce the amount they smoke!

Offer them the tape at say just £29-95 inclusive of P+P and you should get a fair number of people ordering them, which will make you around £27 or more each order profit.

DETERMINATION MAKES THE BIG MONEY!

Read this book again and you will see that the key to our financial success is a combination of clever marketing ploys and sheer determination.

When these techniques are combined in a manner such as this book explains, then at some stage we should be able to convert most if not all of the enquiries we originally get into some kind of financial profit.

The technique's used to market our Smoking Cessation sessions can also quite easily with a little thought and a little research on the world wide web be adapted to advertise in a similar manner any other treatment sessions such as Weight-Loss, Confidence, Phobias etc!

THE BACK UP SUPPORT PACK

The back-up support pack given to them at the end of the session contains nothing more than a copy of our "Smoking Cessation Master" available from ***www.hypnotorious.com*** and a leaflet explaining that they should listen to side A (suggestion therapy session) of this tape every other day ***WITHOUT FAIL*** for the next 28 days to ensure that their new life as a non-smoker remains permanent!

They are also told that they should listen to side B (subliminal's hidden within the music) at least twice a week for the next four weeks.

It also explains that they can then listen to the tape at any time in the future when they may feel under stress to ensure that they never again return to the smoking habit!

And last but by no means least it points out two very important tips,

A A small glass of Pure Orange juice drunk whenever you would, in the past, normally have been desperate for a Cigarette gives a similar kind of "kick" to your body!

B Taking a few rapid deep breathes in and then out for a few seconds, sends a similar rush to our brains as smoking a Cigarette would have done for them in the past!

This back-up support pack is also what we sell people by mail order if we end up having to resort to the phase four marketing attack!

As you will notice the client has to 100% be committed top remaining a non-smoker as they are led to believe that their treatment will only be 100% successful and their guarantee will only be valid if they follow our instructions and the instructions in the back up pack 100% to the letter!

It is this back-up pack ploy which had enabled me to become so successful at Smoking Cessation as the tape listening helps keep them occupied for 28 days and by this time it will have become habit to be a non-smoker!

GAINING TV/RADIO/NEWSPAPER & MAGAZINE PUBLICITY!

The subject of obtaining ***FREE*** TV, Radio, Newspaper and magazine Publicity for your Hypnotic business is one, which I cover in depth on my personal one to one training, courses in Hypnosis.

However I touched on this subject very briefly earlier in this manual and so a few extra words of advice here would not go amiss.

Any press release that you send out should be clearly and neatly typed, double-spaced onto single sided white A4 paper, as this is the format that editors like to receive.

The point of the press release is to offer the editor something of benefit to him, so that he/she will then call you for further information and quite often end up wanting to interview you for their publication or TV/Radio show.

For example you could offer to make one of their journalists a non-smoker for FREE just so long as they publish details of the session and its success in their media, or you could tell them that if they interview you and print the interview, then you will give readers of their newspaper or magazine a massive £150 discount off the cost of a normal session.

Although this would mean you get only £125 per session, such an article would be easy to get printed as it offers their readers something for FREE and also saves their readers money!

From your point of view, it would dramatically kick start your business and give you money to use on future advertising in the manner as detailed in this book!

When you approach Local Publications and TV/Radio stations play on the angle that you are yourself a Local person who wants to help other local people to stop smoking using your NEW SKILLS of Complete Mind Therapy!

Push the fact that you are the only Complete Mind Therapist in your area and they will be even more interested to speak to you, especially if you send them a copy of the "Phase one" marketing pack with the press release and tell them that you will offer their readers, viewers or listeners an even bigger discount off your services!

YOUR 3 TO 5 YEAR SUCCESS PLAN!

Quite simply my advice here is to get Anthony Robbins excellent books "Unlimited Power" and "Awaken the Giant Within" and follow his advice to the letter.

Make out your list of goals and follow his advice and believe me they will become a reality.

And from a financial point of view, seek professional advice from a financial advisor and an accountant.

An accountant will advise you on the tax benefits of registering yourself as a Limited Company and don't forget to ask about the benefits of becoming an offshore Limited Company and legally not having to pay any taxes at all!

A financial advisor will, when you have an amount of a thousand pounds a week or more to invest, (which using this system you could quite easily active) will advise you of the best ways to invest it so that you could quite realistically become a true Millionaire within a 3 to 5 year period of following a structured marketing and business plan such as the example laid out in this manual!

YOUR OFFICE & RUNNING ON AUTO-PILOT

As you will only need an office a couple of days a week, as you will book all of your clients in on these days, it would be my advice to contact other local Hypnotherapists who already have a consulting room and see how much they will charge you to rent their office for just two or three days of the week.

Point out that as you will be so busy and only want to work three days a week maximum, that you will be able to refer an awful lot of clients their way for smoking cessation and that for each client they treat on your behalf you will give them either £175 (so you make £75 for the referrals from phase one) or £150 (so you make £50 for the referrals from phase two) and we are sure that many will jump at the chance!

Failing that, approach local hairdressers and beauty salons, as many of these will have a spare room upstairs which they will be happy to rent out to you for a small daily fee, in this case you also get to display a colour advertising poster in their window for your services and don't be to shocked if they tell all of their clients about your services resulting in more work!

DOCTORS AND PERSONAL REFERAL SYSTEMS

Each client that attends at our offices for a session of Complete Mind Therapy will of course be asked to complete the questionnaire, which makes my system of CMT so successful as explained in my course "The Professional Art of Stage-Hypnosis, Hypnotherapy & Complete Mind Therapy!"

However at this time we also ask them two other important questions,

1. Can you please tell me the name and address of your Doctor as legally I need it for our files?
2. Do you know a couple of people who would benefit from stopping smoking and if so what are their names and addresses?

When the client has left this information will prove itself to be invaluable marketing material as you will use it as follows:

1. You will send a letter to the personal attention of their Doctor, introducing yourself and informing them that you have just helped one of their patients by the name of (here insert the persons name & address) to become a confident, happy, healthy, relaxed non-smoker

with EASE and that you would be happy to do the same for any of their other patients if they would like to refer them to you for treatment. Include a copy of the tape and colour brochure and a note informing the Doctor that if he contacts you, then you will be happy to send him some more audiotapes and brochures which he can then pass on to the patients he has who smoke! This technique alone can over a short period of time build you up a network of Doctors referring their patients to you for treatment!

2. To the clients friends/family details of which they have given you is sent a "personalised" letter telling them that their friend (or son, work colleague etc) by the name of (insert name & address) has just become a non-smoker using your services and mentioned that they may be interested also. Again these people are sent a tape and brochure, but also they are sent the phase one gift certificate, and trust me many will speak to their friend after receiving it and then their friend acts as an unpaid salesperson convincing them to book a session with you!

This technique also means that your clients know that other people will know that they have given up smoking and this adds the very powerful element of peer group pressure and expectancy in ensuring that they remain a non-smoker as they will not want to look like a failure in the eyes of their Doctor, Friends & Family!

You can also cheekily give half a dozen of your business cards to people after their sessions and ask them to give them out to anyone they meet who is a smoker who says they want to stop!

Believe it or not, feeling so good about having become a non-smoker with EASE, these people WILL become your unpaid salesmen and in time, this kind of word of mouth advertising will bring you more clients than from any other source!

OTHER CHEAP ADVERTISING PLOYS

In Publications that are very expensive to place large display adverts, such as National Magazines, I find that a simple classified advert such as the example which follows, can also get the phone ringing with enquiries from people who are then sent the phase one marketing package!

"STOP SMOKING in one Hour and Eliminate the Addiction to Smoking Forever! For your FREE tape and information pack call 07050-377579 today!"

The first two words "Stop Smoking" being printed in Bold Capitals and the rest of the advert as it appears above, this is only 23 words in length and can affordably be placed in many high readership magazines such as Cosmopolitan and similar publications!

Having A5 size colour landscape format adverts (same as press adverts) printed onto bright Day-Glo paper is also a cheap and effective advertising ploy!

For as little as 50p to a £1 a week you can have these prominently displayed in the windows of all the local newsagents and my use of this technique has shown me that the return on investment is well worth while!

After all even if it costs £1-00 a week, that is only £4-00 for the month, this means that for £240 we could have these bright A5 Day-Glo advertisements displayed in the windows of ***SIXTY*** different local newsagents for a full one month period.

As you know newsagents sell Cigarettes as part of their business and so loads of people will enter their shop over the month that the advert is displayed that are potential customers and my experience has shown me that this will result in many phonecalls, which you respond to in the manner already explained in this manual.

Lets face it you only need one enquiry to convert into a paying client in this example for you to have broken even and then after that it is pure profit!

Placing a folded up copy of this A5 advertisement into all of the books at your local library which relate to the subject of giving up smoking can also lead to many paying clients, just make sure they don't see you sticking the leaflets inside the books, otherwise they will take them out again.

Well that's just about it on the subject of setting up a successful smoking cessation clinic, well that's it for this manual, its certainly enough to set you on the right path for financial success.

Should you wish to learn even more though, then I would suggest that you visit ***www.hypnotorious.com*** and consider investing into my other training products, many of which also contain further information on marketing and promoting your Hypnotic business.

Best of all book a personal one to one training course with me and I will reveal of other low cost and effective marketing and promotion techniques.

For now I wish you the best of luck in all that you do and please do enjoy the pages which follow, which explain a simple easy way to make lots of money from the lucrative area of "Stress Management!"

Incidentally I would appreciate hearing your comments and reviews on this book and to this end you can send them to ***hypno@hypnotorious.com***

Yours Hypnotically

Dr. Jonathan Royle – BSc (Hon)

Oh and one last invaluable piece of advice on Marketing your business, Leaflets, yes that's right Leaflets pushed through peoples letterboxes.

If you shop around you can get double sided full colour A5 Leaflets printed in bulk so that they cost next to nothing and then by consulting your local Telephone directory find a company to deliver the leaflets for you.

One colleague of mine has 5,000 yes you read that correctly 5,000 leaflets delivered each week to houses within easy travelling distance of his office.

Even if he only got a 1% response rate that would be 50 telephone calls.

And even if only 10% of those people that called up and got the information packed end up booking a session at £250, that would still be an income of £1250, which is many times what it has cost to print the leaflets and have them delivered.

Believe me my colleague has 5,000 Leaflets delivered each and every week to different areas and his response rate is far higher than the modest examples I have given here!

The Key Secret here is that to make big money from Hypnotherapy people must know you exist and must come to the logical conclusion that you're the best in the area and that's where Advertising, Marketing and Publicity come in.

A final idea regarding Group Hypnotherapy Sessions is to involve a Local Charity as this almost guarantees you Local Newspaper Editorial at no cost and also means that the people running the Charity will sell the tickets for the event.

Indeed they will book the venue, advertise the event and sell the tickets, you just show up and do your stuff on the day and take 50% of the door take with the other 50% going to the Charity.

Re-Read this chapter several times and you will realise that its contents are worth a fortune and with a little thought can be adapted to promote whatever specialist area of therapy you decide to concentrate on.

CHAPTER TWENTY–FOUR

WHY A FAKE HYPNOSIS SHOW??

You may be asking yourself why would anyone want to present a fake hypnosis show? Well the answer is simple really when you consider that every time you are engaged to perform a genuine Stage-Hypnotism show you must obtain permission from the local Council licensing authority for the show to go ahead.

Also consider the fact that to be granted this permission to perform a genuine Stage-Hypnotism show you must have Public Liability Insurance which covers you for the people being placed into trance and it is now very difficult to obtain such insurance and the reasons for performing a fake Hypnotism show become even more apparent.

However if we were to present a show called **"MINDGAMES"** Upon the advertising posters for which it said **"All the fun of a Hypnosis show with NO Hypnosis!"** and stated that you the performer are an **"IMAGINATIONIST"** and/or **"MIND MAGICIAN"** as opposed to a Stage Hypnotist then the question of it being a Hypnotism show would never enter into the equation.

Therefore as you are not advertised as a Hypnotist and are apparently not going to be Hypnotising anybody there is no need to ever apply for permission from the Council for your shows to go ahead.

This means that as you have not needed to apply for permission you are in no way restricted by the 1952 Hypnotism Act which is detailed elsewhere.

In other words just so long that you are never advertised as being a Hypnotist and you never claim to have Hypnotised anybody who volunteers during the show then you are legally allowed to perform such stunts as Catalepsy which would not be allowed under normal circumstances when working as a Hypnotist with permission from the local Council.

From a legal point of view, to cover yourself further I would also have printed upon the posters in very small print (near the bottom where it is almost unnoticeable) the following statement:

"Volunteers who must be aged 18 or over may leave the stage at any time of their own free will during this demonstration which is presented for Scientific & Research purposes only!"

Read the **GENUINE HYPNOTISM LESSONS** elsewhere in this book and you will realise that the above statement is made up of two separate statements linked together.

The first statement of: "Volunteers who must be aged 18 or over may leave the stage at any time of there own free will" is what you would be required by law to have printed on your posters if you were a genuine Hypnotist and were obtaining permission from the local Council.

The second statement of: "During this demonstration, which is presented for Scientific & Research purposes only!" means that you are stating that your performance is a demonstration and not a show! Also it states that you are presenting it for Scientific and Research purposes only.

This means that you are now exploiting the loophole which can be found in section five of the 1952 Hypnotism Act, namely that you do not need any form of permission or license to perform a genuine Stage-Hypnotism show if presenting it for Scientific and/or Research purposes.

As I understand it the dictionary definition of Research is collecting data, therefore if you get all the people who volunteer and participate in your show to fill in a questionnaire at the end of your performance then you are collecting data!

And as I understand it if you are collecting data such as this, with the intention that you will at a later date publish your findings, then you can legally claim to be doing research and as such are legally covered doing a genuine Stage-Hypnotism show even without obtaining permission from the council.

Therefore presenting a fake Hypnotism show, using no genuine Hypnosis in the manner explained should present no legal problems whatsoever!

After your show is finished and before everyone leaves the venue, have all the participants complete a questionnaire asking them such things as:

1. Their Name, Address and Contact Details?
2. Have they ever been hypnotised before?
3. If so was it at a Stage Show, in therapy or both?
4. What was the experience of hypnotising themselves in front of an audience like?
5. Did they find it easy to hypnotise themselves?
6. Would they be prepared to hypnotise themselves again in the future?
7. Would you please confirm that you were fully aware of everything going on around you at all times whilst in a state of self-hypnosis?
8. Finally would you please confirm that you volunteered to participate in this evenings demonstration of the powers of self-hypnosis and as such all sensations/feelings and results of self-hypnosis which you experience are your own doing and own full responsibility?
9. Now please sign and date the form here as confirmation that your answers are true & correct and also to confirm that the performer has given you a FREE "Learn Self-Hypnosis" Audio Tape in exchange for your participation in tonight's demonstration:________________

When placed together to make the statement which is printed at the bottom of your posters in very small wording (almost too small to be noticeable) of:

"Volunteers who must be aged 18 or over may leave the stage at any time of their own free will during this demonstration which is presented for Scientific & Research purposes only!"

YOU WILL THEN BE COVERED LEGALLY IF YOU PROCEED AS I NOW ADVISE!!

The other loophole which we shall be exploiting from the 1952 Hypnotism Act is the fact that it states that it does not in any manner prohibit the use of self-hypnosis.

This also means that it does not prohibit the teaching of self-hypnosis and as such instead of hypnotising people as a genuine Stage Hypnotist would do, we instead just teach people how to hypnotise themselves.

These people are **ALL VOLUNTEERS** and are all **OVER AGE OF 18** (age of consent) and as such the moment they volunteer and agree to be taught self-hypnosis with the aim of becoming the stars of this evenings demonstration you are covered legally.

The questionnaire as worded earlier also protects you against any future legal repercussions as upon it they have given their name, contact details and by signing and dating the form at the end have agreed to all the answers they have given to the questions which as such makes this a legally binding document, as it could be argued in a court of law that if they later denied or contradicted what they had signed to then **THEY MUST HAVE MADE A FRAUDULENT STATEMENT** which would take the legal responsibility away from you instantly.

Read the questionnaire questions very carefully and you will see that they are worded in such a manner their answers prove in writing that you **DID NOT HYPNOTISE THEM!**

They are also worded in such a manner that their answers also prove beyond reasonable doubt that **THEY DID INDEED HYPNOTISE THEMSELVES!**

And best of all question eight is worded in such a manner that once they have signed the form, which of course you retain in your files: **THEY HAVE THEN AGREED IN WRITING THAT ANY SIDE EFFECTS (results) AND/OR CONSEQUENCES (results) WHICH THEY MAY LATER CLAIM ARE THEIR OWN DOING & RESPONSIBILTY!!**

This alone means that they can never make a claim against you for compensation claiming to have been affected by taking part in the show and being hypnotised as you have never hypnotised them, they did it themselves! Also they have signed and thereby legally agreed to take full responsibility for any results caused by the self-hypnosis.

Logically this means that, as they can never claim to have been hypnotised and have agreed to take full responsibility for any results (consequences) then you do not need Public Liability Insurance which covers people whilst they are Hypnotised which is the type of insurance which is now either very expensive and/or almost impossible to obtain!

You would however be foolhardy to perform without any Insurance at all as the unforeseen does occasionally occur. But if you proceed as I have advised then the only Public Liability Insurance cover which you need is that which covers incidents such as people breaking their leg, falling off the stage or a speaker falling on them and suchlike!

This kind of Public Liability Insurance cover is automatically included in your yearly subscription as an Equity member. For more details of the Showbiz trade union Equity and how to gain membership with the greatest of ease please see the **GENUINE HYPNOSIS LESSONS** elsewhere in this Book.

Ultimately though this means that you will as an Equity member have Public Liability Insurance Cover to the tune of Five Million Pounds for a yearly subscription fee as little at the time of writing as £60-00 per annum.

And most importantly as doing things as explained in the eyes of the law **YOU WILL NOT BE HYPNOTISING ANYONE** then this Equity Insurance will cover you for anything that the volunteers and/or audience could legally make a compensation claim for!

It will also look good on your publicity materials when it states that you have Five Million Pounds of Public Liability Insurance and as a professional entertainer are a member of Equity.

Performing shows in the devious (but legal) manner that I am explaining will also mean that you never need to join any so called Professional Body for Hypnotists as when all said and done you will never be advertising yourself as a Hypnotist or ever claiming to Hypnotise anyone.

You can legally cover yourself even more by having a statement (disclaimer) such as the example that follows recorded as a voice over on the music which is played before you are introduced and brought on stage:

"Ladies & Gentlemen, welcome to MINDGAMES the show they tried to ban. In a few moments time we shall be introducing your host for this evening, Outrageous Mind Magician Jonathan Royle."

"During this evenings show we shall be asking for volunteers who are willing to be taught self-hypnosis and then place themselves into a relaxed state using their new skills in self-hypnosis"

"All participants must be volunteers over the age of 18 as you will be required to take full responsibility for your own Physical and Psychological wellbeing before, during and after this evenings show!"

"No one will be expected to remove any article of clothing or do anything which they do not wish to do, as together we can enjoy all the fun of a Hypnotism show without your host ever hypnotising anyone!"

"So please put your hands together and welcome live on stage, Britain's Most Outrageous Mind Magician, The Amazing Jonathan Royle!"

This disclaimer which also serves as your Introduction at the start of your show is as I am sure you have noticed worded to clarify several things:

1. They will be VOLUNTEERS.
2. They must be over age of 18.
3. You will not be hypnotising anyone, rather you will only be teaching him or her self-hypnosis.
4. The Volunteers will all be hypnotising themselves.
5. They must all take responsibility for both their Physical and Mental wellbeing before, during and after this evenings show!

This means that if they volunteer they are doing so in full knowledge that they have agreed by volunteering to take full responsibility for themselves both Mentally & Physically before, during and after the show!

This means that as they have accepted responsibility by volunteering they can not later blame you for anything which they may claim occurs and as such cannot make any form of compensation claim against you.

This fact of course is concreted further when they sign the questionnaire at the end of the show, which you keep and file as your later proof (if ever called for) that they now have no Legal basis for any form of compensation claim against you.

Another thing I do is to have a small portable mini-disc recorder with me at all shows which is wired into my P.A System so that it records everything that is said during the show when it is said through the Radio Microphone which I am using.

I start this recording a few seconds before I start the opening music (with voice over) to my show and let it continue for the first half (one hour duration) of my show.

As the mini discs are not long enough to record the entire show during the interval I change the disc for a new one in order that just as with the first half, after the interval I can record the entire second hour of my performance from start to finish!

This means that I have recorded proof that before my show everyone heard the voice over disclaimer and that everyone who volunteered was a volunteer!

It also means that my opening patter to the audience has been recorded which also serves as another disclaimer and within which would say something such as:

"Well good evening ladies and gentlemen my name is Jonathan Royle and I am both a Mind Magician and also your host for this evenings show!"

"Nobody here this evening will ever be hypnotised, well at least not in a conventional sense. In otherwords I shall not be hypnotising anybody here this evening who volunteers to take part in this evenings show!"

"Instead I will be teaching all the volunteers who must be over the age of 18 how to hypnotise themselves!"

"Yes that's right ladies and gentlemen tonight we are going to enjoy all the fun and laughter of a Comedy Stage Hypnotism show but I will not be hypnotising anyone instead I will teach you how to hypnotise yourself."

"Because of this all volunteers will be expected to take full responsibility for their own Mental & Physical safety & wellbeing at all times!"

"After the show all those who volunteer will be given a valuable **FREE GIFT** *(This acts as an incentive for people to volunteer and take part in the show!)* And will be required to complete a short questionnaire about their experiences during tonight's show!"

"So in short if you volunteer and come up here on stage of your own free will then you are agreeing to this and also agreeing to let me teach you self-hypnosis so that you may place yourself into a lovely relaxed state of mind and body where your imagination is enhanced and your inhibitions reduced."

"Every person in this room here tonight is capable of hypnotising themselves but only if they sincerely want to."

"As such I am looking for volunteers tonight who want to learn self-hypnosis, who are then willing to hypnotise themselves and as a result be one of the stars of this evenings show!"

"So if you have good powers of Intelligence, Imagination and Concentration, are over the age of 18, want to volunteer to learn self-hypnosis and have the Genuine, Sincere and Honest intention of taking part in this evenings comedy show them please make your way towards the stage area now!"

AT THIS POINT GET YOUR VOLUNTEERS UP!

When your volunteers have come up to the stage you must then proceed with your suggestibility test **(see genuine hypnotism course)** making sure that you say something such as:

"Before we continue as our time together tonight is limited I need to find out which of you wonderful volunteers have the best powers of Intelligence, Imagination & Concentration!"

"I also need to work out which of you will be able to learn how to hypnotise yourself the quickest and that's why we are about to do a suggestibility exercise"

"This is not Hypnosis, but it will tell me which of you will be the most co-operative and responsive people to take part in this evenings show!"

HERE YOU DO YOUR SUGGESTIBILTY TEST

Consult the Genuine Hypnotism Course section of this Book and all will be explained regards suggestibility tests and how to decide which subjects to send back to the audience and which to leave on stage for the next part which of course is the hypnotic induction.

YOU DO NOT HYPNOTISE THEM

At this point you would do a normal induction (as explained in genuine hypnotism course section however to cover yourself legally you must make it appear as if the people are hypnotising themselves.

Therefore your patter should always be worded very carefully and along the lines of:

"Just **ALLOW YOURSELF** to let your mind & body relax"

"As I tap you on the back just let it serve as a sign and a signal for you to **ALLOW YOURSELF** to relax completely."

"You are doing a wonderful job of hypnotising yourself, so on the count of three if you decide to **HYPNOTISE YOURSELF** completely and as such **ALLOW YOURSELF** to enter a lovely relaxing hypnotic trance then and only then on the count of three you will fall gently backwards into my arms!"

These few examples of wording for patter should when read in conjunction with the genuine hypnotism course elsewhere in this book enable you to understand how to word all your Induction patter so that it is perceived that **THE VOLUNTEERS ARE HYPNOTISING THEMSELVES.**

This also applies to the patter you use for the deepening of your induction. Again it must be worded in such a manner that it is perceived that the volunteers are hypnotising themselves and allowing themselves to go deeper into trance.

THE POST HYPNOTIC MUST BE ON THEIR TERMS

Once you have them all in a state of hypnosis which everyone perceives to be self-hypnosis then you need to give them the post hypnotic that they will react to your requests during the show in such a manner that it can still be argued that they have hypnotised themselves and as such I suggest something such as:

"For the rest of this evening, just so long as you want to remain in a state of self-hypnosis you will find that you are able to do so with ease."

"You will find that just so long as you want to deepen your level of relaxation and self-hypnosis that every breath you take, every noise you hear, every thought you think and every word I say will merely serve as a sign and a signal enabling you to remain in a state of self-hypnosis and indeed to deepen this state of self-hypnosis further with each second that passes by!"

"For the rest of this evening whilst in this building only those of you in a state of self-hypnosis will find that whilst you allow me to give you signals of what to do, then you will do them as an automatic reflex action."

"In otherwords whenever I say SLEEP as quickly as a snap of the fingers you will ALLOW YOURSELF to reenter a deep state of self-hypnosis, deeper than that you have already placed yourself in."

"Your eyes will instantly close, your heavy head will instantly fall forward onto your chest and you will instantly ALLOW YOURSELF to re-enter the lovely state of self-hypnosis that you have now PLACED YOURSELF into!"

"However whenever I say WIDE AWAKE then and only then you will ALLOW YOURSELF to wake up, open your eyes and will find that just so long as you want to stay in a state of SELF-HYPNOSIS that you will ALLOW YOURSELF to have an overwhelming desire to do almost everything that I say!"

"Keeping your eyes closed at all times I am now talking to each and every person on stage in a state of SELF HYPNOSIS, if you are all prepared to continue as requested with this evenings show then please just nod your head!"

YOU CAN NOW CONTINUE AS PER A NORMAL SHOW

You would now continue as if doing a normal genuine stage hypnotism show as explained elsewhere on this CD-ROM, however when giving suggestions for each of the comedy routines make sure you follow my example which follows:

"In a few moments when I tell you to AWAKEN YOURSELF then and only then you will awaken and ALLOW YOURSELF to come to the realisation that XYZ!"

This again makes it clear that the person has hypnotised themselves, is allowing themselves of their own free will to do everything and that you are merely giving them ideas of what to do whilst in a state of SELF-HYPNOSIS!

Incidentally for those who hadn't already guessed in the previous example you just substitute XYZ with whatever comedy routine suggestion you want them to act out.

From this point on just so long as your patter at all times is consistent with the idea and fact that the people have hypnotised themselves, are allowing themselves to remain in trance and are doing the things suggested of their own free will whilst in a state of self-hypnosis then you will still be covered legally. It is then just a case of waking them from trance in a manner where they appear to have done this themselves:

IT'S NOW TIME TO WAKE THEM UP!

Obviously the manner in which they are awoken from trance must make it appear that they are awakening themselves from trance and therefore have been at all times in a state of self-hypnosis, and as in truth all hypnosis is self-hypnosis this is not at all difficult to achieve.

My example awakening patter is as follows:

"In a few moments time I shall be ending this evenings show, so it is now time for me to teach you how to AWAKEN YOURSELF fully from SELF-HYPNOSIS!"

"If you do as I say as I'm sure you will, then you will find on the count of 3 that you will be able to instantly AWAKEN YOURSELF from this lovely state of SELF-HYPNOSIS!"

"On 1, realising now that everything you have suggested TO YOURSELF this evening will instantly be cancelled out the very moment that you leave this room, in otherwords the moment you leave this room it is as though you never suggested it TO YOURSELF in the first place, and it will never again affect you or make you react in the manner you have ALLOWED YOURSELF to react and be affected tonight!"

"On 2, realising now as 100% Total Reality that just as you have successfully ALLOWED YOURSELF to HYPNOTISE YOURSELF so in turn you can ALLOW YOURSELF to awaken in a few moments time feeling wonderful, refreshed and in fact feeling better than when you came on stage at the start of the show. And just as you were able to HYPNOTISE YOURSELF successfully so you will in turn ALLOW YOURSELF to awaken feeling no headaches, sickness or any other side affects in any way shape or form, in fact you will feel better and more relaxed than you have in years and will discover that if at any time in the future you want to HYPNOTISE YOURSELF again in a safe environment, then you will merely need to close your eyes and count backwards from 10 down to one, and then whenever you want to awaken yourself you merely need to count from 1 to 3 in your minds eye and you will instantly awaken!"

And on 3, that's it everybody its time to WAKE YOURSELVES UP, so wakey, wakey rise and shine!

AT THIS POINT YOU DO YOUR END PATTER

Everybody will now be awake, should anyone not wake up instantly do as outlined in the genuine hypnotism course on this CD-ROM but do it off microphone so that non of the audience hear and so that it is not recorded onto your mini-disc player which has been recording the whole show as earlier mentioned.

All that remains is to plug the sale of your **SELF-HYPNOSIS** tapes which you have on sale for Smoking, Weight-Loss, Confidence, Phobias etc and then to say goodnight!

DO YOU SEE WHAT WE HAVE DONE?

Effectively by proceeding as just explained we would have been able to legally perform a **GENUINE STAGE HYPNOTISM** show without ever needing to apply and/or obtain permission for the show from the Local Council.

Furthermore events have been structured in such a manner that there is no way that any of the volunteers could have a legal claim for compensation based on side effects etc from being hypnotised as amongst other safeguards they have signed a form taking all responsibility for themselves at all times before, during and after the show.

And of course to add the icing to the cake we are insured for incidents such as speakers falling onto the audience member's head by the Public Liability Insurance, which as Equity members we automatically get to the tune of Five Million Pounds cover!

The only potential bad point in this whole example is the unfortunate (but yet still possible) event of one of the volunteers on stage breaking their leg by falling off the stage or some similar type of accident occurring.

The Public Liability Insurance Policy for Equity Members states quite clearly that it does not in any circumstance cover you for any form of accident, which may occur directly involving any of your on stage volunteers who are in any form of hypnotic state at the time!

This of course would also include Self-Hypnosis, therefore it is essential that we find some other legal loophole to cover us, just in case such an unfortunate & unlikely incident occurs.

A statement such as the example which follows printed on the bottom of all your advertising Posters, Flyers and Newspaper adverts for the show should, I believe remove the legal responsibility for anything that happens from you and instead place it on the volunteers themselves for actually volunteering in the first place:

"Volunteers who must be aged 18 or over must take full responsibility for their own Physical, Mental & Emotional wellbeing (before, during & after participating) and may leave the stage at any time of their own free will during this performance which is presented for Scientific & Research purposes only!"

Using this statement printed upon all advertising materials for the show it could then be argued that all those who volunteer were or should reasonably have been aware before volunteering that all responsibility for their Physical, Mental & Emotional wellbeing before, during and after the show remains with them at all times!

Combine this with being able to produce in court a mini disc recording of your show proving beyond doubt that your voice over intro and your opening patter also made it quite clear that all the volunteers must and will be at all times responsible for their own Physical, Mental & Emotional wellbeing and in short I do not see that anyone would have a legal leg to stand on in attempting to ever make a compensation claim against you for anything that happens to them before, during or after the period of time within which they are hypnotised.

That statement, when printed on a poster for example may seem off-putting & negative to potential volunteers but take a look at it again:

"Volunteers who must be aged 18 or over must take full responsibility for their own Physical, Mental & Emotional wellbeing (before, during & after participating) and may leave the stage at any time of their own free will during this performance which is presented for Scientific & Research purposes only!"

Remembering that this is an A4 size page presented to you in Portrait style, all three of these examples would be even less prominent if printed across the bottom of an A3 Poster, which was printed for display in Landscape style.

In fact with this text printed in a less prominent colour than the shows name **"MINDGAMES"** which would be very visible across the top and the fact that 99% of people will then be drawn to the large photograph of you which the Poster bears in its centre and finally to the details of where & when the show is, I can confidently say that well over 90% of people will not even bother reading the disclaimer even though it is still visible enough for all to see.

And as ignorance is no defence in the law it should be true to say that a statement such as this printed upon the posters when combined with the mini disc recorded proof of your voice over intro, your opening patter and the very real fact that you clearly ask the volunteers "Do you wish to remain on stage and take part in this evenings show?" will cover you Legally against the threat of any potential compensation claims.

Also as the mini disc also provides recorded proof that you have told the people who volunteered how to remove all suggestions that either you have given them or as in this example, they have given themselves, then there should never be any basis for a negligence claim.

Therefore when you combine your defences of:

1. The statement printed on all Posters, Adverts & Advertising materials.
2. Your mini disc proof of the voice over introductory disclaimer.
3. Your mini disc proof of your opening patter disclaimer.
4. The mini disc proof that you asked all volunteers if they wanted to remain on stage and take part in the show.
5. Your mini disc proof that all suggestions were correctly removed and cancelled from the volunteers minds.
6. Your mini disc proof that all volunteers were correctly awoken from trance.
7. The signed questionnaire from each of the volunteers which on top of all the other things gives you signed proof from each of the volunteers that they have agreed to take full responsibility for their own Psychical, Mental & Emotional wellbeing before, during and after the show.

All these seven above points when combined provide you with what I personally feel confident is Cast Iron protection against anyone who takes part in your show ever successfully making any form of compensation, negligence or other Legal claim against you.

This only leaves the audience members who do not volunteer to take part in the show and therefore are not in anyway in any form of hypnotic trance and as such are covered by the Public Liability Insurance Policy and Five Million Pounds cover which as an Equity member we automatically get.

THE PRIVATE MEMBERS CLUB PLOY.

As I have previously mentioned the 1952 Hypnotism Act and updates to it do not in any way prohibit the performance of stage Hypnotism shows in Private Members Clubs.

This means that in Working Men's Clubs, Masonic Lodges and the like you need never seek permission from the council to perform anyway & certainly not if you carry out your show in the manner I have just suggested.

This however also gives us another very useful loophole, which we can use to our advantage in several ways as follows:

1. We could set up our own fan club and as there would be a yearly membership fee to join this fan club it would indeed legally be a Private Members Club! A simple website set up and placed on the World Wide Web with details of how to join and rules of membership would act as sufficient proof that such a fan club existed. And of course this website may lead to valuable extra income as many people may actually join the fanclub!
2. We could set the fan club up as a Limited Company and from the moment of the company being set up you would only accept bookings which have been arranged through your fanclub. This as your accountant would advise you offers you several useful Tax Saving Ploys & Methods which could potentially save you thousands of pounds each year.
3. The Fanclub would then get all requests for you to perform and would then supply a contract to the venue stating that the venue has booked you to perform through the "Jonathan Royle Fanclub!" and as such all Legal Responsibility on all levels then falls to the Fanclub as a Limited Company and not you as an individual.
4. The Fanclub then of course issues you the performer with a contract for the show, however this may be for a fee less than that which the Fanclub Limited Company is actually charging the venue which is where the

Legal Tax Avoidance methods come into play which any good accountant would be able to advise you about. This contract from the Fanclub to you as an individual would of course be worded in such a way that the fanclub takes all Legal Responsibility for your actions and what happens before, during and after the show.

5. I gather this would then mean that anyone attempting to take a Legal case against you following the show would have to try and instigate Legal proceedings against the Fanclub which is a Limited Company and not against you as an individual, this means that even in the worst case scenario, the worst that could ever happen is that The Fanclub Limited Company loses a case and perhaps as a result becomes bankrupt and closes down. You however as an individual would never at any time be at risk of this happening to you as all Legal cases would have to be brought against the Limited Company due to the manner in which you have been booked for the show.
6. However present and market your shows in the manner I have already suggested and explained and as a result it should never be possible for anyone to instigate a Legal case against you for harmed caused by Hypnotism anyway!
7. As well as selling Yearly memberships to the "Jonathan Royle Fanclub!" you can also Legally sell one night memberships at a reduced price. This means you could advertise your show in its normal fashion and in very small print state **"This show may be attended by members of the Jonathan Royle Fanclub only!".**
8. With point seven in mind the show is advertised at say £5-00 per ticket and next to where the price is printed is a small * or other symbol. Elsewhere on the poster is this small * again and next to it the statement as follows:

    *The Fee of £5-00 covers your one night membership to the Jonathan Royle fanclub.

    This then means that people are not buying tickets to see the show but are buying one night memberships to the Jonathan Royle Fanclub and as members of the fanclub will be admitted Free to this show, once they have bought their one night membership they too will be admitted to the show.
9. This means that in the eyes of the Law your show is a Private Function organised only for members of The Jonathan Royle (your name here) Fanclub and that only people who have paid for membership to this **PRIVATE MEMBERS CLUB** will be allowed into the show.
10. As the public are not sold tickets, but rather one night memberships to the Fanclub stating that it admits them to the show free during their membership period, namely that night in question only, this one night membership pass (show ticket) makes it Legally a Private Function for members of a private members club only!

11. As Legally it's now a show for a private members club you need never apply for permission from the Local Council for the shows to take place.
12. Also as the one night membership passes (show ticket) and posters could both say in small print the following statement: "Members are admitted subject to fanclub rules & agree to abide by such as listed on ***www. Hypnotorious.com*** or available from P.O. Box 12, Huddersfield" This statement in very small print on all advertising and on the one night memberships (show ticket) makes it clear that they will be subject to club rules and also provides them with a place, namely the club website from which to obtain a full list of rules which by buying the one night membership and entering the venue they are agreeing to abide by!"
13. This is where the most devious bit of all comes into play and that is what the club rules state on the website and also on any rule sheets which on the odd occasion may be requested via the postal service and which to cover yourself 100% Legally you would be obliged to send out.
14. As stated in the Genuine Hypnotism course elsewhere in this book your show should be advertised at the venue etc at least 14 days prior to the performance date in order that your advertising has time to have the correct Psychological effect on those attending of making them as susceptible as possible to taking part and being co-operative.
15. This period of two weeks would also be seen in Law as being a long enough period for anyone to find out what the Fanclub Rules are before buying a one night membership (show ticket) and attending which in itself is their Legal acceptance of the Fanclub rules & conditions of membership.
16. Therefore on the website where it states the rules it can be made quite clear that anyone who attends and/or volunteers agrees by virtue of their membership of the fanclub to never take any form of Legal Action against the performer. It would of course also state that anyone attending a show agrees never to take any form of Legal action against the fanclub itself.

All these 16 points combined mean that:

A You may just generate some extra income from the website from selling Fanclub merchandise & from people who may actually wish to purchase a yearly membership which of course would have to be sold at an extortionate cost as it would entitle them to get into your shows for free. Or with a little thought the rules could limit the number of shows they can enter for Free each year.

B The Potential tax and Legal protection benefits of the fanclub being a limited Company, accepting all your bookings and then employing you the individual to do the show could be great.

C As all attendees at the shows you do would Legally be required to observe the fan club rules you are by nature of the wording of those rules protected against any potential Legal claim from both Volunteers and audience members and therefore in theory don't even need any form of Public Liability Insurance cover! However in reality some venues will not book you or let you hire the premises without this and that's where the Insurance we get as Equity members comes into play!

THE FINAL DISCLAIMER

Although we shall not be presenting our show in a manner requiring us to obtain permission from the Local Council it would still be wise to adhere as closely as possible to the 1952 Hypnotism Act & later updates on this as explained elsewhere in this Book.

For example there is one further disclaimer or warning which you must use during your opening patter and/or voice over intro to the show and that is as follows:

"Basically speaking everybody in this room tonight can be hypnotised, can hypnotise themselves and can learn the art of self-hypnosis in the matter of a few short minutes!"

"Having said this there are several groups of people who for various reasons should not volunteer this evening and these are as follows "

"Firstly anyone who is thinking to themselves I do not want to hypnotise myself or is thinking that this is just not possible, please do not get up when I ask for volunteers as in truth our time together tonight is limited and I'm only looking for people who are prepared to come up here with an open mind, with the idea of letting themselves go, relaxing and giving it a try!"

"Secondly anyone who is drunk as a skunk, and by drunk I mean very drunk should not volunteer as I have always found that Drunk people already think they are hypnotised!"

"Thirdly if you are Asthmatic, Epileptic, Clinically Depressed, suffer from any serious Heart condition or medical complaint then we would advise you not to volunteer this evening. And if there are any Schizophrenics in then you can all F**K Off to one of Paul McKenna's shows!"

"And finally if there are any Pregnant Females in please don't volunteer as jumping around the stage like Madonna may not be the wisest thing for your baby, however if there are any ladies in who are not pregnant but would like to be then see me after the show and I am sure together we can sort that out!"

"So in short I want volunteers who are open minded, have good powers of Intelligence, Imagination & Concentration and above all have an excellent sense of humour and the desire to perhaps become the star of this evenings show."

"So if you want to be Hypnotised, Mesmerised, Pasteurised, Sterilised, Circum (pause) Stances being what they are please make your way to the stage now!"

GETTING THE QUESTIONAIRRE SIGNED

At the end of your show all of the volunteers are told how to awaken themselves from trance and after doing so are sent back to the audience.

Before sending them back I usually suggest that although everything has now been cancelled out of their mind and will never affect them in this manner again once they have left the performance venue, that until they leave they will still react to the bits of music in the same manner that they did earlier in the show.

I also tell them all that when they hear me say "GOODNIGHT", the very moment they hear me say "GOODNIGHT", that very second they will jump up onto their chair and shout out:

"Jonathan Royle is the greatest Mind Magician of them all Hallelujah!"

And then they will sit down and wonder what the hell they have been doing and why they have been doing it.

This means that when everyone is awoken from trance you can send them back to the audience and have a little fun with them there.

By playing some snippets of the music already used earlier in the show the volunteers will react as they did earlier but this time do the funny things where they are in the audience.

Then after a few minutes of this you can start your end of show patter for example as follows:

"Well Ladies & Gentlemen as you have probably already guessed with Self-Hypnosis almost anything can happen."

"All that happens when you are in a state of self-hypnosis is that the imagination is enhanced by 10 times sometimes as much as 100 times, so that what is one minute purely imaginary, the next minute seems very real indeed."

"As I am sure you will agree our excellent volunteers tonight have all been Superstars in their own right and to reward them, could all those people who volunteered during the show please come and see me afterwards as I have a valuable gift I'd like to give you as a thank you for taking part!"

"So once again Ladies & Gentlemen thank you for coming this evening and for those who have enjoyed the show my names Jonathan Royle and for those who haven't my names Paul McKenna!"

"Thank you and **GOODNIGHT**!"

The very moment you say the trigger word (Post Hypnotic) of Goodnight your volunteers will all jump up onto their chairs shouting out:

"Jonathan Royle is the greatest Mind Magician of them all Hallelujah!"

This both draws a huge final laugh from the audience and also gives you the opportunity to leave the stage in a clean, polished and professional manner without the last minute problem of getting the volunteers back to their seats.

When your end of show music (Play Off) is finished you can then make a quick voice over stating:

"Could all those who volunteered during this evenings show please report to the stage area **NOW** (or other suitable meeting point) to pick up their FREE GIFT & fill in a short questionnaire!"

This entices all the volunteers to come back to get their **FREE GIFT,** which means that you can then get them to fill in the questionnaire and sign it before giving them their free gift.

The gift to give them is a FREE copy of your "Learn Self-Hypnosis" audio tape, you can tell them they have to sign the questionnaire first as proof that you have given them their "Learn Self-Hypnosis" tape and indeed by giving them this tape and getting them to sign the questionnaire in exchange for it you have further proof that you never hypnotised them!

As the questionnaire is worded such that they have accepted the FREE audio tape **IN EXCHANGE** for taking part in the show, it may be a valid Legal Argument to say that by signing and accepting the audio tape **IN EXCHANGE** for taking part that they cannot at a later date try and obtain (in any manner) any other form of payment, remuneration and/or compensation from you?

Don't worry if occasionally someone disappears without signing the questionnaire as your mini disc recording will prove that at the start of the show they were informed about needing to complete it and agreed to do so at the end of the show, and also it proves that at the end of the show you did a voice over to remind all participants to return to the stage area.

And above all proceeding as I've suggested you'd still have more than enough Legal defence against any potential claims, but its always better (where possible) to get all the questionnaires signed as these are your proof of collecting data enabling the "Research Purposes" ploy to be used in avoiding the need to apply for Council Permission to perform.

THE PUBLIC'S PERCEPTION

In the genuine Hypnotism course I explain in detail how the success of any Hypnotism show is down to the audience member's and volunteer's psychological perception of what is to take place.

Their Belief and Expectancy of what Hypnotism is, how it works and how it will affect them is in short the only reason why a Stage Hypnotism show ever works!

Therefore it is very important that your posters and photographs advertising the show in the manner I've just suggested are designed in such a manner that visually the general public at large will still get the impression that you are a Stage Hypnotist without it ever stating on the Posters etc that you are ever going to Hypnotise anyone!

My advice is to have two separate posters, both of which must be displayed, at the venue as a condition of booking your show.

On one poster I would have a large Picture of me making mystical gestures at a pretty female who appears to be in a Hypnotic Trance and upon it would be the wording required to make all of the previously mentioned loopholes work.

The photograph of me apparently making mystical gestures at an apparently hypnotised female is a stereotypical one used by many Hypnotists and therefore states that I am a Hypnotist without it ever being printed in black & white!

In otherwords the poster says I am a **"MIND MAGICIAN"** but the photograph psychologically conjures up images of me being a Stage Hypnotist which ensures that people are in the correct psychological state when they attend the show.

On the second poster I would have a montage made up of lots of different photographs of people who have volunteered at shows whilst they are doing various funny things.

Again this poster states you are a **"MIND MAGICIAN"** but the photographs such as a person wearing a big pair of glasses with a shocked look on their faces are familiar to people as things they have seen happen during a Stage Hypnotists show and so once again this ensures that people seeing them are placed into the correct psychological state of mind for the show to be a success.

Phrases on the posters such as:

"Your Trance To Be The Star of The Show!"

"All the Fun of a Hypnotism Show with no Hypnotism?"

These type of phrases also give the public the impression that this is a normal style Stage Hypnotism show without ever stating this in black and white.

People associate the word Trance with Stage Hypnotists and the second statement is ended with a ? Making it a question. This means its perceived by people in such a way that it concrete's their Belief & Expectancy further that they are going to see a conventional Stage Hypnotist perform his show.

This of course is what we want the general public to perceive, as then they will start to Hypnotise themselves before they even attend the show as is explained in the genuine Hypnotism course on this CD-ROM.

However the important thing is that legally in all ways the Posters and advertising materials would still validate the fact that this is **NOT A STAGE HYPNOTISTS SHOW** and instead you are a Mind Magician or Imaginationist.

This means that as you are not advertised as being a Stage Hypnotist and are not booked as such you do not have to hypnotise anybody.

By this I mean if you don't get many responsive subjects you can end the Self-Hypnosis section of your show quicker than usual and complete the rest of your performance time with Mind Reading & Psychic Style stunts similar to those explained in my book "The Bizarre Paranormal World of Jonathan Royle"

It is therefore my belief that you can now perform anywhere, at anytime without ever needing any form of permission from any Local Council and without the need for Public Liability Insurance which covers the volunteers whilst they are Hypnotised.

A useful extra piece of knowledge to know is that even venues such as pubs etc which do not have a full Entertainment's Licence are still allowed legally to book Solo performers or Duo's.

As a Mind Magician you are a solo performer and as such can perform anywhere.

Being able to perform anywhere, anytime (even if Hypnotism is banned in that area) should open up many new avenues for work and as such should increase your income also!

Also as your booking contract would state that your fee is an "Appearance Fee" as opposed to a performance fee it again does not matter if anyone goes into a trance or not as you have still shown up and **APPEARED** at the venue and so an "Appearance Fee" is still payable!

GETTING MORE BOOKINGS!

I would suggest that you compile an advertising brochure within which it states quite clearly that:

JONATHAN ROYLE – MIND MAGICIAN

"HE DOES WHAT APPEARS TO BE A HYPNOTISM SHOW AND YET HE NEVER EVER HYPNOTISES ANYONE!"

In recent years Stage-Hypnotism has received large amounts of bad media publicity and several court cases have occurred as a result of this.

Indeed in 2001 the first successful case was brought against a Stage-Hypnotist after a volunteer at one of his shows claimed that being Hypnotised by him led to her Health Problems!

IS STAGE-HYPNOTISM DANGEROUS??

The short answer to that is NO! The Longer answer is definitely not when used safely & correctly by an experienced Hypnotist.

BOOK A MIND MAGICIAN INSTEAD!!

After over 26 years in the Live entertainment industry of which over a decade was spent performing as a conventional Stage Hypnotist Jonathan Royle has now become a Mind Magician!

As Europe's Leading Mind Magician he skilfully blends Mind Magic & Psychic Feats with hilarious comedy to recreate:

"ALL THE FUN OF A HYPNOTISM SHOW WITH NOBODY EVER BEING HYPNOTISED BY HIM!"

This show which is 100% Safe, Legal & Ethical can be performed at any venue in any town without ever needing any form of council permission.

Although volunteers from the audience appear to enter a Trance and carry out Jonathan's Hilarious suggestions, in truth **HE NEVER EVER HYPNOTISES ANYONE DURING THIS SHOW!**

So for those of you who think Stage-Hypnotism shows are funny which indeed they are then look no further as you can book this show today as it is:

"THE SAFE & LEGAL ALTERNATIVE TO BOOKING A STAGE-HYPNOTIST"

The easiest way to describe Jonathan Royles Unique and Hilarious show is by saying:

"He does everything you'd expect a Comedy Stage Hypnotist to do YET HE NEVER HYPNOTISES ANYONE and then he goes far beyond anything you have ever seen live before!"

Here are a Dozen Good Reasons to Book Jonathan Royle today:

#(01)- Jonathan Royle is Europe's Top **MIND MAGICIAN.**
#(02)- He skilfully blends Mind Magic with Comedy to provide a unique & hilarious show which recreates ***ALL THE FUN OF A GENUINE STAGE HYPNOTISM SHOW*** without him ever hypnotising anyone!

#(03)- As ***NOBODY IS EVER HYPNOTISED BY JONATHAN*** this show does not need any form of licence and/or permission from your Local Council Authority to take place.

#(04)- As ***NOBODY IS EVER HYPNOTISED BY JONATHAN*** this show is completely Safe in every way and as such can Legally be performed in **ANY VENUE** even where Stage Hypnotism is banned!

#(05)- Although this show is 100% Safe, Legal & Ethical, as an experienced professional performer Jonathan Royle is an **EQUITY MEMBER** and as such has Five Million Pounds of Public Liability Insurance!

#(06)- As ***NOBODY IS EVER HYPNOTISED BY JONATHAN*** it is true to say that nobody should ever come to any harm either Psychically, Mentally or Emotionally as a result of taking part.

#(07)- As ***NOBODY IS EVER HYPNOTISED BY JONATHAN*** he is prepared to remove Legal Responsibility for the show going ahead from the venue and/or booker and instead **TAKE FULL LEGAL RESPONSIBILITY ON HIS OWN SHOULDERS**.

#(08)- With literally 100's of TV, Radio, Newspaper & Magazine credits to his name Jonathan Royle is fast becoming a household name and is without doubt a crowd pulling attraction suitable for all **CAPACITY VENUES!**

#(09)- All shows are tailored to suit each venue and booking clients needs, from a 100% squeaky clean family show on the one hand to a XXX Rated Outrageous Adults Only show on the other.

#(10)- From a three minute TV appearance to a Two & a half hour Theatre show Jonathan Royle should be your first choice every time you want top class Comedy Entertainment.

#(11)- Fully self-contained with own P.A. System, Lighting, Special Effects and first class props and costumes!

#(12)- Have Car Will Travel & Have Passport will Fly!

FOR MORE INFORMATION OR TO BOOK NOW:

www. Hypnotorious.com or www. Hypnotorious.co.uk
Tel: 07932-975297 E-mail:shows@hypnotorious.com

A HYPNOTIC SHOW WITH NO REAL HYPNOTISM!!

What you have just read is an example of the kind of wording I would use in any advertising brochure to promote a show such as this.

Obviously interspersed within the text would be colour photographs to make the brochure even more appealing to read.

The main point being that if they want to book a Hypnotist but can get a Hypnotic style show from you without any of the usual aggravation or legal red tape then don't you think its you they are more likely to book?

Just remember that your website would also have to validate the fact that you never ever actually hypnotise anyone during your shows.

However on your website it could go into more details, explaining that instead you teach people Self-Hypnosis.

It may even be an idea to have a section on the site (password protected) which details all the loopholes you are using in order to be able to perform Legally in the manner I've explained.

Then if any venue ever asks for more details or perhaps gets grief off the Local Council who may try to tell them what you are doing is not Legal you can give the person who is making the query the password and they can then enter the relevant area of your website and download details of all the Loopholes you are using.

The fact is that there is absolutely **NOTHING** that any Local council can do to stop your show taking place if it is advertised and carried out in the manner I have suggested.

That is why I am prepared to guarantee the venue/booker that I will remove all Legal Responsibility regarding the show taking place from them as I know there is absolutely **NOTHING** that the Local Council can do except make false empty threats.

When you get false empty threats from a Local Council (as I'm sure you will at some stage) then you can do several things to shut them up:

Phone them and give them your website address and the password to the area where they can download information on all the Loopholes you are using and tell them to get their Lawyers to check it out if they are in doubt as you know they will say the same as your lawyer, namely **THAT IN THE MANNER YOU ARE DOING IT THE SHOW CAN GO AHEAD!**

Fax them a copy of these Loopholes also and to that end send them a copy via the postal service as this way they cannot deny having seen them.

Make it quite clear that under the **HUMAN RIGHTS ACT** you the performer have a Human right to do the show and earn your living by doing shows like this, also the audience who attend of their own free will have a Human Right to visit such shows and volunteer if they so wish to take part in them.

Make it clear that whilst you are doing nothing wrong if they continue to harass either you or the venue then you will instruct your lawyers to instigate Legal Proceedings on them for attempting to damage your career & livelihood and that such a case which you are certain to win would result in **GREAT EXPENSE AND BAD PUBLICITY FOR THEM!!**

THAT SHOULD SHUT THEM UP!!!!

So to recap on our present situation, without Public Liability Insurance which covers you for those people in a Hypnotic State the Local Councils will not grant you permission to perform your Hypnotic show in their area.

And due to the fact that from 1st November 2001 Equity members who are Hypnotists are no longer covered in this manner it is effectively no longer possible for us to obtain permission from any Local Council to perform a conventional style Hypnotic show.

I also have it on good authority that most all (if not all) Insurance companies will no longer insure Stage Hypnotists now or at any time in the future as they feel in light of the 2001 Court Case in which Hypnotist Phil Daemon (Phillip Green) was ruled against and ordered to pay £6500 compensation to his "victim" Lynn Howarth that Hypnotists are in general too much of a risk.

The information I have revealed to you so far means that when carried out correctly you will never need Public Liability Insurance to perform as you will have many other forms of Legal defence working in your favour instead.

However without Public Liability Insurance the Local Councils will not grant you permission to perform a conventional Hypnotic show and that is why I have also revealed how to use all of the Legal Loopholes in the 1952 Hypnotism Act in order that you can **PERFORM LEGALLY** in the manner I suggest!

As a further form of defence you could obtain Public Liability Insurance as a "Hypnotherapist" which as a member of a professional Hypnotherapy organisation can be obtained for Between £50 to £100 per year, giving you at the very least One Million Pounds worth of public liability insurance cover.

To obtain this you may need to take a cheap Hypnotherapy correspondence course, but to pass this will present no problems whatsoever given all the information I teach you about **GENUINE** Hypnosis & Hypnotherapy elsewhere in this Book.

Upon completing the course you would then be able to get "Hypnotherapy" Public Liability Insurance which covers you for those people who are being hypnotised, before, during and after they are in trance.

As many Hypnotherapist's also teach self-hypnosis and give Lecture Demonstrations as part of their work, it may be possible to argue that as you are not performing a conventional Hypnotic show but instead are merely teaching people self-hypnosis that this Hypnotherapy Insurance Cover may Legally cover you whilst giving such demonstrations (never say show) for Research and/or Scientific purposes.

It would certainly mean that you could Legally claim that you hold Insurance Cover which covers you for people before, during and after they enter a Hypnotic Trance even if that is a state of self-hypnosis which you have by teaching them helped to guide them into.

This Hypnotherapy Insurance cover would also prove essential should you decide to set up a Hypnotherapy practice, however you could also avoid the need for Insurance cover in this setting by simply getting all your Patients to sign a disclaimer/release stating that they agree to take all responsibility for the results and/or feelings and sensations caused by their treatment.

Rather like the disclaimer/release that a medical surgeon gets people to sign before an operation this would remove Legal Responsibility from you and as such the need for Insurance cover should be removed.

It is only necessary to exploit one or two of the Legal Loopholes that I have revealed in order to be able to Legally perform a Hypnotic Style show in the manner I have explained, however by combining all of the loopholes and always using them all at the same time your defence should become Iron Clad.

Other interesting points which I would ask you to bear in mind include the fact that, whilst the 1952 Hypnotism is an Act of Law and as such to break it without using the loopholes it contains would be an offence in law, the 1989 Guidelines, 1995 Home Office review and 1996 Government review Are Not Laws!

They are nothing more than "Model Conditions" and as such you are breaking no law by not following them!

I would urge you to use these loopholes as in reality all council districts now have the power to add any conditions they see fit to the process of granting you permission to perform, it is therefore much easier to not bother applying for this in the first place.

If you were to apply for permission to perform and a council ever turned you down, then you would have a Legal case against them under The Human Rights Act!

Whilst it is true to say that the 1996 Guidelines say that Hypnotists must have insurance of One Million Pounds cover, it does not state that this insurance must cover the volunteers whilst they are in Trance. So from this point of view your Equity members Insurance should still be adequate – just keep quiet and say nothing!

When using the Research purposes loophole on its own (e.g. when advertising ones self as a Hypnotist) you must remember that the law is worded such that No Other Form of Entertainment can take place at the same venue on the same night as you and that includes a DJ!

Another loophole is "And for the treatment of Mental or Physical disease". This means you could claim your demonstration was presented to alert the public to the benefits of treating such ailments with Hypnosis?

To ever prove that you had committed any offence under the 1952 Hypnotism Act, they would have to legally prove the existence of Hypnosis, which is impossible! The reason being that for every expert who says it exists you can easily find a dozen who will say that it does not.

For full information regarding al the loopholes of the Hypnotic Laws you are advised to read Chapter 11 of The Course in Complete Mind Therapy which appears elsewhere.

A FURTHER LEGAL DEFENCE

It would also be a good legal defence to point out in court that **THERE IS NO SUCH THING AS HYPNOSIS!**

There are numerous experts in the fields of Hypnosis, Psychology & Medicine who support this view, and whilst there is also an equal number to support the opposite view that Hypnosis is real, in a court case such **EXPERT** testimony would prove invaluable in any defence you should need.

One enterprising British Stage Hypnotist by the name of Alex Tsander performs a show called **"I CAN'T BELIEVE IT'S NOT HYPNOSIS!"** during which he performs what appears to be a normal hypnotism show **WITHOUT EVER HYPNOTISING ANYONE!**

If **HYPNOSIS DOES NOT EXIST** as many people including Alex Tsander say then it is logical to say that as we shall never actually be hypnotising anyone (as hypnotism does not exist) then we should not need any form of licence and/or permission to perform our shows from the Local Councils.

In his book **"Secrets of Professional Cabaret & Stage Hypnotism"** veteran Stage Hypnotist Eddie Burke reveals how he performs his "Hypnotic Shows" and amazingly he admits that **THERE IS NO SUCH THING AS HYPNOSIS ON STAGE** and rather nothing more than Pure Psychology is used.

This book priced £25-00 written by Eddie Burke and available from www.mreenterprises.co.uk is a valuable publication to have in your possession as Eddie has been a Stage Hypnotist for many years and indeed for many years has been a council member of **The Federation of Ethical Stage Hypnotists (F.E.S.H)** making his written statements in this book valuable and powerful defence material if ever you need to prove in a court of law **THAT STAGE HYPNOTISTS DON'T HYPNOTISE PEOPLE!**

Should you just wish evidence to support the view that **ALL HYPNOSIS IS JUST SELF-HYPNOSIS** then numerous books are available to support this claim written by respected experts in their fields.

Using books by such experts confirming that **ALL HYPNOSIS IS JUST SELF-HYPNOSIS** means that we could prove in court that we never actually hypnotise anyone and as the experts say **PEOPLE HYPNOTISE THEMSELVES!**

If people hypnotise themselves this is **SELF-HYPNOSIS** and as the 1952 Hypnotism Act and later updates do not in any way prohibit Self-Hypnotism we do not need permission from the Local Councils for our shows to take place in the manner that I have suggested you present them.

MY BIGGEST SECRET OF ALL

For the first time ever in print I will admit and reveal my most closely guarded secret of all and that is **HYPNOSIS DOES NOT EXIST.**

I would go so far to say that **HYPNOSIS IS THE BIGGEST CONGAME ON EARTH.**

And even further would admit that **ALL STAGE-HYPNOTISTS AND/OR HYPNOTHERAPISTS ARE NOTHING MORE THAN CLEVER CONMEN or CONWOMEN!**

Any so called Knowledgeable Stage-Hypnotist or Therapist who disagrees with this is in my opinion just illustrating **HOW LITTLE THEY ACTUALLY KNOW ABOUT THE SUBJECT!**

I cannot blame many Hypnotists & Therapist for having the **INCORRECT & MISGUIDED** belief that Hypnosis does exist and that they genuinely do place people into trances etc, as they are only repeating what their so called knowledgeable tutor taught them and as such it is what they have come to believe!

In truth Hypnotherapy is only as effective as the actual therapeutic part of the treatment combined with the **PLACEBO EFFECT!**

By this I mean that any form of Hypnotherapy which gets results would either get the same results without the people ever being placed into a so called trance due to the sound basis of the mind therapy techniques which are then used when the person is in a so called trance or **ONLY WORK DUE TO THE PLACEBO EFFECT.**

With Stage-Hypnotism the situation is the same and I would say that **HYPNOSIS DOES NOT EXIST** and that **NOBODY IS EVER HYPNOTISED ON STAGE!** However the volunteers may come to "Believe" that they have been hypnotised and it is only those people who come to "Believe" that they have been hypnotised that have ever got anywhere close to being in a trance, as Hypnosis is nothing more than a Psychological state of self-belief.

Indeed a so called Hypnotic Trance is nothing more than a person "Believing" that they should react in this way because they "Believe" they are hypnotised, and they only end up believing that they are hypnotised because of Psychological tricks we use to enhance the stereotypical false beliefs (expectancy) that they have of what will occur.

It is because of this that nearly everybody who is ever "Hypnotised" says afterwards that they did not feel as if they were hypnotised! **THIS IS QUITE SIMPLY BECAUSE THEY WERE NOT.** And the odd few who say different do so only because of the prior Belief & Expectancy they have instilled into themselves or have had conditioned into them of what they should expect & believe will happen when they volunteer to be hypnotised.

This is also the reason why all knowledgeable hypnotists say that when in a so called Trance that the subjects are fully aware of everything that is going on around them at all times, this is quite simply because **THEY ARE FULLY AWARE** and this is because **THEY ARE NOT HYPNOTISED** they only believe themselves to be in a trance due to the psychological tricks we have used to make them believe this.

Ultimately it is the volunteer's inaccurate perception of things and their false beliefs and expectancy that make them react in the way they do. In otherwords they **MAKE THEMSELVES DO IT ALL!** And it is for this reason that the real experts all say that **ALL HYPNOSIS IS SELF-HYPNOSIS!**

Hypnotherapist's & Stage Hypnotists have both been **GUILTY FOR YEARS OF MISLEADING THE PUBLIC!**

Hypnotherapists have done this because they believe that telling the truth may harm their business and therefore harm their financial security!

Stage-Hypnotists have done this because they know that the more mystical, magical & mysterious Hypnotism appears to be the more powerful a psychological effect the idea of volunteering to take part in a Hypnotism show has and therefore the easier it will be to with a few simple psychological con tricks convince the volunteers that they are genuinely hypnotised.

Read the first chapter of the "Genuine Hypnotism Course" elsewhere in this Book entitled "Back to Front" and the fact that Hypnosis is nothing more than a clever and elaborate con game will be illustrated even further!

To Clarify my claim I will now give you a new **100% HONEST** explanation of the techniques which I teach in the "Genuine Hypnotism Course" and which until December 2001 at time of writing this new book I had always claimed to be genuine hypnotic techniques which would place people into a genuine hypnotic trance.

I APOLOGISE TO ALL MY FORMER STUDENTS

YOUR SUCCESS HAS NOT BEEN DUE TO HYPNOSIS

BUT RATHER AS YOU WILL LEARN DUE TO A

BUNCH OF VERY CLEVER CON TRICKS

WHICH JUST CONVINCE PEOPLE THEY

ARE IN SOME SORT OF "HYPNOTIC" STATE!

IN FACT THERE IS NO SUCH THING AS HYPNOSIS

AT LEAST NOT IN THE WAY IT IS PORTRAYED.

The **TRUE CONFESSIONS** of how these techniques work and are in fact nothing more than pure psychological con tricks to make people believe that something special or strange is happening to them in order that they come to believe that they are being hypnotised and as such come to believe that they have entered some sort of so called trance state will only make any sense when read in conjunction with the detailed explanation of these techniques which is presented elsewhere in this Book.

Yes you are about to learn how Hypnotism is nothing more than **PURE PSYCHOLOGY** and the moment you realise this your understanding of Hypnotism and the **TRUE WAY IT WORKS** will be far greater than many so called professional, experienced and allegedly knowledgeable Stage-Hypnotists and Hypnotherapists **WHO SHOULD KNOW BETTER!**

First we will start with the "Suggestibility" tests which are all explained in the course:

LEMON TEST

You think about sucking on a bitter, horrible sour Lemon and keep imagining this clearly in your minds eye and you will start to Salivate (get a wet mouth), there is nothing strange about this it is a completely normal bodily reaction, however presented as taught, when the people realise that their mouth has started to get wet they come to believe that it is because of your powers of suggestion and skills as a hypnotist!

WARM HANDS TEST

Rub your hands together rapidly back and forth for several seconds and they will naturally get warmer and feel hot, again it's the way that its presented that makes the people come to believe that your suggestions must be working on them as they discover that their hands are getting warmer as suggested.

FINGERS CLOSER TOGETHER TEST

Place your hands in the position I state and outstretch your fingers in the manner as instructed and then just relax. In a matter of a few seconds your fingertips will naturally start to move towards each other until they are touching. Once again its nothing strange its something that naturally happens when the hands are held in this position but we present it in such a manner that it makes the audience believe that our suggestions are having an effect on them!

LIGHT & HEAVY HANDS TEST

Place both your arms out in front of you as it states and close your eyes and then just relax for a minute. After a minute open your eyes and surprise surprise there will be a gap between your arms! The people believe this to be due to your suggestions of a pile of heavy books on one hand and a balloon tied to the middle finger of the other, in fact its perfectly normal and happens all the time as when your eyes are closed its almost impossible to tell if your arms are still in line with each other and as a result they naturally end up drifting apart.

LOCKED HANDS TEST

Place your hands together, fingers interlocked, palms pressed tightly together and fingers pressed against the back of your hands as instructed and keep them in this position for a few minutes. Now try and separate your hands, its appears more difficult than normal dose it not? That's because your knuckles are bigger than each other and as such do not easily slip apart. Some audience members will feel their knuckles knock against each other, take this as a sign their hands are locked together and then stop trying, as such keeping their hands together and identifying themselves as easy people to con further!

GAURANTEED LOCKED HANDS TEST

Exactly as its name suggests this is guaranteed to work, just so long as people put their hands in the position as stated it then becomes psychically impossible to separate your hands whilst they are kept in this position.

EYES LOCKED TOGETHER TEST

Just so long as you close your eyes and then with your eyeballs stare upward through an imaginary hole in the centre of your forehead this will work! The fact is that whilst your eyeballs are in the upwards position focused on the imaginary hole in your forehead it becomes psychically impossible to open your eyes.

WITH ALL SUGGESTIBILITY TESTS

Just as with these examples, all suggestibility tests are built around things, which naturally would happen anyway or are highly likely to happen anyway.

As a Hypnotist we just present these things in such a manner that the audience never get the chance to realise that the same end result would definitely occur or most likely occur without us making any so called suggestions at all!

The law of reversed effort which is a sound proven psychological technique compounds this further and used in the way it is with suggestibility tests makes it even more likely that the desired end result is achieved.

When these things happen to the audience members they instantly believe that they have occurred because of your suggestions to them and therefore this concrete's their false belief that you are some kind of magical, mysterious and powerful hypnotist and as a result they come to believe that you could hypnotise them!

When they believe in this manner that you could hypnotise them then if they volunteer to take part they will expect to be hypnotised and expect whatever you do to work.
On top of all this the suggestions that you actually make when presenting these tests in the manner explained do compound the success of these tests.

This is nothing Hypnotic or strange, but rather is just due to the effect suggestions have on some people which is why these tests work better on some people than others.

To illustrate the **NATURAL** power of suggestion think back to the Lemon Test earlier and imagine that bitter, sour, horrible lemon again, bet your mouth has started to get wetter hasn't it?

Now imagine that you have Ants in your pants, Fleas on your Knees and Nits in your hair. In fact your whole body from head to toe is covered in horrible bed bugs and dust mites, you can feel the little horrible insects biting you as you get itchier and itchier with each second that passes by. I bet you have had to scratch yourself at least once whilst reading this haven't you?

WELL THAT'S THE POWER OF SUGGESTION

SUGGESTION CORRECTLY EXPRESSED IS HYPNOSIS

THIS IS BECAUSE HYPNOSIS DOES NOT EXIST!

It is exactly the same with the hypnotic induction's, we use things which we know will happen every time and then tie our suggestions in to make it appear to the volunteers that these things only happened to them because we suggested that they would.

The volunteers then experience these things (which naturally occur) and as we "suggested" earlier that this would occur come to believe that they must have reacted to our suggestions when in truth these things would have happened anyway.

Therefore convinced that these things happened because we suggested they would the volunteers become even more convinced that they are reacting to what we suggest and therefore **BELIEVE & EXPECT** to continue responding to the things we suggest, in otherwords they have started to hypnotise themselves (convince themselves) into an apparent trance (state of psychological self-belief) state.

As things continue this psychological state of **BELIEF & EXPECTANCY** continues to grow greater and when this is combined with the Sheep Effect, Peer Group Pressure and all the other Psychological things which come into play as explained in Chapter One entitled "Back to Front" in the genuine Hypnotism course it becomes even more obvious why the people behave as they do and why they later claim to have been hypnotised when in truth they have just been playing along with out even realising this is what they have been doing.

It is much easier for them to play along in front of the crowd than to leave the stage and look like they do not have good enough powers of Intelligence, Imagination and Concentration to be a good "Hypnotic" subject.

Yes a large element of the success of a hypnotic show is the fact that those people who apparently become hypnotised are given all the praise and made out to be the Intelligent, Imaginative and Brainy ones, whilst the ones who do not go under are sent back and made to look (and feel) like idiots in the process.

When they hear someone sent back to the audience being made an idiot of (or at least that's how they perceive it) and realise that rather than being treated as idiots those people on stage are being given praise from the Hypnotist and applause from the audience they are now far more likely to remain on stage.

In short what I an saying is some people come on stage and play along purposely because they want to be a star for the night, others come on stage don't enter any trance but realise it is easier and better for them to play along and some genuinely come to believe that they have entered some kind of hypnotic state and that as they have been reacting to all your suggestions so far that they are powerless to do anything other than continue reacting to your suggestions.

In most all cases these people will claim to have been in a genuine state of hypnosis when they return to the audience as "Being Hypnotised" seems the perfect excuse (cover story) for why they were so willingly doing such stupid things on stage.

A rare few will say they were not hypnotised, but then when the audience start taunting them about how stupid they looked will pretend to not remember having done those things and as such admit (falsely) that they must have been hypnotised as this then takes the heat (and blame) off them.

I will now explain the truth behind one of the Induction methods taught in the so-called genuine hypnotism section of this Book, then I will expand further on the Psychology which makes these so called Induction methods work so well:

FALLING BACKWARDS: The way they are stood means that they are off balance. The way your foot is against their ankles means that you can tip them over easily. Drawing your fingertip back from near their nose, across their forehead and then off their head acts as a non-verbal suggestion to move backwards. Tapping them on the back disorientates them and knocks them off balance. Breathing as you tell them to do hyperventilates them slightly and makes them feel dizzy which knocks them off balance even more. In short everything that happens is NATURAL! However the way they perceive it makes them convinced that they are being placed into some form of trance.

WHY DO INDUCTIONS ON STAGE WORK SO WELL?

In each and every case the short answer to this question is that every Induction method used on Stage is designed so that it contains many things which will happen to the volunteers NATURALLY!

In otherwords these things will happen each and every time whether or not the person has a belief in Hypnosis.

However because of the manner in which the Indications are presented to the Volunteers, they never get a chance to analyse what is going on and as such when these natural things occur the people believe that they have occurred because a few seconds earlier you verbally suggested that they would.

This means that they come to the Conditioned Belief that when you suggest that something is going to happen to them, that it then does happen to them!

IN otherwords these NATURAL OCCURENCES are presented in such a manner that the volunteers perceive them as being unnatural and therefore can only explain these things to themselves as the effects of becoming what they perceive to be genuinely Hypnotised!

The easiest way I can prove this to you is to suggest that you get a close friend to learn all the Induction Methods mentioned elsewhere.

Next practise each of the methods on them and afterwards get them to carry out each of the methods on you.

Now go into separate rooms and write down what each of you felt, I bet that when you compare notes your answers are very similar.

Furthermore I now bet that when you then sit down and examine the mechanics of each Induction method in conjunction with your answers that the reasons for you feeling the things you did will become evident.

In otherwords the reason why you felt things you, at the time thought were unnatural (due to Hypnosis) is because in truth they are 100% Natural and that is why the Induction Methods have been designed in that way.

I know this to be true as when I conduct my personal one to one training course, the reason I can teach someone to become a confident Hypnotist in one day is because I demonstrate everything on them.

Then I get them to practise everything on me. Only when you have a full understanding of what each Induction feels like as the Hypnotist and as the subject will you ever become a good Stage Hypnotist.

DELAVAR'S ADVICE ON PUBLIC LIABILITY INSURANCE MATTERS!

As you may be aware Delavar is the past president of The British Council of Professional Stage Hypnotists (BCPSH) and is responsible for having taught some of the worlds leading Hypnotherapists and Hypnotic performers including yours truly!

In early December 2001 I spoke to Delavar (my mentor & tutor) regarding the problems in getting Public Liability Insurance which covers you for the volunteers whilst they are in trance.

We spoke at great length and he confirmed pretty much everything that I tell you to do in this chapter *"The Lazy Mans Guide to Stage Hypnosis!"* as being the correct manner in which to proceed in order to both be able to perform legally without permission from the Local Council and also to avoid ever being sued by anyone!

He also sent me the wording for an example advertising Flyer to display at all venues which from the point of view of not having Insurance, may ensure that nobody could ever sue you in connection with any part of your show.

DELAVAR'S EXAMPLE POSTER WORDING 18/12/01

WARNING

YOU VOLUNTEERED AT YOUR OWN RISK BY ATTENDING

A

ROYLE SHOW

YOU CANNOT APPEAR ON A ROYLE SHOW IF UNDER 18!

ONLY VOLUNTEERS MAY COME ON A ROYLE SHOW

I NEVER KNOW WHAT WILL HAPPEN AT MY SHOWS

THAT IS WHY I URGE YOU NOT TO VOLUNTEER!

IF YOU DO APPEAR IT IS ENTIRELY AT YOUR OWN RISK!

EVEN IN THE AUDIENCE YOU ARE NOT SAFE FROM MY AMAZING HYPNOTIC POWERS

YOU COULD STILL WAKE UP ON STAGE!

THAT IS WHY I SAY LOUD & CLEAR

YOU ARE A VOLUNTEER IF YOU COME TO MY SHOW

YOU COME ENTIRELY AT YOUR OWN RISK

PEOPLE DO COME – SOME LIVE THROUGH IT – IF YOU DON'T NO GOOD SUING ME – I HAVE NO MONEY!

ROYLE

THE IMPECUNIOUS

THE FRIGHTENING

TERRIFYING

HANDSOME

MASTER HYPNOTIST

WARNING

ALL PERSONS ATTENDING MY SHOW ARE VOLUNTEERING TO APPEAR IN THIS SHOW, WHICH IS PRESENTED FOR RESEARCH & SCIENTIFIC PURPOSES, ENTIRELY AT THEIR OWN RISK, YOU HAVE BEEN WARNED! DO NOT BLAME ME IF YOU ARE TITILLATED, AMUSED or ENTERTAINED BY MY SHOW. NOT MY FAULT IF YOU SPLIT YOUR SIDES WITH LAUGHTER, OR ARE TERRIFIED TO DEATH OR YOUR HAIR TURNS WHITE, ETC. ETC.
THE SOLE RESPONSIBILITY & RISK ARE YOURS!

DELAVAR'S ADVICE CONTD.

The previous example is word for word how Delavar wrote it for me, it is laid out differently I admit but the end result is the same.

On the example he sent me Delavar fitted all of this text onto a single side of an A4 Sheet and laid it out in such a manner that it looked like a Professional Poster which you could display at a venue with your Colour Photograph next to it in order to advertise your show.

Re-read the example again and you will notice that the Key Phrases which cover you Legally are:

WARNING. = This makes it clear that something potentially dangerous is going to take place and when displayed at the venue at least 14 days prior to show means all who attend can reasonably be expected to have seen the poster and so by attending agreed to its contents.

VOLUNTEERED. = Means that if they take part they are Voluntarily placing themselves into a position of potential harm and furthermore you have informed them via this poster that it is potentially dangerous!

IF UNDER 18. = This is just normal law and is included for obvious reasons.

VOLUNTEERS. = Same reason as mentioned above.

ENITRELY AT YOUR OWN RISK. = This phrase makes it very clear that if they attend and/or participate at your show they do so entirely at their own risk. Therefore knowing this, they are by attending agreeing to take all Legal responsibility for what may happen to them!

YOU MIGHT WAKE UP ON STAGE. = This means you can place them into trance without even asking for their permission as they have been warned in advance that they may wake up on stage.

VOLUNTEER. Same again as earlier!

YOU COME ENTIRELY AT YOUR OWN RISK. = Same again as earlier to concrete the fact that by attending they are agreeing to take all responsibility on their shoulders.

WARNING. = Again included to draw their attention clearly to the disclaimers and warnings that the information poster contains.

ALL PERSONS ATTENDING MY SHOW ARE VOLUNTEERING TO APPEAR IN THE SHOW. = In otherwords you don't need to get permission to Hypnotize them as they have given it by attending!

ENTIRELY AT THEIR OWN RISK = Same reason as stated earlier.

YOU HAVE BEEN WARNED. = Same reason as why it states "Warning" on posters!

ETC. ETC. = This covers in the context it is presented Everything and anything for which you may need to be covered Legally!

RESPOSNIBILITY IS YOURS. = Presented in the manner it is this, which may place all Legal responsibility onto the audience for attending at your show.

FOR RESEARCH & SCIENTIFIC PURPOSES. = As explained elsewhere in the "Lazy Mans Guide to Stage Hypnosis" this phrase means that you need not apply for permission to perform from the Local Council.

Incidentally Delavar laid this out on an A4 poster layout in such a manner that the text was mainly centered, meaning that some small photographs of me performing could be added down the sides in order to make the poster more visually appealing.

He also suggested that Novel Bill Matter to use when advertising such a show to Agents & Venues would be:

"ROYLE – THE HYPNOTIST WHO TELLS YOU KEEP AWAY FROM MY SHOW!"

Regarding the types of Photographs to place onto the poster Delavars advice was very interesting and when considering his words please remember that as we are not working under a "Permission" from the Local Council **WE CAN LEGALLY** do Catalepsy in our shows!

DELAVARS ADVICE ON PHOTOS

Your Photograph is your first point of contact with anyone. **IT MUST BE DESIGNED TO SELL YOU AND WHAT YOU CAN DO** It is not or at least should not be a self-indulgent Portrait.

My photograph shows a Lady suspended between two chairs (Catalepsy) or a man having hairs burned off him with a blowtorch, or somebody standing on a woman lay across two supports.

These are also printed on smaller sticky back labels for use on all my communications.

I have a small B&W Photograph (Head & Shoulders style) to include with my Bumf that I send to Agents or to print onto Billboard sheets.

I DO NOT SELL MY PHOTO – BUT WHAT I CAN DO!

Make it Dramatic, so that anyone looking at it is Instantly Impressed!

I sell what I am capable of doing so that people want to see my show or to book it for their venue etc!

If you do not have such dramatic photographs and are not capable of doing it, then fake it, I do not need to but it is permissible for Advertising purposes!

Two Chairs, thin plank over the backs of them, lay Lady on plank with head hair to cover one end and heels of her feet to cover the other and of course her dress to come down in a dramatic sweep to cover everything else.

Now take your photographs at leisure with you standing behind the Lady with your arms outstretched, this should give a dramatic picture.

Then stand someone on the Lady (the plank takes the weight) and this also makes for a dramatic photograph!

Take reels of Photographs at every show you do there may be some dramatic ones that you can use later.

Before you use a photograph, look at it carefully to see what the picture conveys to you.

Not so much what it was showing at the time, but rather what it conveys now!

Two men on the floor making Love is just that two men on the floor!

You need atmosphere to create anything else, let your photograph create that atmosphere for you.

A group of people laying back in their chairs is just that, not a group of people under Hypnosis.

YOU CANNOT SEE HYPNOSIS – ONLY ITS EFFECTS

You must grab someone's attention before you can Hypnotise them. Your Photographs on the posters etc must do the same thing!

Posters/Photographs are static, but they must shout out what you are doing and how good you are at doing it.

SUMMING UP ON DELAVAR'S ADVICE

In short I would say that Delavars advice is as always Excellent and you would be wise to consider his words carefully.

Delavar has written an excellent training course in all things Hypnotic entitled **"THE HYPNOTISTS BIBLE"** and it is made up of two parts, one section on Stage Hypnosis and the other on Therapy. This amazing course can be purchased from **www.hypnotherapycourse.net**

ADDENDUM & IMPORTANT WARNING TO ALL READERS

Please be warned and note the fact that neither I Jonathan Royle (formerly Known as Alex-Leroy) or the publishers of this book in anyway, shape or form accept any form of responsibility for readers using any of the ideas mentioned in this guide.

This entire publication is supplied strictly for information purposes and should you choose to use any of the methods detailed herein, then you do so entirely at your own risk.

Indeed I am neither a Medical Doctor or a Lawyer and as such would demand that you seek independent Legal Advice from a trained Lawyer before ever attempting to use any of the information within these pages, I cannot and will not be held responsible for any incorrect usage of the methods explained and indeed am only publishing this guide to illustrate how badly worded the 1952 Hypnotism Act is and indeed what a large loophole Section 5 contains.

However should you decide to use (entirely at your own risk and after seeking independent Legal advice) the techniques detailed herein, then you may also wish to consider the following extra information:

Section 5 of the 1952 Hypnotism Act States: "Nothing in this act shall prevent the exhibition, demonstration or performance of Hypnotism (otherwise than at or in connection with an entertainment) for Scientific or Research Purposes or for the treatment of mental or physical disease."

Section 5 of the 1952 Hypnotism Act totally negates Section 1 and indeed the rest of the Act!

The 1952 Act does not restrict the use of Section 5 to any particular group or persons and as such it may Legally be used by anyone at anytime, until such time as the 1952 Act is amended.

The time of writing this Addendum is April 2003 and at the time of writing Section 5 of and indeed the entire 1952 Hypnotism Act are still in force as originally passed by Parliament and as such Section 5 may still be used by anyone.

Check when considering use of Section 5 that the 1952 Act is still in force and has not been amended in any way since the publication of this manual.

Therefore under Section 5 of the 1952 Hypnotism Act, Anyone can at any time and anyplace give a demonstration of Hypnosis for:

01) Scientific Purposes
02) RESEARCH PURPOSES
03) The Treatment of Mental Disease
04) The Treatment of Physical Disease
05) The use of Self Hypnotism

In the 1952 Act there is no definition as to what is Scientific, also any type of Research may take place as it is not defined or restricted in any manner by the 1952 Act.

What is a Scientific or Research Purpose?

Let us for an example take the Killing of Whales, which is forbidden by The United Nations (1994)...

The Japanese Government allows the killing of Minky & other Whales for Scientific Purposes.

They decide that when a harpoon enters a whale and kills it, that they have scientific proof that a harpoon can sometimes kill a Whale!

They then allow the sale of the meat for Human consumption in Japan!

Similarly take Research. The same Government decides they must kill these protected Whales because they are "researching" different kinds of Harpoons and need to find out which is best.

As you can see from this example the Killing of Whales in Japan is for Scientific and Research Purposes!

Therefore if you advertise the fact that you are "Giving a demonstration of Hypnosis for Scientific and Research Purposes" – then you do not need a Licenses and/or permission from anyone to Legally do so, just so long as no entertainment takes place at the same time!

Your "Research" can be to find out how people react to a hypnotic trance, how/why they go into trance, what they can/cannot do while in trance, how an audience react to people in trance, how they react to each other in trance, what is a trance, why do they do anything in trance, does trance exist, is hypnosis real? Or indeed any other reason that you think fit.

There is nothing in a "Scientific or Research Study" that says that anyone taking part either as a subject under trance or as a subject in the audience, should not find what is going on entertaining or amusing.

It could be entertaining for the audience to watch, also "entertainment" may be what you are researching

E.g: Is it entertaining to watch people in trance do things?

It is not for Entertainment purposes in itself, but rather is only a "Research Demonstration" into the effects of humour in Hypnosis!

The effect on your subjects is also a Research project to you, it may have been done by others before or even by yourself before, but as yet you have not come to any definite conclusions, hence you must continue your Research.

What one person considers entertainment, another may not!

It all depends on each particular person's own individual outlook on things, some would find an accident scary, some bystanders would consider watching it as entertaining.

The problem is that the Government has used a word that has no definite meaning, it is an ambiguous word, the meaning of which changes from situation to situation.

When such a word is used arguments can develop as to which meaning shall be ascribed to that word at any particular time, and is that meaning the one that should be used at that time?

Providing that your demonstration of Hypnosis is for Scientific or Research purposes and is not presented in connection with an entertainment, then you can go ahead and do it without even asking the Council or even giving them notice of what you intend to do.

The word Research covers a multitude of actions without defining any particular action:

DICTONARY DEFINITION OF RESEARCH ETC:

Subject of inquiry, request, search, pursuit, quest, examination, review, investigation, exploration, sifting, calculation, analysis, endeavour to discover new facts by scientific study of a subject.

Scientific = knowledge, systematic, formulated knowledge scientifically – such knowledge in reference to a subject. Pursuit of such knowledge, based mainly on observations, experiment, experts, skill, natural ability, expert knowledge.

AS YOU CAN SEE THE WORDS SCIENTIFIC AND RESEARCH ARE VERY EMBRACING. LOOK IN VARIOUS DICTONARYS FOR YOURSELF!

It now becomes obvious that SECTION 5 of the 1952 Hypnotism Act does indeed have a very large Loophole within it and this is what it is safest to rely on to perform in this modern day as a Hypnotist without need for Council permission.

Remember though that NO ENTERTAINEMNT of any kind may take place at the same time you are appearing, otherwise a license is required.

Not even a Singer can appear with you, if an entertainer of any kind should be at the same venue and at the same time as yourself, your demonstration would then be classed as entertainment, remember this!

The 1952 Hypnotism Act is an ACT OF PARLIAMENT. The wording of the Act restricts it to those words. The spirit of the act is not what needs to be obeyed, only the wording.

These as we have shown, can be interpreted in many ways.

Indeed in a Parliament Adjournment Debate on December 12th 1994 it was stated:

"On the scope of current legislation, consideration should be given as to whether private performances should continue to be exempt from licensing requirements. It may be necessary also to consider whether the provision which exempts performances which are said to be for "Scientific or Research" purposes (Section 5) is sufficiently clearly drawn!"

I would say that those Government Made Comments in 1994 seem to indicate that what I am saying about a massive loophole in Section 5 of the 1952 Hypnotism Act is indeed true, and will remain so until such times as Parliament amend the 1952 Act and do so in such a manner as to make a New Act of Parliament.

To finish this Chapter I would point out that the actual wording which appears at the top of my show posters says:

Theres no Such Thing As A Real Comedy Hypnotist

And at the bottom of the poster it states:

"Volunteers who must be aged 18 or over participate entirely at their own risk, agree to be filmed and waiver all legal rights during this demonstration of hypnotic style phenomena presented strictly for research and scientific purposes only"

On the poster are pictures of me in the classic stereotypical pose of a Hypnotist and also there are images of swinging watches and other things which the public will perceive as saying I am a real Hypnotist even thought the poster blatantly tells them that there is no such thing as Hypnosis.

]And last but not least I have every show filmed as then I have 100% proof of what went on during the show and nobody can make false allegations afterwards as this video could be brought out in court as evidence.

This also provides you with good footage to use for promotional DVDS to send to Agents and best of all gives you a product which you can sell on your Internet Site to people all around the World!

CHAPTER TWENTY–FIVE

HYPNOTISING ANIMALS

There is actually no such thing as genuinely Hypnotising an Animal, what actually occurs is a sort of muscular paralysis which has no ill effects on the animal subjects used.

You can find much information about these techniques on the Internet by using the Search Terms "Animal Hypnosis" – "Hypnotising Animals" and also "Tonic Immobility"

HEN = It is a well known fact that if a hen is placed so that its beak is touching the ground and a chalk line is drawn from the beak, the Hen will not Move, being under the impression that it is tied with this mark!

The eyes of the Hen are focussed upon the mark and the line of vision converges practically at the end of its beak.

HEN = Holding the Hen in One Hand, you can produce a similar effect by gazing intently into its eyes and receiving the return gaze directed into your eyes, bringing the Hen closer to your eyes as you do this!

This Produces an eye-strain which also converges the line of vision as the Hen is brought nearer your face and has the same effect as the chalk line.

ROOSTER = Take a Rooster and place it on a table or on a small stand with its legs folded beneath it.

Then hold its head and beak resting on the table, it will stay there and appear to be in a Trance for a short time.

CHICKEN = A Chicken can be placed into a Sleep Like State by rhythmically swinging it back and forwards.

RABBIT = The Rabbit is held with both hands, the back of the Rabbit being towards yourself.

Now you gently swing the Rabbit up and down, and its struggling will soon cease and the Rabbit will appear to be asleep.

RABBIT = Another easy way is to place the Rabbit on a table, near the edge, on its side, with its head dangling over the side of the table.

You then hold the Rabbit still until any struggling stops and the rabbit appears to be either dead or asleep!

However a gentle touch on its ears will instantly bring the Rabbit out of this state.

GUINEA PIG = These can easily be placed into a Trance Like State by rolling them over and over several times and then placing them on their backs.

Their eyes remain open, it appears to be in a dazed condition and will remain there for a short time.

However any movement in front of its eyes, or a noise will restore this animal to its normal condition.

DUCK = It is possible to hold a Duck in the palm of one hand with its feet uppermost. A gentle swaying movement will appear to place the Duck under Hypnosis, then the Ducks beak can be drawn down onto its stomach and left there for a moment.

DOVES – PIGEONS – VARIOUS BIRDS = Doves, Pigeons and Various other Birds are easy to apparently Hypnotise. You simply hold the Bird in one hand so that the Birds Back is on the Palm of your hand, then you push its head downwards towards the floor and when struggling stops you may open out the fingers of the hand which the Bird is resting on and it will look as though the Bird is "Asleep".

SNAKES – ALLIGATORS – CROCIDILES = All of these are placed into a Sleep Like State when Placed flat on their backs. Hold them in this position for a minute or two and then you can let go and they will stay there as if in Trance.

FROGS – TOADS – CHAMELEONS – LIZARDS ETC = These Can also apparently be placed into a Trance Like State by similarly placing it on its back and holding them in place for a moment or two until their struggling ceases.

However with Lizards and such like, prevent the Jaws from closing and hold its head at the same time.

SHELLFISH = Lobster & Crayfish are both easy Hypnotic Subjects. They may be stood on their heads, using the two forefeet and the head to act as a tripod.

Gently stroke their back towards their head, once the trance like state is visibly noticeable they will remain in most any position until the state wears off.

LIONS – TIGERS – MONKEYS ETC = Most any larger animal can apparently be Hypnotised using a somewhat bizarre method as follows which like all techniques in this manuscript and in this entire book you use entirely at your own risk as all things in life (especially trying to do this on Lions & Tigers etc) carry Risks!

A solution of one half Rose Water, and one half Chloroform is placed into a tightly capped bottle, a tube is led from the top of this bottle to a position on the wrist band around your wrist of one arm.

Another tube from the left hand has a rubber bulb (perfume spray bulb) which when deflated forces air into the bottle, as this is also going into the top of the bottle and as such will drive the odour of the Gas through the second hole in the bottles cap, through the other tube and therefore ejecting the Chloroform Gas out of the tube at wrist level.

The Strong projection of this gas into the Nostrils of any Beast or Animal will create a bewildering effect, passes in front of the animals eyes, together with more Gas ejected, will produce a state of stupification and of course could be carried on until the beast is in a mental daze and apparently in Trance!

Performers in the past have used this method to apparently place Lions, Tigers and other large beast into a Hypnotic State.

You should be careful not to stand in the direction of oncoming wind, otherwise as you spray the Gas out it may be blown back into your face and make you rather than the animal pass out, which could obviously potentially prove fatal with and animal like a Lion or Tiger!

This technique was used for many years, however I feel it must constitute cruelty to animals and as such would be against the Law to use and as such is presented here for information purposes only.

ZOO ANIMALS & DOMESTIC ANIMALS = There are now companies who train animals for TV Commercials and Films and if you were to contact such a company they would be able to train most any Domestic or Zoo Style Animal to react as if asleep and under Hypnosis in response to a simple visual or audio signal.

They could then teach you this signal and you'd apparently be able to place the animal into an Instant Trance, as it would react when it received the signal as if it had gone to sleep.

This piece of information could prove very useful indeed for the Publicity minded Hypnotist.

FLY'S & OTHER INSECTS = You need to catch a fly and freeze it. This puts it in a temporary coma. This can be done by swatting the fly hard enough to immobilise it and then placing it in a small container in the freezer. When it comes to performance time, the fly then needs to be quickly taken to a suitable windscreen IN THE SHADE and placed there. It is important that the car is in the shade to prevent the fly from defrosting too quickly. Then go and find a spectator and take them back to the car, which should appear to be randomly picked. The heat of your hand will revive the fly, which should soon start to move. A lot of this trick is in the actions of you reviving the fly. It may be necessary to practice how long it takes for the fly to revive itself. Freezing the fly with dry ice or even one of these aerosol canned air products for cleaning computers is a better way of freezing the fly as it is quicker and causes less damage to the fly. You of course can start of by showing the Frozen non moving fly and explaining its in a Deep Hypnotic Trance and then as you warm it up and its eventually Flies off you can pretend to awaken it from its Sleep like state! This will also work with some other small insects so try it out with some!

I've included this bizarre chapter both for completeness and also because those of you who are Publicity and Success minded will see what a great Marketing Ploy becoming an Animal Hypnotist could be!

I bet Millions of Dollars could be made selling self-help Hypnotherapy tapes to Animal owners to treat their pets – just an idea!

CHAPTER TWENTY–SIX

HYPNO-TRICKS

(SECRETS OF PSEUDO HYPNOTIC STUNTS)

In short if you ask a volunteer to co-operate and close their eyes and then you say something such as "In order for this to work you must keep your eyes tightly closed at all times unless I say otherwise!" then as they will want things to work they will play along.

However as you combine saying this with running your hand over their face in a Hypnotic manner, the audience perceives this as if you have placed the volunteer into some kind of Instant Hypnotic Trance.

Then when the volunteer returns to the audience and is told what they have just done, they too will be as amazed as the audience as they will have no idea how they were able to have needles thrust through their body with no pain or be supported across the backs of two chairs as concrete blocks are smashed across their chests!

The key secret is that your patter should always sound like that a genuine Stage-Hypnotist would use as then the audience will come to believe that you are a genuine Hypnotist and that the things you are doing are a result of you having placed your volunteers into some kind of Instant Hypnotic Trance!

Most of these demonstrations can be performed anywhere, anyplace, anytime and as they can be performed on anybody, including the world's biggest sceptic they are ideal for challenge situations.

Best of all as they use no genuine Hypnosis, you can advertise yourself as a "Mind Magician" and avoid the need of applying for any form of Council Permission to perform your shows!

By changing the patter just a little, these demonstrations can also be presented as experiments in Psychic Mind Energy or whatever other names you wish to call them!

So lets get started with one of my favourite experiments entitled:

WEAK ARM – STRONG ARM TEST

EFFECT

Volunteer one clenches their right fist and then with their fist in this closed position places their right arm outstretched straight in front of them.

They are told to close their eyes and imagine clearly a time in their life when they felt very weak unloved & unwanted.

They are told to now notice how weak, how drained and how NEGATIVE this makes them feel.

"Feeling weak, drained and negative from the tips of your toes to the tips of your fingers!"

You tell them to TRY to keep their arm straight out in front of them as they allow these NEGATIVE emotions and feelings to flood their entire body from tip to toe.

Then you count to three: - 1,2, and on 3 you cue a 2nd volunteer upon the stage to push down the first persons right arm which they find they are able to do with the greatest of ease.

It is explained to the audience that under normal circumstances the 1st volunteer would have been able to keep his arm much stiffer, much straighter and out in front of him for much longer despite volunteer number two pushing down on his arm.

It is explained that this demonstrates how Negative emotions in our minds can lead to Negative effects in our bodies and as a consequence often lead to unnecessary illnesses and disease.

The good news however, is that by using a form of treatment such as Hypnotherapy we can remove all negative emotions from our bodies and therefore end up with a far more healthy life.

To demonstrate this you have Volunteer number 1 close their eyes once again and have them imagine the warmth represented by the colour Orange that is now flooding into their body.

They are told that just so long as they see the colour Orange clearly that in a few moments time something which was just a few moments ago so difficult will now become so ridiculously easy to achieve.

They are told to notice the inner strength they now feel which is making each and every muscle group in their body from the tips of their toes to the tips of their fingers STRONGER than they have ever been before.

Volunteer number one is then told to resume the same position as before with their right fist clenched and their right arm held outstretched straight in front of them.

Volunteer number two is then told "OK on the count of three just TRY to push his arm down and notice how difficult it is for you and how much STRONGER he has become, 1, 2, 3, That's it just TRY to push down his arm.

Volunteer number two is allowed to continue TRYING for a few seconds or so and then is told to relax. Then volunteer one is told to relax also and take their new-found strength with them.

When asked volunteer one WILL SAY how weak he felt the first time and indeed how much stronger he felt the second time around.

Volunteer two when asked will genuinely comment how much more difficult she found it to get his arm to budge the second time around.

EXPLANATION

Everything is done and carried out 100% exactly as I have just explained, with only a few points being of particular relevance as follows:

The first time around volunteer one has to hold their arm out in front of them from the very start of the demonstration and so it is little wonder that their arm is tired by the time volunteer two comes to push it down.

Also the first time around the psychological effect of thinking of negative things will genuinely make volunteer one feel weaker – its quite simply a simple form of SELF-HYPNOSIS which makes this work without fail with any willing & co-operative subject.

The suggestion of "TRY to keep your arm out straight in front of you!" suggests by that single word TRY that they will be unable to do so!

This is a technique known in Hypnosis as "The Law of Reversed Effort" which states that the harder they TRY to do something the less success they will have!

And finally with reference to the first time round where volunteer one is made to feel weak, because you cue volunteer two to push their arm down on the count of three without person one hearing you it will then come as a shock when it happens!

Because volunteer one does not know when his arm will be pushed down or indeed expect it to happen at all, it will be a complete surprise to him when this happens, he will be caught off-guard and will not have chance to tense up his by now already very tired arm.

The moment this first demonstration is done both volunteers are told to relax as normal. This gives volunteer one time to rest his arm ready for the second time!

This time volunteer one stands with his arms by his side and eyes closed as you tell him to think of the positive times in his life when he felt STRONG, confident and on top of the world.

He is told to notice that as he clearly sees these things in his minds eye so at the same time he starts to feel STRONGER in each and every muscle group from the tips of his toes to the tips of his fingers.

You then start to explain to the audience that its time to make volunteer one much stronger and healthier by the power of Hypnosis and you go into your Mumbo Jumbo at this point!

The moment volunteer one has started to visualise the colour Orange clearly in their mind, then and only then you get them to resume their original position of having their right arm straight out in front of themselves with the fist clenched.

Volunteer one is told "Notice how much stronger you feel, notice how much stronger you are and how much stronger you have become!"

Volunteer two is then told "On the count of three I want you to TRY and push his arm down as you did before, except this time notice how much harder it becomes for you to achieve this."

Then you count 1,2, and on 3 – Just TRY to push down his hand, that's it Just TRY, TRY (continue like this for a few seconds and then say) And now everyone just relax once again.

This time volunteer one has been warned when the pushing will begin and has time to tense their arm, also this second time around it is upon volunteer two that the Law of Reversed effort is used by suggesting to her to TRY and push down his hand.

SUMMING-UP

Do exactly what I have just explained in exactly the way I have said to do it and this demonstration will work EVERY time. Yes the levels of success will vary, but in general 9 times out of ten the visual difference will be VERY DRAMATIC!

And in the other 10% of cases it will still be visual enough to show that "Hypnosis" has indeed made the man stronger the second time around.

This works due to a combination of The Law of Reversed Effort (TRY), the verbal suggestions given to them and the things they think of (self-hypnosis), and the fact that second time around the man (volunteer one) has prior warning of when the woman (volunteer two) will TRY to push down his arm.

He has of course also had a minute or two to rest his arm between tests and this time only places his arm outstretched in front of him at the last second, thus not giving it time to get tired as in the first instance.

This may not sound very impressive when described like this on paper, but visually its very dramatic and makes for a good TV or Stage Show demonstration which both the audience and those whom participate in the experiment will find AMAZING!

BUCKET OF ICE TEST

EFFECT

It is explained to a volunteer seated on stage, that in a few moments time their right arm will be placed into the fish tank next to them which is full of Cold Water and Ice.

They are told to remove their hand from the Iced Water the very second that they feel it is too cold or painful to keep their hand in it any longer.

They are told to close their eyes and you then lift up their arm and place it into the tank of Iced Water without warning.

From the second their hand enters the Water until the very second they remove their hand is timed by a stopwatch which is held and operated by a 2nd Volunteer from the audience.

The time is noted and Volunteer one is told how long they managed to keep their arm under water before the "Hypnosis" begins.

Volunteer One is told to close their eyes and relax as you start the Psychic Mumbo Jumbo.

You suggest to them that "In a few moments time when and only when I count to 3, then and only then I will place your right arm into the water tank beside you."

"This time you will notice that from the very second your hand enters the water you WILL FEEL calm, relaxed and confident in every way!"

"You will notice that something you once thought would be so difficult now becomes so ridiculously easy and you will feel NO DISCOMFORT whatsoever!"

Then you go into the think of the colour Orange Blurb and feel the warmth Patter mentioning to the volunteer that:

"Just so long as you keep seeing the Colour Orange brightly in your minds eye whilst feeling that warmth flooding your entire body YOU WILL FEEL NO DISCOMFORT whatsoever and will be able to keep your hand in the tank for much longer with the greatest of EASE!"

1. Relaxed, Calm & confident. 2- feeling warm & strong inside and on 3 Just notice how, unlike last time you feel no discomfort whatsoever. (As you count three you place their hand back into the water)

At this point Volunteer number two starts the stopwatch and prepares to stop it the very second that volunteer number one removes their hand from the water again.

The times are compared and it is noticed with much amazement from both those involved and the audience that She was able to keep her hand under water for CONSIDERABLY longer the 2nd time around!

She is given a towel to dry her arm and returned to the audience to thunderous applause.

EXPLANATION

Basically if you do exactly what I have explained in the way I have explained it, and say what I have said in the way that I said it then this WILL WORK with great success for you.

The volunteer hypnotises themselves through their belief that "Hypnosis" will work, as don't forget you asked only for volunteers who were willing & co-operate whilst having very good powers of Intelligence, Imagination and Concentration.

Your suggestions to them as detailed in the "effect" section are worded such as to Hypnotise them further into the belief that this will work.

The fact they have had their hand under the cold water once means that the second time around it is not so much a shock to their system and this alone will allow them to keep their arm under for longer than before.

Also second time around the idea of pain is NEVER allowed to enter their head. You see first time around they are told "Remove your hand from the water the very second it becomes too PAINFUL to keep it there!"

This suggests to them it will be painful and with this in their mind it won't be many seconds before they remove their hand from the water.

However second time around the word pain is NEVER ever mentioned and instead they are told to notice HOW LITTLE DISCOMFORT they will feel and how much easier it will be this time.

Lastly the fact they know how many seconds they kept their hand under first time around will usually make them determined to beat this second time around and in a focused state of mind such as this – SUCCESS WILL BE ACHIEVED.

For this experiment I find it works better if the volunteer with the stopwatch is a male whilst a female is used to place her hand into the water tank!

The tank by the way is nothing more than a reasonable sized fish tank, which is filled with 50% cold water, and 50% Ice cubes!

Incidentally it's a proven scientific/medical fact that women have a higher pain threshold than men and that's another reason why I use a woman for this "Bucket of Ice" test.

PSYCHIC STRONGMAN TEST

As a demonstration of "Hypnosis" this experiment has been used by me on countless Television shows, and indeed this test is so good that it has been used by top psychic performer Uri Geller on many of his world-wide TV shows to date, although obviously Uri didn't present it as "Hypnosis" as we will do!

EFFECT

A large volunteer is seated on a stool/chair and four other volunteers are asked onto the stage to participate.

The man on the chair is told to sit upright with his hands on his lap, whilst the four other volunteers are told to interlock the fingers of both hands so that the fingers of the left hand are against the back of their right hand and vice versa.

With their hands interlocked in this position they are then instructed to place their two Forefingers so that they point outwards with their fingertips away from their interlocked hands.

With their hands like this two people are told to place their outstretched forefingers underneath the seated volunteers armpits (one under his left armpit and one under his right).

And the other two volunteers are told to place their outstretched forefingers under the seated mans kneecap area, again one under the left side and one under the right.

On the count of 3 they are all told to TRY and lift the seated man as high as they can noticing as they do how difficult this is to achieve. 1,2,3 – OK just TRY.

They attempt to do this either with no or very little success, which demonstrates how hard the following test, will be to achieve.

The four volunteers who are stood up all overlap their hands in the air so they go, right, right, right, right, left, left, left, left in order so all four people now have their right hands on top of each other in the pile and then their left hands above these!

At this point you instruct each of the volunteers to close their eyes and get them to concentrate on the Orange Colour and the warm feeling for a few seconds.

As you do this it is suggested to them all that "In a few moments time we are going to lift this man again and this time something you once thought would be so difficult WILL become so ridiculously easy!"

"Just so long as you think of the colour Orange at all times you will find that he becomes as light as a feather and that you become as strong as an Ox!"

"On the count of three I want you to all open your eyes, remove your hands from the pile and put your hands back together as they were before so that your fingers are interlocked onto the backs of your hands with only your Forefingers pointing outwards away from you.

Then immediately resume your positions as before, so your fingertips are under the mans armpits and kneecaps as you had them before and then the very second I shout NOW – that very second YOU WILL LIFT HIM UP with the greatest of ease.

1 – Confident, Calm & relaxed, 2- Strong as an Ox and on 3 Resume your positions this very second. (Allow them all to do so and then say) NOW – Lift him up – higher and higher and higher!

This happens and yes the man is almost thrown through the roof the second time to everyone's amazement, before being returned to his chair.

EXPLANATION

Don't even ask me to explain why this works – but believe me it does! I can honestly say that I've been using this test both on TV and Live Stage shows for a number of years now and it has NEVER gone wrong.

Admittedly the patter I use is worded following the rules of NLP and as such actually does have a positive psychological effect on the volunteers.

However even if you carry out this test without using the patter I've suggested then, as you will find for yourself, this test will still work!

The most bizarre thing about this test is that at the end the seated person will swear that they actually felt themselves get lighter, whilst the four other volunteers will swear they felt themselves get much stronger.

Don't underestimate the visual & psychological impact this test has on an audience as I have always found it to be an excellent applause puller, which is long remembered by the crowd!

THE HUMAN PLANK TEST – (FULL BODY CATALEPSY)

EFFECT

A tall volunteer is apparently placed into an Instant Hypnotic Trance and after you have given him a few simple suggestions his body becomes as stiff and rigid as an Iron Bar!

To prove this fact to the audience you place the mans rigid body across the backs of two chairs so that his neck is balanced on the back of one and his ankles are balanced on the back of the other.

Then when the applause has died down, you sit on his unsupported midriff and lift your legs into the air to prove how rigid his body has become!

Then you can stand on a chair and then step onto the centre area of his body and stand on him/her, so that your entire weight is supported by their now stiff rigid body!

Should the occasion be right you could even balance a concrete block on their chest area and then smash it up with a sledge hammer, whilst to everyone's amazement, the volunteers body remains stiff and rigid!

Or you could even place a plank of wood onto their chest and a heavy anvil onto this, which can then be hit repeatedly in time to the music by you and another volunteer, proving beyond doubt by way of your "Anvil Chorus" that the spectator is Hypnotised and is indeed as stiff as an Iron Bar.

My Hypnotic tutor Delavar, even went to the extremes once, by having an Elephant place its front feet onto the volunteers chest whilst they were supported across the backs of two chairs!

I'm sure you can see what I meant now, when I stated that this is by far the most impressive demonstration of apparent Hypnosis that you could ever present and yet it uses no actual Hypnosis whatsoever!

EXPLANATION

A fairly tall volunteer is used as visually this looks more impressive when they are placed onto the backs of the chairs, however other than this, the only other important point is that the volunteer whether male or female must be wearing trousers of some kind.

It would also be wise to ask for a volunteer who does not suffer from back problems or have any other potentially serious health problem, this both makes the demonstration look even more dangerous in the audiences eyes, but also it ensures that you end up with a fairly fit and healthy volunteer.

Firstly I ask the volunteer to lie down on the stage so they are laid down outstretched on their back.

I then position the two chairs in front of the laid down volunteer so that the back of one chair comes in line with the area just above their ankles and the other is in line with the area just below the shoulder blades.

Incidentally the chairs are positioned so that the backs of them are facing inwards towards each other and the seats are pointing outwards, so that someone can still place their body weight on the chairs in order to stop them falling over.

Two volunteers are now positioned one in front of each chair so that they can stand with one foot on the stage and one foot on the chair seat so that their body weight stops the chairs from falling over.

The volunteer is then asked to stand up and asked to close his eyes as you say:

"Just close your eyes NOW and just so long as you keep your eyes tightly closed at all times, then you will find that you feel no discomfort whatsoever and that in a few moments time you will have become the world's strongest man!"

At this point I let the theme from Superman start playing as it hypes the audience and on stage volunteers up even more as I tell the volunteer off mike (so that the audience cannot hear) that they should put their hands down by their sides and grab tight hold of their trousers on the area just below their bum and keep a tight hold of this area on both sides at all times, then on the microphone so I can be heard I say:

"That's it Sir, Feet together, Hands down by your sides and just so long as you keep firmly in this position at all times, then from this moment forward keeping your eyes tightly closed at all times you will realise that each and every muscle in your body from the tips of your toes to the tips of your fingers is becoming stiff rigid, locked, glued, welded and cemented in place so that its almost as if your entire body is now like a solid Iron Bar!"

"Because you now realise that you are Superman himself, the worlds strongest man and from this moment forward just so long as you keep tight hold at all times and just so long as your eyes remain tightly closed, then you will feel no discomfort whatsoever as you are the world's strongest man!"

"OK 3,2,1 and just let yourself fall gently backwards into my arms as you remain stiff rigid, holding tight at all times, eyes remaining closed at all times, you are the worlds strongest man!"

As this last sentence is spoken, I stand behind the person and gently pull them backwards towards me so that I can then place my arms so that they go, one under each of the volunteers armpits, enabling me to lift them up easily from that end, whilst I instruct another of the onstage volunteers to lift the person up by their ankles and help me position them on the backs of the chairs.

This part of the operation should prove fairly simple as you have already positioned the chairs correctly in advance, so it should prove simple to balance the volunteer on the two chair backs, so that at one end they are supported just under the shoulder blade area and at the other end they are supported just above their ankles.

From an audience point of view this looks very much like the person is supported by their neck and ankles, and although this is not actually the case, it is how 99% of your audience members will recall things after the event!

Once the volunteer is in this position I simply say:

"Ladies and Gentlemen the world's strongest man!" and then I pause as this acts as an applause cue which gets the audience clapping.

The moment they do stop clapping, I tap the volunteer on the underside of his back, in effect pushing his body upwards as I say:

"Stiff, stiffer, stiffer still, just like an Iron Bar, just so long as you keep tight hold and keep your eyes tightly closed at all times!"

I then sit down on the volunteer, so that I am sat with my bum on their upper leg area as close to their groin as possible as this allows for even weight distribution to occur, and as I lift my feet off the ground, I stretch my arms out and say loudly:

"Ladies and Gentlemen The Power of the Mind!"

This usually acts as a cue for the audience to applaud and the moment they stop clapping I get off the volunteer and move behind them so that I can now stand onto another chair and then stand on top of the volunteers body.

I position myself so that when I stand on them, my right foot goes onto the area just above the volunteers Knees and my left foot is placed onto their chest (not their stomach) so that my weight is evenly distributed across them.

At this point I extend my arms and say:

"Ladies and Gentlemen (pause) HYPNOSIS!"

And again this acts as another applause cue, and because this for some reason is perceived as being more impressive than sitting on them, it will draw even more applause.

I then get off them and with the help of the other onstage volunteer, I get hold of the top area of their body, whilst the other person gets their ankle area and I say:

"On the count of three lets lift him up off the chairs and lay him gently on the floor, 1,2, and on 3 just lift!"

Once the volunteer has been laid down on the floor I quickly say:

"Eyes remaining tightly closed at all times until I say otherwise!"

I then say thanks you to all the other onstage volunteers and send them back to the audience to a round of applause and then there is just me and the Superman volunteer left on stage!

At this point I go up to them place my hand on their shoulder and say:

"I'm only talking to you if I am touching you on the shoulder, in a few moments time when I count to three, then and only then, your eyes will open, normal feelings will return to all areas of your body and you will return to your normal self in every way!"

"So on 1, everything I have suggested to you tonight completely cancelled out in every way, and on two normal feelings returning to every muscle and every area of your body and on 3, wakey, wakey, rise and shine!"

At this point I help the volunteer to stand up and get them to take a bow before returning to the audience to a huge round of applause!

THE SECRET

Quite simply standing feet together, hands by your side, grab tight hold of your trousers at the area just below your bum and then have someone position you across the backs of two chairs as I detailed earlier and you will discover the secret for yourself.

You see once across the chairs, your head tips back over one chair and your feet hang over the other, which both make the centre of your body arch upwards like a cantilever bridge.

Add to this the effect of grabbing tight hold to the area of your trousers just below your bum and this makes your body arch up even more!

Then just so long as you position yourself where I have instructed when sitting or standing on the person, your weight will be distributed across their body and down the backs of the chairs, in exactly the same way as weight is absorbed by a cantilever bridge, all the patter etc is just pure presentation and is what makes the audience perceive this demonstration as genuine Hypnosis, when in truth it is just a clever scientific trick!

A square plank of wood could also be placed around the area that you would sit and onto this can be placed an Anvil as detailed earlier.

The secret of this being, that the Anvil would be made especially for this stunt so that it was no heavier than an average person (8 stone) as then the effect on the volunteer regards to weight is only the same as someone sitting on them.

If you and your assistant both take a metal hammer and take it in turns to swing these down onto the Anvil, it looks very impressive, and if done in time to the music does indeed become a sort of "Anvil Chorus" but the blows are softer than they appear to be and are absorbed by the "Cantilever Bridge effect!"

The concrete block stunt is how the audience perceives it, however the slab is really a brittle and easily broken sandstone or such like, which with a few gentle taps from a sledgehammer will shatter into bits and fall to the floor off the volunteers chest.

And whilst we don't advise it, you could duplicate Delavar's Elephant stunt by enlisting the help of a good Elephant trainer and some specially made chairs.

The chairs would be made of metal so as to be sturdier, but most important of all they would be made at a height, which matched the height that is necessary for the secret of the Elephant stunt to work.

The secret being, that when an Elephant stands on its two back legs, that is where 99% of its body weight is balanced, so when the Elephant apparently rests its front legs on the volunteers body, in actual fact all of its weight is on its back feet and it just looks as if its front feet are resting on the persons chest as the chairs have been made at the correct height for this to be possible!

Just like all of the other routines and stunts in this manual, we take no responsibility whatsoever for anyone trying out what we reveal herein, as we are detailing these secrets for educational and information purposes only, you have been warned!

THE BLOWTORCH STUNT

EFFECT

A male volunteer from the audience is asked to remove his shirt, he then stands upright with his feet slightly apart so that he is firm and steady and then you pass your hand over his face, he closes his eyes and apparently goes into a trance!

You then lift up his right arm and leave it rigid stuck out at the side of him and then do the same with his left arm so that he looks like a human letter T.

A few Hypnotic suggestions are given to him and then you produce a blowtorch and light the flame, which brings gasps from the audience.

To everyone's amazement you then run the large flame of the burning blowtorch over the arms and chest of the Hypnotised volunteer and they feel no pain whatsoever!

They can then be awoken from Trance and take their applause!

EXPLANATION

The truth is that the burning blue flame of a blowtorch would cause instant skin damage and severe burns, however the yellow flame of a blowtorch, will cause no damage if run over the body at an even steady pace so that it does not remain in one spot too long.

Take a lighter and run the yellow part of the flame steadily and evenly over your hand and you will see what I mean.

The blowtorch is therefore gimmicked, so that the airholes are permanently blocked up and so that it can only ever burn with a Yellow flame, which is relatively safe if run over the body in an even steady manner, just like the lighter is run over your own hand!

However to an audience it looks very impressive indeed, the only thing to be careful of is if the volunteer is very hairy, as the flame WILL burn the hairs off their body and if this starts to happen you will have to rub the area you have just been over with the blowtorch with a wet cloth quickly so that it puts out their burning hair before it gets to hot!

I suggest that you experiment on yourself first if you ever intend to use this demonstration and then you will know exactly what I mean.

The rest is just pure presentation to make it look like the person has been hypnotised to feel no pain and suggested patter is as follows:

"Well thank you very much indeed for volunteering Sir, in a few moments time we shall turn you into the world's strongest man!"

You then run your hand over the volunteers eyes as you say:

"And now just close your eyes and just so long as you close your eyes and keep them closed whenever I tell you to, then and only then this will prove to be 100% successful and will cause you no discomfort whatsoever!"

The volunteer because of the way this is worded will close their eyes and the audience perceives this as though you have placed them into some kind of Instant Trance.

Then off microphone (so audience don't hear) you say to the volunteer, "Be a good Sport mate, do as I say and we'll make you a Star!"

Then you say on microphone (so audience can hear) as you place your hand on the person's shoulder,

"Keeping your eyes tightly closed at all times unless I say otherwise, in a few moments time when the music begins to play, then and only them you will open your eyes and have an overwhelming desire to remove your shirt as if you were one of the world's greatest male strippers, however the moment you have taken your shirt off you will stop and wonder what the hell you have been doing and the moment I say sleep you will instantly close your eyes again and keep them closed unless I say otherwise!"

You then turn to the audience and say:

"Ladies and Gentlemen, Please welcome, better than the Chippendales, better than Adonis, it's the Wimpendale!"

At this moment the music begins to play such as I'm Too Sexy by Right Said Fred and the volunteer will open his eyes and take his shirt off, which by the audience is perceived that you have turned him into a stripper by Hypnosis!

Then the moment he has taken his shirt off, the music stops and you once again run your hand over his eyes as you say:

"That's brilliant and just close your eyes once again, relax and keep your eyes tightly closed at all times unless I say otherwise!"

Then you lift up his right arm and extend it out at the side of him as you say:

"Just allowing your right arm to remain stiff rigid out stretched at the side of you as you imagine now it's a solid Iron Bar!"

This tells the volunteer to keep his arm there in that position, but is perceived by the audience as if he has no choice but to do it as if he is reacting to a Hypnotic suggestion.

The same thing is then done for his left arm as you say:

"Just allowing your left arm to remain stiff rigid out stretched at the side of you as you imagine now it's a solid Iron Bar!"

and then you say:

"Just so long as you keep your arms in this position, and just so long as you keep your eyes tightly closed at all times then you will feel no discomfort whatsoever!"

Then you light the blow torch and run it over his arms and chest in the manner explained before, you continue doing this for around a minute and then turn the blow torch off, face the audience and say:

"Ladies and Gentlemen Mind Over Matter!"

This acts as an applause cue, and as the audience applauds, you tap the volunteer on the shoulder as you say:

"OK now wakey, wakey, ***OPEN YOUR EYES***!"

This concrete's the idea that he was in some kind of Trance to start with!

You then simply give the man his shirt back and send him back to the audience to a huge round of applause as you say:

"Ladies and Gentlemen please give our wonderful brave volunteer a huge round of applause as he returns to his seat in the audience!"

THE HUMAN PINCUSHION EXPERIMENT

EFFECT

A volunteer is placed into an Instant trance and then two Hypodermic Needles are removed from their packages and one is pushed through the back of the volunteers hand, whilst the other is pushed through their arm.

The needles are then removed and the volunteer feels no discomfort whatsoever as they are awoken from trance!

EXPLANATION

Quite simply you get someone from the audience who is not scared of needles.

The secret is that the fleshy skin on the back of his hand is pinched by your fingertips of one hand (which he will feel) and then you say:

"Notice now that the area I have just pinched is turning numb and you feel no discomfort whatsoever!"

As you say this the first needle is pushed through this fleshy skin area of the back of their hand just at the point where you have been pinching.

The truth is that the needle being pushed through this fleshy bit of skin is felt far less than the sensation of you pinching the loose, fleshy area of skin in the first place, which is the same area that the needle is pushed through.

Once the needle is through you can let go of the fleshy area and the needle will visually appear to be stuck through more of their hand than actually is.

When you come to remove the needle, you pinch the skin up again between your fingertips and in this position pull the needle out in a steady motion.

The same thing can be done with the fleshy skin area of arm, near the point on the inside of your arm where your elbow bend is and of course this is done in the same way.

The most painful thing the volunteer actually feels is you pinching their skin before the needle is inserted or removed and as they are warned that you are about to pinch their skin this does not bother them.

As their eyes are closed the needle going in and out does not alarm them, and as the needles are sterilised (new ones for each demonstration) there is no health risk involved.

As with many of the secrets revealed in this manual we take no responsibility for your actions but would advise that you try these secrets out on yourself (with a friends help) before ever attempting at your own risk in public.

The perception of the audience is that you have placed them into an Instant Trance (you just ask them to close their eyes as in the blowtorch stunt) and then that you have via Hypnosis anaesthetised their body so that they do not feel the needles going through their body.

The truth is that the needles hurt far less (especially as they are Hypodermic) than the action of you pinching and pulling on their loose skin areas in the first place!

THE ANIMATED ARM EXPERIMENT

EFFECT

A volunteer is chosen at random from the audience and joins you on the stage where they are seated next to you behind a table in full view of the audience.

A second volunteer is also chosen from the audience and seated at the table as a close up independent witness to the proceedings.

The first volunteer is then apparently placed into an instant trance state and their hand is apparently glued to the table by "Hypnotic" suggestion.

In this state with their eyes closed, you seem to control their mind in some way, because as you point at their hand and lift your own arm into the air, at the same time their arm rises into the air in a most uncanny manner!

You then pause for a short while in this position and when you then start to move your arm downwards without saying a word, so the volunteer also moves their hand back down to the point where it is once again glued to the table.

The second volunteer is then asked to point their finger at the first volunteers hand and told to say nothing but do the same as you just did when and only when they decide to.

Sure enough despite volunteer number one having his eyes closed, when volunteer two decides to lift his arm into the air, volunteer number one does the same at exactly the same time.

And when volunteer two decides to lower his arm again, amazingly so does volunteer one, even though they cannot possibly see what is going on and nothing has been said to alert them to what is happening.

The first volunteer is then awoken from trance and both people are sent back to the audience to a huge round of applause!

SPECIAL NOTES

The effect of this routine looks the same as the one performed by Top British Mentalist Derren Brown during his Live Shows and also on one of his "Mind Control" TV Specials, however I have decided to include my performance method herein as mine uses absolutely no Hypnotic Trance and indeed the Linguistic wording is different in order to achieve apparently the same effect, without the volunteer needing to be placed into any form of actual Hypnotic Trance.

Should you be able to find a copy for sale on e-bay, then I'd recommend that you purchase at any price a copy of Derren's Excellent book "Pure Effect", but please note it is only the original self-published spiral bound version which contains his own handling and method for the routine which he has entitled "Lift" and as this edition is very rare, it is very hard to find to say the least, however the time and expense will prove well worth your while, as will obtaining any of Derren's other excellent works from his site of ***www.derrenbrown.co.uk***

EXPLANATION

This demonstration must either be performed seated at a table which has a tablecloth draped over it, which reaches to the floor so that nobody can see either yours or volunteer number ones feet, or it can be performed whilst stood up at a bar in a pub, just so long as the Landlord will allow you to go to the staff side of the bar so that once again the viewing public are unable to see either your or volunteer number one's feet!

If the audience could see your feet, this could give the secret of it all away as you will be directing the volunteer on exactly when to lift their arm up or put it back down on the table by pressing down on their foot with your foot to signal that they should lower their arm and by releasing the pressure on their foot to signal that they should lift their arm up into the air.

To apparently place the first volunteer into a trance I simply take hold of their right hand and place it over their face as I say:

"As I move your hands towards you, just let your eyes close, that's it just close your eyes and relax, just so long as you keep your eyes tightly closed at all times then this experiment will have a very good chance of working"

I then remove their hand from their face and lower it to the table as I say:

"And as I lower your arm down and place your hand flat on the table, so you keep your eyes tightly closed at all times and allow yourself to relax completely"

"Don't say a word at any time, just let your eyes remain closed, allow yourself to relax and listen to every suggestion that I give you!"

"Noticing now that pressure ***(as you say this your foot presses down on their foot under the table and remains there, whilst on top of the table you are apparently pressing their hand firmly to the tabletop)*** as your hand glues itself to the table top and remains there at all times whilst you can still feel this pressure ***(as you say "this pressure" your foot presses down firmly on theirs to signal to them in a non-verbal manner that it's the pressure on their foot that you are on about!)*** Its almost as though your hand is locked, glued, welded and cemented to the table top at all times whilst you can feel this pressure ***(again as you say "this pressure" above the table you are apparently pushing down on their hand to reinforce things, but under the table you are pressing down firmly on their foot again to reinforce the fact that you mean the pressure on their foot!")*** and whilst you can feel this pressure

(repeat the foot pressure again under table as you appear to press on hand) your hand will remain glued to the tabletop at all times, however when and only when you feel this pressure ***(repeat the foot pressure as you appear to press on their hand)*** disappear, then and only then you will allow your hand to rise up into the air, keeping your eyes tightly closed at all times! Just nod your head if you understand ***(when they nod you know they have understood the foot cues)*** However you will also notice that whenever this pressure reappears ***(again do foot signal as appear to press on their hand)*** that then and only then you will allow your hand to lower down back to the table until it is glued back to the table top! Just nod your head if you understand! ***(Again when they nod you know they have understood the meaning of the foot cues!)*** As I now remove my hand from yours, that pressure ***(do foot signal)*** remains there and so your hand remains glued to the table top until that pressure ***(foot signal again)*** disappears!

At this point volunteer one is sat their with their eyes closed as if they have been placed into a trance and they should now be at a point that they realise that whilst your foot is firmly pressing on theirs (as it is at this time) they must keep their hand on the tabletop, however when you remove your foot from theirs so that the pressure is released they must them lift their arm up into the air.

You should be able to work the rest out now from the description I gave you of how things look to the audience, in essence when you point at their hand and lift your arm up, this is the same time as you release the pressure on their foot so that the volunteer lifts up their arm which looks very spooky indeed.

Then when you lower your arm is the same time as you replace your foot onto their foot and press down which signals them to also lower their arm and hand down back to the tabletop.

When volunteer two points at Volunteer one and apparently takes control of them the secret is exactly the same, the moment you see volunteer two move their arm upwards you release the pressure from number ones foot, and the moment you see them move their arm back down you replace the pressure so that volunteer one places their hand back down to the table.

I am sure you now understand why the audience must not be able to see either your foot or volunteer number ones foot at any time, hence the reason for the draped table or standing behind a bar as detailed earlier.

You then simply place your hand on the apparently Hypnotised volunteers shoulder and say:

"When I click my fingers you will then open your eyes, you'll feel your normal self in every way and you will forget to remember and remember to forget everything that has just happened!"

You then simply click your fingers and apparently awaken the subject before sending them both back to the audience as you say something such as:

"Thank you Sir, you've been a wonderful volunteer and enabled us to witness the true power of the mind, you are a very special person indeed and as such an experience is such a special and person one, I trust that you will keep the inner personal details of your experience to yourself!"

This seems innocent enough to the audience, however it's a nice way of telling the volunteer not to tell anyone what has really gone on and by praising their ego in this manner, they will keep things to themselves.

One other important point is to pick two people who don't know each other and who are seated in different areas of the room as that way they are less likely to talk to each other afterwards.

Even if they do though, as volunteer one had his eyes closed all the time, he will have been very disorientated and will not really have a clue what has gone on as his version of events is a totally different one than from an audience perspective.

This is what we in the business call the "Dual Reality" principle!

Try this out as I have stated and I am sure you will find that this gets amazing reactions from your audience and that they find it very spooky indeed!

THE EYE TEST

A wine bottle with a loose fitting cork is placed onto the table, you apparently place a man into trance and awaken him believing that he is drunk, he is told to place his left hand over his left eye and then to extend his right arm in front of him. You count to 3 and tell him to try and push the cork down into the top of the bottle using only one finger and the more he tries the more he keeps missing as he is of course Hypnotically drunk!

The secret of this is that most all people will find it impossible to hit the cork with their extended forefinger when one eye is closed. But when presented like this the audience perceives it as if you have made the person drunk by Hypnosis.

In order to be able to actually do this yourself to show it can be done when you are soba, you must aim for a spot a couple of inches to one side of the cork, give it a try and you will soon see what I mean!

STRONG WOMAN TEST - A

You get a woman to stand and face the audience, get her to raise her two arms straight out to the sides, then ask her to bend her elbows and touch the fingertips of her hands together. In this position you can now get two men, they each grab hold of one of the ladies forearms and try as they might they will be unable to pull the woman's hands apart! This can easily be demonstrated as turning her into the world's strongest women or perhaps as turning the two men into the worlds weakest men!

STRONG WOMAN TEST – B

Ask a women to place her hand flat on the top of her head (palm downwards) and to push her palm/hand onto the top of her head with all her might. A man is then told to try and remove her hand from her head by taking hold of her forearm! Again this is practically impossible and can be presented as if the result of Hypnosis!

STRONG WOMAN TEST – C

Get a woman to place her hand under her arm, back of the hand under her armpit and in this position it is also practically impossible for anyone to remove her hand from under her armpit by pulling on her forearm!

DRUNK TEST

Get someone to hold both their hands out in front of them, hand wide apart and ask them to extend both their forefingers. Tell them on the count of three you want them to quickly bring their hand together and push the tips of their fore fingers together. Count to 3 and they will try with no success, however you can do it as you are not "drunk" which is of course what you have apparently suggested to them!

You ca do it because you demonstrate doing it slowly, but when the volunteer tries to put their forefingers together, they will experience great difficulty as they have been asked to do it quickly and due to the fact they are attempting to perform a none too easy action under circumstances that the average person will find unnerving.

HYPNOTIC PULSE STOPPING

A great demonstration for a Pseudo-Hypnotic Act is to apparently stop your own Pulses by the power of self-Hypnosis!

With volunteers holding each of your wrists, so that they can feel your Pulses, first one stops and then the other, then one comes back and then the other in a most spooky manner as you Hypnotise yourself!

The secret is that a small rubber ball is held under each of your armpits, this can be held in position with a strap so that it can remain there throughout the show.

Slight pressure on the rubber ball under your armpit will cause that pulse to stop, therefore done in turn you can make one pulse and then the other stop and then bring them back one by one apparently as a demonstration of self-hypnosis.

The audience member's confirming that your pulses have stopped and then started again!

THE WEAKNESS TEST

Ask a man to clench both his hands into fists and then to place one fist on top of the other. The idea is for him to push them both together (one down on top of the other fist) to stop anyone pushing them apart.

You then apparently make him weak with hypnotic Suggestion and using only the tips of each of your forefingers, you easily push his fists apart! This is simply achieved by snapping one finger of either hand against the back of each of the mans two fists as this will separate them every time!

SUPERHUMAN STRENGTH TEST

Take a female and have her stand upright with both her arms outstretched and then place both her palms flat against a wall. Once in this position have a man stand behind her and place his left arm flat on her left shoulder, try as he might and push as hard as he can, he will be unable to push her against the wall. This looks particularly impressive when you line up a row of say 8 men behind the women all of whom place their left hand flat on the persons left shoulder in front of them. Even with a row of eight people in this position pushing on each other against the woman, they will be unable to push her against the wall. You can present this as either the woman becoming super strong or all of the men becoming weak!

HYPNO-HEAT

In this stunt you apparently remove the foil wrapper from some chewing gum, dampen it against the side of a glass and stick it to someone's forehead as you suggest to them that they are Hypnotised and as such the foil will get red hot, so burning hot that they will have no choice but to remove it from their head and sure enough in the matter of a few seconds this happens to everyone's amusement!

You will need two packs of gum, one cinnamon (use Big Red from Wrigley's) and the other a different flavour of the same make and size!

Open the Big Red gun (Cinnamon) and remove a stick, take the other flavour and wrap one of those sticks up in the foil removed from one of the Big Red (Cinnamon) sticks and then place it into the sleeve of the non Cinnamon flavour packet so that it looks like it is just one of them!

The secret is quite simply that the Cinnamon flavour from the wrapper cause the skin to get hot when it gets wet!

So when you are ready to perform this, remove the gum and offer it to a friend to eat who will for example confirm it tastes like normal mint gum (which indeed it is).

Take the empty wrapper and wet the inside of the aluminium foil on the side, which has the Cinnamon coating (not the shiny side).

The easiest way to do this is rub it on the side of a beer glass, which is damp or has condensation on it.

Then just stick the foil on the volunteers head and from here on its all just acting as in about 40 seconds time their head will feel so hot that they will have to rip the foil off as you are suggesting they will do!

CAN'T WALK STUNT

Tell someone to stand by a wall with their right side facing it and to place their right foot against the wall, with their left foot about 6 to 8 inches away from their right!

You now apparently hypnotise them and tell them all strength has vanished from their legs!

To prove this, the subject is asked to raise his left foot without changing the position of his right foot and indeed he can't!

Then apparently awaken him from trance and ask him to step forward with his left foot, he will then be able to walk back to the audience as normal!

STUCK IN CHAIR

Place someone into a chair, have him or her lean well back, place the tip of your forefinger onto the person's forehead and then tell them to try and stand up. They will be unable to do this, especially if their legs are outstretched in front of them as they sit leaning back in the chair!

GIRL THAT CANNOT BE LIFTED

One minute a man can lift up your skinny female assistant and the next he becomes so weak under Hypnosis that he cannot possibly move her!

The secret is to use a skinny assistant, the girl stands sideways to the audience, her arms tight against her body so they are bent up at the elbows.

Now a man steps behind her and has to lean down to take hold of her elbows to lift her by them, this he does and manages to lift her up and then put her back down.

When you want the man to look weak, your assistant who is working with you and is in on the trick, pushes or sways her body backwards just a bit.

This unknown to the man trying to lift her or the audience, throws him off balance slightly so that he does not have his full lifting power and can no longer lift her.

CAN'T BE LIFTED – VERSION B

Get a big strong man to lift you the performer up by the waist, once he has done this get him to hold you in the same position again, but he is to stare you in the eye as you mentally make him weak by telepathic hypnosis. This time he will be unable to lift you and this is for two reasons, a) He has to keep staring up to look you in the eye and b) As he is trying to lift you, the tips of your forefingers are gently touching both sides of his neck, one side touching his Carotid Artery (very lightly only) and for some reason this stops people being able to lift you up!

BROOMSTICK TEST - ONE

This effect is quite startling as it uses the strength of several people. You can use a broom handle, snooker cue or walking stick to perform this effect. Hold this in your open hands about eight inches in front of the shoulders and the same height as your shoulders, the arms being bent at the elbows.

The portion of the arm (from shoulders to elbows), is against the side of your body. The broom is placed into the performers cupped hands and the palm should be facing the audience.

The Broom handle should be placed between the thumb and palm but **NOT HELD IN PLACE** – One or more people are invited to come forward and push against the broom.

The performer now stands on one foot (right foot is suggested), left foot slightly folded back to aid in your balance.
You now challenge the volunteers to push against the broom so that they try to push you completely off balance.

They may grip the broom in any position they wish (but force must be equally distributed) and push with all their might, however they will not be able to push you off balance.

The broom must be placed on a dead level and held there. You must concentrate on holding the broom in position and you will find that only a tiny amount of resistance is required.

In this position its impossible for any number of spectators to push you off balance and so you can present this as if you've hypnotised them all to become very weak indeed!

There will often be a tendency on the volunteer's part to push the broom upwards or downwards, guard against this, do not allow them to jerk or suddenly push.

Because the Broom handle is on the same level as your shoulders, the volunteers pushing can gain absolutely no leverage to counterbalance the slight muscular effort that you exert against their efforts.

This requires practice but is a mind-blowing demonstration when mastered.

BROOMSTICK TEST – TWO

The performer places the palms against the handle of a broomstick held in a vertical position and requests that any volunteer try to push the broom down onto the floor. This is found impossible to do, as they cannot move it down even an inch, yet the performer apparently only supports the broom with open hands!

The secret is that you take the broomstick, with the handle uppermost, keeping the broom in a vertical position, you face the volunteer, keeping them somewhat to your left.

You extend your right hand, fingers extended along the handle of the broom (nearest floor), allowing the handle of the broom to cross open palm along from base of thumb to about tip of your third finger.

The left hand now takes a position further up the handle on the opposite side of the broom, so that when the hand is open. The fingertips will be about 3 inches above the waist.

The handle of the broom passing over open left palm in a similar position and manner to that of the right hand.

You will now find that with the hands in this position the broom is held firmly as though your fingers were encircling it.

Now instruct the volunteer to grasp the upper part of the handle of the broom and without jerking, but rather with a steady downward pull, to try to move the broom down until it touches the floor.

Make sure the volunteer does no jerk and caution them about twisting or hanging on the broom.

If you have an obviously strong person assisting, be sure to allow the hands to assume a position further apart than the one mentioned, it can sometimes be necessary to allow a distance of 24 inches to successfully offset the effort exerted by a muscular assistant.

No matter how strong they are though, you can always prevent them from putting the broom down to the floor. If you use judgement and experience in placing your hands you will always have the greater power of leverage.

The pressing of the two hands towards each other has a tendency to bring the broom into a position that the downward pressure will be null and void whilst they exert themselves to the utmost.

You are rarely required to use but a small amount of your strength to combat this. Always insist on the spectator keeping his hands close together as the further away his hands are from yours and the closer together his hands are kept, the easier this stunt is to perform.

You'll find all of these Hypno-Tricks along with numerous others demonstrated and explained in full on my Ten DVD Hopme Study Couse "There's No Such Thing As Hypnosis" which is available from ***www.hypnotherapycourse.net***

SECRETS OF HYPNOTIC SUCCESS

"Dr. Jonathan Royle Will Make You A Better Alternative Therapist, Show You How to Get More Customers, Sell More Products, Spin Off More Backend Income & In Less Time With Less Effort…."

Dear Fellow Complementary Therapist:

I am absolutely serious. I want to show you exactly how you may be able to add at the very least £25,000, and hopefully £50,000 or maybe even £100,000 profit to your Personal Therapy business during the next year!

And this is the next year we're talking about. The following year will be even more profitable, and the year after that if you take action now and follow our tried, tested and proven to work Hypnotic Business Expansion Techniques – which can work equally as well for any therapist promoting any alternative treatment discipline from A through to Z!

HOW MUCH MORE WILL YOU BE MAKING WHEN YOU LEARN HOW TO:

- **Break into the lucrative fields of Corporate Stress Management & Hypnotherapy for the employees of major Blue Chip Companies.**
- Create a situation where A-List Celebrities and household name TV, Film, Media & Sporting Stars are banging on your door for treatment.

- **Enter the highly paid world of sales training; team building & motivational courses to make big bucks Anthony Robbins style!**
- Get household name Sporting Teams to employ your Hypnotic skills as their personal Hypnotic "Sports Psychologist"
- **Make more money from a single 90 minute group Hypnotherapy session than many Therapists make in an entire month.**
- Attract ten times more one to one clients, never see them in person, and yet help them to solve their problems and make tons of cash into the bargain!
- **Dramatically increase your income treating people over the phone in the comfort of their own home – how to do it and why it works.**
- How to get people like Travel Agents, Driving Instructors and even the Local Zoo to act as your "unpaid" salesmen and help you gain countless new clients for personal treatment & help you to sell a truck load of products at the same time.
- **Royles tried, tested & proven to work techniques to regularly get yourself on Television & Radio shows making exceptionally good money from these appearances.**
- Get Local, National & International newspapers & magazines to give you Millions of Pounds worth of Free Publicity for your business, services and products!
- **Make £10K, £15K, £20K or maybe even £25K (Twenty Five Thousand Pounds) from each weekend training seminar that you organise, who to market these too and how to do this in order to get maximum profit from minimum investment.**

THEN WE'LL SHOW YOU HOW TO:

- **How changing your title from Hypnotherapist to something such as Clinical Hypnotic Consultant can help you raise your hourly fees many times over.**
- How getting a Free BUPA & NHS Provider number can increase your profits!
- **Easily create and/or gain sales rights to sell saleable & highly desirable E-Books, Printed Manuals, CD-ROMS, audiotapes & CD's, training & self-help videos and DVD's amongst many other profitable products!**
- Create multiple streams of income by getting other people to sell these products for you on a basis whereby you keep most all of the profits.
- **Profit from selling other peoples products in a way that takes practically no time or effort on your part and can earn you money 24 hours a day, Seven days a week, 365 days a year – even when your fast asleep!**
- Make a fortune from Merchandising & gain more clients by giving Free public talks, taster sessions & public demonstrations.

- **Generate huge profits from direct mail campaigns & how "target" marketing can increase your profit return on investment many times over.**
- Effectively market your services & products at no cost through email sales letters and postings to Internet Newsgroups and Message Boards.
- **Easily add (at the very least) an extra few hundred pounds a week (over a thousand pounds per month) to your profits by selling self-help products, training materials and related items on Ebay and other Internet Auction Sites!**
- Get major discounts on every advertisement you place in a way that's as easy as 1,2,3!
- **Write Classified Adverts which are cheap to place which can pull in more clients than large display adverts costing several hundred pounds or more.**
- Strategies, techniques and methods to advertise your services at little or no cost in order to Skyrocket your income and give you more funds to invest in other projects.
- **Operate a simple Doctors Referral System which costs less than 50p per client you treat to use and can prove highly effective in getting Medical GP's to refer their patients to you for treatment.**
- Handle telephone enquiries to ensure that you close the sale there and then at least 90% of time or more!
- **The Inside Secrets of Networking, Cold Calling & Successful Telesales for big profits!**
- How to write sales letters, adverts and copy for your Internet Site & other mediums which will pull in the maximum response in minimum time.
- **The real difference between features & benefits, what this means to you and how to create compelling sales copy by using emotion and keeping it conversational.**
- Secrets of compiling a profitable Internet Site & promoting it so you get ranked high in the Search Engines, get more visitors and ultimately make more profits! These secrets alone took Royle several years and several thousand pounds to discover the hard way and when you enrol to attend this seminar right now you learn them all!

AND THAT'S JUST THE TIP OF THE ICEBERG:

- **Which "Power" words instantly increase response, how to write headlines that grab the prospects attention, how to highlight the benefits of your product/service, how to structure compelling offers and closing the sale with ease!**
- How promotional key rings can bring you more clients, More business and more profits than giving out business cards.

- **Tax Evasion is illegal, however Tax Avoidance is Legal! Simple proven strategies which are 100% Legal enabling you to keep far more of the money you earn and how to get it working for you best – a financial adviser would charge huge ££/$$ for this.**
- How finding "Problems" which many people have in life and then providing the "Solution" is the easiest way to get rich rapidly and how you can achieve this!
- **Ways to start joint ventures with other people, secure investment into your own projects from others and generally start to act, think and work like a Millionaire! We teach you the truth behind John Paul Gettys saying, "I'd sooner have 1% of a 100 men's profits than 100% of just one mans!"**
- Even if you have no prior knowledge or experience of Hypnosis, on these tapes Royle will teach you how to conduct Complete Mind Therapy Sessions for Groups and also for individual clients, no stone is left unturned and you could add this valuable new approach to your existing Private Practice with ease, thus increasing profits even more!
- **How to break into "Life Coaching" on a Corporate Level and the story of how one of our colleagues** (who shall remain nameless) **pulled in over £240K (Yes almost a quarter of a Million Pounds) in just twelve months from gaining just 10 regular paying clients! This example alone and the insights and truths it reveals about making the big £££/$$$ with ease is worth many times the tiny price it will cost you to attend this two day training alone!**
- Royle will even teach you the Secrets of "Magical Therapy" – a powerful treatment approach for use with young children which alone could earn you a fortune.
- **Plus Countless Other Tried, Tested & Proven to work Advertising, Marketing, Sales & Promotional strategies, approaches and techniques, exactly how to apply these to your own personal Hypnotic Business and in short how to change your life forever when you take action right now!**
- We know that any intelligent success minded person like yourself will want to order these videos which contain over 10+ hours of mind-blowing secrets and come with a FREE CD-ROM which contains lots of the other Secrets & information referred to herein – we even show you how after watching these videos you could qualify for eighteen (18) Prestigious Diplomas at no extra charge!

SO WHAT'S THE BOTTOM LINE?

How much is your future happiness and financial success worth to you? Read this letter again from start to finish and we're sure you'll agree that if we charged £1,000+ **for these training videos and CD-ROM it would be well worth it – However the introductory price is only a modest** £297!

A REVOLUTION IN PAIN CONTROL

Royle even teaches you his slant on "Noesitherapy" a truly mind blowing pain control technique devised by Dr. Angel Escudero of Valencia in Spain which has been featured on world-wide TV including BBC One's "Your Life in Their Hands" documentary series.

Within seconds you'll be able to ease people's pain and amazingly just like Escudero will be able to use these techniques to enable people to have Medical Operations and Dental work without any form of anaesthetic being used and yet your patients will feel absolutely no pain or discomfort whatsoever!

PHOBIAS CURED IN SECONDS

What's more you'll discover the powerful strategies of "Pain & Pleasure" therapy which combined with NLP and other more conventional Hypnotic techniques will enable you to eradicate the most extreme Fears and Phobias from your client's life's & minds within a matter of seconds!

MERIDIAN THERAPIES – EXPOSED

And just to make sure that your therapeutic tool kit is complete, Royle will teach you his own shortcut approach to learning and using Meridian Therapies such as Emotional Freedom Technique (EFT) – Thought Field Therapy (TFT) and Freeway CER!

He'll even reveal to you how to make a fortune treating Sporting Professionals and High Profile Celebrity Clients over the telephone using these powerful, yet incredibly easy to implement and learn treatment techniques!

THERAPY SUCCESS GUARANTEED!

Perhaps most important of all Royle Reveals how to conduct Group Therapy Sessions, enabling you for example to get an audience of say 100 people to pay you £25+ each to Stop Smoking, resulting in 100 non smokers and £2500+ in your bank account for just over 90 minutes work!

The advertising, marketing & publicity techniques which Royle Reveals on this ten volume video course are worth an absolute fortune and more importantly when used correctly – will earn you one!

From Merchandising at Public Talks to Mail Order Product sales over the Internet on the one hand to gaining Celebrity, Sporting & Corporate Clients on the other – Royle leaves no stone unturned and quite literally teaches stuff never revealed in any other course, which will place you on the right path to becoming a Super Rich Hypnotherapist with ease!

THE TRUE PSYCHOLOGY OF STAGE-HYPNOSIS

For the first time ever Royle Reveals the True **(never before revealed)** Inside Secrets & Psychological Techniques which make the Stage Hypnotists job as easy as 1,2,3!

Many of Royle's colleagues have begged him not to make this amazingly powerful information available – however Royle has decided to lift the lid and teach you techniques which have remained **(until now)** so secretive that many have never before appeared in print or as part of any other training course!

SUGGESTIBILITY TESTS – EXPOSED

No less than 13 amazing Suggestibility Tests are both demonstrated and then correctly explained in such detail as to guarantee you success each and every time you use them!
Yes these experiments when carried out the way Royle teaches are 100% Guaranteed to work on everybody **(even the biggest sceptics)** all of the time!

Even established Hypnotherapists & Stage-Hypnotists of many years experience could learn an awful lot from this section of the tapes alone and as an absolute beginner these videos will take you to advanced Professional Standard with ease!

THE WORLD'S FASTEST INDUCTIONS

A total of 16 tried, tested and proven to work Induction Techniques are first demonstrated and then taught in a simple step by step manner ensuring that you have an armoury of techniques at your fingertips to enable you to place most any person into **"TRANCE"** in most any situation!

Some of the methods taught are also suitable for use in Hypnotherapy, whereas the "World Record Induction" enabling you to place over 30+ people into Trance in less than 60 Seconds is more suited to stage use.

Many of the Induction's taught on these tapes have never appeared in print **(except in manuals by Royle himself)** and therefore even the most established Hypnotherapists & Stage Hypnotists will learn an amazing amount of stuff from this course.

THE IDIOT'S GUIDE TO STAGE HYPNOSIS

In short Royle teaches you absolutely everything you need to know from the moment you start advertising your Hypnotic Show to the moment you walk on stage and make your introduction all the way through to the time when you take your final bow, walk off stage and collect your well deserved fee!

Becoming a Successful Stage Hypnotist is easy when you know how and after watching this ten-volume video-training course you'll know more than many so called established Professionals!

THE 1952 HYPNOTISM ACT

And if that's not enough Royle also discusses in depth the 1952 Hypnotism Act, 1989 Government Guidelines and also the 1996 Home Office Review and then details in depth how you may legally be Able to legally exploit the loopholes which these Laws offer in such a As to be able to perform legally anytime, anyplace, anywhere.

HYPNO-TRICKS – EXPOSED

And as a special added bonus Royle also teaches a total of 24+ yes you read that correctly, a total of 24+ "Hypno-Tricks" which are stunts and routines which can be performed on anyone **(including sceptics)** which are 100% guaranteed to work and which seem both to the audience and assisting volunteer to be a real display of Hypnosis, when in truth no genuine Hypnosis is used whatsoever!

These are the types of stunts & techniques used by people like British Mind Control Expert **DERREN BROWN** to make their reputation, indeed you'll learn enough "Hypno-Tricks" to perform a complete 90 minutes show using these secrets and this section of the training course alone!

And best of all Royle will also demonstrate and explain how to use these techniques as part of your Corporate Hypnotherapy Work, Group Hypnosis Sessions, Team Building Work, Sales Training's & Motivational Classes amongst many other lucrative markets!

NO STOOGES ARE USED – HONEST!

To make your understanding of Stage Hypnosis complete, Royle even teaches you the powerful secrets of **"The Dual Reality Principle"** and then goes on to demonstrate it in action! Using this little known technique which has been closely guarded for years, you will be able to conduct an entire Stage Hypnosis Show using absolutely **NO STOOGES** – Everyone who volunteers **(even sceptics)** will believe they have been Hypnotised and the audience will be convinced they have seen a genuine Hypnotic Show and yet **NO GENUINE HYPNOSIS IS USED!**

ORDER YOUR SET TODAY

To Order your set of this Ten Volume DVD Home Study Course, which also comes with Two Audio Compact Discs and a CDROM containing every book, manual and course ever written by Dr. Jonathan Royle simply use any Credit or debit card and order "The Ultimate Hypnotism Course" for just **£297** sent post Free anywhere in the world from ***www.hypnotherapycourse.net***

Printed in the United Kingdom
by Lightning Source UK Ltd.
110130UKS00001BA/16

9 781846 850523